THE LIFE AND TIMES

OF

ST. ANSELM

ARCHBISHOP OF CANTERBURY AND PRIMATE

OF THE BRITAINS

BY

MARTIN RULE, M.A.

IN TWO VOLUMES—VOL. I.

WIPF & STOCK · Eugene, Oregon

Wipf and Stock Publishers
199 W 8th Ave, Suite 3
Eugene, OR 97401

The Life and Times of St. Anselm
Archbishop of Canterbury and Primate of the Britains
By Rule, Martin
ISBN 13: 978-1-5326-0045-6
Publication date 7/8/2016
Previously published by Kegan Paul, Trench, & Co., 1883

TO

MY WIFE,

BUT FOR WHOSE INDEFATIGABLE SYMPATHY

IT HAD NEVER BEEN WRITTEN,

I DEDICATE

THIS RECORD OF

A PHILOSOPHER, CHURCHMAN, STATESMAN, AND SAINT

DEAR ALIKE TO EACH OF US.

PREFACE.

THE work I now put forth to the world has attained its present size and pretensions I scarcely know how, and in my own despite.

My first idea was that of a very small book indeed, consisting of extracts from Eadmer's 'Vita S. Anselmi,' and such few insertions from his 'Historia Novorum' as might seem necessary for giving a character of continuity to the work; but I soon abandoned it.

My next was that of a translation of the best passages in Eadmer, held together by a brief explanatory narrative; but that was in its turn relinquished.

My third scheme was, still keeping to Eadmer, to reproduce without stint what he has said about St. Anselm in his two works. But that would have been to do what the Dean of St. Paul's had done before me with a grace, a skill, and an appreciation of our hero's character which it would be presumptuous in me to praise, and might have conveyed the impression that I had written under no other inspiration than that of theological rivalry.

Meanwhile, however, my Orderic and my William of Malmesbury were falling to pieces from constant use; I had read over and over again the inestimable but almost unexplored mine of St. Anselm's correspondence; my commonplace book was filling with references to all sorts of odds and ends of eleventh and twelfth century literature; I felt that life was not drifting away in idleness, and I resolved not to hurry myself.

Five years ago, from this very day, I first set eyes on Aosta, and as I had already collected all the serviceable materials to be got for the construction of St. Anselm's pedigree, it was high time I should see his birthplace.

On the 27th of September, then, five years ago, and a few minutes before midnight, my wife and I took our places in the coupé of the diligence which was ready to start from Ivrea to Aosta. The moon was a night or two past the full, the sky was without a cloud, and the weird splendour of the mountainous gorge, up which we sped hour after hour, on the left bank of the dark and sullen Doire, made an impression on the memory of each of us which is not likely to fade away.

And so the hours passed. The road, rising by a slow gradation from the river's brink to the edge of the valley, had brought us to a level space covered with vineyards, when I perceived that another kind of light than the moon's was penetrating the sky, and that a new freshness was in the air; in a moment or two the satellite's effulgence was fading in the dawn; and in a moment or two more, as our course turned suddenly westward, away in the clear distance, like an airy curtain hung across the sky, the sublime range of Mont Blanc, all white and carnation, gleamed and glowed to the touch of the sun's first beam. It was not till the whole valley, from verdant plain to airy pinnacle of snow, was deluged with the day, that I was able to speak. 'How fitting a birthplace for St. Anselm!' I exclaimed: 'No wonder that his soul touched heaven.' And, indeed, I never think of the marvellous union in him of grandeur and simplicity, of majesty and grace, of severity and tenderness, without recalling that sunrise over the Valley of Aosta.

We remained for several days in the valley, identifying the Becca di Nona as the mountain of his mystic dream, and the Pondel as the bridge of the first 'Meditation,' and passed some delicious hours at Gressan.

The following winter was spent in Rome; but four months of desultory research, frequently interrupted, issued in little more of immediate interest to my readers and myself than the conviction—a conviction confirmed over and over again in numberless libraries both abroad and in England—that not a few of the 'Meditations' assigned to St. Anselm by the old editors are not his, least of all the sixteenth.

I was already preparing to leave Rome when a manuscript was one morning placed in my hand, as I sat working in the library of the Vatican. It was the most precious treasure I could have wished to have; for it contained the sweet little anecdote of St. Anselm's childhood—literally an anecdote, for it has never as yet been published—which the reader will find incorporated into my second chapter; and, as if that were not enough for one day's happiness, an authentic list of all the monks professed in St. Anselm's dear Abbey of Le Bec, from the beginning down to comparatively modern times. It would be impossible to overrate the interest, the importance, and the biographical value of this precious document to all lovers of St. Anselm; and I am proud indeed to place a portion of it in the appendix to my first volume, for the service of such of my readers as may be disposed to use it as a key to the earlier portion of St. Anselm's correspondence.

But I was determined to see Schiavi before turning northward, and after some trouble found that the present name of the place is not 'Schiavi,' but 'Liberi,' or rather 'Villa dei Liberi,' instead of 'Villa dei Schiavi,' as from time immemorial till the other day. 'Liberi in Formicola' is, I believe, its usual designation. The old name of the place commemorated an invasion of the Terra Laboris, in the year 926 or 927, as recorded in the 'Chronicon Cavense,' and other like documents.

I cannot help thinking that the famous fresco at Sant' Angelo in Formis must either have been inspired by one of St. Anselm's Meditations, or suggested by himself. One would like to know at whose instance it was executed.

My visit to the spot where the 'Cur Deus Homo' was written was a sort of apparition to the good people there. May such apparitions by their frequency cease to astonish.

It is needless to go into detail about other places made memorable by St. Anselm, unless it be to say that Pont Authou is not far from Rouen, and at the last railway station before Brionne, and that the site of the first monastery of Le Bec is about half-way between Pont Authou and Le Bec-Hellouin. There is a narrow road on a raised causeway across the valley; and on the right of this road, to a traveller turning into it from the high road to Le Bec-Hellouin, is a strip of meadow enclosed by a babbling brook and the beck proper. On that strip of meadow stood the poor little mud-walled monastery where Lanfranc lectured, where Anselm composed his most fervent meditations, and where he constructed the argument of the 'Monologion.'

The story of St. Anselm's archiepiscopal career occupies the whole of my second volume; and I do not blush to confess that this record of the events of sixteen years has cost me more pains than I dared to anticipate when I undertook my task. But, great as they may have been, I cannot hope, and will not try, to say how intense has been my enjoyment, from first to last, of this delightful subject; and now that I come to write my last word on it, I do so with very intense regret, for I am certain that I shall never find its equal.

September 28th, 1882.

CONTENTS

OF

THE FIRST VOLUME.

BOOK I.

THE EARLY LIFE OF ST. ANSELM.

CHAP.		PAGE
I.	ST. ANSELM'S INFANCY	1
II.	ST. ANSELM'S CHILDHOOD	15
III.	ST. ANSELM'S BOYHOOD AND EARLY YOUTH	34
IV.	ST. ANSELM'S EARLY MANHOOD	52

BOOK II.

THE EARLY RELIGIOUS CAREER, AND THE PRIORATE, OF ST. ANSELM.

I.	LE BEC	71
II.	ST. ANSELM'S RELIGIOUS VOCATION	101
III.	THE BEGINNING OF THE NEW LIFE	117
IV.	PRIOR ANSELM'S LABOURS	130
V.	PRIOR ANSELM'S INFLUENCE	144
VI.	ARCHBISHOP LANFRANC: THE MONOLOGION	163
VII.	CONSECRATION OF THE NEW BASILICA: THE 'PROSLOGION'	181
VIII.	THE LAST DAYS OF ABBOT HERLWIN	200

BOOK III.

ST. ANSELM ABBOT OF LE BEC.

CHAP.		PAGE
I.	ST. ANSELM ABBOT-ELECT OF LE BEC	213
II.	ABBOT ANSELM'S CONSECRATION AND FIRST VISIT TO ENGLAND	225
III.	ABBOT ANSELM IN HIS CLOISTER: HIS SECOND VISIT TO ENGLAND	245
IV.	DEATH OF WILLIAM THE CONQUEROR—SUCCESSION OF WILLIAM RUFUS	260
V.	ABBOT ANSELM'S THIRD VISIT TO ENGLAND	279
VI.	LE BEC AND CANTERBURY AT THE CLOSE OF 1089	283
VII.	LE BEC AND BRIONNE IN THE SPRING OF 1090	292
VIII.	ROSCELIN'S HERESY: ABBOT ANSELM'S FOURTH VISIT TO ENGLAND	300
IX.	AN INTERVAL OF SUSPENSE AND ALARM	312
X.	ST. ANSELM'S APPOINTMENT TO THE PRIMACY	322
XI.	THE LAST DAYS OF ST. ANSELM'S ABBACY	337

BOOK IV.

ST. ANSELM ARCHBISHOP-ELECT OF CANTERBURY.

I.	PRELIMINARY CONSIDERATIONS: ST. ANSELM'S ACCEPTANCE OF THE PRIMACY	361
II.	FEALTY AND HOMAGE: ENTHRONEMENT OF THE ARCHBISHOP-ELECT	377

APPENDIX 389

Book I.

THE EARLY LIFE OF ST. ANSELM.

CHAPTER I.

ST. ANSELM'S INFANCY.

ST. ANSELM was born at Aosta, between the twenty-first of April, 1033, and the twenty-first of April, 1034.[1] His father's name was Gundulf; his mother's Ermenberg. Gundulf was, not improbably, a son or grandson of Manfred I., Marquis of Susa, who in his turn was maternal uncle of Arduin, Marquis of Ivrea, and for some thirteen years King of Italy; and thus of the kindred of Boniface, Marquis of Tuscany, and father of the illustrious Matilda. Nor can there be a reasonable doubt that Ermenberg was a grand-daughter of Conrad the Pacific, King of Transjuran Burgundy, and thus first-cousin to the Emperor Henry II., and kinswoman more or less distant to every considerable prince in Christendom. But although St. Anselm was the son of a Lombard, it is scarcely accurate to call him, as he has been called, 'the Italian philosopher,' for the episcopal *civitas* of which Aosta was the capital had never formed an integral part of political Italy.[2]

[1] It was not the custom of biographers in the tenth, eleventh and twelfth centuries to record birthdays, and, with the exception of the first Otho, I know of only one great personage in these times whose birthday is recorded; and we owe the information to the coincidences that it was on anniversaries of his nativity that he went to school, embraced the monastic life, and was consecrated first abbot and then bishop. The personage to whom I refer is Bishop Amadeus of Lausanne, who attained the episcopal dignity in 1145. He was a kinsman of St. Anselm's. Guibert of Nogent tells us concerning himself that he was born on a Holy Saturday, but does not give us the year.

[2] Physically, however, it would seem, early at least in the twelfth century, to have been regarded as part of Italy, if Hugues de Sainte-Marie may be accepted as a witness (Migne clxiii. 847 B). Still, the political geographers, and Anselm himself, refused to assign it either to Burgundy or Lombardy. Thomas Walsing-

The sovereign magistrates of Aosta had from time out of memory borne the title of count, as well as the older and auguster title of bishop, until about the year 1020, when Bishop Anselm II. demised his episcopate to the son of one of his sisters—such, at least, is the most probable account—and his secular honours to a brother-in-law, Humbert the White-handed, Count of Maurienne, and progenitor of the Royal House of Savoy.[1]

In the year 1032, Odo, son of Humbert the White-handed, and first-cousin of St. Anselm's mother,[2] married Adelaide, Marchioness of Susa, who was, as I believe, niece or cousin of St. Anselm's father, and thus added to the county of Maurienne the rich and extended valleys that slope to the east of Mont Cenis and of Mont Genèvre, and possibly the marquisate of Ivrea as well. And it must have been in the very same year that Ermenberg herself was taken to wife by Gundulf, who may, not improbably, have pretended to be the legitimate heir to the domains enjoyed by Adelaide. In which case the marriage of Gundulf and Ermenberg was a political alliance between two families, each of which had reason to be jealous of the counts of Maurienne; Ermenberg's, because two titles hitherto deemed indissoluble had been severed to their loss in favour of the new house; Gundulf's, because an ancient usage had been broken to their loss, and this again in favour of the new house. The author of these griefs was the Emperor Conrad the Salic, who had already obtained possession of the *insignia* of King Rudolf III.,[3] and hoped thus the more readily to secure the Burgundian throne so soon as it should be vacant. For Rudolf III. had two nephews who were about to prove troublesome to his de-

---

ham (*Hypodigma Neustriæ*) describes the saint as 'Genere Langobardus, Augustæ civitatis indigena.'

[1] The county of Aosta was converted into a duchy by Frederick Barbarossa.

[2] The subject of Ermenberg's relationship to the house of Maurienne is discussed at length in the Appendix.

[3] *Art de vérifier les Dates.*

signated successor.[1] One of them was Odo of Champagne,[2] a sister's son, whom the Emperor with difficulty crushed in 1034, by the aid of Humbert the White-handed; the other was Burchard, Bishop of Aosta, who at Lyons fought bravely, desperately, and in vain against the foreigner; and who, had he not been deprived of the military resources of the valley of Aosta upon succeeding to its episcopate in the preceding decade, would, no doubt, have joined his forces to those of Odo, and in such wise paralysed the arm of Humbert as to defer, and perhaps prevent, the absorption of Burgundy into the Empire. The bishops of Aosta, Burchard's predecessors, so long as they were the allies of the House of Burgundy, were of infinite service to the German sovereigns, whose most convenient road into Italy lay across the Great St. Bernard and down the valley of Aosta; but Burchard, now driven into a position of hostility against Conrad the Salic, who by force and craft, rather than by legitimate succession, had stepped into the throne of Burchard's uncle, would have been a dangerous enemy to the Emperor, had the means been left him of blocking the high road to Lombardy. Hence the reason why it was the bishop's doom, as he first grasped the crosier of Aosta, to behold the secular mace pass from his reach into the hands of an uncle by marriage, a creature of the Emperor's.

And further: the bishops of Aosta, allies hitherto of the House of Burgundy and of the House of Saxony, had been most useful in helping the princes of the latter dynasty to suppress that rebellion against their suzerainty over Lombardy, of which the marquisate of Ivrea was the chief theatre; and the reason is not far to seek why Adelaide of Susa should now be betrothed to a son of Humbert the White-handed, the

[1] *Rudolphi Glabri Historia*, lib. iv.
[2] This Odo, or Eudes, of Champagne, was great-grandfather in the male line our own King Stephen, whose father, the Conqueror's son-in-law, was thus, if my genealogical speculations be correct, second cousin to St. Anselm. He fell in battle, contesting his claim (A.D. 1037), and was buried at Tours.

creature of the Empire. For Humbert was thus made master, besides the Little St. Bernard and the valley of Aosta, of Mont Cenis, of Mont Genèvre, and of the vast district conterminous with the county of Aosta, to which the passes of those mountains gave him access.

The history of this district is involved in obscurity; but it is hard to believe that an acknowledged principle of succession was not infringed in settling the fiefs of Turin and Susa on Adelaide; just as the prescription of a century—a prescription, no doubt, intended to endure for ever—had been broken in severing the earldom of Aosta from the bishopric. Humbert the White-handed had a rival at Aosta in Burchard its bishop. Can it be that his daughter-in-law Adelaide had a rival at Ivrea in Gundulf?

If, then, these be correct surmises, it is easy to understand what brought Gundulf to the precinct of the city over which Burchard presided in the double capacity of chief civil magistrate and chief ecclesiastical pastor; and we learn without astonishment that upon fixing his abode there he was courteously constrained to accept the honours of citizenship as a preliminary to his marriage with the prelate's sister.

The newly married pair had a palace in Aosta; and, although tradition does not point out its precise site, there can be no doubt that it stood near the cathedral and the bishop's palace, a quarter which, beyond question, must then have been, as it is now, the best in the city.[1] They must

---

[1] Visitors to Aosta must be on their guard not to believe those who point to a certain house in the *faubourg* as that in which Anselm was born. In that house I was shown a room on the first storey with the assurance that there he first saw the light; a similar story was told me concerning the room below it on the ground floor. One was as true as the other; for an inscription on the doorway declares the house to have been *à fundamentis erecta* A.D. 1505. We shall next be informed that William the Conqueror was born at Hampton Court.

While speaking on this subject to a canon of the cathedral, I ventured to suggest that the present house might possibly replace an older one which had once belonged to the Saint's family; for I could scarcely believe the story to be a mere invention. But I soon learnt the truth. At Gressan there is a tower of

also have had a country-house in the valley, for in that valley must have lain much, if not all, of the *multimoda hæreditas* which Ermenberg at her death demised to Anselm. There are no records extant to prove what may have been the extent or the distribution of this property; but those who point to the manor of Gressan some three miles southwest of the city as having formed part of it, would seem in doing so to represent not the mere surmise of modern antiquarians, but a genuine tradition.

refuge which appears to have belonged in 1200 to a certain Godfrey, the son of an Anselm, who may or may not have been a kinsman of our archbishop's. In the course, I believe, of the last century this tower belonged to a family who also owned the house in the *faubourg*. This is all. And, anyhow, the building at Gressan which has recently been invested with the designation of 'tour de St. Anselme,' even if it existed in Anselm's day, was merely a retreat or refuge used in times of imminent danger from invasion ; it was not a dwelling-house.

A local enthusiast has recently set up an inscription in bad French on a wall of this tower, describing St. Anselm as '*originaire de Gressan ;*' a piece of presumption which I have heard characterised in no measured terms by those who would have had every motive for commending the statement, had they believed it to be true. His family had, no doubt, property at Gressan ; but he was a native of Aosta.

I have in my possession a little manuscript life of St. Anselm, written in the valley, and probably at Gressan. Had there then been a tradition that it was his birthplace, this little treatise might have been expected to mention it. It says nothing.

I was informed when at Aosta that so much of the town as lies east of the *via principalis* is called the *bourg* or borough ; while the remaining, and by far the larger part, constitutes the *ville* or city. It is needless to say that the cathedral, the bishop's palace, and the residences of the cathedral canons are in the *ville* ; the canons of St. Ursus live in the *bourg*, although their church is outside the walls. How long this distinction may have subsisted I cannot say ; but I cannot help thinking that as the *ville* itself has from the very first been divided by the *via quintana* and the main street into four distinct portions, each of these had in feudal times its own destination : the larger section to the north of the principal street being inhabited by the bishop and the cathedral clergy, and the smaller by the *nobiles* of the community. If so, then the house in which Ermenberg and her husband lived may have occupied the site of the Palais Roncas, now used as a prefecture ; and I believe that it is the immemorial site of the best house in the place next after the bishop's palace.

Mr. Freeman in one of his smaller works expresses some surprise that a district outside the walls of Aosta should be called *la cité*, as though the city were outside the city. The surprise would be were the case otherwise. *Cité* is modern French for *civitas*, and the *civitas* of Aosta was the territory of which Aosta was the capital,

The pedestrian who wishes to see Gressan will ordinarily choose the road which, issuing from the southern gate of Aosta, and crossing, after a short but steep descent, the current of the Dora, turns rapidly to the right, ascends the river's bank for some little distance, and then bears off from it to trend its upward way over the sloping spur of rich alluvium that slips from the mountain's foot to the river. Here lies Gressan. Two miles higher up the valley is Les Aymavilles—*Aymonis Villa*—the probable residence of a kinsman of Anselm's who bore the name of Aymon. Above Les Aymavilles again, the road, by this time shrunk to a narrow bridle path, climbs, rough, stony and irregular, the steeper mountain side, till it reaches the edge of a ravine down which the torrent of the Cogne rolls and thunders under the aqueduct of Le Pondel. Gressan, Aymaville, Le Pondel were, probably enough, all of them portions of the ancestral inheritance; but St. Anselm's mother knew less of Le Pondel than of Aymaville, and less of Aymaville than of Gressan, as Gressan was by its aspect the most congenial to her placid and contemplative nature. There is full documentary evidence that some four years after the saint's death there were people living at Gressan, one of whom bore the same name as himself, and another the same name as an ascertained kinsman of his; and Gressan still boasts a domain so singularly favoured by nature that we should be more than sceptical were we to believe it to have belonged to any but the principal family of the valley, and thus to Anselm's, and, within that domain, the relics of just such a residence as the Bishops and Counts of Aosta would have been likely to own. The property is about twenty-five acres in extent; its name is Clochâtel, the vernacular form of *enclos du château*; and there hangs that about it which obliges the heart to confirm the conclusions of the judgment. Sweet peaceful Clochâtel! Nowhere in this favoured valley does noontide heat scorch less fiercely, as nowhere does evening gale or breath of morn blow more refreshingly than here; here where, when autumn days grow short, the neighbouring husbandman wends homeward bending beneath his gathered wealth of maize, and the burnished poplars hang forth to the sunset their foliage of silver and gold, and the chestnut falls soft on the turf, and the bells of the drowsy kine make a mellow discord, and down the vast valley to right and left the giant crags blaze with an amber glóry; whilst far away the clear blue shadow rises, creeping slowly over avalanche and glacier, and, as it rises, the sky-touching snows of Combin, of Velan, and of the nearer Becca di Nona, one by one quicken into rosy splendour, and fade into night.

Here assuredly, if anywhere, was at least one country-house of Ermenberg's family.

Ermenberg's son has drawn her portrait for us; not indeed as others had seen her, in her early bridal beauty, but as he remembered her, a matron in middle life. He describes her as a pious woman, whose goodness was less displayed in the otiose contemplation of an exalted ideal, than in the conscientious observance of the duties proper to her position, in the careful government of her household, in the discreet administration and prudent husbandry of her inherited property, and in the unassuming maintenance of a state suitable to Gundulf's princely rank and to her own. Hers, too, is the sterling praise of a will which ever responded to the government of a sanctified reason; so that if her son's generosity of character was a gift inherited from Gundulf, it was to her that he owed his habit of submitting thought and action to the test of a higher law, and of striving to find the accordance with reason of those revealed verities which are the subject matter of faith. And if we are to believe that the exquisite sensibility of his moral nature was derived from Ermenberg, he surely owed to Gundulf the virtue scarcely less signal of a constancy which nothing could appal.

As to Gundulf, he has been most unjustly treated by the

modern biographers of his son; and were the aspersions but remotely true that have been lavished on him, we should have to describe him as violent and impetuous, as prodigal and imperious, and as the willing slave and infatuated victim of the world's false joys. But there is no authority for any such description. The worst that we know of him is, that he was generous to excess, and loved to spend his fortune rather than to manage it with care. Rank and place asserted claims upon his bounty which were not to be evaded without dishonour; and he responded to them like a thousand worse men and like a thousand better, neglecting

> the lore
> Of nicely calculated less or more.

But that he was a wicked, or, in any bad sense of the word, a worldly man,[1] sobriety dares not conjecture. He was too generous and openhanded, so at least some declared, and spent his fortune heedlessly; whilst Ermenberg, by a singular discretion alike in the disbursement and the husbandry of her own means, played the part of what to this day is, in at least the south of France, termed by lawyers a *bonne mère de famille*. Ermenberg[2] lived in the world beyond blame or adverse

---

[1] He is described, it is true, as *sæculari vitæ deditus*; but no harm is meant by the description. The venerable Count Burchard, contemporary of Hugh Capet, is described thus: 'Cum igitur his et aliis multis Domino placere studeret virtutibus utpote vir *sæculari militiæ deditus* atque in cunctis mundi negotiis implicitus [*i.e.* 'employed,' as I shall prove in a future note] ejus mens Regi regum fideliter devota mundo minime celari potuit.'—Duchesne, *Script. Rer. Franc.* iv. 115.

He is further said to have been by some accounted 'non modo largus atque beneficus sed etiam prodigus atque vastator;' but it is scarcely fair to represent the combined value of these four words by the epithet *unthrifty*. The 'pene prodiga liberalitas' of William Fitzosborn (William of Malmesbury, *De Gest. Regum*) was surely something very different from unthriftiness. Nor would 'unthriftiness' express the princely weakness of Earl Robert of Gloucester, whom William of Malmesbury (*H. N.* i. § 14) describes as 'in dando diffusus, et quod minimè principem decet prodigus.'

[2] This is literally Eadmer's description of her, '*bonæ matris familiæ officio ungebatur.*' I suppose, then, that *un bon père de famille*, or rather its Languedoc or Norman equivalent, was already in vogue in Eadmer's day. Dean Church describes her as a prudent housewife; but in playing the part of the prudent house-

criticism, a prudent and thoughtful woman; but, notwithstanding her predilection for the religious life, died, so a directing Power willed it, in the secular; whereas Gundulf, notwithstanding a bent of character which conformed only too well with his vocation, relinquished in good time the duties no less than the dangers of his state, took the vows and donned the habit of a monk, and, a monk at heart as in garb, died to the world ere yet his end came.[1]

The portraits of Gundulf and Ermenberg are companion pictures, worthy of the son to whom we owe them.

It is very probable that after Anselm's birth Gundulf and Ermenberg remained for a long time without a second child, and that both of them were on that account, although from different motives, the more willing to devote their *unicus filius*[2] to the clerical profession; for an immemorial tradition had taught Christian parents to consecrate only sons to God, either because a solitary issue was regarded as a sort of loan from Heaven which must be restored ungrudgingly, or because such an act of confidence in the Divine goodness would, at any rate, be repaid by the preservation of the child's life, even if it did not win the reward of further progeny to his parents. There can be little doubt that Gundulf regarded the child as a future Bishop of Aosta, and indulged the hope of helping him to regain secular prerogatives lost, but lost, as he hoped, only for a time, to Ermenberg's house and to his own. Er-

wife she discharged but a portion of her duty, and exercised but a portion of her right as *materfamilias*. *Housewife*, I apprehend, is to *materfamilias* what *ménagère* is to *mère de famille*. Again, the Dean calls Gundulf 'a Lombard settler;' but surely *settler* is scarcely descriptive of a gentleman come to take up his abode in a new place. Such a word may be, and in this instance is, as I imagine, too literal to be truthful.

[1] M. de Rémusat and M. Charma must have been feeble latinists. They make 'circà diem obitus sui' refer to Ermenberg's death. The subject of the sentence is not Ermenberg but Gundulf.

[2] Thus we are told of St. Omer: 'Prædictum puerum, secundum Christianæ religionis à cunabulis ritum, ... in ecclesiasticis nutriebant disciplinis, *unicum* enim Audomarum habebant *filium*;' and of Germar, Abbot of Pental: 'Hunc siquidem genitores velut *unicum filium* tenerè diligentes tradiderunt scholis nutriendum atque instruendum doctrinâ Christi.'

menberg, on the other hand, had more generous aims. She knew that, even should her child's career be unchequered by contention and turmoil, the clerical life would for him be an existence of dignity, of wealth, of civic pomp, of ecclesiastical splendour; and her chief ambition was to wrap his childish hands in the altar-covering of some Benedictine monastery, and leave there the flower of her life, now no longer her own but God's, that stealing him thus from a world of sin, of sorrow, and of shame, she might ensure him his celestial crown. For the eleventh century, with all its wildness, all its simplicity, all its unrestraint, was conspicuous for its heroism; and its heroism was sucked from the mothers of the time. If its men had the courage to make vows, its women had the conspicuous constancy that kept them. Guibert of Nogent's father, in an ecstasy of terror, vowed on the day of his child's laborious birth, that the infant, if a boy, should be educated for the priesthood; but the little fellow had not been many months in the world when the infatuated parent, charmed with his child's physical gifts, repented of his promise, and would have broken it had not death interposed between him and his weakness. One Christmas night St. Odo's future father, a notably pious and upright man, prayed that a son might be given him. The prayer was heard, and when the boy was yet in the cradle, the father crept into the nursery, took him up in his arms, and cried: 'St. Martin, jewel of the priesthood, accept this my boy.' True to the dedication, he gave the child a suitable training, and all went well until Odo was fifteen years of age, when, captivated with the boy's beauty and loth to see those divinely-moulded limbs shrouded in a canon's frock, he made him doff the sacred attire, and sent him off to the Duke of Aquitaine's court, to hunt and hawk, and transform himself into the flower of chivalry, if so it might be. But so it might not be. Odo fell ill and was ill for three years, until the father, fairly beaten by the *gemma sacerdotum*, gave up the struggle, exclaiming,

'O Saint Martin, you are as strict to exact my vow as I was once delighted to make it. You are very ready to hear the prayers of your clients, but you make them pay for your patronage.' The fathers were weak, but the mothers were heroines. It was the mothers who prayed for joyous dreams, and who, when the dreams came, sought in simplicity and faith for their interpretation, and they obeyed with hearts brimming over with joy at the thought that for them, and for their children, Heaven should have deigned to disclose its will

During the anxious weeks that foreran Anselm's birth, Ermenberg, no doubt, waited in trembling hope for the consolation of a vision touching the destiny of her child ; like her who in the previous age brought William of Dijon to the birth, and who dreamt, and lo! a Lady of royal mien and in regal attire, who, bending her eyes upon the wonder-stricken sleeper, illumined her right breast with an unearthly splendour. But scarce had the heavenly Queen appeared when troops of angels started into view, who drew the child from the dreamer's arms, and carried it cradled in clouds of light to heaven ; and she in her blissful terror could find no other words than these : 'Blessed Mother of my Lord and Saviour, I give him to you, take care of him!' So crying she awoke ; the vision was not despised ; other presages succeeded, and in due course the two parents, 'with one will and one consent and with the favourable advice of all their kindred, vowed the boy to the Lord Christ, Him to serve perpetually in His house.'

But why cite instances? For any such presages as may have been granted to Ermenberg during her early motherhood were surpassed a few years after Anselm's birth by a dream or vision which, vouchsafed to the child himself, left an indelible impress on his mind and on hers.

Ermenberg, herself as yet little more than a girl, loved to speak to the child of that world on which her own hopes were fixed. Too simple, it may be, or too humble, or too prudent, to perplex herself or him with the twofold meaning of that word which, in her *lingua romana*, denoted at once the heaven of heavens and the lustrous canopy of blue that overhung the valley of Aosta, and seemed to rest on the everlasting hills around, she spoke to him in simple phrase of heaven, and of Him who dwells there; and in speaking of God ventured to represent Him under images suggested by what she herself had seen or heard of all that was noblest and worthiest in this world. Heaven was to her an ideal court, of which her own domestic traditions had afforded her an image; and in that heaven dwelt God, ruling all things and sustaining all things. So she taught her wondering child, in phrase suited to an infancy too tender to grasp other and more mysterious truths; and he in his turn developed her teaching into the conviction that God was willing His abode should be seen by mortal eye. Looking about him, therefore, day by day, for his best mountain way to heaven, he scanned the snowy dome of Velan, the icy flanks of the Ruitors, the slippery pinnacles of Combin, all the aërial heights that stand far off round about the valley of Aosta; but to his untutored vision none was higher than the Becca di Nona, whose noontide shadow lay every day across the valley down below the city, as none was nearer for his untried strength, and none, therefore, when the happy moment should come, less likely to disappoint him. For when at evening all the other mountain summits are already eclipsed, the Becca di Nona [1] gleams bright in the firmament; and whereas they stand wrapped in eternal shrouds

[1] This mountain stands almost due south of Aosta. Its English name would be Noon-tide Peak. Our word *noon* is a corruption of *nona*, i.e. *hora nona*; the word having obtained its present meaning at a time when the ecclesiastical office of nones was said by anticipation at midday, and not about three o'clock. I have no doubt that the Becca di Nona received its name when it was customary to ring the bells for the office I have mentioned, just as the sun stood over it; and my conviction is confirmed by the fact that the older name of the more distant Mons Emilius, which stands a little more to the east, is *pic de dix heures*, or ten o'clock peak. When the unworthy designation Mons Emilius shall have been supplanted by a better, the Valdostans could not do better than give their Becca di Nona the alternative name of Mont St. Anselme.

of snow and ice, time is year by year when the summit of the Becca di Nona is for a few short weeks laid bare by the autumnal warmth. The season was autumn when little Anselm discovered this; and, noting well that at the foot of the mountain there lay a titanic ledge of rock which might be of service to him, called then as now the Gargantua, he nursed his divine ambition till one night as he slept the summons came. He must climb the mountain and hasten to the Court of God. He set forth, crossed the river, scaled the Gargantua, where, grieved at finding the King's maidens gathering in His harvest after too careless and too indolent a fashion, he chid their sloth and resolved to lay charge against them, but passed on forthwith; for he must not delay. So, leaving the region of corn and vineyard, he plunged into the forest, and, threading his way upwards through belts of pine and over lawns of turf and lavender, and scaling precipitous blank rocks, had already reached the summit, when lo! heaven opened. The Invisible, in fashion as a king, sat before him, throned in majesty, and with none near Him but His seneschal, for the rest of the household had been sent down into the world to reap His harvest. The child crossed the threshold; the Lord called him, and he obeyed; he approached, and sat down at the Lord's feet; was asked with royal grace and condescension who he was, whence he had come, what he wanted; answered the questions, and was not afraid. Whereupon the King gave command to the seneschal, who brought forth bread and set before him. It was bread of an exceeding whiteness;[1] and he ate it in the Lord's presence. He ate it and was refreshed, and slept his sleep, and awoke next morning at Aosta, and, remembering his journey, or, rather, not so much remembering it, as retracing

---

[1] '*Panem nitidissimum.*' Thus in one of his eucharistic prayers he says, '*Panis candidissime,* . . . comedat te cor meum, etc.' And in the Life of Archbishop Oswald of York we read that once when that saint was saying mass his guardian angel appeared and supplied him with a *panis candidissimus.*

it step by step, and incident by incident, flew to his mother's knee, and told her all.

Ermenberg wept tears of consolation, but her joy was not like his. Wonder what the vision might mean, wonder whether it was in the body or out of the body that this had happened, added bewilderment to her bliss. But Anselm's was unalloyed; he had been in paradise corporally, and with corporal mouth had eaten the Bread of God.

Thus did Heaven set its mark on the child!

CHAPTER II.

ST. ANSELM'S CHILDHOOD.

IN Lombardy, in Provence, in Burgundy, in Aquitaine, in the comparatively small kingdom of France, it was, in the earlier part of the eleventh century, expected of a gentleman that he should be able to read. The fashion was already taking firm root in Normandy, and the Germans were the only people not deemed barbarous who were insensible to the reproach conveyed by the word *illiteratus*. Our 'illiterate' is now no longer to educated Englishmen the equivalent of *illiteratus;* but there can be no doubt, if the meaning assigned to it by our yeomanry is to be regarded as traditional, that it at one time described the man who had not learnt to read. The day will soon come when by the 'unlettered swain' we shall all mean the swain unversed in literature, and not, as once, the swain who cannot spell. At the present moment no one attaches a definite idea to the phrase; a sure sign that its meaning is undergoing change.

Ladies were not expected to emulate the learning of their husbands and brothers. Thus Guibert of Nogent, when writing of his mother, who was a woman of illustrious birth, informs us, quite as a matter of course, that, although she spoke like a bishop, she was an *illiterata fœmina*.[1]

The scarcity of books rendered it impossible that there should be much reading, whether studious or desultory. Yet

---

[1] *De Vita suâ*, lib. i. cap. xxix. But by the end of the century things were different. The Countess Ida of Boulogne could read; so could Matilda of Tuscany; so could the queen of our first Henry.

we are told of a Duke of Aquitaine that he had a library in his palace which he consulted when the leisure was allowed him, and that he used to pore over the parchment during the long nights of winter, until his head dropped, and toil gave way to slumber.[1] Conrad the Salic knew not letters, it is true;[2] but he was a German. Nevertheless Wippo, in a poem dedicated to Conrad's son Henry the Black, complained that there was only one country in the civilised world whose sons were allowed to grow up *illiterati*, and proposed that the Emperor should make it compulsory on gentlemen that all their male offspring should be taught to read after the example of their sovereign.[3]

The universal text-book was the Psalter. Robert the Pious, King of France, read the Psalms daily, not indeed as a literary but as a devotional exercise; still, there can be no doubt that his choice of the book was guided by the ease which repeated perusals in boyhood had given him in reading it.[4] And we are told of a pious Thuringian, who, resigning the belt of knighthood and assuming the religious tonsure, soon became so famous for his expositions of Holy Scripture that secular clergymen, not allowed by the rule of the order to enter the chapter-house, would hang about its open windows so as to hear his sermons, that he had learned to

---

[1] *Ademari Engolismensis Historiæ*, lib. iii. § 54.

[2] 'Quanquam enim litteras ignoraret tamen omnem clerum . . . prudenter instituit.' Wipponis *Vita Conradi Salici*, § De Itinere Regis per Regna.

[3]
  'Solis Teutonicis vacuum vel turpe videtur
  Ut doceant aliquem nisi clericus accipiatur.
  Sed, rex docte, jube cunctos per regna doceri;
  Ut tecum regnet sapientia partibus istis.'

—*Panegyricus Wipponis.*

Otho the Great a century before achieved the astounding feat of learning to read after he had reached man's estate; and we are informed that he not only read but understood: 'Ingenium ei admodum mirandum; nam post mortem Edidis reginæ cùm autem nesciret litteras in tantum didicit ut pleniter libros legere et intelligere noverit.'—*Widikundi R.G.S.*

[4] 'Eloquentiæ tantùm incumbens ut nullus laberetur dies quin legeret psalterium.'—*Helgaldi Floriacensis Epitoma Vitæ Roberti Regis.*

read nothing beyond the Psalms.[1] The tradition was an old one; for in the ninth century such few boys as were at that time sent to school to obtain some little learning before going to court and entering on military service, were made to learn their alphabet with the one definite aim of being able to read that inspired text-book.[2]

Such children, however, as were destined for the clerical profession must not only read, but sing the Psalter; and such as were to be monks must know every word of it by heart. But with these latter we need not now trouble ourselves; for little Anselm was destined for the white habit of the secular canon, not for the more sober garb of the sons of St. Benedict.

It was the custom of the age that parents who destined a child for dignified clerical preferment should entrust him to the care of a *nutritor*— of a guardian, that is to say, or governor, who was to have the entire charge of him, and train him for his profession. And if pages and maids of honour were the merest boys and girls upon their introduction to the courts of princes, it was in veriest childhood that the clergymen of the generation that was to be were transplanted into the household of some great prelate or high-born canon, under whose direction they were perhaps as carefully tended, and certainly as sedulously whipped, as if they had remained under the parental roof.

The reason of this banishment of the little churchmen of the eleventh century from their own homes to those of great ecclesiastics is obvious. The nurseries of the age were not adorned with those incentives to literary culture which are in

---

[1] 'Nam litteras omninò frater ille nisi tantùm psalmos non didicit, et tamen omnem rationem et intellectum evangelii legis et prophetarum et historiarum quoque . . . mirabiliter percepit.'—*Vita S. Godehardi Hildesheimensis, auct. Wolfero.*

[2] 'Qui . . . studiis litterarum applicatus est . . . ut decurso psalterio mox sæcularibus exercitiis erudiretur.'—*S. Odonis de Vitâ S. Geraldi Comitis Auriliac,* lib. i. § 4.

these days presumed by their presence to stimulate the mental activity of the rising race—such as pictures for meek-souled boys of babes in the wood buried by robins, and, for the iron-hearted, of giant-killers blazoned in bright colours and looking terrible. Nor had the alphabet as yet become a plaything; for there was not a nurse in Christendom, and scarcely a mother, who would have known how to make it serviceable. And since letters are useless without a literary language, how, if the only language spoken by father, mother, and domestics have not a literature, shall the child profit by them? For we should greatly err were we to imagine that either the *lingua sclavonica*, the *lingua saxonica*, or the *lingua teutonica*, was regarded by the scholars of the tenth and eleventh centuries as other than a barbarous patois. Even the *lingua romana* had not as yet a literature. Hence none but Latinists, whether of less or greater ability, would presume to take charge of an *abecedarius*; and ecclesiastics were by an inevitable consequence the sole teachers even of little children.

Little children, indeed! For we are gravely informed that St. Leo IX. was already four years old when his mother sent him to Berthold Bishop of Toul to be educated.[1] And Meinhard, the saint of Einsiedeln, would seem to have been somewhat younger than even that when his father, thinking it high time he should learn the alphabet, carried him away to the unfrequented island [2] of Sulgen, and confided him to the care of a monk who lived there. The good man was a kinsman, and gladly took charge of the child, who is described as an *infantulus*. This was in the days of Charlemagne. It was towards the end of the ninth century that St. Odo, of Cluny, whilst as yet a mere *infantulus à lacte depulsus*, was sent off to a good priest, who treated him very tenderly, no doubt, but not more so than so tender an infancy required;[3] and St.

---

[1] *Acta Sanctorum Bolland.*, April 19.

[2] Vita S. Meginradi; Mabillon, *Acta SS.*, sec. iv. p. ii.

[3] 'Infantulus à lacte depulsus et . . . cunis exemptus cuidam sacerdoti longiùs commanenti traditur nutriendus.'—*Nalgadi Vita S. Odonis Cluniac.*

THE SINGING LESSON.

Robert, the founder of the Cistercians, born some sixteen or seventeen years before St. Anselm, was sent to school as soon as he was weaned.[1] The little ward was no sooner under the roof of his *nutritor* than he was henceforth a *litteris traditus*, a *litteris applicatus*, a *litteris mancipatus*. Going day by day, in at least many instances, to the primary school of some neighbouring monastery, he endured all its traditional woes until, having perused the text of the Psalter to the satisfaction of his teachers, he reached the stage at which children who aspired to military service were allowed to stop, and it became his lot to encounter the more poignant griefs of the singing lesson. What these were may be learnt from the subjoined extract from an unpublished manuscript preserved in the public library at Evreux.

It should be premised that in a certain Cluniac establishment, dependent upon the priory of La Charité, the monks wished the Feast of St. Nicholas to be celebrated with the solemnities used at Cluny, and requested that the saint's history might be sung, not read; that the prior refused; that the monks remonstrated; that the dispute waxed hot and strong; and that the obstinate superior punished his refractory subjects, and even caused them to be beaten with a *scopa*, or birch-rod. This exhausted the patience of St. Nicholas. 'Next night, when the prior had gone to sleep, behold St. Nicholas stood before him with a rod in his hand, and accosted him with these words, "You have had your monks beaten on my account; you shall see what will happen to you for that—Sing!" Then the saint began the antiphon which commences *O Christi pietas*. But the prior refused to sing

---

[1] 'Expletis igitur diebus mulier peperit filium quem ablactatum tradidit litterarum studiis imbuendum.'—*Vita S. Roberti, Cisterc. Fundatoris*, cap. i.
To remove all doubt as to the meaning of *ablactatus*, I will add the following from the Life of St. Odulf:—'Porro ubi desiit ad materna pendere ubera litterarum studiis traditur et sanctis et Deo devotis hominibus, ut at illis canonicâ religione imbueretur commendatus est.'

after him; whereupon he began to give him a sound flogging. .... *Quid multa?* He kept on beating him, and "learning"[1] him, and singing the antiphon over and over again until he should sing it right through from beginning to end without a mistake. Now when the monks who were in their beds all round the dormitory heard the prior sobbing, and singing the aforesaid antiphon between his sobs, they were sore amazed ... but none of them ventured to awake him, for they wanted to see what the end of it would be! So when he had at last succeeded in singing it well and from memory, all alone, the whole of it, he awoke; and perceiving the brethren standing round about his bed with lamps in their hands, as he did not wish to speak to them then, he made signs to them to go to bed again, and spent the remainder of his night without sleeping—he was in such pain and terror. But when it was morning, and the time came for speaking,[2] he called

---

[1] 'Discendo.'

[2] That is to say, on their assembling in the chapter-house after prime. Silence between compline and prime is enjoined by the Rule of St. Benedict (cap. xlii.). 'Exeuntibus à completoriis nulla sit licentia denuo cuiquam loqui aliquid. Quod si inventus fuerit quisquam prævaricari hanc taciturnitatis regulam graviori vindictæ subjaceat: excepte si necessitas hospitum supervenerit, aut forte abbas aliquid jusserit. Quod tamen et ipsum cum summâ gravitate et moderatione honestissime fiat.'

It was customary in some, if not all, monasteries, at the end of compline to say these words: 'Pone, Domine, custodiam ori meo, et ostium circumstantiæ labiis meis.'

The Cluniac monks were famous for a scrupulous observance of this rule. Thus there is a story in the Life of St. Odo of a Cluniac monk who on a journey to Rome allowed a horse belonging to his monastery to be stolen rather than break the rule by raising an alarm. And William of Malmesbury tells us of Lanzo, Abbot of St. Pancras, at Lewes, that, when racked with sufferings which left him no respite and yielded to no expedient, he refused to utter a syllable between compline and prime. 'Nunquam tamen noctibus locutus; rogantibus fratribus ut silentium solveret, non adquievit ... quod nunquam postquam monachicum habitum accepisset à completorio exiens usque ad sequentis diei primam locutus fuisset.'—W. M. *De Gest. Reg. Angl.* p. 675.

While on this subject I will take the opportunity of saying that I think Mabillon must have been mistaken in his interpretation of a passage in one of the Lives of St. Gerald of Corbie: 'Aliquando *post completam* coram altari se effundens in omnium rationum effectus usque ad singultus verba interrumpentes ... tandem laxata vox invenit iter. ... Et gemebundus rediit ad

them together, and said: "The Lord have mercy on you, brethren, for getting me such a flogging last night. Go, sing the history as you want, for, willing or nilling, I suppose I must let you have your way, lest I get another such flogging as I did last night, and perhaps worse."' 'Another such flogging and perhaps worse!' What a plaintive echo from the singing class!

The little schoolboy, concurrently with his lessons in singing, was taught to write. His first efforts were made, not on parchment by means of a pen, but with a style upon a slate of wood, perhaps of ivory, covered with wax. Here, too, must he be cautious; particularly must he remember the difference between his p's and his q's; for he wrote from dictation, and must have his wits about him. There is a difference between *dictare* and *scribere*; *dictare* denotes the writing upon tablets, *scribere* the writing upon parchment, or the copying out of what has been submitted to correction on the wax. But more of this in another place. Enough to know that the three subjects taught in an elementary school in the eleventh century were not reading, writing, and arithmetic; but reading, writing, and the singing of the Psalms to their proper tones.

Children who had learnt thus much, and no more, were termed *scholares* or scholars in the sense of the word still kept up among our rural poor, as when they say, 'I am no scholar,' meaning, 'I cannot write' or 'I cannot read.' They 'knew their letters,' were lettered or *litterati*, and were the precursors of our literates. Our masters of arts, on the other

---

lectum suum, cumque ibi sederet . . . miserabili voce clamavit. . . . Sicque liberatus laudavit liberatorem liberâ voce.' *Post completam* can scarcely mean *post completorium*, for Gerald would not have chosen such a time for praying aloud; and no good monk would have made an audible thanksgiving for no matter what favour during the interval of obligatory silence. Now inasmuch as monks sat up in bed for their mid-day *siesta*, the fact that Gerald was sitting, not lying, suggests the insertion of the word *missam*. He began to pray after mass, *post completam missam*.

hand, had their forerunners in those who, passing from the elementary school of reading, writing, and singing, were in the *schola grammatica*, or grammar school, set to enter upon the study of the seven liberal arts. These were divided into two groups: the *trivium*, which embraced grammar, rhetoric and dialectic; and the *quadrivium*, which consisted of music, that is to say, scientific music, arithmetic or the science of numbers, geometry, and astronomy. A man who had mastered these seven arts was a *homo doctus*.

The schoolboy of the eleventh century who was required to learn grammar—by which, of course, was meant Latin grammar—had as great need as hitherto of his style and tablets. The master or *grammaticus* read what he wished to teach from a manuscript copy of Priscian, of Donatus, perhaps of Alcuin; and his reading, lection, lesson or lecture—whatever we please to call it—was by the process termed *dictatio* inscribed by the pupil on his sheet of wax, and thence by *repetitio* or frequent perusal transferred to memory. Hence our catachrestic phrase, 'to *repeat* a *lesson.*'

Thus were the Latin accidence and syntax learnt; nor can there be a doubt that a great deal of time was spent in declining nouns, conjugating verbs, and reciting rules. There was plenty of parsing too; and, what may perhaps excite some surprise, plenty of composition both in prose and verse. For, indeed, except for the altered condition of institutions well stocked with printed books, we may feel sure that the customs of our own public schools at the close of the last century represented with a general fidelity the practice of earlier ages. 'Apply yourself,' said St. Anselm in his old age, 'apply yourself with all your power to declining and conjugating, and to learning your grammar well; and practice composition, but more in prose than in verse.' 'Try to know your grammar well; get into the habit of composing something every day, especially in prose; and do not grow too fond of an involved style, but aim at a clear and logical one. Always speak in Latin, except when obliged to do otherwise.'¹

St. Anselm's own latinity was so lucid and concise, that we may well believe the literary educators of his childhood to have possessed that rare skill which leaves little to choose between the instructor's pleasure in teaching and the pupil's delight in learning. But if we trust that he was spared much at least of the *infandus dolor* which fell to the general lot of his contemporaries of the schoolroom, we must not imagine that he escaped unscathed; for the allusions in the literature of the age to that ensign of magisterial power which is now fast lapsing into the realm of myth, are such as to render it incredible that any, even the most favoured, can have been entirely spared its infliction; and if the reflections appended to the anecdote with a notice of which this chapter will conclude may be taken in evidence together with what Eadmer tells us of St. Anselm's endeavours to mitigate the severity practised by the best of men amongst his contemporaries, there can be no room to doubt that he was in his childhood made to suffer even as others. What sort of suffering it was we learn from Guibert of Nogent, whose private tutor, the kindest-hearted and best of men, treated him with a severity scarcely credible but by those who are fortunate enough to have time to spare for reading the whole of his account. Here are the concluding passages: 'So sincere was my return of his affection, notwithstanding the many stripes my skin carried from his numerous and gratuitous castigations, that I forgot all his roughness, and paid him the homage, not of my fears, but of a love deep as the very marrow of my being. And my mother and my master, observing that I rendered due respect to each, made not a few

¹ *Ep.* iv. 31, 114. The speaking of Latin in our university-schools and senate-houses is the perpetuation of a custom which lapse of time has abolished elsewhere, partly, perhaps, in consequence of the elevation of English to the dignity of a literary language. But I imagine that Latin was usually spoken in our schools as late as the end of the sixteenth century.

experiments on my fidelity, to see if I would presume to prefer one to the other. . . .

'At last an occasion arose, alike unprecedented in its occurrence and unmistakable in its issue. One day I had had a flogging in the school-room; the school-room had been made out of a parlour in our house. My studies, such as they were, having come to an end, as it grew late in the evening, I approached my mother's knee, still mindful of my very severe, but quite unmerited chastisement. She began, as usual, by asking me if I had been punished during the day. I promptly replied in the negative, not wishing to look like a teller of tales out of school; when, will I or nill I, she pulls off my under garment, which they call a *subucula*, that is to say, my shirt, and beholds my poor little back livid from the switching of the birch-twigs, the skin in ridges all over. The bowels of her compassion yearned, for I was a delicate little fellow, and had been rather too roughly used, no doubt. She trembled exceedingly, and her eyes brimmed over with grief, as she exclaimed, " Never, never shall you be a clergyman. Scholar or no scholar, no longer shall you pay like this for scholarship." Whereupon I turned round, looked her full in the face as reproachfully as I possibly could, and replied, " If I have to die for it, I intend to go on learning, and I *shall* be a clergyman." She tried to bribe me with the promise of a splendid suit of armour, and all the rest of it, would I only consent to become a knight; but I was not to be bribed.'[1]

Thus victory declared for the *grammaticus*. He was an incompetent teacher, no doubt. Whilst, however, we make every allowance for his incompetency, we must remember that he would be unlikely to chastise a high born and delicately constituted child with what he in his heart deemed an excessive severity, and that he can scarcely have far exceeded

[1] Ven. Guiberti, Novigent., *De Vitâ suâ*, lib. i.

the custom of his age. Precisely so. He represented a universal tradition, which made whipping as necessary to the formation of a child's character as blood-letting to the health of persons of mature age. The tradition was an old one; for have we not all heard the story of St. Isidore of Seville, who in his childhood suffered so terribly from whippings administered by his elder brother as to run away from him in sheer terror, but who repented himself and came back to be whipped more cruelly than ever, if so be whipping was to make a man of him? It was an old one; for St. Benedict in his Rule enjoins that a false note or a false quantity in the Divine office is to be atoned by castigation.[1] It was an old one; for St. Paul seems never to have heard of a child who escaped: 'Quis enim est filius quem non corripit pater?' (Heb. xii. 7). St. Anselm himself, when Prior of Le Bec, notwithstanding his unrivalled sweetness and repose of nature, and an affectionateness that has almost passed into a proverb, refused not to correct with rods a lad whom he was educating into saintliness, and whom he loved with a love unparalleled in history for its depth, for its purity, and for the sympathy with which it was returned. And the monks of Cluny, than whom a more respectable body of men never existed—no, never—thus describe the general practice in their monasteries:—'At nocturns, and at all other hours, if a boy makes a mistake in singing a psalm or anything else, if he falls asleep, or, in short, does that which he ought not to do, no matter what, he is taken to task at once, and without a moment's delay, as soon as he gets into the schoolroom, is stripped of frock and cowl, and either by the prior or by his own master birched with a rod provided for the purpose.'[2]

---

[1] 'Si quis dum pronuntiat psalmum, responsorium, aut antiphonam, vel lectionem, fallitur .... vindictæ subjaceat. Infantes vero pro tali culpâ vapulent.'—*S. P. Benedicti Regula*, cap. xlv.

[2] *Adalrici Consuetudines Cluniacenses*, lib. iii. cap. viii.

This extract—and others like it might be quoted—may perhaps throw an unexpected light upon a usage which the unwary student of the middle ages is tempted to regard as barbarous. Severe it was, as indeed it was meant to be; but it was meant to be passionless, though strict; and though inevitable, as the good men thought who inflicted it, yet always just. Hence parents, the best and tenderest of parents, were only too ready to subject their children to it; and these latter, knowing only too well of Whose providential government the men they revered thought it a copy, responded to its sobering influence with a return of love not altogether unlike theirs who have been sanctified and sweetened by the afflicting hand of God. ' Ego quos amo, arguo et castigo.'

Thus we are told of our own St. Hugh of Lincoln, that, committed when not seven years of age to the care of some canons regular near Grenoble, 'the pedagogue's scourge in such wise plied upon his *infantile corpusculum*, and in such wise did the shackles of discipline restrain in him the motions of boyhood, that his virtues outstripped his vices'—poor child—'and that his entire life from its morning to its decline [*a sui ortu usque ad occasum*] was one perpetual martyrdom.' 'In good truth,' used the saint to say, 'I never meddled with the joys of this world; I never learnt to joke; I could never join in sports.' For an aged canon, the very man who seems to have administered the whippings, conceived a special interest in him, and, persuading him to have no part in such vanities, prepared him for a loftier destiny than that which awaited his thoughtless schoolfellows. 'My dearest child,' he used to say, 'do not let yourself be led away by all this silly and unmeaning levity. Let them alone. These pursuits are not in keeping with your destiny.' And then he would add, 'Little Hugh, little Hugh, I am training you for Christ; to play the fool is no work of yours.' (' Hugonete, Hugonete, ego te Christo nutrio; jocari non est tuum.')

Anyhow, the ideal wielders of all this rigid severity were,

in their turn, models of self-chastisement and self-control; and, however unhappily it may in this or that instance have been exaggerated or misapplied, it was not incompatible with a very deep and earnest love. For it evoked love, and with love an emulation of the self-discipline, the self-restraint, the minute and conscientious watchfulness of men who dared to be merciless to their own flesh. Thus little Hugh as time passed longed for something severer than the canonical life, ran away to the Grande Chartreuse, took the habit there, and eventually established the first Carthusian monastery in England.

But enough of this. Suffice it on the one hand to know that this terrible discipline was fashioned to a passionless ideal; suffice it on the other to remember that grave historians of the eleventh and twelfth centuries seem to have regarded the sufferings of a school-boy under the ferule of his master as the very *acme* of human woe. And we may well believe it; for, if no less careful a speaker than St. Anselm himself used in his old age to protest that rather than be Archbishop of Canterbury he would prefer to be a little boy in a monastery school quailing under the master's rod, the declaration was deemed by Eadmer so strange, and antecedently so unlikely to have been made in earnest by any man who knew what he was saying, that he has thought it necessary to call God to witness that the Archbishop had indeed made it, and that he had himself heard him make it over and over again in most sober earnest.[1]

Let us now, therefore, provided with some general notion of the education of children in St. Anselm's time, trace the course of his, guided by such special information as has survived the accidents of time.

He can scarcely have been more than three years old when he dreamed the dream recorded in the preceding chapter;

[1] 'Deum testor me sæpe illum sub veritatis testimonio audire protestantem quod liberius vellet.'—*Vita*, lib. ii. cap. i.

and the awe with which that dream inspired his parents and kinsmen must have been sensibly enhanced by the desire which the child soon expressed of being allowed to go to school. Ermenberg, knowing what was meant by going to school, resisted with all the arts and artifices of a fond mother; but, from whatever cause, and for whatever reason, her unwillingness was made to yield; and little Anselm was transferred to the home of one or other of her brothers, Lambert and Folcerad, who, besides being godfathers[1] to the boy, now began to share in his behalf the responsibilities of *nutritor*.[2] Day by day he went to school—what school cannot easily be determined; but on the whole it is likely that, as the collegiate church of St. Ours and the cathedral were only provided with institutions for the training of choristers, he was entrusted to the educational skill of some Benedictine fathers, who had a monastery within the city not far from its southern wall. Morning by morning he set forth, accompanied, as became his rank, by a *clericus*,[3] one of those ill-paid but not always ill-taught gentlemen in minor orders, who, though sometimes termed *clericuli* in sport, were found to be very useful personages in the palaces of kings and the higher nobility. Evening by evening the little fellow returned in charge of the same attendant, to prepare his lessons for the morrow. And if the modest usher ere day declined alleviated the drudgery of the task in hand, he had when the morrow came a slight burden enough to carry—at first an *abecedarius*, and later on the wax-lined diptych of boxwood or ivory with its accompanying *stylus*. Unless, indeed,

---

[1] He calls himself their godson in *Ep.* i. 18.

[2] St. Anselm's is not the only case in the eleventh century of a child whose sponsors were charged with this additional duty. Thus he himself (*Ep.* iii. 106) says to one of his correspondents, 'Si tota vestra congregatio . . . consilio reverendorum episcoporum Ivonis Carnotensis et Galonis Parisiensis, *qui patres vestri fuerunt et vos nutriverunt*, vos instanter elegerit.' And Archbishop Halinard, of Lyons, was his godfather's *nutritus*.

[3] Thus St. Leo IX. in his childhood has his *clericus*. We read in his Life, 'Adalberonem suum clericum tunc tantummodo ejus assidentem lectulo allocutus.'

custom required even a child of Anselm's rank to do as humbler schoolboys did, and carry his own *tabulæ* slung by a strap over the left shoulder and resting on the right hip; but this is not likely.[1]

After he had for a year or two pursued his studies in the elementary school, Lambert and Folcerad confided him to the care of a private tutor, a kinsman perhaps of their own, and certainly of his, and, therefore, a kinsman either of Ermenberg's or of Gundulf's. His name has not been recorded, an omission all the more provoking as we know that other godsons of Anselm's uncles had a *magister* named Lambert,[2] who gave lessons when Anselm was approaching middle life, and who may quite be the *Lambertus levita* of a document drawn up in the year 1040 at Aosta, and still extant. I suspect, indeed, that Lambert the deacon, Lambert the tutor of other young gentlemen after Anselm, and Anselm's own *magister*, were one and the same person.

Be this as it may, the little boy's tutor, whatever his name, had probably been selected in virtue of that clearness and accuracy of thought and phrase which characterised a school of teachers recently sprung into existence in the neighbouring Lombardy. Their *coryphæus*, their exemplar, and their guide was the illustrious and incomparable Lanfranc —Lanfranc, the grandest scholar of his age, its admiration and its envy; and it is no slight praise of the eleventh century that it should have known how to envy and admire such an intellect as his.

It would seem that for some fifteen or twenty years before the period of Anselm's birth Lanfranc had dazzled Italy by an acumen without precedent in its Christian annals; had given a new character to the jurisprudence of

---

[1] 'Duas solùm tabellas manu bajulans, scribendi officio aptissimas, fabrili opere ita connexas ut possent patefieri non tamen disjungi, quibus scholastici dextro femore solent uti.'—*Vita S. Odonis* auctore Joanne (Mabillon, *Acta SS.*, Sæc. V.).
[2] *Ep.* i. 17.

Lombardy, and had informed and moulded the choicest minds not of Lombardy alone, nor of Italy, but of almost every country in Europe, by the accuracy, the vigour, the grace, and the amplitude of a scholarship which the citizens of Pavia long accounted, and still account, one of the proudest titles to renown which their annals have preserved to them. But Pavia was well known to Gundulf, kinsmen of whom had worn the iron crown within its walls; Pavia was in all probability, so long, at least, as Lanfranc flourished there, a nursery of classical tutors for, at any rate, the best families in the valleys and plains which were watered by the Dora Baltea, the Ticino, and the Po; and to have heard Lanfranc—as the phrase then ran—in his lecture-room at Pavia, constituted an advantage of even comparatively greater value than in these days it is to have had the special assistance of the best of private tutors in the more accurate and more critical of our own universities. And when we remember that St. Anselm, before he reached the age of thirty, was, in at least some departments of learning, deemed scarcely second even to Lanfranc, and that the desire of making Lanfranc's acquaintance had been his principal motive for travelling from the Alps to Normandy, we may well believe his earlier studies to have been directed by some teacher from Pavia, who knew how to recommend to him the genius and the talents of that illustrious scholar.

But not only did Anselm's birth entitle him to a private tutor; he seems, when as yet quite a boy, to have held a rank in the ecclesiastical hierarchy which rendered it seemly that he should no longer be sent out to school. There can be little doubt that he was a canon as early as his fourteenth year, and I suspect he had worn the habit from the early age of seven. He could sing the Psalms, and was old enough to receive the tonsure; well, therefore, might he be a member either of the cathedral chapter or of that of St. Ours; or even of each. Lambert and Folcerad appear to have been pluralists,[1] and their nephew may also have enjoyed double preferment. He certainly was a canon of the cathedral church in early manhood, but it does not therefore follow that he had never occupied a stall in St. Ours. On the contrary, destined, as he was, for the mitre, nothing would be more likely than that the first canonry to be had in either church should be conferred upon him, child though he were. Anyhow, the junior canon of St. Ours in the year 1040 was an Anselm. Why should not that Anselm be ours?

If so, then as canon of St. Ours he wore a little white habit, white from head to foot; as canon of St. Ours he day by day took his place in his stall and sang the divine praises.

[1] There are two documents in the *Historiæ Patriæ Monumenta* which not only confirm the conjecture which I had made long before seeing them, that Lambert and Folcerad were canons, but render it probable that they had canonries in both churches. The deed of exchange between Bishop Burchard and a certain Frecio, executed in the year 1025, has a group of six signatures, which must be those of the six canons of the cathedral. They are Guntardus, Lambertus, Folcho, Vulgrinus, Volfordus, Ugo. If I could only be sure that the third of these names should be Folceradus and not Folcho, and nothing is less unlikely, then I should have no doubt that each of Ermenberg's brothers was a member of the cathedral chapter in the year 1025.

The other is a deed of gift from Humbert the White-handed, in 1040, to the canons of St. Ursus, and is attested by five names, those, no doubt, of members of the chapter; namely, Bovo, Boso, Folceradus, Arnulfus, Anselmus. Now there were six canonries, and I suspect the missing name is Lambert's.

Light may yet break upon the subject; meanwhile we must be content with the probability that Lambert and Folcerad were pluralists. Two provostships and twelve canonries might well invite plurality in a family like Ermenberg's; for I cannot too strongly insist upon it that Ermenberg's was the ruling family of the *villa* and *civitas*, the 'city and county,' of Aosta. One of Ermenberg's brothers was Bishop of Aosta; another of them was his *coepiscopus*; and, as none but persons of birth, and high birth, might hold the twelve canonries, half of which would seem to have been founded by her collateral ancestor, Bishop Anselm I., her eldest son would naturally receive the first of them that offered. The reader will find the subject of Ermenberg's pedigree pretty fully discussed in the Appendix.

Of course the junior canon of St. Ursus in 1040 may have been another Anselm; but our little friend was unquestionably a *clericus* as early as his fourteenth year, and there would seem to be no reason why he should not have resembled St. Odilo, who was made a canon of Brioude '*inter ipsa primordia.*'

It was, however, as a canon of the cathedral church—unless, indeed, like St. Oswald, he had higher preferment still—that he was known upon his arrival at Le Bec. The *Ecclesia Augustana* of Gilbert Crispin can only be the cathedral.

The Church of St. Ours is at this moment in many respects as it was then; but eight centuries can have witnessed no lovelier sight within its walls than that of the innocent white-robed child thus engaged. Surely the listening angels can have had no sweeter task than to improve his timorous efforts and carry them all musical to heaven.

But we must leave the choir for the school-room.

Tutor and pupil began their labours with equal zeal; but the zeal of the former was greater than his discretion. He had been too well taught, and was himself too good a teacher, to exaggerate the customary rigours of the school-room, and may even have relaxed them in no inconsiderable degree. But he had so good a pupil, that, bent upon converting the thoughtful, meditative, ever-reasoning child into a prodigy of learning, he entered upon a course of discipline which prudence should have warned him was for such a child the cruellest that could be contrived—a course of discipline in comparison with which the purple lashes on Guibert of Nogent's little back were very mercy. Guibert, when his case was at the worst, could, at any rate, look his mother in the face and say, 'If I die of my whippings, I mean to be whipped;' but, when Anselm's was at the worst, the brightest star of the eleventh century had been well-nigh quenched in its rising. The infatuated pedagogue confined him to the house in the fond hope of forcing him by incessant application into a premature intellectual ripeness; and, deeming it waste of time that so active a mind should be allowed to relax a tension to which it was only too prone by temperament, kept him prisoner over his books, and paid little heed to the attenuated features and throbbing pulse of his willing victim, and to all the other indications of an overwrought brain. At last the brain refused to work, and the precocious little student felt as if reason were toppling from her throne. The uncles, appealed to in this emergency, tried all the rude skill then in fashion, but to no purpose, and were fain in their perplexity to send him home to Ermenberg. Here fresh alarms awaited the poor child. He had forgotten the bustle and pomp of that princely home; the attentions of men-at-arms, of retainers, of lacqueys, of servile and officious dependants, terrified him; he sought solitude, shunned the looks of others, and, when father and mother plied him with solicitous tendernesses, turned away a flushed face and said nothing. On one such occasion, Ermenberg, unable to control herself, cried out, 'Ah me, I have lost my child!' But even in this extremity her characteristic prudence was not at fault. How she governed her own conduct we are not told; but she gave peremptory orders to her servants that the child was to be allowed to do whatever he pleased, thwarted in nothing, and implicitly obeyed in all that he should choose to require. Her injunctions were respected; time and care did the rest.[1]

In future years it was remarked that never had nurse like Anselm entered an infirmary; that he possessed a tact and tenderness surpassing woman's. Ermenberg had taught him the science of the sick-room.

[1] See Appendix.

CHAPTER III.

ST. ANSELM'S BOYHOOD AND EARLY YOUTH.

HAD Anselm come into the world a century later than he did, he would have found in the canons of St. Ours a cloistered brotherhood resembling in its essential features a community of monks; for precisely a hundred years after his birth that corporation relinquished the secular life to enter upon one ordered after a religious model; and the antiquary who now treads the cloister[1] which their feet once wore, will find upon the capital of one of the exquisite little pillars of its colonnade this inscription:—

Anno ab Incarnatione Domini m.c.xxx.iii. in hoc claustro regularis vita incepta est.

But though Anselm did not live long enough to witness the reform of that society of which he had, not improbably, been a member in his boyhood, he may have remotely contributed to the change both by early example and by exhortations addressed at a subsequent period to some of its members. These shall engage our attention presently; for it is first necessary to recall the fact that the secular clergy of the west, at least in its higher ranks, underwent a most signal change for the better during the latter half of the eleventh century.

In the year 1063 Pope Alexander II., well noting the symptoms of amelioration for which good men had long sighed, summoned, in terms partly of command, partly of invitation, partly of entreaty, all such corporations of secular

---

[1] The cloister of St. Ours at Aosta reminds one of that of Saint-Sauveur at Aix-en-Provence, and of Saint-Trophime at Arles.

canons as were not infected with the graver evils of the time to take their meals together, to sleep in a common dormitory, and to attempt a general approximation to the apostolic ideal of a life in community;[1] some five-and-twenty years later monasteries of canons regular were already scattered thick over the face of Christendom;[2] and early in the twelfth century secular ecclesiastics, not of the highest grades only, but of all, by their response to the cry of Norbert from his wilderness in the Vosges, gave ample proof that their ancient lethargy was coming to an end.[3]

But the earlier half of the eleventh century had inherited a universal indolence; and when Anselm was a child secular canons, like his uncles Lambert and Folcerad, were blind, or all but blind, to the ideal which required that such as they should possess nothing which they could call their own, but have all things in common; an ideal which St. Augustine had endeavoured, but with indifferent success, to maintain in its proper lustre amongst his clergy;[4] but an ideal which as age succeeded age had faded languidly from sight, till at length a college of canons was the merest synonym for a company of tonsured gentlemen of all ages down to very childhood who owed their dignity to birth, to purchase, or to favour, and who regarded the revenues of a deanery or a canonry as so much private income to be expended, free of all

[1] 'Et præcipientes statuimus ut hi prædictorum ordinum qui iisdem prædecessoribus nostris obedientes castitatem servaverint juxta ecclesias quibus ordinati sunt sicut oportet religiosos clericos simul manducent et dormiant et quicquid eis ab ecclesiâ competit communiter habeant. Et rogantes monemus ut ad apostolicam communem vitam summopere pervenire studeant quatenus perfectionem cum his consecuti qui centesimo fructu ditantur in cœlesti patriâ mereantur adscribi.' See Baronius, *Annales*, s. a. 1063.

[2] This, at least, is a fair deduction from letters of Urban II. written in the year 1089.

[3] 'Norbertus . . . vineam plantavit quæ . . . jam implevit terram.'—*Hermanni de Mirac. S. M. Laudun.*, iii. § 1.

[4] 'Me hoc noverit charitas vestra dixisse fratribus meis qui mecum manent ut quicunque habet aliquid aut vendat aut eroget pauperibus aut donet aut commune illud faciat. . . . Ecce in conspectu Dei et vestro muto consilium.'—S. Aug. *Sermo de Moribus Clericorum.*

restraints, and free of all conditions not imposed upon men of the world in general.[1]

But it would seem as if St. Anselm, when as yet a mere boy, was already anticipating that great reform which he was not to witness for many years to come; for before he had completed his fourteenth year [2] he was debating within himself how best to fashion his life to the Divine will, and, after what certainly appears to have been an impartial and adequate comparison of the different modes of human converse open to him, came to the conclusion that the monastic state was the most fitting. To do this he must have set side by side in the field of mental vision the monastic state and the canonical; but if so, he must have set them side by side as they should have been, rather than as they were. The canons of St. Ours, the canons of the cathedral church of his native city, and such other members of collegiate bodies as lay within the circle of his limited knowledge, may not, it is true, have lived unchaste lives; may not have loved to doff the ecclesiastical habit and wear the military in its place; may not have loved, as St. Peter Damian says was the wont of some, to live in frequented thoroughfares, to chaffer with hucksters in the market place, to examine with dainty curiosity the mystic products of the milliner's skill, and discuss with epicurean nicety the gastronomic marvels of the cookshop; [3] for there never

[1] Thus St. Odilo, 'inter ipsa primordia . . . clericali sorte est donatus' at Brioude; and Guibert of Nogent was a canon of Beauvais when as yet a mere boy. But let the following suffice: 'Scholares pueri et impuberes adolescentuli ob sanguinis dignitatem promoventur ad ecclesiasticas dignitates et e sub ferula transferuntur ad principandum presbyteris; lætiores interim quod virgas evaserint quàm quod metuerint principatum.'—S. Bernardi, *De Moribus et Officio Episcopi.*

[2] 'Necdum attigerat ætatis annum quintum decimum.' He had not attained his fifteenth year, therefore he had not completed his fourteenth.

[3] 'Hoc autem tempore clericis quod de quibusdam loquor parum videtur si suo Deo vivendo carnaliter subtrahant; nisi etiam ab ecclesiasticæ procurationis excubiis per angiportus et nundinarum stationes habitare secedant; nimirum suavius judicantes si cauponum tabernas olfaciant quàm si divini sacrificii quotidie limen terant, magisque delectat eos textricum gynæcea conspicere quàm cœlestis eloquii paginis incubare. . . . Nunc autem è contra ii qui divinis sunt cæremoniis mancipati ecclesiæ sacraria remota contemnunt, habitare vero inter forensis strepitus

was an age in which the clerical caste was composed of none but uxorious, idle, or gluttonous parsons; and the best as well as the worst of us are prone to exaggerate both the number and the heinousness of such grave scandals. Nevertheless, when Anselm was a boy, the canons known to ordinary experience could not for a moment be set in comparison with the average members of the Benedictine order;[1] and it may well be questioned whether over the whole face of Christendom there was as yet a single college of canons who lived as St. Augustine would have wished that they should live, at the moment upon which the child undertook the investigation which now engages our notice. Thus, his comparison of the monastic life and the canonical was a comparison of ideals. In a man of matured intellect such comparison would not astonish us; but that a boy of thirteen years should, by an inductive effort of the reason, have succeeded in setting side by side two ideals evolved from ecclesiastical literature, or from whatever accessible source; that, having set them side by side, he should have tested them, each in its turn, by all that he knew of the Divine will; and that, convinced of the goodness of his decision, he should then have lost no time in endeavouring to give it practical effect, is wonderful indeed; and we scarcely know whether more to admire his moral or his intellectual intrepidity.

Eadmer describes the event with suitable brevity, and if we are inclined to blame him for not telling us at what precise date the little philosopher began to institute an inquiry which must have been characterised by not a little of

murmura concupiscunt.'—S. Pet. Dam. *De Communi Vitâ Clericorum.* And Warner, of St. Blaise, speaks thus: 'Hæc est vita clericorum qui litigant in conviviis ac disceptationes habent in trufis.'

[1] The first step in the direction of clerical reform was taken as late as the year 1039, when four canons of the Cathedral of Avignon, 'touched by the love of God,' formed themselves into a religious community under the shadow of a ruinous and deserted church outside their city. But, even so, we must remember that there is a wide difference between the holy defection of a few and the corporate reform of all.

the originality, the subtilty, and the boldness that marked the profounder efforts of his manhood, we must remember that the reticence is not his own, but Anselm's.[1] Like those profounder efforts, it was an exertion of the speculative intellect, cold and scientific. There was nothing in it of inspiration, as the word inspiration is generally used; neither was he urged to it by impulse, led by example, or directed by persuasion. What, therefore, we are to contemplate is a child, forgetful of the exterior accidents of princely birth, and absorbed in the prosecution of an abstract inquiry, the sole aim of which is the discovery of the mode of life most pleasing to God. This is all; but it is enough.

Would, then, that some magician would show us this tall, white-robed boy, of refined features, delicate complexion, and abundant light hair shorn at the crown with the clerical tonsure; show him to us, now perusing the sacred page of Scripture, now unclasping a volume of St. Gregory or St. Jerome, and transcribing here a text, and there some glowing phrase of ancient wisdom; show him to us day by day poring over the unfolded treasures of a much loved literature, and lost in a research too sacred for words; show him to us alone with his own heart, alone in the sight of God, alone in his quest of the highest destiny attainable here below. And would that Eadmer had been allowed to describe to us what followed; for this he could have done easily enough. He could have told us something about the monastery which the lad chose for his new home, and the name and aspect of its abbot, and supplied us with means for realising the most thrilling scene in that young life. He could have told us how the boyish canon was ceremoniously ushered into the guest-chamber; how he prostrated himself on the ground

---

[1] We must not make Eadmer's words mean more than they tell us. He seems, however, of set purpose to have suppressed not only the boy's precise age at the beginning of his inquiry, but his age when he presented himself to the abbot. Anselm would certainly be *sui compos* on the completion of his fourteenth year, and I suspect that he awaited that event before going to the abbot.

when the abbot entered; and how the holy man, bidding him rise, soon learnt with mingled astonishment and dismay that this descendant of emperors, of kings, of dukes, and of marquises, this great-nephew of the last of the grand old line of the Counts of Aosta, possessed by one enthralling conviction, was longing to throw aside the trappings of the secular state, to resign all present and prospective pomp and dignity, and, poor amongst the poor, assume the habit of a novice and die to the world!

The postulant told his story with all the modest assurance and quiet unreserve of one who took it for granted that to receive he only had to ask; but was presently stupefied to learn that he had miscalculated, or, rather, had quite forgotten to take into account, the perplexities and the needs which beset even religious communities here below. The abbot was only too well aware that to entertain the request would be to invite his own ruin, since Gundulf, who had a power and influence in Aosta, which none of its inhabitants were likely to think of questioning,[1] was not the man to allow his only child—the child in whose fate were involved the historic interests of his own family and Ermenberg's, the child who was to inherit his own claims against the Marchioness Adelaide, and Bishop Burchard's claim against the Count of Maurienne her husband, would not allow such a child to be shut up in a cloister without his consent; and, sooner than give this, would transform the cloister into a heap of stones.[2] The abbot was peremptory,

---

[1] The relation of the Counts of Maurienne to the valley of Aosta can scarcely have given them a claim to meddle in the internal economy of the city. The bishop and citizens were free of any such interference, and the bishop had sovereign rights inside the walls, and probably over a limited area outside.

[2] A similar instance is to be found in the case of Hervé, who subsequently became archpriest or dean of Tours, who sought the monastic estate, but with like ill success. 'Qui, ut generosioribus mos est, nobiliter educatus, dehinc verò scholis artium liberalium applicatus . . . Relictis autem pompaticæ scientiæ studiis, ad quoddam monasterium clam ingrediens, monachum se fieri satis devotè postulavit. Sed quoniam, ut diximus, clari erat generis idcirco parentum minas pertimescentes nullo modo acquievere . . . fratres ejusdem monasterii.'—*Rodulf. Glabri Hist.* iii. § 4.

and the postulant in despair. Nothing could be done, and there was nothing more to say on either side; unless, indeed, the good man, touched by the child's woe, gave him the forlorn consolation, that He who was calling him to the religious state would not suffer him to die in the secular.

A forlorn consolation indeed; for Anselm knew that the power, the authority, and the influence, which were sufficient to paralyse the courage of the Benedictine, were the power, the authority, and the influence of a man who knew how to assert in his son's name the right of succeeding to the ancestral throne of the bishops of Aosta. And how, in such an event, would it become that son to act? Must he, to please his father, violate conscience and consent to wear the mitre? Or must he fly betimes the scene of so great a danger? And if, reviewing in this crisis the steps of the argument which had directed him to the religious life, he consulted once more the text of the Gospels, to learn, if learn he might, what the Divine Author of Christianity would teach in this emergency, he certainly found three or four passages in the inspired volume which, since they are familiar to the reader, need not be quoted, but which it would have required some sophistry to explain away. Or, if he traced through his tears such records of the Church's legislation as regulated the practice of the age, he must have seen that he had not been mistaken in believing, as all the world then believed, that there was not a law in Christendom which forbad him to relinquish his canonry and become a monk.[1]

All this was perfectly true and very interesting; but the logic of facts can be as inexorable as any other, and poor little Anselm was at his wit's end.

No; not quite. There was one resource left. He was set, it is true, in the crisis of a supreme perplexity, and had

[1] Thus the fourth Council of Toledo enjoins as follows (Can. 49): 'Clericis qui monachorum propositum appetunt, quia meliorem vitam sequi cupiunt, liberos ab episcopo in monasterio largiri oportet ingressus.' This is quoted by St. Anselm, *Ep.* iii. 12, 13, who also adduces the authority of Gregory the Great.

no human counsellor to help him ; but he could at least turn to One whom he loved to call the *magni consilii Angelus*, Him whose will he desired to do. He turned and prayed that at whatever cost that will might be accomplished in him. A slight thing indeed was health, and a slight thing life itself, when set in comparison with the execution of those counsels of perfection to which he conceived that will to be calling him ; and, as if to assure Heaven of the sincerity of his vow, he prayed that an illness might be granted him,[1] if so be an illness might introduce him to a state of life, second only to the angelic, a state of life as far superior to all other on this earth as is that of the Cherubim to the rest of the heavenly host.[2]

The story is best told by Eadmer : 'Persisting in his design, he prayed God for the grace of an illness, that so he might be received into the monastic order for which he yearned. A wonderful thing then happened. God, as if to show him that even in other emergencies he might surely trust to be heard by the Divine compassion, gave favourable heed to the prayer, and visited the boy with an overmastering weakness of body. Reduced to a grievous sickness, Anselm now sent word to the abbot, assured him he apprehended death, and prayed to be made a monk. But the abbot's fears were obstinate, and the request was not granted. So does human sight scan the ways of God ; but erringly. He whose foreseeing eye can by nothing be deceived was unwilling that

---

[1] William of Malmesbury's account is slightly different : ' Petierat et acceperat adeò gravis morbi incommodum quò parens uterque perterritus Deo filium voveret.'

[2] Bishop Yves, of Chartres, says (*Decreta*, vii. 22) : ' Sacerdotes igitur monachi atque canonici . . . angeli vocantur. Sed unusquisque angelicus ordo quantò claritatem Dei viciniùs contemplatur tantò dignitate sublimior affirmatur. Nam, uti cherubim, monachi sex alis velantur.' And an oft-quoted poem on the monastic state concludes thus :—

> ' Qui semper *Sanctus* triplicatâ voce resultant,
> In terris monachi qui modulantur idem.
> Sic cherubim cœlo, monachi tellure manentes,
> Unum dant uni servitium Domino.'

His servant should have share in the religious life of that place;[1] because He had some others hidden in the bosom of His mercy, whom, as became evident in due time, He was preparing to be informed by Anselm to the doing of His will.

[1] 'Servum suum ipsius loci conversatione noluit [Deus] implicari.' I am constrained to draw attention to the unfaithful fidelity of Dean Church's rendering of these words: 'It was not God's will that he should be entangled in the conversation of that place.' Nothing could be more infelicitous; for *conversatio* has a technical meaning all its own, and *implicari* should not be translated as if it were *irretiri* or *illaqueari*.

I. The modern use of the English word *conversation* is entirely wide of Eadmer's *conversatio*. The word with him means *life as member of a religious community*, in opposition to the *communis vita*, or life in the world (see *Cur Deus Homo*, lib. ii. cap. iii.). I could fill pages with instances. This use of the word is a commonplace of mediæval Latin.

II. The word *implicari* is of less frequent occurrence; but I trust that I shall make its meaning clear.

1. When St. William of Dijon was a child his nurse once left him at the door of a church while she and some other servants entered a neighbouring house to take some refreshment, '*in quibus necesse erat illis quædam victualia quærere.*' Whilst they were thus employed, not entangled—*dum in his diutiùs implicarentur*—the child crawled into the church, when he was cured of a troublesome weakness.—*Vita S. Guill. Divon.* lib. ii. cap. i.

2. St. Salaberg was sought in marriage by a certain Blandinus, but much against her will, since she had made a vow to employ, not entangle, herself in the Divine commandments—*divinis præceptis se implicare voverat.*—*Vit. S. Salabergæ*, cap. vi.

3. Arnold, the author of the *Miracula S. Emmerami*, says of himself, '*Subduxi me libris paganis, et, saniore consilio, implicabar divinis*' ('I spent my time in the study of sacred literature').

4. The like is said of another: '*Cum isdem vir sacræ scripturæ studiis attentissimè fuerit implicitus*' ('Engaged or employed in the study of holy scripture').—*Angelran. Centulens. Vita*, § 20.

5. '*Implicari exsequiis*' is 'to take part in a funeral,' as where we read of a disciple of St. Angelran's that '*desiderabat . . . optimi patris implicari exsequiis.*'—*Ibid.* § 21.

6. And in the Life of St. Hugh of Lincoln we find the phrase '*honestis implicari exercitiis.*'

In short, the word is colourless as water and tasteless as white of egg. Not so *irretiri* and *illaqueari*. Eadmer uses the former where he remarks, in his Life of St. Oswald, '*quàm difficile sit hominem inter mundi illecebras gradientem ipsis illecebris non irretiri;*' and an unpublished MS. to which I have already alluded, gives us *irretitus in amore*.

But enough: unless indeed I add that whilst *implicari* is the precursor of the French *s'employer*, and the corresponding Italian, we have in *implicamentum* the precursor of the English *employment*: '*Sæcularibus implicamentis ex more humano detentus est et adstrictus.*'—Arnoldi *de Miraculis S. Emmerami*, lib. ii.

Let this suffice.

After a while health returned to the lad, and what he was unable to do then he determined by the grace of God to do at some future time.'

He had knocked at the gate of an earthly paradise, and knocked in vain; at the gate of the heavenly cloister, but only to be disappointed. His place, for a time at least, must be the secular state; and he must adorn as best he might his rank of secular canon.

It was not long after his recovery that the wintry silence of the Valley of Aosta was broken by the approach from the side of the Great St. Bernard of a numerous cavalcade, one amongst whom, the humblest of men, with a face furrowed by tears, and lips that moved evermore in silent prayer, was evidently treated with no ordinary respect by his fellow travellers. That respect was the only intimation of his rank, for, contrary to the usage which forbad prelates to travel without some show of pontifical state, he was enveloped in an ordinary cloak and hood. It was Bruno, Bishop of Toul, who had recently been appointed Pope by an abuse of the imperial power, and who is known in history as St. Leo IX.[1] His stay in Aosta was a brief one, for he was worn with anxiety, and could have no peace till he should know that, the clergy and people of the Eternal City concurring in his election, Rome, and with it Christendom, were to be spared the scandal of a disputed succession to the Papacy. The stay was brief, but it was signalised by one of those presages which the time so religiously noted; for there it was, and then, that Bruno heard angelic choirs weaving sweetest harmony to the words, 'Thus saith the Lord, I think thoughts of peace and not of affliction, and you shall call upon me and I will hear you, and I will bring back your captivity from all

---

[1] I scarcely need remind the reader that, if my genealogical speculations be correct, St. Leo IX. and St. Anselm were *affines*, Ermenberg being sister of the Pope's sister-in-law; in which case Leo would not improbably be the guest of Gundulf and Ermenberg during his stay at Aosta.

places' (Dicit Dominus, Ego cogito cogitationes pacis et non afflictionis : invocabitis me et ego exaudiam vos, et reducam captivitatem vestram de cunctis locis '). A pretty legend : it reminds us of the 'Regina cœli lætare' which the angels sang in the hearing of St. Gregory, and of the mystical pomp of that chapel at Einsiedeln which the King of Glory consecrated, saints and angels ministering to Him. Bruno resumed his journey, and the city relapsed into its usual stillness. No more angelic songs have been set on record ; and yet, if Anselm strained his ear to catch a promise of the peace which he had failed to secure, and of redemption from his present state and the gilded terrors of the episcopate, who shall say that he listened in vain?[1] Little did he think that he was himself to play a part in the great drama to which that angelic melody formed so exquisite an overture ; but when the lapse of years at last brought him into the thick of the action, he must often have remembered that close to the Pope-elect as he drew nigh to the city there rode an unassuming monk from Cluny, and that the name of that monk was Hildebrand.[2]

This took place in the January of 1049.

Anselm had now entered upon a studious, innocent, and exemplary youth, which was to be spent partly under the direction of his uncles, and partly in the ancestral palace of his mother's family.

His youth was studious ; for only then can he have formed those habits of profound and carefully sustained argument and of accurate and lucid diction which characterised his manhood ; then it was that, in the perusal of all the literature sacred and profane within his reach, he acquired that skill in critical analysis which none better than he knew was scarcely to be attained but by the scientific study of the laws of

---

[1] Otto Frisingensis, *Chronic.* lib. vi. cap. xxxiii. *Acta SS.* Apr. 19.
[2] If I wished to dramatise the saint's life I should feel no scruple in making the palace of the Anselms the scene of this celestial overture, and there should be three persons on the stage : the Pope elect, Leo IX., Prior Hildebrand, and the youthful Canon Anselm, the hero of my play.

language, where language was to be found in its choicest form; then it was that he stored his mind with the maxims of ancient wisdom which adorn so many of his letters, and with the poetical allusions which lend a grace to so many of his philosophical treatises. Nor can we doubt that his thirst for knowledge was alternately stimulated and allayed by the perusal and transcription of works borrowed from the libraries of neighbouring monasteries, from Ivrea, from Fruttuaria, from Chiusa, and from St. Maurice-en-Valais, which had property in and near the city, and whose annals recorded the name of his great-uncle, Archbishop Burchard, of Lyons, in its list of abbots, and that of his uncle, Bishop Burchard, of Aosta, in its list of provosts.

His youth was innocent; for Eadmer, when discoursing of his Meditations, tells us that those compositions, designed mainly for the use of others and written, not in his own person but in that of the penitents or disciples for whose benefit they were composed, were acts of reparation for the sins of other men and for his own, 'if indeed he had any,' a reservation of no slight value in our estimate of his character when a young man; and William of Malmesbury gives testimony still more valuable when he assures us that after Anselm had emerged from boyhood not once was the purity of his soul ruffled by an unguarded look: 'Pueritiam egressus nunquam vel lasciviori aspectu castimoniam turbavit.'

And it was exemplary; for during these early days he practised one of the distinctive virtues of the ideal canonicate in distributing his personal estate and the income of his canonry amongst the poorer members of his order, and formed those habits of life which, on his arrival at Le Bec, led the inmates of that monastery to regard him as a model of the clerical character.[1]

There is a passage in Eadmer's Life of St. Oswald of York

---

[1] 'In omni clericali officio apprime eruditus.' Eadmer (*Vit.* § 33) dwells at some length on this characteristic in Anselm when he was yet a secular.

which agrees so nicely with what we know of Anselm's character at this period of his career, as to read like a discarded page from the first draft of his 'Anselmiana':[1]—'He was a canon amongst canons; and, if the reader ask what sort amongst what sort of canons, a canon regular amongst irregulars. With indefatigable industry he carried out all that the ideal of the canonical life teaches and enjoins; whilst they, disdaining it, walked according to the desires of their own heart. Hence, by reason of the plenitude of the Divine grace, which shed all its lustre on his character, he was deemed worthy of the admiration of them all. . . . But they, choosing rather to hold on by the lax habits of a long degenerate life—although, seeing that he was so good and his way of living so good, they paid him the homage of a courteous respect and a good will not to be denied—plainly told him that on no account would they become his disciples in an affair like this. He, however, cared nothing for their empty praises, but grieved without ceasing day and night, and prayed God to give him counsel for his salvation.'

Nothing can be more probable than that young Anselm should even thus have striven to rouse his fellow canons, and especially his uncles, from a secular lethargy to that severer mode of life which their successors three generations later were to emulate. We have two letters of his addressed to his godfathers and *nutritores* many years later, and at a time when they must already have been far advanced in life. These letters prolong the strain of his youthful expostula-

---

[1] And the more so as what goes immediately before reads like the first draft of what we actually have in the *Vita*. We know that some passages of the *Anselmiana* were cancelled, and we know that Eadmer was loth to see perish what he had composed with great pains. I think it likely that much of what he tells us of St. Oswald's early days was the transcript *mutatis mutandis* of what he had written about Anselm's; this is to say, the whole of the passage, from the words, 'Unde et ab omnibus diligebatur,' to 'singulis horis meditatur.' And further, it is not impossible, and I think it more than probable, that the passages 'Quid amplius? Fit canonicus . . . gradiebatur,' and 'Sed illi . . . precebatur nocte ac die,' are salvage from the *Anselmiana*, inserted without any alteration.

tions, and to their plaintive music Lambert and Folcerad pass from our view.

The first is as follows :—

'To the most noble lords, his much loved guardians, and dearest uncles; May they so pass through temporal goods despising them, as to endure in eternal goods enjoying them.

'Oh that when my uncles read this letter they may feel the emotion to which my eyes give witness as I indite it; for my heart is readier to prompt the tear than my pen to print the syllables. If no lapse of time and no stretch of space can take from my bodily frame the lineaments it received from your race, and the stature it attained under your fostering care, neither can any employment of my soul lessen the love I bear you, a love engendered in my very being and sustained by your goodness. And as unremittingly as my heart burns with love for you, so ardently does it ever thirst for your true happiness. . . .'[1]

The second, which has a similar superscription, is to this effect:—

'Certain I am that you have the same love for me as I for you, and that your love is as firmly rooted in your heart as my love is in mine; and not less sure am I that you always long to have news of me as ardently as I to hear news of you. But you will be much better able to learn the one and to send the other with all the fulness we desire through the medium of the bearer of this sheet than by letters, which are necessarily scanty. Still, there is one longing in my heart, and what that longing is may He from whom it comes, to whom it goes, and who alone knows of it, communicate to you with all the intimacy and all the persuasiveness which He knows to be for your good. And yet fain would I let you know something of the fulness of

[1] *Ep.* i. 18.

my heart. It is this. I greatly fear lest you go on loving the world, and living in the world, sleeping even to the end ; and so find nothing, or all too little, in your hands, when with the men of riches you awake after the end.'[1]

They were near the end when these words were written. Let them go.

There is a spot in the Valdostan territory which has supplied St. Anselm with a parable of the dangers of the present life, and of the spirit in which those dangers should be encountered. The spirit he recommends was precisely that which governed and consecrated his youth, and, since he, no doubt, had paid many a visit to the spot during the period embraced by the present chapter, it may not be improper here to add some slight notice of it.

It is in one of his Meditations that he illustrates the uncertainties and perils of our state by the figure of a bridge not more than a foot in width, thrown across some deep and gloomy chasm ; a bridge along which the traveller walks, not knowing whither a step may carry him. No such structure was ever yet erected as a means of human transit, and yet he writes as if he had seen some such. He had ; and no one who loves his memory should visit Aosta without paying a visit to Le Pont d'Aël.

Le Pont d'Aël, or Le Pondel, two years older than our era, is all that now remains of a Roman aqueduct which, purposely dismantled of its upper arcade, has thus been converted into a means of communication between either bank of the Cogne, at a point where the bed of that angry torrent narrows into a gorge hemmed in by two precipitous flanks of rock. Into the live limestone of these Roman skill has inserted a masonry all its own, a masonry that rises in adamantine walls to a height of some forty yards on this side and on that, and then knits itself into a bold but narrow

[1] *Ep.* i. 45.

semicircular arch athwart the chasm, rising thence in squared masonry to a level some ten feet above the key-stone, when it stops short, now no longer an aqueduct, but a foot bridge.

The traveller approaches Le Pondel by descending the grassy sward that slopes to the eastern edge of the chasm, a sward thickly planted with chestnut trees, in pleasing contrast to the steep and barren fall of the opposite cliff, a fall so steep that no shadow lies on it at noonday, and so barren, that nothing grows on it but a few thin blades of rye, cultured with infinite pains by a thrifty peasantry. On reaching the bridge, he finds that it is a long and narrow causeway, five feet in utmost width, and protected on either side, if protected be the word, by the slightest of parapets, half a yard in height, the work of the fathers of the valley. And if, adventuring on the bridge, he stops half way across to look up the gorge, he experiences a sensation of terror not easily to be surpassed. Down headlong precipitous stairs of rock, now sweeping in smooth cataracts, now dashing against boulders of limestone, the trophies and the witnesses of its fury; now breaking into stormy spray; and evermore bellowing forth the wrath of a thousand thunders, the torrent flies down into the chasm; and the fascinated spectator quakes as he overlooks his rickety parapet, and tries to measure the abyss. But time was when the passenger had not the solace of so wide a causeway, or even of so slight a parapet; time was when, the superincumbent range of arches still intact, the structure gradually narrowed at its successive stages, till the slabs which covered the trough of the aqueduct were scarcely more than a yard in breadth; and when a reach of pavement much narrower than the present, and by reason of its enhanced elevation not only much narrower, but very much longer, must have tried the courage of even the most courageous. By St. Anselm's day, however, the covering slabs had, no doubt, been removed, and, whilst the interior of the trough remained as a strait but secure path for the timorous, those who courted danger might walk along the coping that crowned either of its sides.[1] Such coping would present precisely the kind of bridge described by St. Anselm, a long, narrow, and extended way, not more than one foot in width, across a deep and gloomy abyss; and, if he ever ventured to take a few steps along it, he must have experienced sensations terrific enough to suggest the picture which he has left in his first meditation, a picture as dantesque as anything outside the pages of Dante.

'Think that you see some deep and gloomy ravine, with every kind of torment down in its bed. Imagine over it a bridge, stretched across the yawning space, and measuring only one foot in width. If anyone were compelled to go along a bridge so strait, so high, so dangerous, and to go along it with eyes bandaged so as not to see his steps, and with hands tied behind him so as not to feel his way with a staff, what fear, what anguish would possess him! . . . Nay, more, imagine monstrous birds of prey sweeping round about the bridge, intent on betraying him down into the gulf; will not his terrors be enhanced? And what if, one by one, the paving tiles slip from his heels as he advances? Surely he will be stricken with greater and greater anxiety the further he goes.'

Le Pont d'Aël, the dizzy bridge over the Cogne, must have suggested this terrible picture. Here is its lesson:—

'That perilous bridge, from which the awkward traveller is launched, is the present life; for he who lives ill drops down to hell. The paving tiles that slip away behind the wayfarer are the days of this our state, which so pass away as never to return, but, by the shortening of their tale, ever urge us to the end and compel us to hasten to our goal. The birds that sweep round about the bridge and baulk the pas-

---

[1] This is no fanciful account. It is based on careful examination and study made, for that purpose, of the Pont du Gard. Of course the Pont du Gard is immensely larger than the Pont d'Aël.

senger are malignant spirits, whose whole study it is to cast us down from the direct path we tread, and plunge us headlong into the deep abyss. We, we are the travellers. . . . Will you not, then, set as you are in such danger, cry to your Creator, that, defended by His protection, you may sing with confidence, though troops of foes beset you, "The Lord is my light and my salvation, whom shall I fear?"'

Yes, indeed; though the inhabitants of the city and valley of Aosta inherit no tradition of Anselm and his family, the eternal heights of the Becca di Nona are the ladder by which in infancy he clomb to heaven; and the masonry of the Pont d'Aël shall for many and many a generation remain as his own parable of the holy fear which set its consecrating mark upon his studious, his innocent, and his exemplary youth.

CHAPTER IV.

ST. ANSELM'S EARLY MANHOOD.

OF all the metaphors employed in the eleventh century to illustrate the excellence of the monastic state, none is more usual than that in which its repose and security are likened to those of a haven, whence the rescued mariner beholds unhurt the fury of the elements from which he has been delivered by the unmerited favour of an ever-watchful Providence. No metaphor could have been happier than this, as none could be in more intimate accordance with the monastic spirit; for are not the dread forces of wind and wave as truly the creation of an Almighty Hand as the rock to which the breathless mariner clings, vowing never again to adventure the perils of ocean? Nor did it lack the guarantee of antiquity, for it was as old as the age of Gregory the Great, whose comparison of the secular life and the religious must have engaged young Anselm's attention during the inquiry recorded in the last chapter.

'One day,' writes St. Gregory, 'tired with the turmoil of secular cares, I sought a quiet spot, friendly to grief. .... As I sat there, weary and silent, my dear son, Peter the Deacon, came to me; .... who, finding me consumed by my heart's malady, said, "Has any new thing happened, that a sadness greater than ordinary possesses you?" I replied, "The grief, Peter, which I day by day endure is by its consuetude old enough, but by its increment ever new. My soul suffers from all this distraction, and smarts from her wound. She remembers what she was in the cloister; she remembers how all worthless things then lay far below, and how she stood superior to the fleeting pursuits of life. In those days she thought of nothing and cared for nothing but heavenly things. Mistress of the body, she rose superior in her contemplations to all the bonds of the flesh, and thus even courted death and yearned for it as the beginning of life and the requital of all her toil. But now she is, under pretext of pastoral responsibility, exposed to the distractions which beset men in the secular state, and has dropped from the ripe beauty of the eternal world to gather stains from the dust of earthly employment. . . . Too well do I know my loss; and in exact proportion to my distress for what has passed away is the weight of the burden that I carry. Behold me buffeted by the waves of a vast sea; the ship of my soul is beaten by the billows and the storm. As I reflect upon my past life, like one who casts a backward glance at the harbour he has left, I groan for very sorrow. And, what gives keenest poignancy to my grief as I drift out to sea, the plaything of the mountainous waves, is this: that I almost fail to descry the haven I have left. Such are my trials. And truly, truly, may I say that the very existence of those who forsake this present world and climb to the height of the angelical life is a perpetual aggravation of my woe; for when memory puts me in mind of the elevation of their state, I know and feel and own how low, how very low, I have fallen!"[1]

So deplorable a lot did Gregory the Great esteem it to have exchanged his cell upon the Cælian Hill for a throne in the Lateran. Living in the former, his soul enjoyed the security, the serenity and the repose of a harbour unvisited by storms and pacified with unbroken visions of perennial bliss; seated on the latter, he was involved in cares which, however inevitable and however sacred, were so many secular employments that harassed his soul with distractions as pitiless

---

[1] *S. Greg. Magn.* Dialogi, *sub initio*.

as the persecutions of a tempestuous sea. In another place he says : 'Men look upon me as the chief administrator of the Church ; more true were it to say that I am tossed about on the billows of the world, and am too often only not overwhelmed by them. Do you who pass a tranquil life in the serenity of your retired home, do you who stand upon the unthreatened shore, stretch forth your hands in prayer for me, as I sail upon the waves, or rather, as I sink beneath them ; help me, I implore you, with what addresses to heaven you can, whilst I am struggling to reach the land of the living. So shall you have an eternal reward not only for the life you are leading, but for your salvation of me.'[1]

Nor was it only by themselves that good and saintly men whose lives lay outside the precincts of the monastery were described as storm-tossed mariners toiling against the angry elements. The metaphor was used of them by others. Thus Waso, Bishop of Liège, is pourtrayed as one who, beset by the tempests of the treacherous world and engaged in governing secular persons, was set entirely upon the thought of heaven, and mortified to all exterior things.[2] And we are told of Boso, a disciple of St. Anselm's at Le Bec, that he had been so carefully brought up by his parents as, although set in the very midst of the waves of the world, to have contracted no worldly stains.[3]

[1] *S. Greg. Magn. Ep.* xi. 1.
[2] 'Licet inter fluctuantis sæculi procellas . . . . divinâ tamen contemplatione suspendi solebat.'— Vasonis Leod. *Ep. Vita* (*Patrol.* cxlii. 761).
[3] 'Boso sic bonis artibus pietateque est imbutus ut in mediis fluctibus mundi nihil prorsus immundum contraxerit.'—*Guil. Gemmet. Hist. Ducum Northman.* cap. xxi.
'Cum diu (Guilbertus Boso et Raynaldus) inter suos honestam vitam duxissent amore Dei succensi, quasi post marina pericula, portum sub sancto Anselmo abbate Beccum petierunt.'—*Vita Ven. Bosonis* (*Patrol.* cl. 724).
Here are other instances :—
1. 'Sicut olim columba Noe cum foris non invenisset ubi requiesceret, ad arcam et ad ipsum Noe redibat ; sic iste vir inter hujus sæculi fluctus ad secretum cordis recurrens in Christi delectatione quiescebat.'—*S. Odonis de Vita S. Geraldi Comit. Aurillac.* § 16.
2. Of Odo himself we are told that 'Naturæ violentiâ cogebatur, ut parentibus

But this recalls us to St. Anselm, who, so far from contracting a stain from living in the world, remained in it consoled with an inward peace which could scarcely have been profounder had he been dwelling among saints in a cloister, remained in it, in such wise dead to it, that Eadmer, not venturing to speak of him under the figure of a ship at sea, describes him by the pretty and exceptional metaphor of a ship in port, of a ship fixed to her moorings, of a ship safe from the rage of the billows. And well he might, for Anselm has left it on record of himself, that although he could not enter religion for many years after he had formed the sacred resolution of his boyhood, yet to do so was ever the sole desire of his heart, and the one end which he held steadily in view: 'Vobis consulo quod me mihi cùm sic essem sicut vos nunc estis singulariter consuluisse . . . cognoscitis.'[1]

And if it here be asked, why then did he not break with home and preferment, fly beyond the reach of his father's territorial and political influence, and bury himself in some distant monastery, it may be enough to reply, not that such an idea would have suggested to him a very grave theological question, which he could scarcely answer to the satisfaction of his conscience except by remaining where he was; not that his was too reposeful, too hopeful, too wise, too simple a nature to resort to any unnecessary casuistry; but, simply, that his health was not yet robust enough to endure the usual discipline of the cloister. Of this there cannot be a doubt; let it therefore be enough for us. The strange illness which had befallen him in his boyhood left him for a long time in a state of health the very opposite of robust; and if after an interval of convalescence he appears to have been strong enough to

---

quos periculis mundi hujus reliquerat innatantes debitum suæ visitationis offerret.'
 3. William of Dijon 'cœpit . . . . cogitare qualiter suum genitorem à fluctivagâ istius sæculi curâ subtraheret.'
 In short, the metaphor was a commonplace.
[1] *Ep.* i. 36.

endure slight, but scarcely more than slight, fatigue, it was not till his twenty-seventh year that he had so far outgrown his weakness as to be able to enter some cloister where the rule of the Benedictine order was observed with a considerably moderated rigour. So that for a long course of years he must have been content to remain as he was; to follow the Divine Office as a secular ecclesiastic with as punctilious an exactness as he could bring to the task; to read his Virgil, his Horace, his Persius, his Plato, perhaps, and his Aristotle, with such assistances as he could command; and, above all, to guard the sanctuary of his heart. As to this last particular he would seem to have left us no other record than the passage just quoted; but it is a passage of inestimable value when read in conjunction with the evidence already adduced from William of Malmesbury: 'Pueritiam egressus nunquam vel lasciviori aspectu castimoniam turbavit.'[1]

Thus pure, studious, recollected, and hopeful, he passed the days of his youth; when, as he entered on manhood, a change, if change it may be called, came over him, which challenges our careful attention; for some fluent foreign writers have made of it a text for period after period of useless rhetoric, and for one of the most astounding calumnies to be found in the annals of all history. They have not, indeed, converted a molehill into a mountain, they have done worse: by the strangest of alchemy they have converted a diamond into a dunghill, and transformed a blameless adolescence into that which the pen refuses to describe. Nothing could be more cruel, as nothing could be more false, and there is not the shadow of a suggestion from end to end of Eadmer's account to lend excuse to it. This is what Eadmer says: 'As bodily health, early manhood, and a successful secular career welcomed him with their smiles, the fervour of his heart, which had been set upon embracing the monastic estate, began by slow degrees to cool; so much so that he

[1] *De Gest. Pontif. Angl.* lib. i.

rather wished to pursue his course along the paths of the secular life than leave them and become a monk.' Then comes a passage, intelligible enough as written by such a man as Eadmer: 'He also began insensibly to neglect those literary pursuits, of which he was by habit a very enthusiastic student, and to turn his attention to manly sports.' This is all: 'He began.' Pray, is it so very wicked in a young man of twenty, though he be a subdeacon, or even a deacon, to study the bias of a bowl, or the curve described by a javelin? But let Eadmer tell his story: 'After all, however, his love and his devotion for his mother held him back somewhat from these pastimes. But on her death, like a ship that has lost its anchor, he narrowly escaped drifting utterly off into the billows of the world'—the billows, that is to say, among which the lot of a saintly pope like Gregory the Great, a pious bishop with heart set on heaven like Waso of Liège, a blameless youth like Boso, and numberless other holy souls had been cast, throughout every age from the foundation of Christianity.

The case is clear and simple enough: Anselm was not yet a monk; but he had resolved to become one. To him, as to his future friend Hugh of Cluny, the cloister had hitherto been a home for which his young heart yearned,[1] and the paradise from whose enclosure he trusted some day to look back upon his life in the world as a period of banishment and exile.[2] And hence, when in old age he reviewed his mortal career, it was not without regret that he pointed to one period of it in which the intensity of his desire for the religious profession was allowed to relax; to one short interval in which,

[1] 'Suspiranti ad patriam.'—*S. Hugonis Vita*, auctore Hildeberto, cap. i.
[2] 'Didicit quanta sit differentia inter delicias paradisi claustralis et exilium vitæ sæcularis.'—*S. Anselmi Epp.* iii. 38.
'Claustralem paradisum et religiosam conversationem . . . deseruistis sed non clausit Deus ostium paradisi . . . sed potiùs vos misericorditer coegit ut ad requiem relictam rediretis.'—*Ibid.* iii. 102.
'Verè claustrum, fratres mei, verè religio est paradisus.'—*S. Bernardi Sermo de Verbis Domini.*

mortification not being his sole joy, he suffered his heart's barque—to use his own phrase—to ride indolently at anchor and run risk of drifting out to the open sea. But, be it a thousand times repeated, he was never out of harbour, and he has nowhere accused himself of what never happened. Perhaps he could scarcely in his old age declare, like Hugh of Lincoln, 'Revera, ludere nunquam scivi,' or, like Hugh of Cluny, that though he might have brandished a javelin in his youth, or crossed the saddle otherwise than of necessity, he had done so from sheer compulsion.[1] But possibly enough he could even say as much; and his utmost extravagance of conduct may have been that he once provided himself a pair of hawking gauntlets; but even so it is more than likely that ere he could go forth and whistle the falcon to his wrist his mother, whose prayers had long attended him in the austere and religious seclusion of his study, saw them and persuaded him not to put them on.

For, indeed, if it be unreasonable to apply to such terms as *fluctus sæculi* a meaning utterly wide of the sense assigned to them by those who had used them for five centuries from the days of Gregory the Great, it is inexcusable to forget that St. Anselm was a *monachus monachorum*, and fervent enough in his love of monasticism to deem it a disadvantage to have lived a year, a month, or a day, in the world after having once formed the resolution of leaving it, and a diminution of merit to have responded even for one thoughtless hour to the smiles of health, such as his was, of youth, and of secular fortune; for the entertainment of those sinless solicitations, during however brief an interval, had snapped the continuity of that *juge martyrium*, that perpetual immolation, which has been the holy vaunt of some partakers of our common nature.

But, even so, I have not yet exhibited his estimate of the loss he had sustained in spending his boyhood, innocent and angelic as that boyhood was, in the world rather than in a

---

[1] *S. Hugonis Cluniac. Abbatis Vita*, cap. i.

cloister. At the age of fifty he wrote as follows to his friend Gilbert Crispin, the newly-appointed Abbot of Westminster:—

'Better hopes must be entertained for you and the like of you, whose life was nurtured in the cloister, than of me and the like of me, whose life was for a time wasted in the secular state. For you the hope must be, that by your promotion to the cure of the souls of others your own conformity to right will be brought to its ideal perfection as you instruct others to conform themselves to your likeness; for us the fear must be lest, oppressed by so great a burden as the cure of souls, our own inconformity be aggravated in the balance of God's hidden justice.'[1]

What a strangely pathetic contrast! Here are two abbots charged with the cure of souls; but, whilst much may be hoped for the one, much is to be feared for the other; not that the one had been always a saint and the other erewhile a sinner, but solely because the one had entered the cloister in infancy, the other in manhood. And the fervour with which Anselm wrote thus to his friend at Westminster may help us to understand, little as we appreciate them, the tears he dropped upon Eadmer's account of the brief interval that now engages our attention. For what, pray, is the purport of that account? Not that for one brief day or hour he definitively relinquished the idea of becoming a monk, but that his boyish fervour began insensibly to cool; not that he deliberately consented to a temptation to live henceforth in the world, but that he entertained the thought that a life in the world might be the preferable state; not that he discarded his studies and threw his energies into sports innocent in themselves, but that he was on the point—only on the point—of doing so. Do we ask, then, what can be the secret of all this emotion? There is only one thing that can

[1] *Ep.* ii. 16.

explain it, and that is his estimate of the blessedness of the religious state. Whether or no we one by one and all of us sympathise with him, matters not; our only present business is to understand him. He held it a supremely blessed thing that a soul created for God should in the earliest morning of life be transplanted to lawns of paradisaical security, there to put forth its blossom and its fruit, unhurt by chilling winds and nipping frost, and he deemed it a grievous loss to have been surrounded, for however short a time after reaching the age of reason, by any other accessories than the alternate prayer, and chant, and silence, and discipline, and labour, and penance of the cloister.

Now, fortunately enough, we can illustrate not only the general purport, but the very words of Eadmer's strangely misinterpreted account of young Anselm's temporary vacillation by two letters written by Anselm himself in his later life. In the year 1093 the cantor of Paris cathedral—it was not as yet a metropolitan church—sought and received the religious habit in the monastery of St. Martin des Prés, but his diocesan recovered him by force. To that diocesan Anselm, now just about to be consecrated Primate of Britain, wrote as follows:—

'You know what St. Gregory says in the case of a man who, urged by Divine inspiration, had obtained the grace of conversion to the religious life; how he warns the man's bishop by no means to thwart his design (*propositum* [1]), but rather to foster the flame with utmost endeavour, lest the fervour kindled in the man should relax (*ne fervor conceptus in eo tepescat*)[1]; and tells him that one who has once sought the haven of the cloister (*monasterii portum*) ought never again to be involved in the turmoil of ecclesiastical cares. . . . God forbid, my lord, that on a bishop

---

[1] So Eadmer says of Anselm, '*coepit paulatim fervor animi ejus à religioso proposito tepescere.*'

should fall that sentence of His mouth, "He that gathereth not with Me scattereth," and "He that is not with Me is against Me." It is a fearful thing to hear that those whom Christ has chosen from out of the world a bishop should chain back to the world; that those whom Christ brings home to port from the storms and tempests of the world a bishop should drag out of harbour to be wrecked in the whirlpool of the world; that those whom Christ has sheltered in the fold from a host of scheming wolves a bishop should filch from the fold and expose to the wolves.'[1]

But the letter to the cantor himself is still more interesting, for it gives us some idea of what may possibly enough have passed in Anselm's heart during the critical epoch of his youth with which we are at present concerned.

'I fear the crafty fiend is trying to deceive your soul, and your soul is very dear to me; I fear he is putting it to you that, since you are forced against your will from the execution of your holy design (*a sancto proposito*), you are free to go on living in the clerical state (*in clericatu*) lawfully and without blame as heretofore. Be sure, my dearest friend, that you cannot possibly do this and be free from blame ('nullo modo hoc potest anima tua sine reprobatione suscipere'); for Christ says, "No man putting his hand to the plough and looking back is fit for the kingdom of heaven." And your mind is looking back from the plough of Christ, if, growing lukewarm, it by any means fail of the design to which Christ has called you, and on which you have entered ('si a proposito ad quod te vocavit Christus, et quod incepisti aliqua occasione tepescendo deficit'). . . . If by reason of bodily persecution we are to fly from city to city, how much more by reason of spiritual? . . . You could not have attempted anything more conducive to your

---

[1] *Ep.* iii. 12.

salvation: nothing would be more dangerous than to relinquish the attempt.'[1]

Young Anselm's case, therefore, was, briefly, this: Forbidden to enter a monastery prior to the completion of his fourteenth year, and prevented from doing so subsequently by obstacles he was unable to surmount, the fervour of his desires began after some considerable interval to cool; he began to think that, not being a monk, it might be well not to live so much like one in his father's house as he had hitherto done; and further, he began to familiarise his mind with the thought of passing his life as a secular clergyman rather than as a Benedictine monk. But these beginnings, after all, were checked and never carried out in practice; nor do they bear the faintest trace of a moment's conscious sin.

This is all. For a little space the fervour of his long-cherished hopes abated; and, looking back in his life's evening on that critical time, it seemed to him—such were his views of the blessedness offered, and the responsibility incurred by the religious vocation—as though while safe in port he had for one instant of strange vacillation had half a mind to put out to the treacherous and tempestuous ocean; as though, after so long carrying the cross with joy, he had only not set it down, in that case, it might have been, never to be enabled to take it up again; as though, after having put his hand to the plough, he had almost turned to take one perilous sidelong glance at the forbidden world, and thus imperil his fitness for a higher destiny.

And as he read Eadmer's record of that crisis—unless indeed, the words be his own—tears fell upon the parchment; tears of regret, but of speechless gratitude; tears that compel the homage of our own bewildered and awe-stricken respect

---

[1] *Ep.* iii. 13. This case resembles St. Anselm's. The gate of the cloister had been barred to him; he thought, therefore, that he might remain a secular clergyman without blame, or rather he began to think so. 'Cœpit paulatim *fervor tepescere.*'

and of our indignant sorrow for the gross injury done in these latter times to a spotless memory.

But another memory here claims our notice, that of Ermenberg. The information which we possess about her is so scanty that we must be content to guess where we would only too gladly know; but the following account has at least the recommendation of probability. I think it likely that, whether because Anselm was her first child, or because when in labour she had resolved to devote him to the special service of Heaven, or for whatever other reason, her highest ambition had from the first been to consign him to a cloister; that, thwarted in this desire, she noted with joy the first tokens of her child's religious vocation, and never failed to buoy up his hopes against Gundulf's contrary resolution; that being blessed, as years rolled along, with no other issue, or rather, that being year after year unblessed by children that survived their birth, she beheld in these successive afflictions the corrective hand of Him who claimed the entire surrender of her first-born son; that she hung all her maternal hopes upon an event so consonant with her views of right as his entrance into religion; that as time drifted on, and those hopes were still unfulfilled, she exerted her best endeavours to conciliate Heaven by keeping him true to his resolution; that at last she was consoled by the happy birth of a daughter, but that the life of the child was only secured at the sacrifice of her own.[1] She passed away on the second day of November in the year 1056.[2]

It was now of little avail for Gundulf to reflect that, had he been generous to Heaven three-and-twenty years ago, his

---

[1] This only sister, or only surviving sister, of Anselm's was still the mother of infant children at the close of the century (*Epp*. iii. 43; iv. 34, 52, 114). She must, therefore, have been his junior by many years. I shall have to revert to Richera on another occasion.

[2] I owe the day of the month to one of the Colbert transcripts (*Lat*. 13905) in the National Library at Paris. The year is, I regret to say it, conjectural. It cannot have been 1057; it may have been 1055, but 1056 is much more likely.

generosity might have been rewarded by the blessing of other sons, who would even now have been growing up into manhood; and after so many disappointed hopes for living offspring it was a bitter mortification to see his wife sink into the grave bequeathing to him not a son, but a daughter. Anselm, among the other things which he did well (*quæ benè faciebat*), tried to console his father. But why so? Who but Anselm could put an end to his distress and turn his disappointment and compunction into happiness by consenting to make a figure in the world? During his more cheerful intervals he no doubt desired his son to essay a feat of horsemanship, or practise some of the sports which were so eagerly pursued by the gallants of that age; and the young man complied—complied, but with a hardly checked tear at thought of her who had once been to him what the anchor is to the wayward skiff; complied, but with an inward regret after the gardens of Divine recollection and repose which invited him, but all in vain, to their sacred shelter; complied, and did his best to please; but succeeded so indifferently well (*perperam faciebat*) that the furibund father, who had cursed his son's bootless consolations, cursed now with tenfold bitterness an inaptitude which told him only too plainly that the time had passed away for transforming the studious, contemplative, ascetic youth into a mere man of the world.[1] Anselm, thus assailed, was unwise enough to administer the anodynes of sanctity to transports of rage. Had he confronted upbraidings and reproaches with anger or sullenness, Gundulf, if surprised, might at least have ventured to hope for some measure of eventual success;

---

[1] 'Ut æque vel certè magis ea quæ *bene* sicut quæ *perperam* faciebat insequeretur.' The correlative of *bene* is *male*, that of *perperam* is *rectè*; but *rectè* and *perperam* have no necessary moral meaning. Eadmer doubtless chose *bene* and *perperam* of set purpose. *Ea quæ bene faciebat* means *his good actions*; *ea quæ perperam*, *his inadvertencies* or *mistakes*. Thus, if you put a shoe on the wrong foot, or touch a piece on the chess-board without intending to move it, you act *perperam*.

but, alas! Anselm was a saint, or at least a saintly youth, and indiscreet enough, like David harping before Saul, to imagine that gentleness would disarm a fury which almost assumed the symptoms of demoniacal possession; indiscreet enough to display an exasperating patience; indiscreet enough to make it evident that the piety practised, and practised unbrokenly, from the time of his celestial vision, stood him now in good stead. Precisely so; his piety was all so much oil poured upon a conflagration. True indeed it is that, when persecuted, to pray for the persecutor, or, when struck on one cheek, to present the other, are acts of infinite value to the sufferer; but they are acts which convince the persecutor that sanctity is incorrigible, and have not unfrequently lashed exasperation into frenzy.

Gundulf was at length driven into such extravagances of conduct by his ungoverned and perhaps ungovernable violence, that Anselm, fearful lest some injury to his father's good name or to his own should come of it, resolved to quit home and country and adventure exile. To that resolution he in later years reverted with profoundest thankfulness; for had he prolonged his abode under the princely roof of his forefathers, still incapable of living in a cloister, but no longer succoured by that maternal sympathy which had hitherto kept alive in him the hope of doing so, he might insensibly have drifted off—so deemed his timorous conscience—into new habits of life, and by the time of his father's death, which took place at the Michaelmas of 1059, been ready deliberately to choose the career of a great secular churchman in preference to that heroic ideal on which Heaven had set his contemplation.

He set forth, however, not in haste nor indecently, but equipped for a long journey and for a protracted sojourn in distant homes; attended, as became his condition, by a clerk,[1]

---

[1] This clerk was perhaps his *clericus de terrâ*, part of whose duty it was to accompany, or rather follow, him to and from the cathedral when he went there

whose business it was to anticipate and supply his wants on the road; and accompanied, not improbably, by four other members of his household, who had caught the fire of his enthusiasm for learning and religion, the *alii quidam* whom God had 'disposed to be informed by him to the doing of His will.'

The travellers descended the Valley of Aosta, and pushing on from Ivrea to Susa, made for the foot of Mont Cenis, where the baggage of the canon and his attendant was transferred to the back of an ass purchased, or more probably hired, for the occasion. They then pursued their way more slowly, each with utmost care leading his timid horse up the treacherous ascent.

In crossing Mont Cenis Anselm did more than traverse a geographical barrier; he put term to an old period of his life and entered on a new. That life had indeed opened brightly, with the advantages of splendid pedigree and of peculiar favours from Heaven; but the cloud that gathered over it in the disappointment of his longing for a life of religious devotion had become thicker and darker during year after

---

for Divine service. His proper place was on the floor of the choir below the stall occupied by his *dominus*.

I suspect that Anselm's *clericus* was none other than Hernost, the future Bishop of Rochester.

If it be objected that he must have had only one companion on his journey, since he was '*uno* qui sibi ministraret clerico comitatus,' it may suffice to reply that the others would not accompany him as *ministri*. But, after all, *unus* need serve no other purpose than that of our indefinite article; *unus clericus* being *un clerc*, not *un seul clerc*; a clerk, not *one clerk*. This use of *unus* is not unfrequent. Thus we are told of St. Odilo (Migne, *S. L.* cxlii. 923*c*) that 'in Romuleâ urbe . . . *uno* in tempore morabatur.' And again, '*Unâ* igitur dierum venient ad mensam.' St. Anselm himself speaks of '*una* religiosarum personarum ecclesia' in the sense of '*a* religious community' (*Ep.* iv. 53); and in his description of the perilous bridge (*Med.* i.), 'Cogita desuper pontem *unum*,' 'Imagine to yourself *a* bridge.' And Ptolemy of Lucca says in his annals (s. a. 1066), 'Alexander ad instantiam dictæ comitissæ tradit eidem *unum* clericum sibi familiarem,' 'gave him *a* clerk of his household.'

It may be well to apprise the reader that in any references I may henceforth make to the *Series Latina* of the Abbé Migne's reprints, I shall omit as unnecessary the notification 'Migne, *S. L.*'

year of feeble health, and thicker and darker still as he shrank beneath the coldness and the aversion and the hatred of a father whose love he would willingly have died to win. What, what could have been more cruel than the hailstones of a father's wrath on such a son? And in the midnight and blackness of that tempest he set forth, whither he knew not.

No wonder, then, that after so much anguish, after all that it had cost him to resolve on flight, after his adieux to all who were dear to him on earth—to Lambert, to Folcerad, to his unconscious infant sister Richera—after his anxious flight from Aosta to Ivrea, and from Ivrea to Susa, and at last the laborious ascent of Mont Cenis; no wonder that when the reaction came it came with vehemence.

For a time he pursued the passage of the mountain with sufficient cheerfulness. But the physical exertion was new to him; he was unequal to great fatigue; the provisions for the journey were exhausted; and as unmeasured, monotonous wastes of snow stretched drearily above, below, around, his strength failed. The memory of his griefs revived, his heart sank, and the heat that succeeds emotions too deeply stirred began to burn in proportion to his weariness; he spoke little, for speech was difficult with a tongue so parched as his, and clutched up handfuls of snow if even so he might slake the fire that was raging in his veins. His alarmed attendant, who knew that in regions of trackless snow hunger and fatigue, faintness and drowsiness, exhaustion and sleep may steal upon the traveller in all too rapid a succession which he shall never awake to describe, was persuaded that only food could save him; but food from whence? For their wallets were empty. In very despair and terror he dragged their scant baggage from the ass, and ransacked a sack of provender that had been thrown across the animal's back, when—had some recent traveller forgotten it, or had an angel from heaven bestowed it there?—lo! a manchet of bread, and the bread was of an exceeding whiteness, a whiteness like that of the celestial food wherewith his childhood had once been refreshed in the presence of God. Anselm ate of it, and was restored to life, and resumed his journey weeping tears of thankfulness and hope. Shall we wonder if in so singular an interposition of the Divine compassion he discerned a presage of blessing on the new career opening out before him?

Book II.

THE EARLY RELIGIOUS CAREER, AND THE PRIORATE, OF ST. ANSELM.

CHAPTER I.

LE BEC.

NOT long before the date of St. Anselm's birth there flourished at the court of Gilbert, Count of Brionne, a knight called Herlwin.[1] Count Gilbert was cousin-german to Robert, the contemporary Duke of Normandy, whilst Herlwin could boast that he was sprung on the side of his father, Ansgot, from the first Danish conqueror of Neustria, and related through his mother with the reigning dynasty of Flanders. He was the highest of all at court in his lord's favour; he was in the very vigour of manhood; to unusual natural endowments he added a skill in arms which, even in that martial age, won him universal and unqualified applause; the great Norman houses pronounced him the flower of their chivalry, inasmuch as to the prowess of a model soldier he united the high and refined ideal of a finished gentleman; and their verdict was confirmed by Duke Robert and by princes beyond the duchy, whose gates always opened as if by enchantment to Herlwin.

He was the very pink of knightly honour, and it is hard to suppress a regret that so few stories have been preserved about him; but what we have show sufficiently what sort of man he was. Here is one of them.

At one time Count Gilbert did not behave to Herlwin as he should have done; and the latter, to his lord's discomfiture and chagrin, retired from the court. His absence

---

[1] The materials for this chapter are derived from Gilbert Crispin's *Life of Herlwin*, from Milo Crispin's *Life of Lanfranc*, from an unpublished codex in the public library at Evreux, and from the *Nomina Monachorum Becci*.

was the more regretted when, after some little time, an occasion presented itself upon which the earl, deeming himself injured by some of the most powerful of the Norman nobility, conceived it his duty to wipe out the grievance in blood. For Gilbert was a man of haughty temper; somewhat pretentious, perhaps; and so exceedingly vain of his relationship with the reigning dynasty that if the world ever forgot that he was great-great-grandson of Rollo, first Duke of Normandy; great-grandson of William Longsword, second Duke of Normandy; grandson of Richard I., third Duke of Normandy; that, furthermore, he was nephew of the fourth and cousin of the fifth and sixth Dukes of Normandy—the world was to be commiserated for its neglect of some very important facts. On the present occasion, too, he was not a little vain of his army; its numbers were positively worthy of such a leader; and heralds were despatched to advertise his foes that on such and such a day, at such and such an hour, and in such and such a place—he gave them due notice, that they might have every opportunity of incurring an honourable defeat—he would convince them that he was not a person to be trifled with. Accordingly, on the eve of the day fixed, the field was approached by two mighty hosts, the one commanded by Duke Rollo's great-great-grandson and the other a confederated force formidable enough to present all the requisite conditions for frightful carnage on either side; when, as Count Gilbert was already conducting his forces up the flank of a high hill, he descried twenty fully armed knights crossing the plain below. A hostile demonstration, he thought. No; it was a choice troop of horse collected and headed by the noble-hearted Herlwin, who, however much injured, was not a man to stand aloof in the hour of danger from the prince at whose board he had been nurtured; a return of good for evil which astounded the earl, who received him back at once into favour and restored to him his forfeited estates.

But a change was soon remarked in Herlwin.[1] A Divine flame had been kindled in that heroic breast, and already the gallant knight's attachment to the secular state was growing weak and cold. He passed his days in unbroken fast and his nights in protracted vigil; the church was his chief haunt, prayer his principal pursuit, and his only pastime showers of tears. He was less than heretofore at court, and indeed his only reason for not breaking with it entirely was that he desired to dedicate his estates to the service of God. When duty enjoined his presence there, he was found in his place; but not otherwise. His zeal for knightly accomplishments was gone.

There is little need to say that in time his position proved to be both false and irksome, and he would willingly have renounced the world without further delay did he but know whither to betake himself or what form of the religious life to adopt.

For the state of Normandy was exceptional and peculiar. From the day in 912 on which Rollo and his fierce hosts were made Christian in the fonts of Rouen the Dukes of Normandy had not, it is true, been unmindful of at least their public and official duty to Christianity; but we must not forget that a people, whose fathers at no remote period had amused themselves by tossing infant children in the air and catching them on the points of their spears, and could convert human skulls into drinking-cups, were scarcely to be humanised in one short century, and that so long as their spiritual leaders were men taken from among themselves, they were likely to advance along their new paths at a very slow pace. Hence it was that their bishops affected the matri-

---

[1] Here is Orderic's account of its occasion: 'Ingelrannus Pontivi comes cum valida manu ei (Gisleberto) obvius fuit. . . . Tunc ibi quidam miles nomine Herluinus periculum metuens, totqque nisu pro suâ salute fugiens, Deo vovit quod si de imminente periculo sospes evaseret, nulli ulterius nisi soli Deo militaret.'—*Orderic*, ii. 13. In quoting Orderic's *Historia Ecclesiastica*, I shall refer to M. Le Prévost's edition.

monial state,[1] under plea of perpetuating the princely or noble families to which they belonged; and that their monks, men from the ranks most of them, however good at heart—for there is no reason whatever to think them other—enclosed a kernel of piety under a husk of exceeding harshness.

Hence, too, a difficulty of no inconsiderable gravity for Herlwin. He knew not whose guidance to seek in the choice of a new home and a new mode of life; and, postponing his entry into religion, lived on in the world as unsecularly as he could. He laid aside his spurs, dressed himself in cheap and ordinary clothes, allowed his hair and beard to grow untrimmed, sat at the same table as heretofore, it is true, in the earl's dining-hall, but nourished himself with coarse bread and a cup of water, while Gilbert and the courtiers fed on dainties. Conduct like this excited no little amusement, and something more than a suspicion of mental aberration; much that he did looked mad, and all was accounted such. The earl, fond as he was of him, took part with his other knights in administering the treatment usually adopted in such cases—threats, promises, jeers, and blandishments—but to no purpose; until, perhaps as a last resource, the pious culprit was sent on errands to courts where once he had been the universal favourite, in the hope that either pride or shame might induce him to remove the beard, to trim the hair, to resume the ensigns of knighthood. It is a touching story. He went

[1] I think, however, that it would be more correct to say that in most instances married laymen were elevated to the episcopal dignity, not that bishops took to themselves paramours. Thus Gilbert Crispin, Herlwin's biographer, says, 'Sacerdotes et summi pontifices [i.e. bishops] liberè conjugati et arma portantes, ut laici erant, veterum ritu Danorum universi adhuc vivebant (*Vita B. Herluini*, p. 33). By *laici* he means laymen turned clergymen, just as Herlwin after his profession was called a *laicus*, that is to say, a layman turned priest and monk; the idea being that they had not been educated for the ecclesiastical state. It would seem as if a feudal lord who was also a bishop was not deemed singular in regarding a wife as a suitable adjunct to his secular fief; thus Archbishop Robert, son of Richard I., 'conjugem nomine Harlevam, *ut comes* habuit.'—*Orderic*, ii. 365.

obediently; but he went not only with tangled hair, unkempt beard, and ignoble apparel, but seated on that humble beast of burden whose more familiar name has been repudiated by our great lexicographer. Thus mounted, thus disguised—yet not disguised, for there were keen eyes at every court that soon recognised the most polished man in Normandy—his approach excited as much pain as amusement wherever he went. But he was unamenable to contempt and unamenable to compassion, and, being of invaluable service to Count Gilbert, who had no wish to lose him, remained at court even as he was; not permitted to leave, and not willing to leave without permission. To please his earthly lord he frequented the castle at Brionne; but to please his heavenly he rode on an ass.

At length an occasion occurred on which he found it impossible to reconcile the claims of the two masters. Earl Gilbert wished to injure one of his neighbours, and desired Herlwin to carry a mischievous message to Duke Robert, whose interest in this business was identified with his own. Herlwin refused; Gilbert insisted, entreated, threatened, but to no purpose; for the juncture was of too critical a kind for Herlwin even to hesitate. He therefore rudely broke the bond that had so long tied him to the service of an earthly lord, by once more and finally refusing to carry the message and by retiring from the court. Gilbert, little dreaming that the good man was in earnest, took it for granted that the commission had been executed, and allowed a day or two to pass before going to receive his cousin's answer; when, to his infinite mortification, he found that no message had been delivered. This was too much for Duke Rollo's great-great-grandson, who in a transport of rage ordered Herlwin's estates to be escheated, and the goods and chattels of Herlwin's poor dependents taken from them.

For himself, Herlwin could not take this to heart; but the

prayers and tears of his poor people left him no rest. He therefore, after a few days' interval, presented himself before the earl to plead their cause. The whole court was assembled, and the recalcitrant knight had to endure a volley of reproaches from men who vainly thought that he had come to justify himself for his late disobedience. He quietly set aside a few irrelevant charges, and then continued, 'As for my possessions, take them and distribute them, no matter how, if only these poor people, who have done nothing to deserve your displeasure, have their things given back to them.' The earl's heart swelled, for wonder and pity had taken hold of him; and, calling Herlwin aside, he implored him to explain this great change in his conduct. What did he mean? What was he bent upon? 'I have, by loving the world,' was the reply, 'and paying court to you, all too much neglected God and neglected myself; my heart set upon the concerns of the body, I have received no discipline for my soul. So then, if ever I have deserved well of you, let me pass the remainder of my days in a monastery. Let me but keep your love, and devote to God with me all that I once had.' The sitting of the court broke up; for Gilbert could restrain himself no longer, and, retiring to his own room, broke into a flood of tears. The earl wept for his faithful follower; the knight wept for the lord he wished to quit. The desired permission was only gained by dint of long and earnest entreaty; but no sooner did the 'love strong as death' win its victory than Gilbert, who had once lavished affection upon Herlwin as his favourite dependent, not only gave him full power over his own person and estates, but, treating him with as careful a respect as if he had been a social and territorial superior, kept him at Brionne in the quality of a guest to whom all honour must be paid, and finally bade him farewell, invested with the absolute ownership of the estates he had inherited from his father, and, in addition to that, with seigneurial authority over his two brothers, Odo and Roger; 'because, although by birth they were Herlwin's equals, it was no insult to their rank or to their persons that he should be made their legal superior now that he was raised to a higher rank than they (in virtue of absolute ownership of what had hitherto formed part of the Earl's *alodium*), and in virtue of a true nobility (the *vera nobilitas* of such as leave all and follow Christ) set above them.'

All this took place in the year 1031.

Amongst the other estates of which Herlwin had the propriety was Malleville, the dowry of his mother, Eloise, on her marriage with Ansgot; and a third part of the adjacent manor of Burnencville or Burneville,[1] a place some five miles east of Brionne. It was upon the second of these that he soon resolved to build a church and establish a religious community.

He was at once master of the works and workman. He dug, as well as marked out, the trench for the foundation, and carrying off the dug-up soil, collected his own building material; material plentiful enough then, as now, all over the vast upland plain on which Burneville lay, and now, as then, employed generally by the masons of the district, siliceous nodules, gravel, and chalky marl; and carrying them on his own shoulders to the site, sorted and arranged them, and finally built a church of them, flint predominating in the lower part of the walls, and in the upper part clay. He took but one scant meal in the twenty-four hours, and that after his manual toil was over; except, indeed, on fasts, when he ate nothing; and then set to work again in another way; for to be a monk he must be familiar with the Psalter; to know that he must be able to read, and to be able to read he must begin with the alphabet itself; a lesson learnt to such

[1] *Burnencville.* This is undoubtedly the spelling in the Evreux codex. The modern name Bonneville, like many others, is a manifest corruption, suggested perhaps by Malleville, the name of a neighbouring village. Thus the name of the neighbouring wood or *boscum* 'quod dicitur *Roboretum*' has been transformed into Bosrobert.

effect that, in course of time, scholars like Lanfranc wondered not only at his acquaintance with the text of Holy Scripture, but at his intimate knowledge of its hidden wealth. And when, far in the night, his studies were brought to a close there were prayers to be said, which left him little time for repose before the morning's labour should begin again of carrying flints, gravel, and marl for the erection of his poor little church.

But his architectural labours, if architectural they may be termed, for nothing could have been humbler and ruder than the whole thing, were suspended from time to time, at least in frosty weather. On one of these occasions he resolved to visit a monastery, the name of which is not recorded, so as to gain some experimental knowledge of the claustral life, and, invoking the benediction of Heaven, set forth, penetrated with a sense of respect, which improved into trembling awe as he approached the sacred edifice, and then, as he at last found himself at the very gate of the cloister, into palpitating terror; fitting emotions for the mortal who is presently to have a glimpse of paradise. The gate was open, and in he stepped; for who would ever think of asking leave, should he find the gate of paradise ajar?[1] He trod lightly, and was breathless; for he thought he should see a vision of angels, gravely scapulared indeed, and to outward eye not unlike the children of humanity, but to the cleansed vision beings of supernatural sort, all tranquilly enclosed in a low-browed corridor. Alas that the truth must be told! His expectations were disappointed. Those monks were men, and very disorderly men to boot. He stood rooted to the pavement, bewildered and not knowing what next to do; when the gate porter, who had watched his tiptoe invasion and made no doubt that he was a thief, emerged quick as lightning from his hiding-place, struck him with one hand a sound blow on the nape of the neck, and with the other hand clutched him

[1] 'Velut ad ostium paradisi.'

by his long hair as he tumbled forward, dragged him to the gate, and then, to borrow the biographer's phrase, 'extruded him.'

The flower of Norman chivalry was not accustomed to this sort of thing; but, remembering that, after all, the gate porter was a monk and he a mere laic, he controlled his tongue and his temper, 'deeply grounded in the charity of Christ, the charity which beareth all things.'

Bent on monastic studies, he made his next expedition to a house of no small renown; and, selecting a pacific season, that of Christmas, approached its gates with a full sense of the respect due to gate porters, and was received civilly enough. The procession had already begun; but there was much about it that sadly shocked his refined tastes. The fathers who took part in it were evidently very vain, vain from the vanity that comes of a vulgar mind. But vulgarity is not a celestial attribute; and Herlwin's imagination could hardly grasp the idea of angels in procession distributing nods and smiles among the saints that line their path, which was precisely what the fathers, in the midst of their hymn, did to the laity who stood watching them; nor was it seraphic in the wearers of the handsomest copes to make an ostentatious display of their finery. Gilbert Crispin very properly remarks that the Normans, as a people, were not yet civilised. But Herlwin was. Hence his dismay when, as the procession regained the church, the reverend fathers made a general rush to see who could get in first; and his horror when, in the thick of the *mêlée*, one of the monks, who found himself too closely pressed by another, turned round upon the offender and dealt him, with clenched fist, a blow that sent him reeling till he measured his length on the ground—flat on his back, as we should say, but in Gilbert's choicer phrase 'teeth upward' (*supinis dentibus*).

All this levity and impropriety so scandalised him that he, perhaps, valued it at more than its real worth. But God is good. The next night he remained in the oratory after matins—matins were said in the small hours—and, when the rest had all gone, retired into a remote corner to pray unobserved. In a few minutes some one came close to where he was. Herlwin remained still as death, and watched him. The new comer, deeming himself alone, now stretched upon the ground, and now resting on his knees, prayed and wept, and wept and prayed all through the wintry night, and until broad day lighted up the church.

Reassured by an experience like this, he returned to Burneville, and, pulling down some cottages on the paternal estate, proceeded to build with the materials what was necessary for the completion of his monastery, now that the church was finished.

It was in the year 1034 that, the whole structure being now erected and fit for use, Herbert, Bishop of Lisieux, consecrated the church and clothed Herlwin, who had by this time completed his fortieth year, in a cowl and hood of unbleached, undyed, coarsely-woven wool; a quaint exaggeration, it may be, of the typical poverty of the sons of St. Benedict, but only too just a token of the extreme indigence of this new *miles Christi*. Two of Herlwin's own people, Walter and Hervey by name, received that humble livery together with their master; but there were others ready to join the triad; and at their head Baldric de Servaville, Herlwin's brother-in-law, whose name stands fourth on the list of the monks of Le Bec; the eighth being that of Baldric's son, Hugh, born about the year 1030, and professed in 1037, at the same time with his father. Then, too, it was that Herlwin was raised to the priesthood, and consecrated abbot of a house so miserably poor that no one else could be induced to accept the post.[1]

---

[1] It is thus that I account for the white habit peculiar to Le Bec until the year 1626. Dugdale, in his *Monasticon*, ventures upon some strange nonsense concerning this white habit in his account of St. Neot's. Leland (*Collectanea*,

Later ages, whilst respecting the site of Herlwin's first monastery, have perpetuated the memory of its earlier history in the name of La Baronnerie. La Baronnerie is a plot of land, an acre in extent and of irregular form, adjacent to the churchyard of the village, which bears the modern name of Bonneville, and is surrounded by precisely such a wall as Herlwin built, a structure composed in its lower part of flint and in its upper of a mud-like compost held together with gravel and straw; the whole surmounted by a packsaddle coping of thatch. The enclosure contains a barn of comparatively modern date, used by the monks of Le Bec during a long series of years down to the Revolution; a row of humble cottages, which, no doubt, occupy the site of Herlwin's dwelling-place; and a pond, vocal with frogs, the perpetuation of his reservoir for such water as it might yield him. For this morose upland plain has no fresh springs, and not the least of the trials of the poor little community was the necessity of fetching the limpid fluid from a source which lay five[1] miles away; whilst their estate, a very wilderness of thorns and brambles, boasted a soil so thankless that nothing but unrelaxing and severest toil could elicit from it a scanty return of thin rye or a few herbs; and the heroic band deemed it a godsend if ever a little cheese, a little pulse, or a loaf made of some finer grain found its way into their store-room.[2]

After some time, however, Herlwin was admonished in a dream to relinquish his arid, incorrigible, and monotonous wilderness for another site.

To reach this he must make for a point on the edge of

iv. 13) is much more to the point. Dom Bouquet (viii. 459) gives evidence from Le Bec itself that *vestimenta alba* were worn there early in the fourteenth century; and the portraits of Lanfranc and St. Anselm, preserved in the parish church, represent them in cowls of a dirty white colour.

[1] The distance to the source of the nearest stream, the brook presently to be reached, was four miles 'as the crow flies.'

[2]   Vestibus hutis, sumptibus arctis, membra domando,
    Herbis vescentes crudis laticemque bibentes,
    Pane sed adjecto quandoque siligine facto.

the plain some two miles distant to the west-south-west, and descend the wooded slope that dips into the valley, down which babbles the historical rivulet of Le Bec. Here, just where the long strip of meadow land begins to broaden, and, degenerating into a marsh that spreads north-westward, merges into the basin of the Risle; here, on the right bank of the rivulet, there stood three water-mills, built upon piles and separated by a narrow piece of rank mead from as many cottages, which had been planted as far back from the brook as was permitted by the narrow limits of the enclosure. Why the enclosure had not been made higher up stream must now be explained.

The Castle of Brionne stood on a rocky island in the Risle; whilst round about it as from a centre, and stretching away to the average rectilineal distance of full three miles on every side, there lay a territory over which the Count of Brionne exercised sovereign jurisdiction, from the levying of a petty custom at Pont Authou to the hanging of malefactors upon a gallows which adorned the local Golgotha of the Champ de Geoffroy. The limits of this territory had been determined by measuring with a cord for the distance of some four miles in all directions from the castle, now to one point, now to another, now to another, and so on, the points lying at a convenient interval each from each, and then by tracing a boundary from point to point until a rude circle was completed, of which Brionne was, of course, the centre. It is scarcely necessary to say that if the boundary line had been exhibited on a map it would have displayed some very marked divergencies from mathematical symmetry, by reason, not only of the deviations from theoretical rectitude of the track along which the cord was carried at each successive measurement, but of the irregularities of hill and dale.

The boundary line of this privileged domain crossed the Risle near the confluence of the beck with that river, and at some little distance above the stone bridge of modern days. There was Pont Authou, or Pons Altoi, the Bridge of Autoy. On leaving the river the line traversed the open for a quarter of a mile, and then, trending eastward, ascended the tributary for about the same distance, after which, crossing abruptly to the right bank, it at once plunged into forest and mounted the overhanging hill, not again to cross the rivulet, whose source lay within the domain.

Thus the part of the stream whither Herlwin went his way in quest of a new site was precisely that at which it escaped from Earl Gilbert's immediate jurisdiction. The site, it is true, was a swampy one, but he had no choice of a better.

The land was Herlwin's own out and out; but he had no interest in one of the three mills, and only a third share in the others, his brothers Odo and Roger being co-proprietors with him. They, however, and the owner or owners of the first either gave or sold him each his respective share of the whole property, and he was thus put in possession of an area barely large enough for the erection of a small convent.

He began by building his church, and as soon as all that was necessary had been erected brought his community down from Bonneville.

His church was nearest the brook, lying from east to west; at right angles to it was the chapter house, the rafters of which he almost touched with his head as he stood in it, and in an attic over the chapter house the dormitory, to which he gained access by a steep ladder with six or seven rungs. On the northern side of the little quadrangle stood the refectory; and on the western a cellar surmounted by a loft, which was meant to serve as a granary, but was probably converted in course of time into a second dormitory. Besides these there were kitchen, bakehouse, lavatory, and the other offices, all built of the materials in vogue in the valley; mud, however, predominating considerably over flint; whilst the walls were supported and held together by timber from the adjacent forest. The walls of the cloister, which was not built before the church had been consecrated, consisted of a timber framework filled in with plaster, except where there were openings for the admission of light; but the thatched roof must have been too heavy for them, as they tumbled down the very night after the completion of the work. They were rebuilt in flint.

The church was consecrated in the year 1040, and on the 23rd of February, by Mauger, Archbishop of Rouen, in the presence of Herlwin and his monks, whose numbers had by this time swelled to a full score. Next night, so the story goes, Dom Gotbert, or Gothbert, on rising to call the brethren up to matins, observed that the church was so brilliantly illuminated that the streams of light which poured into the sacristy, where he slept, would have shown him a needle had there been one on the floor. This was strange, for the community were so poor they could not afford an altar lamp and were wont to sing the night office by the gleam of a light brought from the kitchen.[1] But scarcely had the alarmed sacristan jumped out of his bed when he heard voices singing very, very gently. He stepped to the door, which opening into the church near the high altar,[2] thus commanded a view of the choir; when lo! in the abbot's stall there stood 'Mary, the most glorious and blessed Mother of

---

[1] Or from the bakehouse. These two offices usually adjoined one another.

[2] In monasteries of greater size and possessed of treasure the sacristan slept within the sacred fabric. I find from an unpublished manuscript preserved at Evreux that in the new church of Le Bec the *secretarius* had his bed in the church, close to the door of the treasury. Guibert of Nogent (*Vita*, i. § 25) tells of a procession of ghosts, who entering a church, walked past the bed of the *custos ecclesiæ* and crossed the building between the choir and the high altar. And in the early days of St. Martin's at Tournay, when there was as yet no treasure to guard, the monk who was to ring the bell for matins, *sicut ejusdem officii moris est procuratoribus*, had his bed within the walls.—Herman, *De Rest. Abb. Sti. Martini Tornac.*

our Lord, and in front of her the most blessed Apostles Peter and Paul, and a third saint whom he did not recognise, singing matins before her.' Seeing this, he thought he would go round to the choir gate so as to have a nearer and better view of those most glorious persons and enjoy the singing. He did so as gently as possible, 'and on tiptoe as it were;' but before he could reach the choir-gate the light vanished and the voices died suddenly away. 'But there was such a sweet perfume in the air that when the brethren came in for the office they were fain to make signs to each other to ask what it meant.'

Two or three years later—that is to say, in the year 1042 or in 1043—Lanfranc, the illustrious Pavian, who had for some time been lecturing at Avranches, set forth from that city on a journey to Rouen, attended by a single companion, a *clericus* or clerk, whom he seems to have employed to relieve the drudgery of his school or lecture room. His baggage seems to have comprised all his movable property; in which case he can have had no intention of returning to Avranches, and was not improbably bent upon carrying into effect the resolution which he had now for some time made, of exchanging the secular state for the religious. He was uncertain, however, whether to live as a recluse, as a hermit, or as a monk, but had made up his mind that, should he choose the cloister in preference to the hospice or the hermitage, he would enter some obscure little monastery, none of whose inmates was likely to know who he was. So then he set forth on his journey.

Several days had passed without disturbing incident, when one evening, as the furtive gloom already closed over the basin of the Risle, warning him to hurry on to Brionne, he was surprised by robbers, who took from him all he had,[1]

---

[1] '*Cuncta quæ habebat*,' '*omnia quæ habebat*,' '*omnia mea.*' These phrases and the general tone of the several narratives lead me to think that he had taken final leave of Avranches, and what the bandits took was literally all that he had in the

except that, whether out of rude chivalry or from respect for his clerical character, they spared him an old cloak as defence against the weather and let him go forward on his way. But he had not taken many steps before his active memory recalled a story in St. Gregory's 'Dialogues,' which tells how some good man in Italy, on being robbed of his horse by highwaymen, called after them and offered them the whip; how the robbers on reaching the Voltorno could by no means cross it, and how, persuaded that their victim must be a saint, they came back and restored him his quadruped. 'Let me do the same sort of thing,' said Lanfranc to himself, 'let me turn back and offer them what they have spared me, and then they will give me back my all.' He acted accordingly, overtook them, *mitis ut agnus*, and offered them the cloak. There was an Italian refinement about the act which they failed to appreciate; so they gave him a cudgelling for his impudence, tied his hands behind his back, pulled his hood well down over his eyes, led him off to a distance past all possibility of discovering the bridle path, and then lashed him to a tree, but with no old cloak to protect him against the weather. His clerk was fastened to another. Thus checkmated, Lanfranc began to bewail his misfortune, and well he might, for wolf and bear roved at will through the forest, and foxes hunted their prey in packs and made short work of worrying belated travellers. But as the night grew still and deep his very terror was hushed and overawed by the hollow silence. Hour after hour passed, but nothing approached to hurt him; hour after hour passed, and his thoughts turned from the contemplation of his present distress to the changefulness and transitoriness of this world's glory and the vanity of human toil; hour after hour passed away, and, unless the overhanging foliage was sparse enough and the sky clear enough

world. A sad loss to the learned of that age; unless, indeed, they contrived to sell his books.

for him to see the constellations, he must have guessed but vaguely the progress of the night, when, to his joy, the faintest, tenderest gleam of reviving day lived in the air, and he, with the devotion of one who was already at heart a religious, began to recite the two offices of *laudes nocturnæ* and *laudes matutinæ*, now termed matins and lauds; offices comprising, apart from hymns, versicles, responses, and antiphons, two lessons out of St. Paul's epistles and twenty-one psalms, besides the Te Deum, the Benedicite, and the Benedictus. But the task was too much for him, and he broke down, and breaking down cried, 'O Lord God, how many years have I spent upon this world's learning! I have wearied both body and soul with secular studies, but I have not yet learnt to recite the office of Thy praise. Deliver me from this trouble, and I will try so to correct and order my life as to learn how to do Thee service as I ought.'[1] His prayer reached Heaven,

[1] 'Voluit Domino laudes debitas persolvere. . . . Laudis officia tibi persolvere non didici.' Surely the phrases *laudes debita, laudis officia* and the double *persolvere* are sufficient to guide a careful reader to the real meaning of the passage. The following passages are sufficient illustration of the text; they are taken from the lives of King Robert, St. Odo, the Countess Ida, B. Emmeram, and B. Simon of Crépy. 'Quodam tempore . . . . adveniente horâ quâ *laudibus* laudaretur deus, surgit à lecto et ad ecclesiam ire disposuit;' '*nocturnas laudes* fraterna devotio *persolverat*;' 'factum est cùm quâdam nocte *matutinis laudibus persolvendis* fratres interessent intererat et deo dilectissima Ida;' 'circa horam diei tertiam celebrante illo canonicos hymnos et *debitum officium* solvente;' 'nocte quâdam priusquam fratres ad *debita* servitutis officium processissent.'

Nor did the robbers tie Lanfranc *naked* to a tree. Virgil's husbandman is *nudus*, but not naked;

'Nudus ara, sere nudus.'

St. Anselm, in one of his dialogues, says that a monk without his tunic is *nudus*, but the monk had under garments. Guibert of Nogent (*De Vitâ sua*, iii. 9), describes a man who has thrown away his armour as *nudus*; 'arma projecit nudumque se eorum misericordiæ in modum crucis exposuit;' and our saint, on his first exile from England, is said to have landed *nudus* on the opposite coast. But enough of this.

The words which I render 'to do Thee service' are *tibi servire*—'ut tibi servire valeam et sciam.' *Servire* and *servitium* are words proper to the Divine office; and the familiar phrases *service* and *Divine service* are a literal translation of the monastic *servitium* and *servitium Dei*. Thus in the Life of Boso, fourth abbot of Le Bec, we are told that Anselm, observing him to be *sollicitum ad opus Dei . . . . instruebat eum in Domini servitio.* I shall have some-for presently he heard the sound of travellers and shouted to them; but they, haunted no doubt by visions of hungry wolves, were so terrified that he was obliged to redouble his appeals for help and thus assure them that the voice they heard was a man's voice. They made for him, and, on learning who he was and what had befallen him, loosed his bonds. He now begged them to direct him to the meanest and humblest monastery in the country-side. 'There is none humbler and meaner,' they said, 'than one which a man of God is building not far from here,' a little bit of a place, they explained, extremely poor, poor even to contempt. The monk who was employed on it—and it was a sorry bit of building—had not long quitted the world; his name was Herlwin.[1] So saying they pointed out a track which led down to the river towards the sunrise, and pursued their journey. Goodbye, then, to the world. Let the dead bury their dead.

The track pointed out by the travellers led him down to the *Pons Altoi*, which I have already mentioned as facilitating the passage of the Risle where the boundary line of the *comitatus Brionensis* crossed that river, and, gaining the opposite bank, made for Herlwin's little encampment, which lay half a mile off in the marshy open. The time was early

thing to say about *opus Dei* in another chapter; that and *servitium Domini* are one and the same thing.

When Bishop Wulstan on a well-known critical occasion was favoured with a brief interval of seclusion for the preparation of his defence, he, instead of thinking about such mundane trifles, exclaimed, 'Why, we have not sung nones yet!' His friends remonstrated; let them first settle the business in hand; there would then be time enough, and more than enough, for singing nones; the King and his great men would think he was playing the fool with them. 'No, no,' said Wulstan, 'we will first do the service of God (*Dei servitium*), and then turn our thoughts to men's quarrels.' Whereupon they sang their *hora nona*. The 'Divine service' which they performed was the canonical office.—W. M., *De Gest. Pontif., De Ep. Wigorn.*

In snort, Lanfranc's *servire tibi* means 'to say my office.' And, indeed, this is manifest from the sequel. 'Non oblitus quod in nocturna captione promiserat . . . *in discendis officiis* . . . . curam maximam impendere voluit, ut sciret Deo *laudis sacrificium persolvere, sicut voverat.*'

[1] 'Cœnobiolum quoddam pauperrimum et despicabile, quod à quodam monacho nuper converso de sæculo quoquomodo edificabatur, qui dicebatur Herluinus.'

morning, and lauds had been said in the church, but not prime. He entered the precinct and asked for the abbot. Some one pointed to an outlying structure, and he approached it. It was merely a one-room cottage of modest dimensions, intended for a bakehouse, and it had in the further wall an opening too small for a doorway. When Lanfranc reached this outhouse, Herlwin—so chance would have it—had crept through the aperture just mentioned and was constructing a rounded chamber or lean-to of mud.[1] This little chamber was to be the oven; Herlwin was standing upright in it, for its low hemispherical roof or coping was not begun; but neither of the interlocutors could see the other. The stranger approached the opening and asked who was the abbot. 'I,' said Herlwin from his retreat, his hands covered with mud; 'but why do you ask?'[2] 'Because,' answered the stranger, 'I wish to become a monk here, if it be God's will and yours.' 'Are you clerk or layman?' inquired Herlwin. 'Clerk, a teacher in schools, an Italian; my name is Lanfranc.' Herlwin stooped down, took a scrutinising view of his visitor through the mouth of the future oven, and replied, 'In the Lord's name I receive you;' upon which the other bent himself lowly down to kiss the feet of the abbot, who refused the premature homage and only allowed him to kiss his muddy hands. No more was said, for the rule of the order forbad conversation at that period of the day; but Lanfranc threw off his habit and set to work with a will, notwithstanding the adventures and fatigue of the night, to help Herlwin and such others as were there to build the oven. The work was finished by the hour for prime; office was said; and then the brethren in chapter assembled heard from their abbot's lips of the demand that had been presented by their clerical visitor.

[1] Precisely thus are ovens built to this day in the valley of Le Bec.

[2] This account, taken from the Evreux codex, differs from the other two hitherto published; it is incomparably the most probable of the three. It was written by a Le Bec monk, who had received his information from contemporaries of Lanfranc.

Their concurrence granted, Herlwin gave the postulant the formal welcome which that concurrence warranted him in according, and presented him the book of the rule to read. When Lanfranc had had time duly to peruse the rule he was admitted to the novitiate, and after some few days his name was inscribed in the list of the professed monks of Le Bec. It was the thirty-fifth.

Mindful of his vow in the forest, he now spared no pains in learning the day and night offices with even greater accuracy than the rule of the order required, and rejoiced in the thought that at last he was an unknown man. He lived as men may in small communities, very much to himself; and, though thrown with others, was almost a solitary; for there were only one or two in the house to whom he ever spoke, and that he did very rarely. And his brethren, as they noted him day by day in the cloister, seated apart and alone, sometimes lost in thought, sometimes shedding tears over the sacred page that lay on his knee, but always the model of meekness and a placid melancholy, little dreamt that he had once made a noise in the world. They used to speak, poor simple men, in later days of this pious fraud of the Italian, sustained through three long taciturn years, and how, for example, he would never read a lesson in the church unless he had first rehearsed the task under the guidance of the cantor, or how once, when desired by the prior to mispronounce a word, he had mispronounced it.

Still, those years of *incognito* were years of peculiar trial to Lanfranc. Undoubtedly the men amongst whom he lived were anxiously desirous to fulfil the object of their creation; but, only as yet in part reclaimed from barbarism, the majority of them were by an inherited necessity absolutely incapable even of approaching, however awkwardly, the ideal which his life displayed to them; and the lesson which the refined and courtly Herlwin had a few years before so rudely learnt was now taught to the high-souled and accomplished

Lanfranc; namely this, that gentlemen and scholars are not the only people destined to take a high degree in the next world. It was inevitable that their equanimity should be chafed by the presence of a man who, as their own rude instincts told them, had been cast in a different mould from their own; a foreigner too, and of all foreigners a foreigner from Lombardy—from Lombardy, the home of the arts, of learning, of commercial resource, of maritime adventure, of high political ambition, of all the influences which, consecrated by religion, were to give impulse and a character to the new civilisation of Christendom; and some of them were even haunted by the apprehension that at no distant time he might be set in authority over them. He bore his trial for a time and then resolved to fly. He feigned an infirmity of the stomach and induced Fulcran, the gardener, to give him a daily supply of thistle-roots, which he ate in order thus to grow inured to the sort of food he would find in the desert, and was already laying his plans for departure in the dead of the night, when the abbot sent for him. The two men sat for a time in silence. Herlwin would fain have spoken, but his heart was full; the words refused to come; his face, at all times singularly mobile and expressive, gave token of some unusual sorrow, and at last he burst into tears. Lanfranc, much bewildered, threw himself at his feet and implored him to say what was the matter. After a pause the abbot recovered himself sufficiently to exclaim, 'Woe is me that God should threaten me with such a loss! Alas! I have lost my counsel and my help! Often, and with sighs and tears, did I pray and supplicate the mercy of God to give me a man like you to advise and help me. . . . And when, brother Lanfranc, He brought you here, I felt sure that my prayers had been answered. I have even thought of shifting my burden upon you; I have hoped you would carry all its load for me. And now, I know not why, you are going to leave me and run away; you want to fly into the desert.'

Lanfranc was soon at the abbot's feet again, inquiring in amazement how he knew all this. The shade of Herlwin's sainted nephew, Hugh de Servaville, recently deceased, had come to him in the night, clothed in white garments, as he lay in his bed, and had warned him of Lanfranc's design. The surprised culprit at once confessed his fault, received a penance and absolution, and vowed never to forsake his abbot, but to obey him well for the future.

He lived on, therefore, at Le Bec, still unsuspected by his brethren. Herlwin had, it is true, either known or suspected the quality of his visitor from the very moment of their first encounter, one standing in the bakehouse, the other in the oven; but not so the rest of the community. Many of those men must have entered religion before Lanfranc opened his school at Avranches; but in any case what should people of their class know of such a man as he? The inhabitants of the remotest village in our island know much more about the Master of Trinity than the monks of Le Bec, shut up in a cloister and isolated from the world by marsh and forest, can have known of Lanfranc. They, though at the best they were *non multùm litterati*, could read after a fashion; but they had nothing to do with the rhetoric, the dialectic, and the other liberal arts once taught by him at Avranches. Had some distinguished clergyman, indeed, followed him into religion at Le Bec, or some schoolmaster, or some member of the *haute noblesse*, Lanfranc the Lombard might have been recognised; but such were not the men to pass by Jumièges and Fécamp, and Mont St. Michel, and a host of other great houses, and search for a place without even a name; a place hidden from human sight, a place the very synonym to the few that knew it for all that was poor, and obscure, and mean.

He lived on, therefore, at Le Bec, the world forgetting, by the world forgot, when one fine day the world was startled out of its propriety to hear that the dead was alive, that the lost was found; that Lanfranc, the great *magister*, who, leaving

Avranches three years ago, had fallen a victim to a wolf or a bear somewhere on his way to Rouen, had reappeared on our earth; that he had grown very thin, that he was very emaciated, very sparing in speech, and not a little sanctified; that he had reappeared in quite a new character, a Benedictine of Benedictines; but still that he had reappeared. From that day his unknown, unnamed retreat was the most famous place in Normandy; from that day the lowly walls and thatched roof of Le Bec were familiar objects to the noble and the learned of all Western Christendom; from that day its gates were sought by scions of the best families of Normandy, Brittany, France, Flanders, Gascony, and Provence, and by the most famous schoolmasters in Christendom; all anxious to hear the resuscitated Lanfranc lecture, and all eager to carry away the sacred flame and communicate it to other minds and other hearts.

The Prior of Le Bec—for he seems to have been appointed to the office about this time; and the appointment was approved by the unanimous suffrage of the monks, who could now admire and revere the object of their recent mistrust and aversion; so true is it that men in false positions are always disliked—the Prior, thus invaded, was constrained to open a school for externs so soon as lodgings could be provided for them.

It flourished for some seven years, although they were not seven years of uninterrupted teaching. For Lanfranc spent part of the autumn of 1049 at Rheims, where he took part in the famous council convened by Leo IX., in which that pontiff, amongst other efforts for the restoration of ecclesiastical discipline, and so for the reformation of the public morals,[1] forbad once more the espousals of persons connected by the tie of consanguinity, and issued a special prohibition against the contemplated marriage of Duke William and his kins-

[1] 'Ipse igitur . . . concilium tenuit . . . et salubria decreta quæ jam antistites et presbyteri nesciebant renovavit.'— *Orderic*, i. 183, 458; ii. 398.

woman the Princess Matilda of Flanders.[1] Early in 1050 we find him at Rome, summoned thither on occasion of the recently divulged heresy of Berengarius, and he remained in Italy until the assembly of the Council of Vercelli in the following autumn. Nevertheless his labours, although uncontinuous, were sufficiently active, not only to sustain the new character he had given to Le Bec, but to win to its cloister postulants from the social and the intellectual aristocracy of Europe—not many indeed, but still enough to hold things in readiness for what in modern phrase would be called a new departure.

Meanwhile Duke William saw much of Lanfranc during part at least of his long siege of the Castle of Brionne,[2] whither Guy, Count of Burgundy, had retired after his defeat at Val ès Dunes,[3] and the two men soon established a friendship in which the wise counsels of the monk were repaid by the filial reverence and dutiful obedience of the prince.

But no sooner had the Duke, in the year 1053, consummated his uncanonical espousals, than Lanfranc's horoscope betokened an approaching crisis. Men were not wanting who made it their business to inflame the prince against his best friend; and, unless history has maligned that lady, Matilda herself directed her spiteful regards towards the Prior of Le Bec. Chief, however, amongst the mischief-makers was a court chaplain, 'a man of small mind' and scanty culture, whose reputation for learning, at one time great, had suddenly paled on Lanfranc's first appearance in the duchy. His name was Herfast.

[1] The reader who is interested in this subject will find something about it in the Appendix.
[2] This famous castle was on an island in the river. The road from the railway station to the main street of the modern town crosses the island. On the destruction of the castle in 1090 a new site was chosen on the cliff which overhangs the eastern bank of the river. Orderic says that William reduced it *in tribus annis*; by which, as I hope to show in the next chapter, we must understand two years and a fraction.
[3] Herlwin's old friend, Count Gilbert, died by violent hands in 1040.

But a few words about the abbey are here necessary by way of explanation. Count Gilbert had now been dead for more than twelve years; but before his death he had given Our Lady of Le Bec the whole of the wooded hill-side which overlooked the right bank of the stream for a distance of three miles above the monastery. At the upper or southern extremity of this strip of land, and where the hill-side subsides into a gently sloping glade, across which the high road from Brionne to Rouen now runs, there was a grassy enclosure shut in, save on the side washed by the stream, by a thick-set fence or palisade. There a few cattle grazed; there, in a barn, the monks' harvest was, year by year, stored up, for this spot was easy of access from all their arable land as far as Bonneville; there, in a mill on the water, their corn was ground; and there, in a chapel dedicated to St. Martin, the holiest rites of our religion were constantly celebrated for the benefit of the neighbouring peasantry. It was called the Park. A church path led from the chapel, the chapel of St. Martin du Parc, to Neuville, which lies a few miles off above the course of the beck, and Gilbert's successor at Brionne, Guy of Burgundy, gave Herlwin all the land that lay between the church path and the water. But enough. Let us return to Duke William.

It would seem that, in the autumn of 1053, the young prince brought his uncanonical bride down to Brionne, having in his train Herfast, who lost no time in announcing his intention of attending Lanfranc's lectures. Term must just have commenced when one morning the chaplain rode up in great state to the poor little monastery of mud and thatch, accompanied by a troop of courtiers all splendidly mounted. Lanfranc appreciated the plutocratic effontery, and it is refreshing to learn that he knew how to chastise it. Convinced, by the very first remark with which the gracious auditor deigned to favour him, that he knew next to nothing, the Lombard, with grave and exquisite politeness, set an alphabet before him, 'ferociam hominis Italicâ facetiâ illudens;' and oh that we had been there to see the sight! The exasperated clergyman flew from the lecture room, posted back to Brionne, summoned his brother chaplains, entered the Duke's presence, and set forth his grievance with such adornments as convinced the prince that it was not so much Herfast, the chaplain, as himself, William, Duke of Normandy, who had been mocked and flouted by the stranger. An order was forthwith issued banishing Lanfranc the duchy. But, alas! William was even thus unable to satisfy the demands of a wrath which at times spared him as little as it spared many others of his race, and, adding cruelty to rage, he further commanded that the grange up-stream at Le Parc should be burnt to the ground. The order was mercilessly executed.

Whilst the Park with its little store of grain for the next year's consumption was collapsing into one miserable heap of ashes, Lanfranc, the joy and solace of his brethren, set forth; set forth provided with 'a three-footed horse,' the best beast of burden they had to give him for his baggage, and a serving man who was to bring the creature back when its work was done. Crushed with stupid grief, they knew not what to do, save 'wait in silence for the salvation of God.' Nor did they wait in vain. As Lanfranc, on his way towards Brionne, walked along by the side of the poor beast—it dropped its head to the ground at every step—he descried the Duke, who must surely have gone forth anticipating an encounter; and when he got near enough to salute him, did so as one who had no reason to be ashamed. William turned away his face—perhaps from pride, perhaps from confusion, perhaps from both, perhaps from neither, for he was inwardly convulsed at the sight of the lame hack—but presently looked round and smiled good-naturedly. He was an accurate reader of men's character, and the dignity, the candour, the openness, the moral beauty of Lanfranc's countenance convinced him that he had been deceived. The monk was the first to speak.

'I am going on foot out of your province, worried with this worthless quadruped. Give me at least a better horse, that I may obey your orders.' 'And pray,' rejoined the Duke, smiling, 'who is this that asks presents of his offended judge before he has cleared himself of the charge laid against him?' The Prior seized his opportunity; begged for a hearing; pleaded his case, and pleaded it to such effect that he was taken into greater favour than ever; was assured that never henceforth should he be condemned without a hearing; and then received and returned the Duke's embrace and the Duke's kiss of reconciliation.

On going back to the monastery he found his lecture room empty, and empty it was destined to remain for the space of some four or five years, Herlwin being indisposed to provoke a repetition of the late disaster. Neither does there seem to have been during that interval more than one accession, if indeed there was even one, to the list of professed monks. The truth is that although only thirty professions had been made in the course of the eleven years just passed, the poor little cloister must have been already pretty full when Lanfranc entered it 1042, and now that a sixty-sixth inmate had been introduced the capacity of the house was tried to its very utmost. The refectory was too small for a party of three score, the dormitories were inconveniently crowded, and Herlwin seems already to have set about enlarging his borders, notwithstanding the opposition of Lanfranc, who represented to him that few sites would be more unfriendly to health than that watery hollow, and that the moment had come for erecting a first-class monastery[1] on some more salubrious spot. But Herlwin dreaded the excitement which would attend so vast a work; he was no longer young, and wished to end his days tranquilly. Lanfranc, on the other hand, plied him with encouragements, with entreaties, with importunities, and always, as a last resource, with remon-

[1] A *majus monasterium*.

strances; the present site was not fit for the habitation of monks, a site so moist that every foot, at least every human foot—for the devil had once appeared in the guise of a secular clergyman and left no print behind him—made a mark in the spongy soil. But the Norman had the gift of obstinacy if the Lombard had that of pertinacity, and refused to be persuaded, growing callous even to the incessant and unanswerable plea that such a swampy site was not fit for the habitation of monks. And obstinacy would have conquered but for an unanticipated interposition in favour of the Prior. 'The Lord Abbot,' he once said, 'is wasting time and energy on this watery site, and refuses to believe me when I tell him he should desist from his works here and begin others in a healthier place. May Almighty God put such an impediment in his way as may make him listen to me and desist from wasting his efforts on such an unsuitable site.' The idea was worthy of the man, very devout and very much to the purpose; and in due time it was realised, for in or about the year 1057 a sad accident befell the church in the collapse of a chamber on the south side of the sanctuary, which served the double purpose of oratory and of chapel to St. Benedict. Evidently the foundations were in a very perilous condition.

'The abbot, in his grief and great agitation at this mishap, found his own best comforter in Lanfranc, who approached him and begged him now at least to acquiesce and consent to begin building on a larger scale. Overcome at last, and placing an unshaken trust in God, and setting an unbounded confidence in his counsellor, by whose aid all his undertakings proved successful, he began new works on a spot at once much more healthy and much more suitable—a monastery church, with the other necessary buildings; a great architectural pile built up in course of time, not so much of the revenues of the house, which were still very inconsiderable, but of a firm faith and an unswerving trust in God.'

It was in the spring, then, of 1058 that Herlwin and

Lanfranc and their three score monks set forth with cross, with censer, with holy water, and with book to the newly chosen site of their future home. That spot was a mile higher up the valley, and on the same side—that is to say, on the right bank—of the rivulet, whose waters in that part of their course danced merrily down from south to north under the protecting shade of forest trees. A clearing had been made in the wood, part of it on the very declivity of the hill-side itself; for damp must be shunned, and, besides, Lanfranc had brought with him from Italy, and particularly from his own Pavia, majestic ideas of ecclesiastical art, and he meant to avail himself of this rise in the ground to give a dignified elevation to the sanctuary, and behind that to the high altar. With cross and censer, with holy water and book, they come singing through the glade; they enter the open space; they range themselves in two lines, on this side and on that of the trench, into which Herlwin will presently place the first stone of his new church, and then Lanfranc the second. As we scan them one by one we recognise each in his turn, for we know their names. We know which is Walter, which is Hervey; here they are, close to the abbot. We know Baldric of Servaville; he is not far off. There, too, fourth from Herlwin, on his left, is Roger, who will some day be Abbot of Lessay, and who, twenty years hence, will close Herlwin's eyes. Fourth, again, from Roger's *vis-à-vis* is a young man of some three-and-twenty years, with an earnest, intellectual face; no common person. Ever since he was ten years old Lanfranc has been teaching him; he is just now his favourite pupil, and some fifty years hence, when the abbot and the prior shall have passed away, will have something to say about both the one and the other of them which no one now suspects. At like distance, again, from Dom William, stands Dom Norman, another of the younger generation; he too is training under Lanfranc for high place, and will one day be Abbot of Ivry. Almost opposite him is Fulcran, who for thirteen years has marvelled at Lanfranc's wonderful recovery from a severe indisposition and sudden abstention from the thistle-roots which were curing him. Let us hope that Fulcran's garden has fewer specimens of that esculent now than then. Yes, indeed, we know, or can easily determine, the name of each of these sixty men as we look down the lines, and we know more than the names of not a few of them. There we recognise Albert and Farman, the courageous defenders of the rights of their house at a future time; there, again, is Durand, another Abbot of Ivry, and Walter, who shall govern Evesham, in foggy England across the sea; and here, amongst the singing boys, is Gilbert Crispin, a sweet lad of thirteen. Little dreams Gilbert of an abbey he shall one day govern hard by the Thames; little dreams he that through slowly rolling centuries his tomb shall be pointed out in the cloister of Westminster.

But the first stone is laid, and the second; and the pageant passes out of sight with cross, with censer, with holy water, and with book. One of the most momentous of human undertakings was now fairly begun; thanks for this in a great measure to Gilbert Crispin's father, who, in devoting him to the service of religion, had with him given the abbey no insignificant endowment in land, and who was to keep up a lively interest in its welfare during the remaining years of his life; thanks, too, and in still greater degree, to Lanfranc, who was not long in gaining permission from Herlwin to reopen his *exterior schola*. The fees would help to pay the workmen, who, no doubt, were countrymen of his own.

But Lanfranc had not been many weeks engaged in his lecture room when his labours were discouraged, and possibly suspended, by the arrival of very depressing news. The Pope had laid Normandy under interdict for the offence committed by William and Matilda now nearly five years ago. The next news to be feared was that the offenders had been excommunicated.

CHAPTER II.

ST. ANSELM'S RELIGIOUS VOCATION.

THERE is a passage in Robert of Torigni which seems to imply that Lanfranc had not long been lecturing at Le Bec,[1] when Anselm, still a mere boy, set his heart upon the journey which, as we have seen, was only to be undertaken ten years later; in the early spring, that is to say, of 1057.

But why undertake it when he did, if Lanfranc's school had been closed ever since the autumn of 1053? An answer to the question is supplied by William of Malmesbury, who informs us that when Anselm, after traversing the Alps, was anxiously debating with himself whither to go, the Divine compassion soothed his distress by directing him to Lanfranc.[2] Precisely so; the great Lombard was not keeping school when Anselm gained the foot of Mont Cenis, but the fugitive was at that critical moment inspired to direct his course towards Normandy, so as to receive early news of the resumption of lectures, which he now felt sure had not been discontinued for ever.

He therefore made for Lyons. Lyons was still famous for her school of philosophy, and there was not a city on this

---

[1] 'Sanctus Anselmus . . . disertorum studiis magistrorum in brevi Deo donante coæqualus, et per divinam visionem ad sedes cœlicas denique in spiritu raptus, salutis suæ arcana verba confestim audivit quæ non multo post tempore devote complevit audiens igitur famam magistri Lanfranci.'—Rob. Tor. *Chron.* s. a. 1060.

[2] 'Evasis Alpibus cum volutaret anxius animi quo tenderet divina dignatio fluctuantem serenavit Northmanniam ad Lanfrancum eundem cum quo si moraretur et patriæ necessitudine et litterarum fomite incolatum levigaret.'—W. M. *De. Gest. Pont.* lib. i.

side of the Alps in which secular teachers and lecturers could be found at once more efficient and more numerous.[1] But it is not likely that he lingered there, for an aspirant to the cowl of St. Benedict would be indisposed to frequent a school taught by any but monks, and, besides, his most trustworthy information about Lanfranc's movements was to be had in monasteries. His first resting-place, therefore, must have been Cluny, which lay at no great distance from Macon. Cluny was the pride of Burgundy, and ranked as queen among the numberless houses of religion that for a century past had sprung up, as if by enchantment, between the Alps and the Contentin. Founded in 910 by William the Good, Duke of Aquitaine, it had been enlarged and partially rebuilt by St. Odo, its fifth abbot, the *archangelus monachorum*, and was destined, under his successor, St. Hugh, who now ruled it, to assume proportions and a grandeur as yet without precedent in the annals of Christian architecture. The austerity of the life led by its inmates, who in winter allowed themselves but one meagre meal in the course of the day and remained in the church by night from twelve o'clock till sunrise, was only equalled by the rigour with which they observed their rule; and yet that rigour and that austerity drew to Cluny such crowds that, when Anselm went there, it was well-nigh impossible to conduct the processions[2] in seemly order, or even

---

[1] St. Mayeul's biographer tells us that '*non timuit accedere Lugdunensem ad aram.*' This allusion to the well-known lines of Juvenal—

'Palleat ut nudis pressit qui calcibus anguem,
Aut Lugdunensem rhetor dicturus ad aram'—

must not be too strictly interpreted, it is true; but, as the writer goes on to call Lyons the 'nutrix et mater philosophiæ,' and declares that there the 'arx totius Galliæ' was to be found, and as there is no doubt that in the thirteenth century it boasted a famous school of law, we may reasonably, I think, believe that during the interval it retained its reputation as a secular seat of learning.

[2] Cluny was famed for its processions. As Bethlehem was famous as the birthplace of our Lord, Jerusalem consecrated by the Holy Sepulchre and for ever illustrious as the resting-place of so many martyrs, so Cluny was described by the founder of Fontevral as the 'supremum monasterium' in which 'pulchræ fiunt processiones.'—*Vita B. Roberti de Abrissello.*

to find standing room in the choir. Wise men and simple, nobles and commoners besieged the gates of Cluny, yearning to share the penances and the joys of its tranquil inhabitants; and in their train were children eager to call the young abbot their father—Hugh was at this time little more than thirty years old—and bind themselves to him by the tenderest, the purest, and the most enduring of bonds.

But Anselm might not be numbered among its inmates, for he must soon have discovered that such health as his could never endure the severities of its terrible discipline, and that, even though its cloister were composed of sub-Alpine marble,[1] and the high altar of its church were covered with a baldachin of silver, no æsthetic charms could avail to disenchant a feebleness which it was his fate to carry with him to the grave. But he bore the mortification and hoped on. Perhaps, however, he attended a course of lectures in the *schola clericalis* of Cluny; although it is more likely that whatever lengthened stay he made in Burgundy was made not there, but at Dijon; for the monks of St. Benignus, in that city, seem to have been the intellectual leaders of the duchy, and never failed to welcome, with a special affection, visitors from beyond the Alps. Some of the most illustrious members of the community had been Italians, who, attracted by the piety of St. William, its second founder, had come from all parts of their peninsula to practise religion under his austere guidance; had come from Rome, from Capua, from Genoa, from Milan, from Ravenna—amongst the latter St. Romuald, the founder of the Camaldulensians—and had brought with them not a little of the acumen and the taste of their countrymen. And although Anselm was scarcely an Italian, he was in all probability a kinsman of St. William's, and had plenty

[1] St. Odilo found the cloister of wood, and replaced it by one of more precious material, conveyed in barges from some spot in the north-east corner of Provence, down the Durance, and thence up the Rhone as far as Macon; probably the green marble of Guillestre, perhaps the pink found in the same neighbourhood. A prodigious undertaking.

to say about St. William's ancestral city, Ivrea. The monks, therefore, of St. Benignus were more than willing to set at his disposal all that they had to offer him of oral teaching, of written documents, and even of instruction in the fine arts. For if letters flourished at Dijon, so did architecture; and St. William's church, or rather system of churches,[1] with their pillars and columns nearly four hundred in number, and their hundred and twenty windows fashioned in a style hitherto unknown in Gaul, had not long since marked the opening of a new era with the architects of northern Christendom.

But neither might he remain at Dijon. He might not remain there as a monk, for, severe as was the life at Cluny, St. William had introduced something, if possible, severer still in all houses of his creation or of his reform;[2] nor might he remain there as a student, for Le Bec was his lodestar.

The simplest interpretation of Eadmer's too brief account of this period of Anselm's life is that the traveller spent a little more than a year, from the beginning of 1057,[3] in Burgundy, and then resumed his long journey towards Normandy. This interpretation tallies admirably with the fact that Lanfranc reopened school soon after the ceremony in which he and Herlwin laid the first stones of their new church in the spring of 1058. And, if it be not hypercritical to interpret Eadmer's phrase, as meaning that Anselm's journey was not so much one journey as two, the second sudden in its beginning as the first had been sudden in its ending, the interpre-

---

[1] An elaborate description of these is to be found in the *Chronichon S. Benigni Divionensis*. Some remains of the lowest church have recently been brought to light.

[2] His strictness earned him the *surnom* of 'supra regulam.'

[3] We must not misinterpret Eadmer's words, 'Exactis dehinc . . . ferme tribus annis,' and T. Walsingham's 'In Galliâ liberalibus disciplinis studuit per triennium.' Both one and the other mean two years and a fraction. Thus St. Anselm himself, writing in the autumn or early winter of 1099, early, that is to say, in the thirteenth year of William Rufus, as having reigned 'jam per tredecim annos' (*Ep.* iii. 40); and in his second exile he describes the church confided to him as 'jam fere per tres annos desolata' (*Ep.* iii. 175), when the real time was about two years and a half.

tation is justified by the obvious reflection that he can scarcely have reached the borders of Normandy before the terrible news of the interdict arrested him like a 'shadow of eclipse,' and Normandy was, for the present, forbidden ground.[1]

He remained, therefore, till clearer skies should shine in France—the France, that is to say, of his age, the limited territory of Francia Latina, at the centre of which lay Paris, with Orleans near its southern frontier towards Aquitaine; for Le Bec was still his lodestar, and, having come so far, he could not well go back. Nor was France without attractions; it had its St. Germain des Prés at Paris, and above all Fleury, which boasted the relics of St. Benedict and was a devotional centre of attraction to all Gaul, besides being famous as a school of learning.

But, however, the summer of 1058 lapsed into autumn; and, whilst winter held his icy reign, Anselm had already entered on his third year of exile. At last Easter came; hope revived with the blooming spring; and, before many weeks had passed, the Prior of Le Bec was on his way back from Rome, with a conciliatory message for Duke William. Anselm was soon on the move, and Orderic describes him as travelling in the wake of the Lombard, because wherever Lanfranc might teach—and his heart told him that teach again he soon must in the swampy hollow near the Risle—there to him was his land of promise.[2]

But Anselm reached his Canaan too soon, either because the prior was detained at the Duke's court, or because there was a customary vacation between Midsummer and Michaelmas. He therefore retired to Avranches, where he passed

---

[1] This is, of course, conjectural; for the precise date of the interdict is not known. For my own part, however, I have little doubt that the interdict was published by Stephen IX. in the Lent of 1058, and a few weeks before his death; after which event the pontifical throne remained vacant for nine months. Nicholas II. assumed the tiara in the December of 1058.

[2] 'Lanfrancum secutus Beccum expetiit, et instar Israelitarum auro divitiisque Ægyptiorum, id est sæculari eruditione philosophorum onustus terram repromissionis desideranter adiit.'— *O. V.* ii. 256.

an interval of eager expectancy, and on the very day that term opened at Le Bec was waiting betimes at the door of Lanfranc's lecture room.

He was not alone, however, for undoubtedly his clerk was at his side; and, besides his clerk, there were several other of like rank, who had either accompanied or followed him from Aosta.[1] Alas that their names are not precisely known; but, if a guess may be hazarded, there is, perhaps, a Rudolph, perhaps a Frodimund, perhaps an Ansfred, perhaps a Maurice among them.

His heart beat high as he stood outside that lowly shed of rude timber, flint, mud, and thatch. And, if it be true that, after hopes alternately thwarted and deferred during many years, his enrolment amongst Lanfranc's disciples was an event of utmost interest to himself, it is impossible for us to forget that issues of enduring import in the moral and intellectual destinies of mankind were to follow from the relation now established between the illustrious teacher and his illustrious disciple. The disciple was to succeed the teacher first as Prior of Le Bec, then as Archbishop of Canterbury; and the friendship of the two men during nearly thirty years, the part which each of them played in the same stirring events, their intimacy with the same great personages, have placed them side by side on the page of history. But though we regard them as contemporaries, we must not forget that at their first meeting the younger man had barely completed his twenty-sixth year, whilst the older was already in his sixty-third. Nor did they present a less remarkable difference in respect of character and of endowment. Lanfranc was the greatest teacher of the eleventh century; Anselm was to be distinguished as its profoundest thinker. Lanfranc's intellectual mission had been to rectify, arrange, and illustrate the learning which his age inherited from the past; Anselm's vocation was to lay open new tracts of thought, and hold on high a torch for the guid-

[1] 'Cum aliquantis familiarium clericis.'—*Robert of Torigni.*

ance and illumination of the great thinkers of modern time no less than for the frequenters of the mediæval schools. The one was famous for breadth and accuracy of learning, the other for the subtilty and elevation of his speculative intellect. And if Lanfranc had already challenged the confidence of mankind by his prudence as a counsellor, his knowledge as a jurist, his consummate generalship in times of disturbance and conflict, Anselm would soon win their reverence by the clearness of his moral vision, by his exalted ideal of right, by his transparent simplicity of purpose. Lanfranc had more than once shown himself great upon slight emergencies; it was impossible that upon great ones Anselm should be other than heroic. Lanfranc conciliated the general respect by his genial temper, his brilliant repartee, his adroitness of management, his versatility, his knowledge of the world; Anselm, by an exquisite delicacy of feeling, a profound humility, and an inexhaustible charity, would, in due time, challenge the love of thousands even though his inflexible adherence to duty should provoke the hatred of a few. The piety and prudence of the one ensured him a welcome and a hearing in the cabinet of princes; the wisdom and the holiness of the other were to be his avant-couriers to their sick chamber and their death-bed.

The Prior of Le Bec had long taken scrupulous care to confine his studies to Holy Scripture and the Fathers of the Church, and to use the former as his principal text-book. Whatever he had known in earlier days of pagan literature had for some twenty years been made to hold an ancillary and subordinate place, as compared with those graver and critical employments with which history has associated his name.[1] And his new pupil seems to have followed his

[1] This statement of the biographer's is confirmed by a letter from Lanfranc himself. 'You have sent me some questions on subjects appertaining to secular learning. It ill becomes a bishop to spend time on such pursuits. Long ago, and in my earlier days, I took no little interest in them, but upon my promotion to the pastoral care resolved to have nothing more to do with them' (*Ep.* 33). The priorate was a *pastoralis cura*, and on his accession to it his *juvenilis ætas* had passed away.

example at an early date ; he certainly very soon began to emulate his industry in the correction of corrupted texts of the Old and New Testaments, and of other sacred books. Already his rival in secular learning, he was not slow in obtaining an almost equal renown for critical acumen and for habits of most intense industry. And the more brightly the flame burnt in the ardent mind of the enthusiastic student, the more eagerly did his master and guide add fuel to it, giving him as many lessons as he chose to take,[1] and thus making his nights as laborious as his days; whilst to these in their turn more than a fair portion of toil was assigned, for he acted as assistant lecturer, and was at all times ready to aid the studies of his less gifted companions.

Change of scene, movement from place to place, congenial occupation, had been of so much benefit to Anselm for the last two or three years that he could now attempt what would have been beyond the compass of his physical capacity at the time of his mother's death; and a better physician, perhaps, than any of these things was the consolatory news lately received from home, which informed him that his father had died well, and in the monastic habit. Gundulf passed away on September 29, 1059; and the fact that Gundulf had thus died was an assurance to Anselm that now, at last, his was a united family.[2]

But pleasantly prosecuted intellectual employments beguiled him into a severity of living which he had little contemplated on his arrival at Le Bec; and it soon occurred to him that, were he ever to be a monk, the cruelty of the cold which it was now his lot to bear could hardly be surpassed by the severest temperature ever likely to befal him ; and that his diet need not necessarily be more scanty, or his

---

[1] 'Non solum quæ volebat à Lanfranco legendo.' '*A Lanfranco legere*' does not mean 'to read books lent by Lanfranc,' but 'to attend Lanfranc's lectures,' or 'to read with Lanfranc.'

[2] The obituary of Beaumont-le-Roger contains this entry : 'iii., Kal. Octob. Gondulfus pater Anselmi archiepiscopi.'

nightly vigils more wearisome, within the precincts of a convent than they now were in the world.

'As soon as this idea occurred to him he began to fix the bent of his being upon pleasing God, spurned the world with all its allurements, and desired to be in very deed a monk.'

'What means the habit of a monk?' asks St. Gregory the Great; 'what does it mean but contempt of the world?'[1] Here let us pause for a moment to note a peculiarity in Eadmer's narrative at this stage of the history. He breaks the thread of the biography in order to set on record the considerations which engaged Anselm's mind so soon as he had formed his resolution. But that is not all; his account of those considerations is given in the very words of the saint himself as he used to tell the story in his old age, and is accompanied with a description of the saint's manner in the telling of it. Nothing could be more graphic.

We must, therefore, violate the dramatic unities, and bidding our laggard imagination fly from Le Bec to Canterbury, shift our date from 1060 to 1108 or thereabouts. The scene is a room in the monastery of Christ Church, and the principal *dramatis persona* not a secular clergyman of twenty-six, but a Benedictine monk who has already entered on the eighth decade of his life—a monk, yet more than a monk; for he wears on his white, slender hand a ring which distinguishes him from his surrounding religious. He is seated in his chair; and, together with a countenance of inborn nobility and sweetness, every line of which indicates a rare susceptibility of feeling, he has an eye lightened with a fire that always glows, but seldom, if ever, flashes, and hair that lies snowy white in tonsured ring over brows deeply marked by thought and the buffetings of an adverse fortune. It is Archbishop Anselm, now near his end, and he is speaking:—

'I said to myself, "Now I am going to be a monk; but

[1] 'Quid est autem habitus monachi nisi despectus mundi?'

where? If at Cluny, or if at Le Bec, the time I have spent in study will have been lost. The life at Cluny is so severe that I shall soon make a sorry figure of myself, for I have not the strength to endure it; and as to Le Bec, Lanfranc's is too towering a genius for me there to be of use to anyone. I shall, therefore, best carry out my purpose in a place[1] where I may display my knowledge and be of service to many others."'

So does the old man speak, or rather not so much tell his story as soliloquise his old soliloquy over again and turn his youth's heart inside out, little dreaming that anyone present cares to treasure its contents and describe them. So does he speak with a sort of playful smile at his own expense, and then relapse into a reverie, half muttering, 'No, I was not yet broken in; my contempt for the world was only in the bud, and that accounts for my not seeing the danger. I thought all this came from charity to others.' Then, resuming the old strain, he continues, 'But what am I saying? A monk! To be a monk; what! is it to wish to be set before others, honoured more than others, made much of at their expense? No! no! Down, then, with your pride and thought of self, and turn monk in a place where, as is just, you will be set last of all for the sake of God, and accounted least and unworthiest of all, and in comparison of all the rest not cared a straw for! And where can this be done? Why, at Le Bec, if anywhere. At Le Bec I shall be of no importance; for at Le Bec is a man who shines with the light of a transcendant wisdom which is enough for all of them. He will do for them all; they will all honour him and make much of him. At Le Bec, then, shall my rest be. At Le Bec shall God, and God alone, be the beacon of my life; at Le Bec the love of God, and that alone, shall be my study; at Le Bec the thought of God, the

[1] I suspect he had his mind on Fleury, or Saint Benoît-sur-Loire, as it is now called.

blissful and undying thought, shall be my solace and my satisfaction.'

If Eadmer wrote this with dry eyes, he was less of a monk, less of a man, than posterity has been fain to think; and a biographer who has studied his subject may disdain to reply to the impious and utterly unjustifiable travesties that have been made of it.[1] 'Such,' continues the historian, 'were his musings, his longings, and his dearest hopes;' such, too, his victory over the temptation of a moment most precious to the enemy of souls. If the moment was critical, the victory was complete.

There are two short words in this wonderful soliloquy, so touchingly made vocal after an interval of half a century, which invite a moment's attention; I mean the words *scire meum* in the phrase 'in tali loco in quo scire meum possim ostendere et multis prodesse.' These very words occur in a letter written by Anselm soon after his profession in answer to one which must have been despatched to him while he was yet in the secular state; or, at any rate, about that time; for his correspondent addresses him as a secular person. This correspondent, Avesgot by name, was an inmate of the monastery of La Couture at Le Mans, and seems to have been a scion of the house of Bellesme. Be this as it may, Anselm had not been long at Le Bec when Avesgot, hearing that he was Lanfranc's assistant lecturer, perhaps that he had a sort of dame's house close to the monastery, wrote, begging him to undertake the classical tuition of a nephew in whom he was interested, saying amongst other things, 'I can send him to other masters, but I have greater confidence in you than in any other man living, and should feel no anxiety about him if he were only in the same place with you;' and

---

[1] Thus M. Charma could bring himself to write words like these: 'Ce n'est pas la religion qui, dans son cœur, a triomphé du siècle; c'est une passion qui a vaincu une autre;' and again, 'alliant par un impur mélange à son amour des saintes pratiques l'orgueilleux désir de s'élever au-dessus de ses frères.' And there are others beside M. Charma quite as bad.

then adds, 'How is it that Lanfranc and Guitmund make more noise in the world than you? Why will you persist in hiding your light under a bushel? Do you not remember what the poet says—

> Your skill is nought if others skill not that you skill
> (Scire tuum nihil est, nisi te scire hoc sciat alter)?

It would almost seem, then, as if Persius's *scire tuum*, thus recalled to Anselm's memory, had suggested the *scire meum* of his soliloquy; it certainly finds a pretty place in his reply to Avesgot. 'I am very sorry,' he writes, 'that on the first request you make me I am unable to give proof of my desire to serve you. The truth is that I am not now free to undertake the charge, nor do I contemplate or see any likelihood of a return to my former employment, or what your charity is good enough to regard as having been my employment.[1] ... And now for the quotation in your letter:—

> Scire tuum nihil est nisi te scire hoc sciat alter.

'Persius wrote this to fan the love of self-display, not to smother it; still I make bold to answer—

> Scire meum nihil est, si quale sit hoc sciat alter
> (My skill is nought if others skill what I do skill).

'You ask why Lanfranc's renown and Guitmund's are wider spread than mine. The reason is, that not every flower has the scent of the rose, cheat the eye though it may with a blush like the rose.'

This was not the real reason. The superscription of his letter tells us why it was that his fame was not flying through

---

[1] The compilers of the *Histoire littéraire de la France* have entirely missed the meaning of Anselm's reply. Their remarks on it will not bear analysis, and I need only observe that Avesgot's nephew was between twenty and thirty years of age; that the request was a personal one to Anselm himself, not to Herlwin or Lanfranc; and that what was wanted was that he should be always under Anselm's eye. 'Habeo quendam meum nepotem *jam juvenem* . . . desidero eum *manere tecum* . . . valde securus fierem *si moraretur in loco in quo es.*' The letter is to be found in Baluze's *Miscellanea*, lib. ii. p. 174.

the world on the wings of every wind. He was no longer
'Anselmus,' but 'frater Anselmus;'[1] no longer his own,
but another's; and as for making a name, so far from
asking leave to lecture any longer in Lanfranc's *schola
clericalis*, so far from having even the intention of doing so,
he had purposely chosen a cloister whose *schola clericalis* was
under so illustrious an administration that there would be no
occasion that his services should be evoked in its behalf, a
cloister in which God alone should be the occupation of his
thoughts and the employment of his time.

No, no; the reason he assigned was not the true one.
The learning, if we may employ his own floral metaphor,
slowly accumulated by intense and enthusiastic study from
very boyhood, was dear to Anselm as is the first expanded
bud of some rare rose-tree to the gardener who has directed
all its capacity of loveliness and fragrance to the production
of one choice flower; but, mindful of Him *qui semetipsum
exinanivit*, he had culled the flower and laid it at the foot of
the Crucified.

After he had chosen, and for these reasons, the monastery
of Le Bec as preferable to all others, the very question
occurred to him which had once occurred to Lanfranc,
whether, after all, the cenobitical life was for him the best.
He had heard of those vast silentious tracts on the confines
of Maine and Brittany where anchorites were practising
austerities that surpassed the ancient wonders of Upper
Egypt; scantily clad in sheep-skins, and sheltered—if
sheltered be the word—by rickety pent-roofs of osier which
the next storm might rend and dissipate in irrecoverable
fragments.[2] He had heard, too, of such charitable founda-

---

[1] The superscription of Avesgot's letter is, 'Avesgotus cœnobii Sancti Petri Culturæ monachus Anselmo, salutem.' The superscription of Anselm's answer is, 'Domino et amico charissimo Avesgoto frater Anselmus, salutem.' It is the earliest of Anselm's extant letters.

[2] 'Erant autem in confinio Cenomauniæ Britanniæque regiones vastæ solitudinis, quæ tum temporis quasi altera Ægyptus florebat multitudine eremitarum per diversas cellulas habitantium,' &c.—*Vita B. Bernardi Turonensis*, cap. xl.

tions as that of St. Bernard of Menthon, who, chasing their false gods from the Alps, not far from his own Aosta, had there established a refuge from the glaciers; and although he could scarcely emulate such rigours as those—for his frame was too fragile to tempt the storms and inclemency whether of open plain or desolate mountain—there yet were tempered spots easy to find where he might live all alone, with even less risk to health than he would encounter at Le Bec; and he might found a hospice in an Alpine valley as meritoriously as on an Alpine pass. His determination, indeed, was on the whole to the life of the cloister; but still he questioned with himself whether he might not do better by living either in a hermitage or in some such institution as a hospice founded out of his own inherited estates.

'Knowing, therefore, that it is written, "Do thou nothing without counsel, and thou shalt not repent when thou hast done" ("Omnia fac cum consilio, et post factum non pœnitebis"), he was unwilling to commit himself without due advice to any one of the modes of life on which he pondered, lest in anything he should seem to disobey the precepts of Holy Scripture. He had many friends, indeed, but out of them all he chose as counsellor to whom unreservedly to commit himself one, and only one. That one in a thousand was Lanfranc'— the Lanfranc, be it noted, who has been depicted as a sort of freezing mixture, such as might be compounded out of college don and home secretary. 'Going to Lanfranc, he told him that his purpose hung undecided between three alternatives, and that he wished to take his advice and choose that of the three which he should pronounce the best. "I want to be a monk. I desire to be a hermit. I am strongly inclined to live on my patrimony, and, for the love of God, minister of it as best I can to some few needy people.[1] My will, Dom Lanfranc, is tossed to and fro between these three

[1] The author of the *Histoire de l'Eglise Gallicane*, in addition to several grave mistakes about Anselm's early life, has made a curious blunder on this

subjects of choice. I beg you to determine me to that one of the three which is best."' Lanfranc declined to give an opinion, but advised him to refer the case to the decision of Maurille, the venerable Archbishop of Rouen, their diocesan. Anselm, long ago a monk at heart, yielded to the advice, and, accompanied by his counsellor, set forth to present himself before the prelate. But he did not therefore relinquish his confidence in Lanfranc, for had the Prior, whilst they were traversing the wooded heights that overhang the valley of Le Bec, said to him, 'Remain here in this forest, and take care as long as you live never to leave it,' undoubtedly, as he used to say, he would have obeyed him and turned anchorite then and there. Can more be said for Lanfranc than such a confidence?

Maurille, Archbishop of Rouen since 1055, had been removed to that see from the princely foundation of Fécamp, where he had said many a prayer at the tomb of St. William, the reformer of monastic discipline and patron of religious architecture. He rendered his twelve years' pontificate illustrious by the completion of his cathedral, parts of which are still extant.

The Prior of Le Bec and his pupil laid their case before the Archbishop, who promptly declared in favour of the ordinary monastic life. His word was law, and his visitors were ready to return to Le Bec on the morrow.

In those days the Seine at Rouen, taking its tortuous

---

third alternative: 'Mais il délibérat entre trois états, sçavoir, *s'il demeurerait dans le monde* .... ou bien s'il se ferait moine ou hermite' (livre xx.). The learned Jesuit must surely have known that a man may live in a convent, in a hermitage, or in a hospice, but that nobody can be out of the world and at the same time in it. Nevertheless Longueval's mistake has been most industriously perpetuated by subsequent writers. Surely in cases like these, if intuition does not suggest a probable solution of a difficulty, we should have recourse to reflection. But, curiously enough, Longueval and his followers had no need to trust to the one or resort to the other. John of Salisbury says, 'An enim expeteret eremum, an claustrum monachorum, an ex proprio patrimonio domum construens peregrinis, pro facultate, et pauperibus ministraret, habebat incertum.'—*Vita Sti. Anselmi*, cap. ii.

course further to the north than now, washed the very precinct of the metropolitan church; and it requires but little effort of imagination to see the Prior of Le Bec and his pupil putting off in a ferry [1] on the morrow of their interview with the Archbishop from close under the sacred pile, and slowly making for the southern bank of the river. That ferry carried no ordinary freight—Lanfranc and Anselm, each bound to the other by the ties of a new and supernatural sympathy; Lanfranc and Anselm, monks both of them, in heart at least, for the difference of garb will not last long; and in a few short hours Anselm will have exchanged the white dress of the secular clergyman for a coarser habit. It is a morning in spring, and three winters have passed since he crossed Mont Cenis. The passage of Mont Cenis then, and that of the Seine now, what a contrast! That was a deliverance, undoubtedly, from thraldom, from suffering, from the shadow of death; but it was a perilous journey over solitudes of snow, and, to one sick at heart and jaded in body, a venture into blank uncertainty; but this is a peaceful transit from suspense and deferred hopes to security and a terrestrial heaven. And peaceful influences fill his pure heart with an ineffable happiness. No sound breaks the pervading calm save the confused and harmonious din of hammer, chisel, and crane, plied by the builders of Maurille's cathedral. He turns and gazes on its massive but unfinished tower. Clear and hard it strikes against the pearly sky, and stretches in vain pursuit its tremulous reflection across the flood. A peaceful reverie to Anselm. Lanfranc gazes on him with brimming eyes and an interest too deep for words. Nor he alone; others are watching. Ermenberg stoops from her blissful throne, and Gundulf, who once in weakness and rage drove him from his old home, now pursues him with blessings to his new.

---

[1] I frankly own that on revising these pages for the press I cannot find an authority for the suggestion that there was no bridge across the Seine at Rouen in the spring of 1060. I have no proof either way. So, *quod scripsi scripsi.*

CHAPTER III.

THE BEGINNING OF THE NEW LIFE.

ON reaching the southern bank of the Seine, the travellers plunged into the forest, and followed a track just wide enough to allow one horseman at a time to thread his cautious way over a russet carpet of dead leaves; a long and tortuous lane, where sweet and reposeful gloom reigned by day, and by night awful darkness.

The ceremony of Anselm's introduction to the novitiate was not long delayed, and was very simple. Led into the chapter-house by the guest-master, the white-robed postulant threw himself upon the floor before Herlwin, who demanded of him what he wanted. 'I beg,' he said, 'the mercy of God, association with you, and membership in this family of brethren; and I desire to become a monk and serve God in this monastery' ('Dei misericordiam et vestram societatem et fraternitatem hujus loci requiro, in hoc monasterio monachus fieri et Deo servire desidero'). The abbot replied, 'Almighty God grant you association and a lot with His elect;' to which all present responded, 'Amen.' This, of course, was no answer to Anselm's petition; it was a prayer dictated by piety and prudence, and served as an encouragement to him to listen not altogether in despair to an account of the hardships and austerities embraced by all true monks, and of the still heavier severities held in store against those who might violate the rule of the order. But Herlwin was too well acquainted with the antecedents, the character, and the temperament of his postulant to say more than a few necessary words on those topics. Anselm replied in fewer still, and promised to endure all that might await him. Upon which the abbot replied, 'May our Lord Jesus Christ so perform in you what for love of Him you promise, that you may have His grace here and eternal life hereafter' ('Dominus Jesus Christus sic perficiat in vobis quod pro amore ejus promittitis ut ejus gratiam et vitam æternam habere possitis'). The monks again said 'Amen,' and the abbot continued, 'And we for love of Him hereby grant you what you so humbly and steadfastly ask' ('Et nos pro ejus amore hoc tenore concedimus vobis quod tam humiliter et tam constanter requiritis'); but the words had scarcely escaped him when Anselm was lying at his feet,[1] and imprinting on them kisses, such as were offered by subjects to their spiritual or territorial superiors. When he had kissed Herlwin's feet he was permitted to retire to the church, where he remained alone until the chapter broke up and brethren appointed for the purpose of clothing him in the dress of the order entered and cut short his meditations. They exchanged the clerical for the monastic habit, the *vestis nuptialis*, as it was prettily called, for the cheaper tunic of undyed and unbleached wool proper to Herlwin's monastery. To this was stitched the *capitium*, or hood; for the large and ample garment to which the hood properly belonged was withheld from novices, inasmuch as, although its assumption was proverbially incapable of conferring the

[1] We stiff-kneed English, who fail to appreciate this sort of thing, should remember that the age in which Anselm lived was nearer to the days of Constantine than ours is to it, and that prostration was one of the numerous Oriental usages of the later Empire which were still generally observed in every corner of Western Christendom where the Latin civilisation had been established. It was not peculiar to Churchmen. A certain Count Aginulf once persecuted a poor knight with such inexorable ferocity that his victim scarcely dared to show himself out of doors, and would have persisted to the bitter end had he not the very night after rejecting a most touching appeal for mercy seen the devil blowing the fire and warming himself at leisure in his very bedroom. Frightened out of his wits, he began to recite the psalter from beginning to end, and continued reciting until daybreak, when he hurried off to the other, and falling prostrate on the ground at his feet offered to be at peace with him.—*De Mirac. S. Emmerammi*, lib. ii.

monastic spirit, the *cuculla* was the peculiar note and badge of the monastic profession.

During his novitiate Anselm, like other novices, was not allowed to read the lessons, or to sing anything in choir alone, or to offer at the mass, or to receive the *pax*; and when he was in the cloister took his place apart from the professed monks, and under the eye of the master of novices, whose office it was by word and example to instruct him in holiness of life and the duties of the order.

But his transitional life was of no long duration. Short novitiates, even in cases less promising, or rather less mature, than Anselm's, seem to have been one of the distinguishing features of Le Bec in later years, when he was himself abbot; and there is hardly room to doubt that the ceremony just described was within a very few days [1] succeeded by the more solemn act of profession. Scarcely had a week elapsed, or at the utmost a month, when, between the breaking up of the chapter, which assembled immediately after prime, and the ringing of the bell for mass, Anselm was invited to write out his profession on a small strip of parchment; the hood was then detached from the tunic and taken away, to be fastened to its proper *cuculla*; and he awaited the further instructions of the novice-master.

The mass was sung by the abbot; and the usual order was observed until, at the conclusion of the Gospel, the choir gates unfolded, and Anselm entered, conducted by the novice-master. This was the signal for the beginning of the *Miserere* by the *dexter chorus*; whilst the novice, with downcast eye and composed mien, made for the steps of the altar, where he lay prostrate as verse by verse, now from this side of the church and now from that, that plaintive and incomparable cry rose to heaven. The psalm ended, he stood up and read

---

[1] Thus Lanfranc was professed *non post multos dies* from the beginning of his novitiate. Other instances will occur in the sequel.

from his slip of parchment, 'Ego, Anselmus, promitto stabilitatem monachi et conversionem morum meorum et obedientiam secundum regulam Sancti Benedicti coram Deo et Sanctis ejus in hoc monasterio quod est constructum in honorem Beatæ Mariæ semper virginis in præsentiâ Domini Herluini abbatis.' He then ascended the steps and laid the document upon the altar, there to be preserved. Returning to his place at the foot of the altar steps, he next called upon God, singing the simple and pathetic words of the psalmist, 'Suscipe me, Domine, secundum eloquium tuum et vivam, et non confundas me ab expectatione meâ;' whereupon, with that inexplicable sympathy of which our holy religion so well knows the secret, the words were taken up and repeated by the whole assembly, he kneeling the while, 'Suscipe me, Domine, secundum eloquium tuum et vivam, et non confundas me ab expectatione mea,' 'Uphold me, O Lord, according to Thy word, and I shall not be confounded in my expectation.' He then rose, and with growing fervour and in a higher key once more raised his soul's cry to Him who alone could bless, as He had inspired the surrender. Again were his words echoed through the lowly church. Nor was this enough. After the example, it may be, of Him who 'prayed again a third time,' he urged his petition once more, singing this time in a still higher key. Once more was it repeated by men, who know but too well that not the least part of the monastic ideal is fellowship, not less in each other's hopes and anxieties than in each other's joys and griefs. After a few short prayers, the *Paternoster* being said in silence, the abbot intoned the *De Profundis*, whilst Anselm could do little else than lie with his heart beating at the cold ground, in the speechless anguish of a bliss all new to him; a bliss and an anguish most fittingly embodied in that unique psalm which, if it express with equal felicity the yearning of humanity for its Redeemer and the trembling hope of the redeemed but unbeatified Christian,[1] is no less happy as the interpreter of such emotions as must needs possess the heart of one about to pass into such a life as it is the aim of monasticism to foster and develope. ' Out of the depths have I cried unto Thee, O Lord ; Lord, hear my voice. . . . My soul hath waited on His word ; my soul hath hoped in the Lord. . . .' Thus far the ceremonies of profession at Le Bec were precisely the same as those used at Cluny and other famous monasteries, nor was there any difference in the three prayers which followed the *De Profundis*. At the end, however, of these— perhaps by a happy inspiration of Lanfranc's, whose joyous nature could ill brook its absence on such an occasion—the use observed at Le Bec directed the abbot to intone the pentecostal hymn, *Veni, Creator Spiritus*.[2]

All caught and prolonged the strain with an unanimity and a fervour which those who have witnessed such solemn acts are not ashamed to own themselves unable to describe, and which as far transcend this meagre account as the sonorous majesty of the original puts to shame the following attempt[3] at translation :—

> Come, O Creator Spirit, come,
> Make in Thy servants' minds Thine home ;
> And fill our breasts with grace Divine,
> Thou didst create them, they are Thine.
>
> Lo ! Paraclete, we name Thy Name,
> Thou Gift of God the One Supreme,
> Thou living Fountain, Fire, and Love,
> And sacred Unction from above.

[1] The *De Profundis* forms part of the Christmas office as well as of the office for the dead.

[2] There is, I believe, no evidence to show that the *Veni, Creator Spiritus* was anywhere sung at ordinations before the close of the century, and I suspect that Le Bec was the very first monastery in which it was sung at professions. Can it be that Anselm's was the first profession in Christendom thus adorned ? Who shall say ?

[3] I trust the learned may not disdain my version. It is, I think, the closest which has as yet been made in our language.

Gifts sevenfold wait on Thy command,
Thou Finger of the Father's hand,
The Father's very Promise Thou,
Who dost our lips with speech endow.

Shed on each sense light's kindling beam ;
Pour on each heart love's quickening stream ;
Inform our corporal mould so frail
With virtue that shall never fail ;

Drive off, and keep afar, the foe ;
And peace—Thy peace—even now bestow :
So shall we, following Thee our Guide,
Turn from all harm our steps aside.

Through Thee the Father may we own ;
Grant us to know through Thee the Son
And Thee of Both the Spirit sole
Confess whilst all the ages roll.

Glory to God the Father be !
Glory, O God the Son, to Thee,
Ris'n from the dead ! Like praise Divine,
O Paraclete, be ever Thine ! Amen.

The melodious tumult expired, and a prayer was said. Anselm rose and was sprinkled with holy water, and the cowl being brought to the abbot, he blessed and aspersed it and then proceeded to perform the crowning act of the solemnity. Removing the novice's tunic, he said, 'May the Lord put off from thee the old man with his deeds ; ' and then, clothing him in the cowl, added, 'May the Lord put on thee the new man, who according to God is created in justice and holiness of truth.' Anselm was a monk at last ; at last, in the bold but suggestive phrase of his order, he had received his second baptism.[1] The abbot kissed him, and, drawing the hood

---

[1] This is a very usual name for the monastic profession. St. Odilo's biographer exclaims of him, 'Quàm jocundum erat tunc videre ovem mundano vellere detonsam de lavacro baptismatis iterum ascendentem ; ' and one of St. Anselm's disciples, in a letter addressed to him, speaks of the 'filiorum caterva quos in lavacro secundæ nativitatis ipsa (ecclesia) genuerat' (*Ep*. iii. 2).

over his head, dismissed him in his delirium of new-born joy to go the round of the choir and kiss in turn each of its members.[1] He then resumed the mass.[2]

And now that the young monk has entered upon his hidden life, the unavailing regret may once more be forgiven that Eadmer should not have completed those *anecdota*, the compilation of which was so peremptorily interrupted by his master; for some of them belonged to the first three years of Anselm's monastic life. All that he has allowed himself to tell us is that no sooner was Anselm admitted into the cloister than he set to work to study the lives of such among his new friends as observed the rule of the order the most strictly, and valued as contributions towards a model which he must copy all that he recognised in those lives as being most conformable to that rule. He had long since apprehended the ideal of religious life, but had not as yet had opportunities for studying an exemplar. Such exemplar as he wanted he was not long in securing, but it was an exemplar of his own constructing.

[1] An opportunity for impressing upon the mind of the newly made monk the idea, an idea as old at least as St. Jerome, that this solemn investiture with the *cuculla* symbolised a new death to the world, and introduced him to a life of higher aims than were ordinarily contemplated in the secular state, was afforded by the discipline which required that he should wear the cowl and keep his head covered with the hood for three days and nights. This was one of those *factitiæ consuetudines* of which St. Anselm speaks in his *Similitudes* as by no means essential to monasticism but 'quibusdam de causis rationabilibus' worthy of observance. The hood was removed by the abbot or a deputy at the *pax* of the third day's mass. We need not be surprised that in this continuous wearing of the hood for some days after profession a resemblance was noted to the carrying of the chrism cloth by a newly baptised infant; but that was, no doubt, an afterthought. If a strict analogy be sought, it may be found in the custom which required a newly made priest to wear the stole day and night uninterruptedly for a certain time after ordination. Witness the following passage from Nalgod's *Life of St. Odo*. 'Diem consecrationis ejus insecuta nox fuerat in quâ vir Domini post quietem evigilans et suæ consecrationis non memor stolam sacerdotalem collo suo reperit circumflexam.' A like account is given by another biographer, who inserts the words *sicuti mos est*.

[2] For the particulars noted in this description see and compare Udalric's *Consuetudines Cluniacenses*, Lanfranc's *Decreta*, and John of Avranches' *Liber de Ecclesiasticis Officiis*.

No character was ever formed—no man ever attained the excellence of *totus teres atque rotundus*—by servile imitation of another, or by the mimicry of a method here and a manner there. Anselm, with the true genius of a philosopher, and, be it added, with the true genius of a poet, made no such commonplace attempt, and thus escaped the inevitable issue of a commonplace failure.

> Æmilium circa ludum faber unus et ungues
> Exprimet, et molles imitabitur ære capillos,
> Infelix operis summâ, quia ponere totum
> Nesciet.

He imitated no one; he copied nothing. What he did was, first, by an instinct of unerring selection, one of the rarest of gifts, to choose out of the lives of the fifty men about him precisely the sort of details which were most conformable to the speculative ideal which he had constructed for himself by a careful study of the monastic rule; then, by the exercise of another and as rare a gift, to form out of all these diverse and incongruous excellencies a consistent and harmonious model; nor only that, a consistent and harmonious model suitable to his own capacity; and then, possessed thus of his speculative exemplar, laboriously to fashion his life into conformity with it. Aristotle would have worshipped him.

Thus did he form his character; nay, so accurately and minutely faithful was he to the religious ideal that 'whosoever in all that community desired to live a wholly religious life, found before long much in Anselm's way of living which it was worth his while to imitate. And Anselm, advancing day by day for the space of three years nearer and nearer to perfection, came to be deemed a hero of goodness whom it was meet that all should respect and honour.'

Alas that Eadmer should have told us no more than this! Alas, indeed! for if the little that we learn from another source concerning these three years helps to supply, as indeed it does, the blank which he has left, it also serves to enhance our regret that he should have left the blank at all.

A certain Dom Gundulf had been a denizen of Le Bec for some twelve months when Anselm made his profession there. Sprung from one of the best families in Normandy ten years before Anselm saw the light, Gundulf at an early age received preferment in the cathedral church of Rouen, where, by the purity of his life and by austerities worthy of a monastic cloister, he engaged the regard and won the friendship of Archdeacon William and of Maurille the metropolitan. It was in the interval of Anselm's detention in Burgundy and France that the canon and the archdeacon made a pilgrimage to the holy places and reached Jerusalem, 'accounting as nothing the fatigues of their journey, so entirely were their hearts inflamed with the love of the Jerusalem that is above.' But being overtaken by a terrible storm whilst crossing the Mediterranean on their return, they made a vow to enter religion in the unlikely event of their escape. Their prayer was heard, and Gundulf, upon reaching Normandy, lost no time in finding his way to Le Bec, where his name and that of Anselm stood[1] next each other on the 'boards;' and during the short three years which they there spent together, so intimate was their friendship, and so well contested the rivalry of their endeavours after holiness, that it is as difficult to separate the memory of Gundulf the monk from that of Anselm the monk as it is for the naked eye to divide the joint lustre of a double star.

When Lanfranc, in 1063, left Le Bec and assumed the government of St. Stephen's at Caen, Gundulf accompanied him as his prior, Anselm rising to the like dignity in his own convent; and when Gundulf was raised to the see of

---

[1] In my first draft of this chapter I wrote 'seem to have stood.' The *Nomina Monachorum Becci*, with which I have since made acquaintance, shows that my surmise was correct. They had neighbouring beds in the dormitory, and neighbouring places in the cloister.

Rochester, in 1077—for Dom Gundulf was none other than the famous bishop of that diocese—the pastoral staff of abbot was already passing into the hands of his best and dearest friend, who had not long before written to him in the following terms :—

'You beg me by your messages, you exhort me by your letters, and by your presents you importune me, to remember you. Remember you! " Let my tongue cleave to my jaws if I do not remember you ;" yea, if I have not long ago given Gundulf the first and chief place in my friendship! . . . Why, how can I forget you? Graven on my heart as the seal is printed on the wax, how shall the thought of you fade from my memory? . . . When you are silent, I know that thou lovest me (*ego novi quia diligis me*), and when I hold my peace thou knowest that I more than love thee (*tu scis quia ego amo te*).'[1]

Gundulf was still at Rochester when his friend became Archbishop, near the close of the century; and the contiguity of the dioceses, and the peculiarly close official relations of their incumbents, cemented anew an intimacy and a devotion which, as no separation had loosened, so now no trial could shake. United in life, they were not long divided by death; for Anselm buried his friend in the Lent of 1108, and by the Easter of the following year was sleeping his own sleep at Canterbury.

Hence the interest presented to us by the early days of their friendship—one of those elevated friendships of the cloister that for pure and supernatural love rival the unsullied charities of heaven. 'Bound each to each so intimately, the younger of them would say, and rejoice to hear it said, that he was another Gundulf[2] and Gundulf another

---

[1] *Ep.* i. 4.
[2] In conformity with this idea one of Anselm's letters (i. 33) opens thus :— 'Et meus Gundulphus et tuus Anselmus testis est,' &c. An exquisite touch which some of the editors have strangely disfigured.

Anselm; "for they had in God but one heart and one soul" (Acts iv. 32), and indulged in frequent converse on spiritual things and in many showers of tears, whilst thus they communed in mutual incessant exhortations to climb to higher heights, and in a sacred rivalry which curtailed their very sleep out of zeal to do the service of God.[1] Anselm, as

[1] 'Sancta ut se invicem ad *opus Dei* prævenirent æmulatio.' Let us first understand what is meant by *opus Dei*. I have translated it 'service of God,' but its meaning is less general. *Servitium Dei* has the technical sense of 'Divine office,' a meaning perpetuated in the well-known phrase 'Divine service.' When Lanfranc made his vow in the forest, 'sic vitam meam corrigere et instituere curabo ut tibi servire valeam et sciam,' he meant by 'ut tibi servire sciam' 'that I may know how to say my office.' Thus in St. Anselm's Life we have 'matutinæ et aliud servitium Dei,' and in the *Miracles of St. Emmeram*, 'Cum presbyter .... ad horam divini servitii veniens .... psalmodiæ in erviret.' And *opus Dei* has a similar, though perhaps a less curtailed, meaning. Witness the following passage : 'Videns abbas novum militem Christi revera Deum quærere, *sollicitum esse ad opus Dei*, ad obedientiam et ad alia quibus novitius debet intentus esse, lætabatur corde, *instruebatque eum in Domini servitio* jugiter accendens animum ejus ad virtutis amorem.' (*Vita Ven. Bosonis Abb. Becc.*) Eadmer tells us of St. Wilfrid that when he was a boy 'non ardor æstatis non frigus hiemis (eum), ab instantiâ operis Dei detorquere valebant.' (*Vita S. Wilfridi*, § 28.) In each of these cases *opus Dei* means the Divine office. In the following passage from the *Life of St. Gerald of Aurillac*, *opus Dei* seems to be equivalent to *missa*. Seems to be, I say, for we must not be precipitate ; it may really mean the office which followed mass. 'Facto autem in castro strepitu vociferantium milites qui ad missam .... aderant exsilire volebant. Quos ille .... *donec opus Dei completetur* nequaquam exire permisit.'

Opus Dei, therefore, like *servitium Dei*—unless, indeed, it may sometimes be used for the mass, which I doubt—means the Divine office. See note on p. 85.

And now that we know the general sense of the 'sancta ut se invicem ad *opus Dei* prævenirent æmulatio' of Gundulf and Anselm, I must draw the reader's attention to the following passage from the *Rule of St. Benedict*. In the chapter 'Quomodo dormiant monachi' are these words : 'facto signo absque mora surgentes festinent *invicem se prævenire ad opus Dei*.' These are the very words employed by Gundulf's biographer in the passage which engages our attention ; they are my justification for rendering, as I have done, 'they curtailed their sleep out of zeal to do the service of God.' That is to say, each tried to forestall the other by jumping out of bed at the first stroke of the bell for matins.

I believe Gundulf's biographer has employed the words of the Rule because the two friends slept in adjoining beds ; for the chapter just quoted also provides as follows : 'Surgentes vero ad opus Dei invicem se moderate exhortentur,' the first to rise tapping at the beds of the rest, as Turrecremata explains. I have no doubt whatever that each of the two friends kept an account of the number of times he had had the pleasure of awaking the other.

the better versed in Scripture, spoke more than Gundulf, who, being the proner to tears, was drenched with profuser showers of emotion. The one spoke, the other wept; the one planted, the other watered; the one brought forth treasures of divinest speech, the other heaved sighs of deepest feeling; the one played the part of Christ, the other that of Mary.'

Alas, that not a vestige should remain of a home hallowed by that saintly converse! It paid in due course of time the penalty of its too fragile structure, and the church itself, religiously preserved for four centuries, fell at last before the fury of our own countrymen in the reign of Henry V. But imagination easily beholds the little grassy quadrangle, and round it the lowly cloister of flint and timber, covered by a shallow roof of thatch and lighted by a range of little windows of semitransparent glass. The various rooms and offices on the ground floor open into the cloister. Close to the refectory is the lavatory,[1] supplied by a duct of water from the neighbouring rill; we know it by the long towel hanging close to the door, and by another accessory of all monasteries —I mean a whetstone, suspended from a joist in the roof by a chain of iron. For each monk carried his knife at his girdle, and from time to time he must sharpen it. The whole of the arrangements are simple and homely to the last degree. But everything, even to the whetstone, supplies the two friends with illustrative material in aid of their conversation. 'Anselm would sometimes say to Gundulf, "Do you

---

[1] 'Appensum autem ante lavatorium esse debet manutergium, . . . debes autem habere cotem juxta lavatorium ad quam exacues cum opus fuerit cultellum tuum. . . . Cultellum tuum est ingenium tuum, . . . exercitium adhibe ingenio et cotem adhibe cultello. . . . Pendere autem debet cos ex alto quia nisi exercitium de sublimi æternum intentione pendeat, cultellus ingenii ad scindendum panem factus scripturæ non præparat sed potius habetat. Catena ferrea quæ cotem ligat,' &c. . . .—From a curious little tract, *De Claustro Animæ*, in the Vatican Library; by whom composed I cannot say.

Anselm no doubt borrowed the metaphor of the whetstone from Horace's
'fungar vice cotis, acutum
Reddere quæ ferrum valet, exsors ipsa secandi.'
(*A. P.* 304.)

wish always to sharpen your blade at my whetstone, and will you never let me sharpen my blade at yours? Come, come, say something wherewithal I too may profit. In good truth I am only too like a whetstone, blunt and dull from my many sins; I have no edge at all, whereas you set your heart and your desires so ardently upon the love of our heavenly home (*ad amorem cœlestis patriæ*)—what a sweet phrase is this *cœlestis patria*; common as a field flower in spring, we meet it on every page; peculiar to no clime, it is the accepted formula, the plaintive *dulce domum*, of all St. Benedict's children—you set your desires so ardently on the love of our heavenly home that from always musing on God your edge is always sharp." Then the other said what good things he could. So were both their hearts set on fire; so were both of them refreshed with the sweetness of heavenly longing. Such was the intercourse of the two men;' such was their life in the cloister of Le Bec.

A strange glimpse, our only glimpse, of the hidden life of Anselm!

CHAPTER IV.

PRIOR ANSELM'S LABOURS.

HERLWIN'S biographer informs us that the good abbot could be very severe upon indolent, idle, and slothful monks, and would ask, 'What is the use of a man who can neither read nor keep the commandments of God?' But his face would lighten up with an expression of more than paternal fondness when he observed that some member of his community was especially punctilious in the performance of the Divine service, especially devoted to literary pursuits, or especially painstaking in the cultivation of a virtue. 'To such an one he was not a superior, but a servant.' Not a few of Herlwin's monks were urged to habits of study, more from a desire of pleasing him than from a love of knowledge; and he made it his business to learn who 'amongst Lanfranc's auditors in the *schola claustralis* had the best cultivated mind and the most tenacious memory. . . . If any lettered man came to him wishing to enter the order, there is no describing the joy with which he welcomed, or the kindness and consideration with which he afterwards treated him.'

Anselm, therefore, was a marked man; and Lanfranc was not likely to leave the abbot long in ignorance of his genius, his attainments, and his piety.

In truth, Anselm had committed a blunder in chosing Le Bec for his home. He chose Le Bec, hoping there to slip the more easily into the shade; but in choosing Le Bec he cemented his friendship with the one man in Christendom who could best appreciate him, and than whom no man living could be more firmly resolved that his light should not be hidden under a bushel.

Hence it was that he had not worn the habit for three years when his destiny overtook him, and overtook him by the very avenue which he fondly thought most effectually blocked against it; for in 1062 Lanfranc was appointed Abbot of St. Stephen's at Caen, whither he removed, taking with him Gundulf as his prior and leaving his vacant stall to Anselm.

In the early days of monasticism the difference in dignity and rank between an abbot and his *præpositus*, or provost, had proved too slight for the maintenance of that unity which is the first condition of domestic happiness. St. Benedict proposed, as a remedy, to suppress the office of provost, and establish deaneries in its place—one dean to every ten monks in a community—but at the same time permitted the appointment of a provost in extraordinary cases, provided only that that officer should be nominated by the abbot, the monks having no more than a consenting voice in the business; and that the abbot himself, not the bishop, should give him the dignity and be free to depose him for misconduct. Long, however, before the eleventh century experience had ascertained the impracticability of the decanal system, had changed the title *præpositus* to *prior*, and had established numerous safeguards in addition to St. Benedict's for the assertion and protection of the abbot's supremacy. At Cluny, whose customs in this particular were followed with a general fidelity by the most considerable monasteries of the West, the prior was the abbot's deputy or vicegerent in all that concerned the interior police of the house; not less, but not more. He held the place of honour in the *sinister chorus*, as the abbot did in the *dexter chorus*; but, unlike the abbot, had neither chalice nor *ornamenta* of his own, and was not permitted to occupy the abbot's stall when the latter happened to be absent from the monastery, although on such occasions it was his business to preside both in the chapter-house and in the refectory. Whenever he set forth to perform official duties at a distance, as on visits of inspection to dependent houses or *obedientiæ*, he was accompanied by two brethren at the least, and a serving man who had charge of the baggage assigned to him; but none of the baggage was his own, such was the Cluniac horror of *proprietas*. The customs of Le Bec, however, exhibited an interesting variation from those of Cluny, for Lanfranc had a chalice which he left behind him as a legacy, or at least a loan, to his successor, as he bequeathed to him certain marks of honour which seem to have been denied to the prior of the great Burgundian monastery. Thus at vespers and matins Anselm as well as the abbot was incensed by the officiating priest, and when he appeared in the cloister all rose and remained standing until he had taken his place; nor would anything seem to have been omitted which could show that the dignity hitherto held by Lanfranc and now conferred on Anselm was, if second, yet only second to that adorned by Herlwin.

But the earlier days of Anselm's priorate were not without trouble. There were some who questioned the fitness of the appointment; not that any deemed him morally incompetent, for all admired his virtues; or thought him too young, for it was no rare thing to raise still younger men than Anselm to the abbatial chair itself. The grievance was, not that he was young, but that he had been only two full years in religion; whereas the next senior man in residence had already worn the habit for ten years at the very least.[1] 'They saw, and seeing grew jealous, that one who, as a recent convert, should, in their opinion, have been kept below them, was now set above them. Troubled in themselves, they troubled others, offended consciences, sowed dissension, fostered party spirit, and fomented dislikes. But with them

---

[1] Only such of my readers as may care to study the *Nomina Monachorum Becc* in the Appendix can form any just idea of the light it sheds on what I have been able to glean of Anselm's life at Le Bec.

that hated peace Anselm was peaceable, and in return for their detraction paid back offices of brotherly love, choosing rather to overcome evil by good than to be overcome by evil; and, by the mercy of God, he succeeded so well that they, remarking the purity and singleness of purpose with which he persevered in all his doings, and noting that there was not a trace in him of anything that could justly be blamed, were turned from ill will to good, and at last began, to envy indeed, but to envy with a holy jealousy all that he said and all that he did.' Eadmer, as might be expected, gives us no particulars of this little transitory scandal, for the name of Osbern, whom he introduces in connection with it, if it be the name of a rival, is the name of a rival without followers. Poor Osbern—a mere boy of some fifteen years, he was his own leader and his own clique; for three years he had savagely gloated over the thought that he had right of precedence over two such model monks as Gundulf and Anselm, and he now as savagely made it his business to persecute the new prior. But Osbern's story must be told elsewhere; and since we know nothing about the other malcontent or malcontents, we may pass on at once to more agreeable topics.[1]

Now that Anselm's time was in great degree at his own disposal, he could prosecute with greater freedom than heretofore his more cherished employments. One of these was prayer; either the prayer in which the soul addresses herself to God and the celestial hierarchies, or that in which, contemplating the mysteries of the faith, she seizes and records the images presented to her gaze; in correcter phrase, either prayer or meditation. The homage is one, the forms are distinct. But Anselm passed from one to the other with a

---

[1] 'Quidam fratres ipsius coenobii facti sunt æmuli ejus.' My knowledge of Eadmer's style obliges me to say that these *quidam fratres* need not have been more than two in number; and, but for the context, I should say that there may have been only one of them. I beg the reader to make note of this instance, for we shall meet with others, some of them of considerable importance, in the course of the narrative.

facility, and indulged in both with a fervour, which leave it hard to determine whether of the two he preferred.[1]

But he had another favourite employment, an employment with which his name will ever be associated; I mean the consecration of the speculative intellect to the quest of Divine truth. Owning in reason as in faith a gift from God, he was assured that the legitimate researches of the one can never be in conflict with the divinely authorised convictions of the other; and made it his task, not indeed to give a rational analysis of Christian doctrine—for his method was not analytical—but laboriously and fearlessly to follow up the deductions of reason, as knowing that their ultimate conclusion would be in perfect harmony with revealed dogma.

'Thus did he wing a flight so lofty as that he reached and unlocked the cabinet of problems which until his day had lain unresolved, problems about the Divine Being and the subject-matter of Christian faith, and penetrated and disentangled them, and by trains of luminous reasoning made good both the intellectual and the theological soundness of his method. Such was his faith in the Holy Scriptures that nothing could shake his heartfelt belief that there is nothing in them that lies ever so little wide of the pathway of solid truth. Inspired with this conviction, he directed all the efforts of his soul to one end, that up to the measure of his faith he might be privileged to penetrate by the eye of reason such things in Holy Scripture as he found lying involved in much obscurity here and there upon its page.'

Such is Eadmer's account, and it agrees with the account given by the philosopher himself in the 'Proslogion.' 'I do not try to sound Thy depths, O Lord, for I cannot match my understanding to such an effort; but I long to understand in

---

[1] Hence in one of his letters he speaks of his *meditandi sive orandi opportunitates*; in another he refers to *orationes sive meditationes*, which he had composed; and in a third he characterises one of his devotional compositions as not so much a prayer as a meditation.

some degree Thy truth, the truth which my heart believes and loves. I do not seek to understand as the condition of believing, but I believe as the condition of understanding. For this is my belief, that if I believe not neither shall I understand.'[1]

And in another place he says, speaking in the person of a disciple—

'As on the one hand right order requires that we believe the deep things of the Christian religion before presuming to subject them to the analysis and test of reason, so on the other hand it looks to me like an indolent neglect if, already established in the faith, we do not take the trouble to gain an intellectual intimacy with what we believe.'[2]

'Hence it was,' continues Eadmer, 'that, illuminated by the searching light of an inner wisdom and guided by a discriminating reason, he could analyse characters of every age and sex with such an accuracy that when he came to speak you perceived that he had lifted a curtain and was showing each one his own heart.' And his biographer goes on to say that he was peculiarly happy in tracing the mixed and tangled upgrowth of those moral habits which constitute the difference between man and man to their ultimate source and root; that he penetrated nothing which he did not illumine; that whatever he said carried with it the authority of an inspiration, as though the words he spake were not his own, but Another's; and concludes his account by saying that if a prophet's lips had in olden time been inspired by the live coal from the altar, we surely need not wonder that the tongue which was once in childish vision blessed by the Food of heaven should thus have distilled lessons of Divine wisdom.

I need not say, however, that the industry which he expended upon his monks in that little half-lighted cloister down in the damp valley of Le Bec was not solely occupied

---

[1] *Proslogion*, cap. i. [2] *Cur Deus Homo*, lib. i. cap. ii.

in spiritual direction, and that the discipline of the intellect was, in his judgment, if of secondary, yet only of secondary, importance to the discipline of the heart. It would perhaps be impossible to ascertain the extent of his acquaintance with the works of Plato; but, whatever the field it embraced, there cannot be a question as to its depth and accuracy. And if the form of some of his philosophical treatises may be a guide to us, we shall have to own that he followed Plato's great master by adopting an interlocutory method of instruction. We have several specimens of his application of dialectic to theological inquiries; but of his lessons in dialectic itself, or the art of analysing and classifying ideas, he has only left us one example. Nevertheless this little treatise, 'De Grammatico,' proves that the walls of Le Bec often heard the name of Aristotle, and affords us a more than favourable notion of the power, versatility, and subtilty of the analytical method which Anselm had borrowed from the Stagyrite. A detailed account of this, or of the 'De Veritate,' the 'De Libertate Arbitrii,' and the 'De Casu Diaboli' would be out of place in these pages; but no one who takes the trouble to read them with the attention they require and deserve can be surprised to learn that the monks of Le Bec who had profited by Anselm's teaching came to be renowned through Christendom 'for their zeal and skill in the investigation and solution of sacred enigmas,' and were so fond of these studies that the name of *Beccensis cœnobita* was almost a synonym for philosopher. Perhaps the second of the three treatises just named is the happiest of the group; and if the reader who is beguiled into opening its pages find it necessary to peruse them more than once before he masters the argument, he will derive solace from the fact that even St. Anselm's auditors were in like case. 'Do not be surprised,' says the disciple, 'if things upon which I have not been in the habit of pondering are not always all of them together in the field of my mind's vision when I have only heard you propound them once.' His definition of free-will is 'the power of preserving rectitude of will for its own sake;' and the following short account of it may not prove uninteresting:—

'*Master*: It remains now for you to tell me if you have any exception to take to our definition of free-will. *Disciple*: There is one thing which raises some little difficulty in my mind. We often have the power of possessing a thing, and yet that power is not a free power; it may, that is to say, be hampered by influence from without. When, therefore, you say that free-will is the power of preserving the rectitude of the will for that rectitude's sake, should we not add that the power is a free power and superior to external influence? *Master*: If the power of preserving the rectitude of the will for that rectitude's sake were sometimes to be found without the freedom which we have seen to be proper to it, it would be well to make the addition you suggest; but since the definition we have framed is in such wise a perfect one as that it includes neither less nor more than the freedom of which we are in quest, we may satisfy ourselves that there is nothing to add to it and nothing to take away. For power is a kind, form, or mode of freedom. It is a *power* then. And we say further that it is *a power of preserving*, to separate it from all power that is not a preserving power, as that of laughing or walking. We say, further, that it is *a power of preserving rectitude*, so as to exclude the power of preserving gold, or whatever is not rectitude. We then add the word *will*, to distinguish it from the power of preserving the rectitude of other things, as the rectitude of a rod[1] or of an opinion. And when we limit our definition by subjoining the words *for that rectitude's own sake*, we distinguish free-will from the power of preserving the rectitude of the will for the

---

[1] In allusion to a passage in the preceding treatise, the *De Veritate*, in which he limits the application of the word *rectitudo* as the synonym of *veritas*.

sake of any other thing, as when it is preserved for the sake of money or in obedience to a physical law. A dog preserves rectitude of will in obedience to a physical law when it loves its young or a kind master. Since, then, there is nothing in our definition which is not necessary for outlining the freedom of will of a rational and voluntary being, and for bounding out all others, the freedom with which we are concerned is included within its terms, and all other is excluded. Does it seem so to you? *Disciple*: It seems to me to be an exact definition.'

But enough of this; unless, indeed, we venture to reflect that his acquaintance with Greek philosophy was the Egyptian treasure which he is described as bringing with him from Aosta to Le Bec. He had owed its possession indirectly to Lanfranc, no doubt, and to Lanfranc's intercourse with the East through the merchant vessels which came thence across the Adriatic, and up the Po and the Ticino to Pavia; and to Lanfranc was he indebted for its subsequent assortment and valuation. These pagan spoils were woven by Anselm into that philosophical theology which it is his peculiar glory to have been the first to throw, as adornment at once and as protection, around the sacred ark of Christian dogma.

Anselm's days were so ruthlessly consumed by these labours in behalf of his monks—to say nothing of the claims made upon him by applicants, whether religious or secular, from without the precinct of Le Bec—that a few precarious minutes were often all that was left him of leisure for his own proper employments. He, therefore, was wont to filch for meditation, study, and prayer hours which, by the rule of the order, were devoted to sleep. Rarely, if ever, did he retire to rest with the community after compline; rarely, if ever, did he allow himself more than a brief interval of oblivion before the bell for matins warned him that midnight had come.

Nor was this all. The critical acumen in which he had proved himself the rival of Lanfranc was not allowed to lose its edge by want of practice; and another employment was ever open to him in the interminable toil and *labor improbus* of correcting manuscripts, which had hitherto been much corrupted by the indolence of transcribers, or by successive but injudicious efforts to repair blanks created by the slow corrosion of the parchment through lapse of time. Many were the nights in which he thus laboured on, peering over crabbed texts, moving his capricious, ineffectual candle from one codex to another, comparing and collating their differences, and digesting their conflicting evidence; at one time tracing back the history of a corruption until there could be no question as to the original reading, at another pondering over some intricate and knotty fault in hope of the moment when his genius should inspire him with the only possible method of unravelling it.

But other work awaits him. Some one, whose soul is bound to his own by the sacredest of sympathies, has implored him to compose a meditation, or a prayer, or something in part prayer and in part meditation, which he may treasure and carry about him and refer to from time to time when he finds that his love of heaven is growing cold; something wherewith to rekindle his longings for the *cælestis patria*. He therefore lays aside the wearisome parchments, and, taking out his tablets of wax, and a style which use has polished to a silvery brightness, trims the smoky candle, whose feeble ray, though it scarce reach wall or ceiling, fully illuminates his pale eager face and sensitive lips, and then engraves the opening sentences of that wonderful *Terret me vita mea*[1]

---

[1] 'Deinde: *Terret me vita mea; namque diligenter discussa*, cum eo quod sequitur; scriptum hoc et præter hoc alia piissima de contrito spiritu tuo et de pietate contriti tui cordis edita et scripta, pias præstant nobis lacrymas tuas legere, nostras edere; ita ut utrumque miremur, et in corde tuo redundare tantæ rorem benedictionis et sine susurro descendere inde rivum in cordibus nostris.'—*Ep.* i. 61.

concerning which the monks of Chaise-Dieu made bold to say that they fancied they could read the writer's tears upon the parchment of their copy, and declared that they knew not which was the more marvellous, the dew of benediction with which Anselm's heart was drenched, or the subtilty with which the thrill of sympathetic emotion passed from his soul to theirs.

Another of his most remarkable pieces is an *oratio meditativa*, written in the person of one who, having sadly fallen, cries out in grief and terror at the view of his sin, regrets an innocence gone for ever, complains no less of his irreparable loss in the past than of the intolerable torments which await him in the future, and, in an ecstasy of woe, flies to the brink of hell, there, from the punishment of sin, to learn its guilt and to gain a motive for challenging the mercy of his offended God.[1] It exhibits in a singular if awful manner the sympathy and sensibility which constituted the secret of St. Anselm's extraordinary influence; for it fascinates, not by its fervour, its poetry, or the skill expended in its composition, but simply by its reality. As the reader reads on he finds it hard not to think himself the penitent, and well he may; for the writer writes as though the case were his own. And when one has read it one wonders what the hour must have been when it was tremulously committed to the tablets; an hour of tears and more than tears, an hour of overwrought nerve and throbbing brain, an hour of ecstatic horror, when the very birds of night were hushed lest they should recall the writer from his vision.

'Let my mind go down, down to the region of darkness, the region covered with the shadow of death; and let her scan the torments that there await my guilty soul; let her gaze on them, and study them; let her see, and be sore

[1] It is the third in Gerberon's edition. Its proper title is *Deploratio male amissæ virginitatis*.

troubled. What is it, O God, what is it that I descry in the land of misery and gloom? Horror! horror! What is it I behold there, where no order, but everlasting horror dwells? Ah, the jarring shrieks, the tears and hurly-burly, the gnashing of teeth, the disordered advance of multitudinous wailings, wo, and wo. How many wo's! how many and how many wo's, and wo's on the heels of wo's! Ah, the sulphurous fire, the flame from the nethermost deep! And you, ye volumes of blackest smoke, with what frightful roaring do I see you wreathe and roll! You worms, alive in fire, what strange appetite for gnawing thus inflames you, you that the fire of fires does not burn! And you, ye demons, glowing through and through, chafing with rage, gnashing your teeth with frenzy, why so merciless to them that are writhing in the midst of you? O all and every kind of torments, measured by justice, but measureless to power of endurance, is it so that no controlment, no respite, no end is ever to subdue you? Are these the things, great God, that have been prepared for fornicators and despisers of Thee, of whom I am one? I, yes I; I am one of them.'

But let us read on:—

'Shudder, O my soul; and faint, my mind; and break, my heart. Whither do you drag me, O punishers of my guilt? Whither dost thou thrust me, O my sin? Whither dost thou drive me, O my God? If I have contrived to be Thy culprit, say, could I have contrived not to be Thy creature? If I have robbed me of my chastity, say, have I bereft Thee of Thy mercy? O Lord, O Lord, if I have let that come whence Thou canst damn, hast Thou let that go whence Thou art wont to save? Do not, O Lord, so look upon my evil as to forget Thy good. Where, O God of Truth, where is Thine "I desire not the death of the sinner, but that the sinner turn from his way and live"?

O Lord, who liest not, what means Thy *nolo mortem peccatoris*, if Thou bury down in hell a sinner crying unto Thee? To plunge a sinner into the bottomless pit, is this Thy *volo ut convertatur*, Thy *volo ut vivat?* . . .'

In course of time these incessant labours in numberless interests told upon a constitution far from robust; both mind and body were fatigued; he regretted the lost calm of earlier days, and resorted to his Archbishop. He entered Maurille's presence with no further intention than that of seeking advice; but whilst he set forth his case the prelate's sympathy and his own weakness forced an unwilling tear to his eyes; the sketch which he had begun to draw of his present distracted life enlarged and exaggerated itself into the picture of some irreparable disaster; sobs broke the continuity of what had been designed as the coldest and clearest of statements, and the poor prior, losing all control of himself, divulged the secret of his heart as he had never meant to do, abandoned statements for entreaties, and in an agony of emotion implored the Archbishop to relieve him of a burden which he protested was unbearable. Maurille was more than a builder of cathedrals, or Anselm would not have unbosomed himself so soon and so passionately. 'My dearest child,' replied the prelate, 'do not ask this of me, do not ask it. Do not wish to lay down your burden and care only for self. I assure you I have heard of many, and known many, who, for their own quiet's sake, have declined to undertake the pastoral care and watch their brethren for their good. I have known them saunter along in sloth, get into a bad way, and at last hurry on from bad to worse than bad. This must never be the case with you (God forbid it); and, therefore, by your holy obedience I require you to keep your present preferment, and never under any pretence, or for any reason whatever, relinquish it, except at the bidding of your abbot; and, furthermore, on no account to refuse a higher one, should you ever be called to it. For I am sure that you will not remain very long where you are; you will soon be promoted to a higher charge.' 'Ah, poor me,' cried the sobbing and distracted prior, 'I am not strong enough for what I carry now, and if a heavier load is laid upon me I dare not shake it off.' But all to no purpose; the Archbishop repeated the injunction, and under pain of sin forbad him to transgress it.

His fate was sealed.

CHAPTER V.

PRIOR ANSELM'S INFLUENCE.

WHEN the Prior of Le Bec went to Rouen on the worse than bootless errand just recorded, he was accompanied, it appears, by a secular clergyman named Albert, whom he had for some time known and loved, but whom, by reason of some confidence revealed during their ride through the forest, he was henceforth to regard with still greater interest than heretofore.[1] Albert the physician was certainly not an Englishman, nor, in all likelihood, a Norman, but probably a Lombard, whom Lanfranc, with his fatal talent for attracting all that was most excellent, had induced to forsake the medical school of Bologna and live close to Herlwin's monastery, thus completing its encyclopædic renown. It was a pleasant distraction for Anselm to have such a companion on such a journey; for the growing interest which the one felt for the other, as each unbosomed all that was nearest to his own heart, did much to soothe the Prior's spirits and recruit his overtasked energies. But Albert did not return to Le Bec with him; for he was on his way to Caen, where he was henceforth to reside in the neighbourhood of St. Stephen's Abbey.

Anselm's journey back to Le Bec, therefore, must have been a weary one. With the disheartening prospect of a life burdened with its own proper responsibilities there blended the nearer view of a growing community deprived of the services of an accomplished physician. The fault was Lanfranc's; but Lanfranc may have thought that the healing art at

[1] *Ep.* i. 28, 36.

Le Bec would suffer little by the substitution of the Prior for Dom Albert;[1] and so many of the great ecclesiastics of the time studied medicine that some skill in diagnosis and in the exhibition of drugs must surely have been expected from men in a position like Anselm's. Great prelates like Fulbert of Chartres and Lanfranc of Canterbury have left behind them letters which evince not only a knowledge more than empirical, and an anxious care that their remedies should be properly applied, but that which must best recommend both the knowledge and the care—sympathy, vigilance, and thoughtfulness, all engaged in the alleviation of human suffering. Baldwin, Abbot of St. Edmund's, and at Fécamp Johanellinus, or 'Little John'—thus named by men who wondered that so diminutive a frame should enshrine so many and such various gifts as his; Guntard of Jumièges; Gilbert Maminot, Bishop of Lisieux—were all of them *medici*; and the Prior of Le Bec can scarcely, since his promotion to the priorate, have either escaped or evaded the obligation of studying a science so noble in itself and so benign in its aim.

But Eadmer, who in writing the 'Vita' wrote as a hagiologist, has not deigned to recommend the medical skill of St. Anselm by any instances of its successful exercise. The little that he tells us, and the little that can be gathered from Anselm's correspondence, show that the good Prior was a careful observer of symptoms, and a painstaking student of the works of Galen and Hippocrates.[2] But it would seem that whatever technical skill he may have displayed elicited from his patients even less admiration and less gratitude than

---

[1] What may really have constituted a good physician I will not undertake to say. 'Eodem tempore Rodulfus cognomento Mala Corona Uticum venit. . . . Hic . . . Galliæ Italiæque scrutando scholas secretarum indaginem rerum insigniter attigit. . . . Physicæ quoque scientiam tam copiose habuit ut in urbe Psalernitanâ, ubi maximæ medicorum scholæ ab antiquo tempore habentur, neminem in medicinali urbe, *præter quandam sapientem matronam*, sibi parem invenitet.'—Ordeni, ii. 70. This *sapiens matrona*, by the way, suggests the *sage-femme* of the French.

[2] See especially *Epp.* i. 31, 51.

those moral gifts which he brought to bear upon the mitigation of physical suffering. 'He spent much of his time in the infirmary, and used to investigate most carefully the symptoms of each one of his patients. Whatever each one's case required he promptly, ungrudgingly, and cheerfully administered. He was a father to the whole and a mother to the sick; nay, father and mother in one both to the sick and the whole. No one had a secret in his heart that he did not wish to confide to Anselm, as a child entrusts its confidence to the keeping of a tender mother.'

His characteristic sensibility was never at fault, so inventive was it of palliatives for both the moral and the physical distresses of his patients. 'Oh,' cries Eadmer, 'how many already given up for lost in their sickness were by his sympathy and watchful care restored to their former health!' Here is an instance: Herewald was broken with age and sickness; age and sickness between them had drained the vigour from all his limbs, and paralysed every organ except the tongue. But Anselm was ever at his side, minutely feeding him with the juice of grapes squeezed, berry by berry, from one hand into the other, and thence distilled into the sufferer's mouth. It was the only food the old man could take, and, as he explained on his recovery, he could only take it from Anselm's hand.[1]

Among the senior members of the community there was one who had never ceased to resent the foreigner's promotion to the priorate. He fell ill, and in his hour of weakness brooded over the injury that had embittered his later years, until one day, when the house was plunged in silence—for, except the attendants in the infirmary and Anselm, who was in the cloister correcting manuscripts, the community were

---

[1] To what precise date this incident is to be assigned I cannot say. Eadmer does not always observe the chronological order, nor need we expect that he should; for it is improbable that as he wrote he had a *Nomina Monachorum Beccensium* to guide him, as I have. Herewald was professed in 1072 or 1073; but he may, of course, have had a very long novitiate.

taking their midday *siesta*—he became suddenly delirious. Anselm was summoned, and after a short delay repaired to the room where the sufferer lay, and as he went in made the sign of the cross, invoking the Holy Trinity. The sick man was instantly tranquillised, and owned his deliverer in Anselm, who now seated himself at his side and spoke to him as only saints can speak, and by the unconscious force of sheer Christian meekness constrained him to pour into his ear all the sins and sorrows of a long and chequered life, and then composed him to meet his end. And why not? The charity of Christ had won its victory. Why should the poor man linger? As the community were rising from their repose to go to nones they were startled by a sharp quick sound from a wooden rattle. They knew what it meant, hurried to the infirmary, and, crowding in, found Anselm's old inveterate foe expiring, forgiving and forgiven, in the arms of Anselm.

If the Abbey of Le Bec was now old enough to see men who had entered it in their prime drop off as leaves drop in autumn, the institution had gained sufficient renown to number among its members the children of people of rank, who discerned in it the best home and best refuge for their offspring. Some of these *nutriti* were by this time emerging into youth, and the story I am about to borrow from Eadmer shows that, even before coming into directer relations with the Prior—for boys under fifteen were kept apart from the rest, and had a master of their own—they must have enjoyed in large degree the benefit of his gentle administration.

Once a certain abbot, whose name and preferment need not be given, but who was accounted quite a monk, was talking aloud to himself about matters that concerned the monastic profession, and, amongst a number of other subjects, found something to say about his *monachi nutriti.* 'What will become of them?' he exclaimed, addressing, but scarcely addressing, the Prior in his querulous monody. 'They are perverse and they are incorrigible; we flog them night and day incessantly, and they are always worse for the flogging than they were before.' The Prior, with an air of surprise, rejoined, 'You flog them incessantly! And when they outgrow their boyhood what sort of lads are they?' 'Stupid brutes.'

'You have not very good luck in the training of your *nutriti*,' suggested Anselm; 'you found them human, and you nourish them into brutes!' 'What can we do, then?' was now the abbot's challenge. 'What can we do? We brace them in all sorts of ways that they may get on, and we end by not getting on ourselves.' 'You brace them!' rejoined the Prior; and, after a pause, 'Tell me, my lord Abbot, I pray you, were you to plant a young tree in your garden, and so hem it in betimes on every side as to prevent its stretching forth its branches, and were you, after some years, to remove the impediments you had set about it, what sort of tree would it then grow into?' 'Useless timber, of course, with gnarled and crooked branches.' 'And, of course, no one would be to blame but you, who had gone to such extremes with your restraints upon it. Surely this is what you are doing with your boys. They have been planted in the garden of the Church, by their parents' oblation of them, to grow and bear fruit for God; but you carry the system of terror, threats, and whippings to such a pass that you cramp them and leave them no chance of expanding and developing; and the consequence of all this indiscriminating repression is that they contract such a base and—what shall I say?—such a crooked moral habit as reminds one of the tangled branches of a thorn tree; they foster and indulge it, and not only indulge, but grow obstinate in it; so that whatever is afterwards done for setting them straight they purposely shun. And so, thinking that you have no such thing in your hearts as love, sympathy, kindness, gentleness for them, they at last cease to believe that any such virtues can possibly exist in you, and fancy that all you do comes of hatred and spite against them. The consequence is very sad. As they grow in years hatred and a suspicion of all kinds of mischief grows with them, and they become inevitably biassed to what is evil; for having been trained in nothing like genuine charity, they can look at nothing you do for them without a scowl and a sidelong glance.

'But do, for the love of God, let me know why it is that you are so set against them? Are they not human? Are they not of the same nature with yourself? Would you like to be served as you serve them?' Here the moody abbot no doubt muttered something, part of which reached the Prior, who, perhaps, had not the acutest of hearing. 'If you were what they are! Be it so. Do you expect to form them to goodness by nothing but blows and rods? Did you ever know a goldsmith form a beautiful intaglio out of a plate of gold or silver by nothing but blows? I think not. Why, what? To work out his design upon the plate of metal he now gently presses and strikes it with his tool, now still more gently, and very, very carefully raises it and works it into form. So with you. If you desire your boys to be lovely characters, you must, together with the depressing discipline of the rod, administer to them the support and succour of gentleness and fatherly kindness.' 'What support? What succour?' demanded the discontented and somewhat defiant interlocutor. 'Our task is to brace them to solidity and ripeness of character.' 'Quite so,' said the Prior, 'quite so. Bread and other solid food are useful and nutritious for children that are strong enough to bear them; but give them to an unweaned babe instead of its proper nourishment, and you will find that, instead of feeding, you choke. And why? No need to tell; the reason is clear. Be sure that just as the human body, in its weakness and in its vigour, has its proper food suited to its state, so the soul of man, in its time of weakness and in its vigour, has its own appropriate nurture. The vigorous soul is refreshed and nourished by solid food, such as patience in tribulations; not coveting neighbours' goods; when one cheek has been struck, offering the other; praying for enemies; loving those that hate, and such like. But a soul frail as yet, and weak in the service of God, requires milk; for example, kindness from those about it, benignity, sympathy, a cheerful mode of address, a loving tolerance, and much more of the same kind. If you adapt yourself thus to your weak and to your strong, by the grace of God you will win them all to God.'

'*You will win them all to God.*' These words broke the poor abbot's heart, who exclaimed, with a groan, 'Truly we have erred from the truth, and the light of discernment has not lighted on us;' and, falling on the ground at the Prior's feet, confessed that he was wrong, begged pardon for the past, and promised amendment in the future.

A word for Eadmer, who tells the story. His introduction of the abbot, with a great reputation for *religio*, a sort of typical monk, talking aloud to himself, and speechifying about his little grievances, until he came to his naughty boys, when the good, tender-hearted Prior took care to throw in a word so as to open conversation; the curt replies which he puts into the poor man's mouth; the muttered something, not expressed in the text, but intended to be read between the lines, in response to Anselm's appeal, '*Would you like it?*' the dogged adherence to the same unhappy word 'brace,' and the adroit change of meaning from 'we brace' in the rustic and still extant sense of 'we flog' to 'our business is to brace' in the sense of 'our business is to invigorate;' the advantage Anselm takes of the abbot's *équivoque* and shifting of position; the good Prior's crushing conclusion, '*You will win them all to God*;' and the sudden contrition and melting of the other's heart, who, every inch a monk, fell at his feet begging pardon and promising amendment—all this is told with a skill and a picturesque effect which the acknowledged masters of biography have scarcely ever reached and assuredly never excelled.

'I write this,' he adds, 'that we may have an idea of the Prior's kindly discrimination and discriminating kindness in his treatment of others, no matter who.'

But to us the story is otherwise of value. Anselm's kindness and Anselm's discretion had ample opportunity of exercise, indeed, but they were exerted in the execution of his great mission, which was to humanise, to civilise, to christianise the untamed but not indomitable ferocity of his Scandinavian neighbours. Thirty years ago Herlwin had sought, but sought in vain, for some monastery in which that ferocity should have been sufficiently subdued for him to have some reasonable prospect of a peaceful lodging within its walls, but finding it untamed, had been constrained to shrink from contact with it. The gate porter who handled him so roughly was a Christian, and a Christian who, as Herlwin deemed, and no doubt rightly deemed, had voluntarily relinquished many a gross allurement in hope of gaining a happy immortality; and, just as we should be ashamed to rebuke a child for thinking that angels in heaven eat sugar plums, so Herlwin would have scorned to indulge uncharitable censure of a porter who had not the slightest doubt that St. Peter at the gate of heaven was in the habit of clutching intruders by the hair with one hand, and dealing them a sound blow on the nape of the neck with the other, by way of ejecting them. The minds of the best men in Normandy were childish, and their manners barbarous, even though their hearts were set on heaven; and Herlwin dared not condemn them, though he felt obliged to abstain from their society. And the little group who gathered round him first at Bonneville, and then at Le Bec, even though they may not have been as rough as some other religious, were yet so intolerant of salutary control that he almost despaired of taming them, unquestionable as was the goodness of their intentions; whilst Lanfranc, in his turn, found them to be exceedingly disagreeable neighbours, notwithstanding his expectation and his hope of meeting them hereafter in a better and a gentler world.

Still, Lanfranc's priorate had been of invaluable service to the house of his adoption, in compelling the respect and the distant emulation of its inmates, and in drawing to its cloister a few men of refined manners and cultivated intellect; and Anselm's priorate was to complete the work thus begun. It was, as I have said, Anselm's mission to humanise, civilise, and christianise whatever of the old barbarous element still survived within the walls of his monastery. A noble mission, indeed, but not an easy one. The good abbot who had been so stupidly unmerciful in his treatment of his *nutriti* was soon converted from his error, for, grievous as was his mistake, he had been prompted to it neither by rivalry nor malice; but the handful of men who kept alive their jealousy of Anselm were too deeply prejudiced to yield a ready submission to his arts of gentle suasion. The prejudice is easy to understand. If they had once been jealous of Lanfranc, because, unaware of the estimate which Christendom had formed of him, they knew no more about him than that he was refined as they were not, high-souled as they were not, and a foreigner, they no sooner learnt what sort of man he really was than their admiration set him out of reach of their spite, and they were proud to have him for prior. But Anselm had not made a name in the world, and Anselm was a foreigner. The reason they gave of their dislike was that he was their junior in religious profession; but that can scarcely have been their chief as undoubtedly it was not their only grievance; and it is the habit of jealous people to give a false account of their griefs. Some five or six years, it is true, had elapsed between the profession of his immediate senior in religion and his own; but the very fact that his immediate senior was his most inveterate rival would in itself have sufficed to disarm their discontent by exhibiting its absurdity. For that immediate senior was, after all, the merest stripling; and the contrast which they noted between Anselm and Osbern was not merely a contrast between three years of religious profession and ten, nor a contrast between monks by conversion and monks by bringing up; it was a contrast between refinement, gentleness, elevation of character, and the as yet unexorcised demon of the old barbarism. Poor Osbern! A Norman, and not improbably a son or nephew of William Fitzosbern, the kinsman and counsellor of the lately crowned Conqueror, he in his strangely mingled good and evil exhibited the conflicting qualities of the Norman people, the Norman nobility, and the princes of Normandy at this critical epoch. Possessed of a singularly keen and accurate perception, and a remarkable skill and ingenuity in the mechanical arts, he had moral gifts which would have made him attractive at an engaging age, but for a certain perversity which detected mischief with all the accuracy of an instinct and did wrong with all the energy of a passion. The keen-witted boy was not slow to detect the resentment which Anselm's promotion had evoked, and, with the assurance and audacity sometimes to be found in children of an age and temperament like his, avowed himself a sharer in the grievance of his elders. Such an ally may be of great service to a group of malcontents, who watch his tricks with more than an amused interest, and are gratified to perceive his facility in seizing the proper part to play and his adroitness in playing it. Osbern was admirably qualified for his task, for to the intelligence of a dog in reading, as such young gentlemen so well know how to do, the human face, he added the rage of a dog that is set on worrying his victim. His active mind delighted in the difficult and exciting enterprise of worrying the placid Prior; whilst the placid Prior, untroubled indeed on his own account, but grieved at the contrast between the moral and the intellectual qualities of his persecutor, was quietly resolved upon reforming him. The community looked on. Anselm began by coaxing the wild creature with little acts of kindness; by tolerating his pranks with a benignant condescension; by conceding in his favour such little indulgences—and they were not a few—as could be granted without positive breach of discipline. The strange wolfish creature, thus pleased and occupied, began by insensible degrees to lose much of his erst unmanageable ferocity, and, giving faint tokens of a heart that, after all, beat generous and true beneath that untamed exterior, slowly responded to his tamer's caresses with a coy, uncouth respect, with submission to his counsels, and with manners rudely formed upon a civilised model. The Prior perceiving this and pursuing his advantage, now admitted him to the interchanges of an intimate and familiar friendship, tended and fostered his new affections and his new virtues, and seized every opportunity of improving, whether by instruction, encouragement, or advice, what was so well begun.

After some considerable time, but very warily, he retrenched one by one the concessions once yielded to his puerile age; for indulgences proper to a savage boyhood were unsuitable to a youth who had at last consciously owned the charm of the civiliser.

Years passed on; and so well did the young man lay Anselm's instructions to heart that the latter, assured of ultimate success, at last made it his business to root up with unsparing hand whatever of boyish folly might come to the surface in Osbern's character. What was worthy of reproof he now vigorously punished by verbal reprimand, and even by that physical chastisement which the age deemed necessary to the formation of character. The reclaimed, educated, almost polished Osbern bore all these corrections with a quiet patience; for he was at last a monk in soul, in act, in will; and, inspired with a very passion for holiness, soon showed himself a model of Christian meekness. It was now his turn to suffer as Anselm before him had done. The refining change wrought in him provoked many a hard word from men who, being too old themselves to undergo the like, were jealous of it in him, and were unwilling to condone his apostasy from their ranks. But they were soon subdued, for they soon owned that the reformation which nettled them was no superficial change but a moral conversion, a transformation of the spirit of the young man's mind to the ideal of a perfect Christian humanity.[1]

Henceforth Osbern was more to Anselm than a favourite disciple, an intimate companion, a bosom friend; he was a typical instance of that civilising, humanising, christianising change which it was the mission of monasticism to effect in the world. And henceforth Anselm could confidently hope that in the humble cloister of Le Bec, its inmates now one at heart and all engaged together in endeavouring to realise the fulness of the stature of the Christian character, a peace would soon reign that should make Le Bec like the more favoured cloisters of the south, an earthly paradise. Hitherto it had not been that.

Was it to ensure the issue of the conquest that Heaven now so strangely interposed? When Anselm in his old age reached this part of the story, tears came to his eyes. His young friend had already displayed a wealth of moral and intellectual capacity and endowment such as even in Anselm's estimate gave promise of a career rich in abundant service to Christendom, when—so does a cruel frost nip our blossoms and shed them to earth—some undescribed malady laid its sudden hand on Osbern, and he took to a bed in the dormitory from which he was never to rise again. The young man was very happy in his illness, for Anselm had taught him the secret of a content that rises victorious over every pain and every regret, and was at his side day and night incessantly. Whatever nourishment he took was administered by Anselm; whatever needful attentions were bestowed on his suffering and emaciated frame were all bestowed by Anselm, who, leaving nothing undone that the most provident care could suggest, supported and consoled the patient both in his body's

---

[1] In this account I follow Eadmer's as closely as may be, short of a literal translation.

and in his soul's necessities to the very end. As that end drew near Anselm, loth to have such a friendship snapped so soon, and yearning to trace the soul's passage, though an assured one, yet through what storms he knew not, hence to the eternal shore, bent over his dying friend and whispered an entreaty that he would, if it were possible, let him know when he was gone how it fared with him. 'He promised, and passed away.'

The body was washed, clothed, composed on the bier, and carried into the church, the whole community preceding it and singing the 'Subvenite, sancti Dei.'[1] When the usual rites had been performed—it seems that he died about midnight, and was carried into the church after matins—the monks all sat round about the corpse, to watch it and sing psalms for the departed soul incessantly, until it was time for the next office.

But the Prior wished to be alone, and withdrew to an unobserved part of the church. There, as he prayed and wept, his strength failed him from fatigue and grief, and he closed his eyes, when lo! beings of reverend aspect, and clothed in the whitest of white garments, had entered the room where Osbern died, and seated themselves in judgment round the spot where, stretched on the sackcloth, he expired. But their sentence was hidden from the dreamer, who tried in vain to learn it. Presently the scene changed, and Osbern himself, pale and haggard, and like to one coming to himself from a fainting fit or from excessive loss of blood, appeared in sight. 'What! you, my child?' cried Anselm. 'How are you?' And the vision replied, 'Thrice the old serpent rose up against me and thrice he fell back again, and the bearward of the Lord God has delivered me.' 'Anselm opened his eyes, and Osbern was no more seen. But observe,' continues Eadmer, 'how the dead showed the same obedience to the living which, living, he had been wont to show.'

[1] 'Subvenite, sancti Dei, occurrite, angeli Dei, suscipientes animam ejus: offerentes eam in conspectu Altissimi. Suscipiat eum Christus qui vocavit et in sinu Abrahæ angeli deducant. Offerentes.'

For an entire year the Saint said mass daily for the repose of his friend's soul, except when he was prevented from doing so, in which case he bade one of the monks say a *missa familiaris* for this intention, repaying the debt at as early a date as he could, and then saying a second mass for Osbern.[1] He sent letters, too, in all directions begging prayers for the soul so dear to him. Thus he wrote to his old friend Gundulf :—

'Salute Dom Osbern, who is with you, as a dear brother of mine, for my own dear dead Osbern's sake. . . . Wherever Osbern is, his soul and mine are one ; so much so that whatever is done for him in my lifetime I will accept as the tribute of friendship which I might trust to have for myself after my death, that my friends may not trouble themselves about me when I am gone. Good-bye, good-bye, my dearest friend ; and, to repay you your importunity with me, I beg, and I beg, and I beg again of you, remember me, and do not forget the soul of my dear Osbern ; and if I seem too troublesome, forget me and remember him.'

About the same time he wrote to another friend at Canterbury :—

'Take my letter to Dom Gundulf, as written to you, *mutato nomine*, and think yours to be for him. But, as I cannot pray to God enough, or implore my fellow men

---

[1] To say two or even three masses a day was not unusual. It is now done only, I believe, on Christmas Day throughout the whole of Christendom, and on All Souls' Day in Spain and Portugal and their colonies. Ademar, in his letter on the Apostolate of St. Martial, says, 'Duæ missæ quas hodie . . . continuas . . . celebravi.' In the Life of St. Ulric we read, 'Respondit quia virum Dei tamdiu expectasset donec ter missarum solemnia peregisset.' Bishop Gundulf of Rochester used generally to say two masses a day, the second of them for the dead. St. Hugh of Cluny said two masses daily, both of them for the living. Alexander II. (Ep. cxxxii.) had expressed himself as follows on the subject : 'Sufficit sacerdoti missam unam in die celebrare. . . . Non modicum est unam missam facere, et valde felix est qui unam dignè celebrare potest. Quidam tamen pro defunctis unam faciunt et alteram de die si necesse est.'

sufficiently for the dear, dear soul of my departed brother Osbern, I must again assure you that whatever I say to Dom Gundulf in my letters, that I say to you. The Lord Abbot and the whole of our congregation salute you and Dom Gundulf, rendering you hearty thanks for your presents, and still heartier for your zeal and goodness. Good-bye, and think of the soul of Osbern, my second self, not as his soul, but as mine.'

And, in another letter to Gundulf, we have the following :—

'Since all who are dear to me are dear to you, place in a group together with me in the chamber of your memory, where I always keep my place, those friends of mine of whom I have told you, as wishing to be bound by the same links of friendship with us; set them in a circle with me; but, oh! my dear friend, place Osbern's shade in my bosom; place him, I beg you, in my bosom, nowhere else.' [1]

Osbern must have died in the earlier part of 1072. Before the tale of their year's masses was told Anselm's victory was insured. Surely it was for this end that Osbern had been called away, for all jealousies were now hushed and quelled in presence of so supernatural a love. The spectacle of that love subdued all hearts, and there was not a man at Le Bec who did not take shame to himself as he contrasted his own character with all this capacity of heaven-born sympathy; not one who did not bewail his lot when he contrasted it with Osbern's happiness and joy, a happiness and a joy which the heavenly-minded Prior had insured him by his attachment in life and his succours after death; not one who did not commit himself and his dearest interests to Anselm, in hope of inheriting Osbern's privilege. 'And he,'

[1] *Epp.* i. 4, 5, 7.

says Eadmer, 'giving thanks to God, became all things to all men, that he might save all.'

Thus a new era was about to begin at Le Bec, and Providence had so ordered things that the change should be symbolised and illustrated by the removal of the community to their new home.

The foundations of Lanfranc's basilica were laid, as we have seen, in the spring of 1058; and the fabric would seem to have been completed in 1066. Alas for us that it should have perished! for, if I am not mistaken, it marked a new epoch in the history of ecclesiastical architecture in Normandy. Alas, too, that the name of the architect should not have been preserved, nor any account of him! for I suspect that he was a master-builder from Pavia and a relation of Lanfranc's. Nevertheless, although the fabric has perished, and although we know not whence its designer came, time and change have spared us one or two *data* which seem to prove that in at least some of its more important details it was constructed on the model of the basilica of San Michele in Lanfranc's native city; and I trust that I am not presumptuous in turning those *data* to account and attempting a theoretical reconstruction of its ground plan.

The nave, then, was, as I have reason to believe, some hundred and fifty feet long by thirty-two feet wide, and was flanked on either side by an aisle of twenty feet in width; the western limb of the building was thus a hundred and fifty feet long and seventy-two feet wide from wall to wall. Nave and aisles were divided into seven bays by two rows of semicircular arches which rested on moulded shafts eight feet thick or nearly so, as measured from north to south or east to west, breast high above the level of the floor. The pillars, however, which stood at the junction of nave and transept were much more massive than those to the west of them. The clear distance from pier to opposite pier across the nave was slightly over twenty-four feet; the clear distance from pier to pier up the church was slightly under twelve feet. East of the nave and its aisles was the transept, thirty-two feet deep and a hundred feet from north to south. The eastern limb, like the nave, was separated from the transept by two massive piers, and consisted of two bays terminated by a semicircular apse, and flanked on either side with two collateral bays similar in area to those on either side of the nave. Each of these collateral bays in the eastern limb was a separate chapel with an orientated altar. There were also four altars in the transept, two on either side of the choir arch.

The three easternmost bays of the nave were enclosed, except on the side nearest the sanctuary, so as to form a choir for the monks, who had two entrances to the church, one from the cloister into the south aisle, and another in the southern extremity of the transept.

The four massive piers at the central portion of the church supported a tower of no great height, in which the bells were hung. I suspect that there were no towers at the western end, which was pierced with three doorways—round-headed of course, for the style was Lombard romanesque—and by one row of small windows. The sills of the windows which lighted the aisles were about twelve feet from the floor.

The whole of this work, including, perhaps, the decoration of the ceiling, which was flat and panelled in wood, was completed, as I have said, in about eight years after the laying of the first stone by Abbot Herlwin in 1058.

In 1067[1] he began the other buildings of the new abbey. These all stood south of the church and were arranged on

---

[1] I am indebted for this piece of information not to any documents proper to Le Bec, but to the *Chronicon Sancti Maxentii*, published by Dom Bouquet (xi. 220). 'A.D. mlxvii. Herluinus fundavit suum monasterium.' This is the only notice of the fact which I have seen, and the context gives a curious proof its accuracy, for it states that in 1067 Quadragesima Sunday fell on February which it did.

the usual Benedictine plan. The chapter-house, which had an interior dimension of some forty-two feet square, stood alongside of the eastern limb of the basilica, and opened by a large door in its western side into a hall or lobby, the north side of which was formed by the southern termination of the transept. The western exit from this hall opened into the cloister, and from its south side, as I conjecture, rose the staircase to the dormitory, whilst its north was pierced with a doorway into the transept. Each side of the cloister measured from ninety-five to a hundred feet, its northern side corresponding with five bays of the nave.

By the summer of 1073 the work was sufficiently advanced for Herlwin to resolve on moving his monks to their new home before the approach of winter.

On the last day, then, of October in the year 1073 Herlwin and Anselm and their monks, after partaking of a slight refection—for the day was a fast—went into the church and ranged themselves into processional order. That humble temple was endeared to them by sacred and varied associations. It was there that Gotbert beheld the Queen of Heaven, and apostles singing before her in a blaze of glory; there that Gundulf, another sacristan, had a special place assigned him, whither at will he might retire to pray and weep unobserved before Our Lady of Le Bec; there that Anselm nearly fourteen years ago made his memorable profession, and quite recently beheld the pale shade of Osbern. And Osbern's ashes lay hard by, in the cemetery that sloped slowly to the rivulet. As they all stood there awaiting the signal to depart, many a heart swelled and many an eye grew dim. But enough; the western door unfolds, the cross passes on before, and the shortening day and falling leaves of autumn are gladdened by a hymn in which all regrets for the past and all hopes for the future are together swallowed up in a common sentiment of humble and thankful adoration. 'Tibi laus, tibi gloria, tibi gratiarum actio in sæcula sempiterna, O beata Trinitas.'[1]

That hymn is not so well known as it deserves to be, and but for some few fragments preserved in the Roman Breviary its name would fall unfamiliarly on the ear of most of us : *O beata Trinitas*. But it is an august and magnificent composition ; and nothing could more accurately have accorded with those rare speculations in which Anselm was already employed, and which must engage our own attention in the next chapter.

[1] The *O beata Trinitas* is attributed to Alcuin, and is to be found amongst his works. It is a lengthy but exquisite composition ; a profound theological treatise in rhythmical form. I am sorry that it is too long for transcription.

CHAPTER VI.

ARCHBISHOP LANFRANC: THE MONOLOGION.

IT was at an early part of the period embraced by the last chapter that three theological students in a recently erected monastery in Lower Normandy entertained, or rather employed, themselves—for they were less in jest than in earnest—during a brief cessation in a lecture on Holy Scripture by endeavouring to peer into the future after a fashion which, quaint as it was, has not even yet died altogether out in our own country. The book of the Gospels being in the hand of one of the three friends at a moment when the lecturer's attention was called off from his work, they resolved that each of them in his turn should open the sacred volume at random, and in the passage first offered thus to his notice accept a Divine intimation of the lot that was to be his own, it being their special wish to learn which of them was to be an abbot and which a bishop.[1] The first to investigate his destiny was rewarded with the words, ' Fidelis servus et prudens, quem constituit Dominus super familiam suam ; ' and the second with others not unlike them, ' Euge, serve bone et fidelis ; intra in gaudium Domini tui ; ' but the third, whose name has not been recorded, was unlucky enough to light upon a text which, whatever it may have been, galled and fretted him. The other two, either amused at his discomfiture or entertained by the words which had caused it, broke out into fits of laughter, loud

[1] ' Experiamur, inquiunt, revolutione foliorum, quis nostrum futurus sit abbas, quis episcopus.'—Gml. Malm. *De Gest. Pontif. Angl.* lib. i. *De Ep. Roff.*

enough to bring back the lecturer, who no sooner heard what had taken place than with all gravity and seriousness he foretold that the first would some day be a bishop, and the second an abbot; but that the third would retrace the steps which had brought him to the cloister, and lapse into the slippery ways of the secular life.

It would, of course, be both unjust and unphilosophical harshly to censure this rather solemn diversion of three theological students who belonged to an age in which the use of any substitutes, provided only that they were Christian, for the sortileges of paganism was in itself a victory for Christianity, and to a country only separated by a narrow streak of sea from that England whose faith was still disfigured by many remnants of heathenism. But this consideration is scarcely adequate to the case; for the lecturer accepted the three prognostics with perhaps even a fuller confidence than his disciples, and the lecturer was not a Norman. Nor were his hearers immature and thoughtless youths. One of them, the future bishop, was between forty and fifty years of age, and was none other than St. Anselm's friend Gundulf; the future abbot was Walter, who subsequently administered Evesham; the abbey to which they belonged was St. Stephen's at Caen, and their lecturer no less a man than Lanfranc himself.

Of all prognostics—prognostic was the proper technical name for these forecasts drawn from the inspired page—none was more sacred than that which at the consecration of a bishop gave mysterious hint of what was now to be. I need scarcely say that there is an interval in the course of that function during which, whilst the bishop elect kneels at the foot of the altar, the book of the Gospels is held open across his shoulders, but with the text towards him. The book is opened at random, and the prognostic of Lanfranc and his contemporaries was the first passage on the left-hand page. When Hernost, Anselm's immediate junior at Le Bec, was in 1075 consecrated to the see of Rochester, the book opened at the words 'Citò proferte stolam primam.'[1] As soon as the chief officiant heard this, he replied that Hernost would not live long; nor did he. The chief officiant was Lanfranc.

But Lanfranc's own *prognosticon* on August 29, 1070, is of peculiar interest to all who love to trace his relations with Le Bec during Anselm's priorate. It was this: 'Date eleemosynam, et ecce omnia munda sunt vobis.'[2] The bystanders received it with murmurs of delight, and he himself no sooner heard the words than he cried, his countenance lighting up with joy, 'Let us, then, contend one with the other, Thou, O God, in giving, and I in giving away,'

[1] 'Bring forth quickly the first robe,' as the Douay version has it. The phrase *stola prima* was held to symbolise the state of the beatified soul pending the resurrection of the body. See S. Greg. Magn. on Job xlii. 11; S. Bernard, Serm. de Diversis, xli. § 12, and Serm. iii. *in Fest. omnium Sanctorum*; St. Anselm, *Med.* ix., and *Med.* xvii., falsely attributed, however, to him ('Postremò et mundâ sindone primæ stolæ spiritum meum involve in quâ requiescam . . . . die autem tertio . . . . me indignum resuscita ut in carne meâ videam claritatem tuam.' 'Expectant fideles . . . . ut in die resurrectionis duplici stolâ, scilicet corporis et animæ perpetuâ felicitate fruantur'); Radulf. Ardens, Homiliæ in Ep. et Evang. Domini P. I. hom i. ('corpus cum animâ stolâ gaudebit immortalitatis'). In the tract *De Inventione Sanctæ Crucis Walthamensis*, published in Michel's *Chroniques Anglo-Normandes*, we read of Edward the Confessor, 'Dissolutâ igitur hujus habitationis domo, domum non manufactam accepit rex ille gloriosus in cælis . . . . decoratus unâ stolâ, securusque de reliquâ.'

[2] Milo Crispin says, 'Repertum est *super caput ejus* evangelicum dictum Date eleemosynam,' &c. . . . It seems just possible that the book may have been held over the head, and not across the shoulders, in the case of an Archbishop of Canterbury. There certainly were differences of detail which distinguished the consecration of the Primate of the Britains from that of a suffragan. Abbots as well as bishops had their *prognosticon*, which might be sought on other solemn occasions besides that of consecration. Guibert of Nogent (*De Vita sua*, iv. 3, p. 491) gives a curious account of his own on his taking possession of his monastery. Guibert tells us of a Bishop of Laon at whose consecration the book was opened at a blank page 'ac si diceret. De eo nihil vaticinabor cùm nulli pene futuri sint actus,' and who died in a month or two; and of another—and he was not the first to whom this happened—whose *prognosticon* was, 'Tuam animam pertransibit gladius.' He was still alive when Guibert wrote. 'What bad luck awaits him, God knows,' exclaims the writer (*ib.* pp. 499, 514). St. Wulstan's *prognosticon* was 'Ecce verè Israelita in quo dolus non ' (clxxix. 1747D).

and from that moment obeyed the consolatory precept with no less alacrity, no less fervour, and no less constancy, than if an angel had planted finger on the text. Witness his charities to the poor, which were boundless so long as prudence set no limit to them, and particularly such poor as by relationship to any of his own monks seemed to have peculiar claim on his bounty ; witness his spontaneous largesses to poverty-stricken monasteries and to needy clergymen ; witness his famous recovery to the see of Canterbury of estates wrested from it by a kinsman of the Conqueror's ; witness the churches and manor houses which he built or reconstructed throughout his domains, and religious and eleemosynary edifices erected in the primatial city, the metropolitan church of which would alone have sufficed to perpetuate the name of Lanfranc as the restorer of the ancient glories of Canterbury and the author of its new.

Nor was Le Bec forgotten by his generosity—the home in which he had spent full twenty years of his life. For although its inmates could in 1073 boast the possession of a church which had, perhaps, but one rival in the duchy, the builder had been paid out of numerous small pecuniary contributions, and their income from real property was scarcely greater then than it had been in 1058, when Lanfranc's school was reopened, or in 1062, when it was permanently closed. The house was not without benefactors, it is true, but the benefactions took the form of alms, not of endowments; and Le Bec, so far from being a wealthy institution during Anselm's priorate, was not even self-supporting when he was elected abbot in 1078. Its fortunes were eventually secured by endowments in England ; but until these were settled on it, its best, indeed its only considerable, benefactor was Lanfranc, whose messengers never crossed the Channel empty-handed,[1] but always brought presents in money, and sometimes gifts of other kinds for

---

[1] On one occasion he infringed the rule, but sent such an apology for the omission as drew from Anselm one of his own characteristic letters (*Ep.* i. 41).

the embellishment of its church, such as the embroidery described by William of Malmesbury, in which, precious as was the material, the skill of the worker had given it a new value all its own, and the eye of the beholder wandered from floor to roof, charmed and dazzled by contrasted play of colour, by brilliancy of tint, and by exquisite harmony of composition.[1]

And Lanfranc's attachment to his old home was displayed in other ways than in direct contributions to its money chest or its treasury. Thus there was at Arras[2] a *monetarius* named Girard—minter, no doubt, to the Abbot of St. Vaast—who was very anxious to assume the religious habit of Le Bec, but was unable to do so on account of certain grave pecuniary embarrassments. When the Archbishop heard of the case he at once proposed to contribute no less than a hundred *solidi*— a sum equivalent to two hundred pounds sterling of our modern money—in liquidation of Girard's liabilities. Girard went to Canterbury, and there, after giving the prelate, under oath as it would appear, an exact account of his pecuniary condition, received not only what was wanted for the discharge of his debts, but enough besides to make a handsome donation to the monastery of his choice upon his reception as one of its members.

The correspondence upon Girard's case is too long and discursive for reproduction in these pages, but it shows, past possibility of mistake, that if Anselm was all aflame with desire to receive into his community those who for the good of their souls were anxious to form part of it, his true and faithful friend Archbishop Lanfranc was not less eager to gratify the spiritual yearnings and relieve the temporal neces-

---

[1] *De Gest. Pontif. Angl.* lib. i.
[2] There seems to have been a famous guild of goldsmiths—a *caritas monetariorum* - at Arras. One of them made the famous reliquary which contained the relics of the Blessed Virgin preserved at Laon (see Hermann, *De Miraculis S. Mariæ Laudun*). There is also record of a *vicus monetariorum*.

sities of the saintly Prior. Girard's was the last profession made in the old or second monastery.[1]

And, not satisfied that Girard should go to Le Bec with a full purse, the generous Archbishop about the same time committed to Anselm's care two young men sent by him from Italy to Canterbury whilst he was on his journey to Rome for the pallium in 1071. The correspondence relating to one of the two can scarcely fail to interest the reader. The first letter is from Anselm:—

> 'We are debtors without hope of discharge to the paternal kindness which keeps us ever present to your thoughts; and if we cannot always give tongue to our gratitude, the moment has come when we may not impose silence on it. Such is the exuberance of your kindness that you have now at last by the most convincing of arguments proved it to be, what we well know it was, most real and genuine; and have by the sacredest of pledges shown it to be, what we had no doubt of ever finding it, unalterable. For you have sent us your dear nephew Lanfranc, and have desired that he should enter religion in our monastery in preference to all others. None would willingly entrust his dearest kinsman to any but such as are themselves dear to him; and it is unlikely that he should not love the home where that dear one dwells. So that in sending your nephew hither you have evinced not only the constancy of your attachment to us, but, what we equally prize, your conviction of our attachment to you. Thanks therefore do we render first to Him from whom is every good, and then to you (*paternæ vestræ sublimitati*) that you thus love us, thanks that you thus trust us, thanks that you thus confide to us so precious a pledge of your love and of your

---

[1] Girard's affairs were settled by the Archbishop in the early part of 1073, and he seems to have entered upon his novitiate soon after the following Easter. It was in the intervening Lent, the Lent of 1073, that young Lanfranc and his friend Guido reached Le Bec. They were professed without delay.

trust. Accept this expression of gratitude not only as mine, but as that of our whole community.

'But I am now fain to add in my own name, and in few words, and as to one who understands all my meaning, that even though of late you have enhanced the unequal burden you once laid on me, the heavy burden of the priorate, you have lightened its weight most materially; and, at a moment when my weakness groaned beneath the load, you have made me, I will not say unwilling, but as nearly unwilling as may be to set it down.'[1]

The Archbishop, than whom none could better appreciate the solid argument that underlay what a careless reader migh regard as a mere rhetorical flourish, replied as follows :—

'*Domino, patri, fratri, amico Anselmo, Lanfrancu peccator, perpetuam à Deo salutem.*[2]

'What is best for me you well know (*Quid mihi expedia beatitudo vestra optimè novit*), for on my return to England as on my journey to Rome, I communicated to you (*sanctitati vestræ*) all that the occasion seemed to require from me. Pray, therefore, pray, and ask your friends and all you love to unite with you in praying, that Almighty God may be pleased either to make me more fruitful for His glory than I am, or to remove my soul from this prison of the flesh in the confession of His holy name. For this land in which we are reels under the daily shocks of so many and so great afflictions, is defiled with so many adulteries and other abominations, that there is scarcely any order of men who care for their own souls, or even so much as care to hear the salutary teaching which might instruct them to improvement in the sight of God.

[1] *Ep.* i. 19. Guido, Lanfranc, and Girard would seem between them to have made the poor Prior quite a rich man for the moment. Hence, perhaps, the completion of the new building in the course of the following summer.

[2] Nothing was more usual in Lanfranc's letters than such descriptions of himself as *indignus antistes, indignus vocari antistes,* and *peccator.*

'It was a pleasure to me to receive the letter you sent me by Dom Robert,[1] and a still greater one to read it. Indeed, I read it again now, and treasure it; and treasuring it read it even once again, with how much delight I cannot express to you in writing; because, as that letter informs me, you have received my dearest nephew,[2] whom I love as I love my own soul, with no small pleasure, as discovering in my committal of him to your care a fresh assurance of my love for you (*amoris mei*—a pretty change from Anselm's *dilectio*) and, though last not least, because the burden of your office, which before seemed too heavy to carry, has been lightened by his arrival. I declare to you without waste of words, and what I truly feel, that even if he were living in the same house with pagans I should have a kindlier feeling (*plus diligerem*, not of course *amarem*) for pagans than for any other, and any worldly goods I had should be at their disposal. So that I render all the thanks of which I am capable to God, to the Lord Abbot, and to all of you; for I always find you to be towards me and all who are dear to me such as I hoped to find you.'[3]

The Prior of Le Bec replied:—

'*Domino reverendo, patri vere diligendo et dilecto*[4] *catholicæ matri amplectendo archiepiscopo Lanfranco frater Anselmus suus, quod dignius potest, totus suus.*

---

[1] Dom Robert seems to have been a confidential messenger between the Archbishop and the Prior.

[2] '*Dulcissimum mihi fratris mei filium.*'   [3] B. Lanfranci (Ep. 43).

[4] Our conventional *dear*, as when we say 'dear sir,' 'dear madam,' represents fairly enough the Latin *dilectus, dilecta*. Thus St. Anselm writes to Queen Matilda, 'Dominæ et filiæ in Deo dilectæ,' and to Archbishop Hugh of Lyons, 'Domino et patri cum dilectione reverendo et cum reverentiâ diligendo . . . . Hugoni.' Precisely thus Spenser, dedicating the *Faery Queene* to the sovereign, says—

'The which to heare vouchsafe, O dearest dread, a while.'

The word *dread*, again, in this line represents the Latin *reverentia*, and the well-remembered 'most dread sovereign' is a perpetuation of the mediæval *reverendissime*.

'Whenever you are pleased to learn that I am pleased, I myself experience a new pleasure, and what was at first a great pleasure becomes a greater pleasure still. You tell me that you are happy in finding that I, not to say others also, was delighted to receive our dearest Lanfranc, your nephew. My first joy therefore is enhanced by yours, and the satisfaction which I proved in the person of one so loved by you, though ever fresh, is renewed by that enhancement; an enhancement this, and a renewal, measurable, I do not blush to say, by nothing else than my own satisfaction in finding how well it has fared with my Maurice, whom you are severing, and severing for yourself, from one by whom he is loved more than by another, and whom he loves as he loves no one else. Do you yourself judge, therefore, what a debt you are contracting to him. For, be the subject and object of so singular a love no matter how worthless, still you owe it to Maurice that he neither love less nor be less loved than heretofore. But, in short, I know the right measure of your justice, and you know the degree of his love and mine one for the other. I say no more in recommendation of him to your care. As to his headache, it is my first and chief request to you, and a request which I press with all possible urgency, that for the love of God and your eternal reward you will have the case at your own instance as thoroughly examined and attended to as may be by your dear friend Dom Albert.'

This short correspondence may not have been without interest to the reader, for it is a fair specimen of the best epistolary style of the age; it gives us a glimpse of the state of England in the year 1073; it shows the affectionateness and unreserve of the friendship that had for fifteen years subsisted between Lanfranc and Anselm; it displays the generosity of Lanfranc's attachment to his old home; it convinces us that to that generosity the community of Le Bec owed their ultimate deliverance from a condition of prolonged and pinching penury; and it introduces to us one whose name has been already mentioned in these pages, a *conscholasticus* of Anselm's who accompanied or followed him to Le Bec in 1059—Dom Maurice.[1]

Lanfranc had been in quest of a monk, young in years but not immature in character, of irreproachable life and cultivated intellect, who should take in hand some special work for him; what work we are not informed, but in all likelihood, if the sequel may be trusted, that of collating and transcribing manuscripts. The required conditions were all united in Maurice, the favourite disciple and from his very boyhood the inseparable friend and companion of Anselm.[2]

Dom Maurice, therefore, was shipped off to England, carrying with him a budget of letters all wet with the Prior's tears; letters to the Archbishop, to Prior Henry, to Gundulf, his old friend and rival in sanctity—another of his many losses due to Lanfranc, to Dom Herlwin—another migration from Le Bec, and to Dom Albert the physician; letters overflowing with a tenderness, a delicacy, a considerateness, and a pathos such as surprise even the reader who thinks he knows something of St. Anselm into new admiration of a character whose sweetness is without a parallel.

But the regret of Anselm and Maurice at parting from each other was something more than the mutual sorrow of two singularly susceptible and sympathetic natures; it had

---

[1] The compilers of the *Histoire littéraire de la France* say that the title *dominus* 'ne s'accordait alors qu'aux moines d'un mérite distingué ou constitués en charge ou en dignité.' There could not be a greater mistake. Albert the physician was not a monk; the younger Lanfranc was called Dom before he was even a postulant, so was Roger of Caen, so were many others.

I fear these gentlemen were not very accurate, or it may be my own peculiar misfortune never to open their work without finding a mistake.

[2] (1) Anselm had known him from his boyhood; (2) St. Maurice was the patron saint of Transjuran Burgundy, and was no doubt the personal patron of the young man who (3) was professed at Le Bec either with Anselm or soon after him (see Appendix). I suspect that Rodulf, Ansfred, and Maurice all accompanied or fololwed him from Aosta.

an intellectual as well as a moral element. If Anselm was the most original teacher, the acutest reasoner, and the profoundest philosopher of his age, Maurice was the teacher's, reasoner's, philosopher's favourite disciple. Lanfranc, it is true, had long ago gauged the Prior's intellectual stature, and estimated his capabilities of enterprise; but Maurice knew more than Lanfranc had even suspected of his speculative flights. To say that Maurice had not only been instructed in collating, correcting, and transcribing the literary treasures which Anselm lost no opportunity of culling from whatever source, but had learnt from him the value of accurate scholarship, of severe and exact theology, and of scientific criticism, would be saying much indeed, but after all too little; for he had been taken into the confidence of Anselm's genius with an intimacy shared by few within the walls of Le Bec, and by none, absolutely none, outside them; and he had done justice to that confidence. It was not therefore without one pang more that Anselm saw Dom Maurice transplanted to a new home, where, always excepting the Archbishop and a few others, he would be doomed to live among barbarians. The word sounds harsh, but the men who used it saw no injustice in it; for, blind our judgment as we may, the facts remain that the grain of the Saxon nature was coarse, that the English at the period of the Conquest were addicted to pagan superstitions, that their tastes and habits were gross, that they loved to eat enormously of ill-selected dishes and drank strong ale to scandalous excess, that their public monuments were mean and inartistic, that their scholarship, or such ill-digested knowledge as may be adorned with the name, was contemptible, that in morals and intellect the secular clergy were only not worse than their stupid brethren of the laity, and the regular clergy only not worse than the secular, boorish and unschooled.[1] It was therefore from intellectual

---

[1] *Agrestes et illitterati.*

as well as from moral sympathy with his young friend that the bereaved Prior wrote to Dom Herlwin of Canterbury:—

'I commend Dom Maurice to you. You well know how fond we are of each other, and I should like him to be happy enough to have found in you a brother whilst living amongst *barbari*,[1] and you to make it evident that, far removed though you be from me, you have retained your place in my catalogue of friends.'

But, dear as Maurice was to Anselm by reason of his moral and intellectual endowments, his name claims a very special interest from us, inasmuch as there can be little question that but for him the argument of his master's 'Monologion' would never have been committed to parchment, or that, even if committed to parchment, it might never have been allowed to pass beyond the walls of Le Bec. He had not failed to remark that Anselm's arguments concerning the existence and being of God appertained to a domain of thought unattempted by St. Augustine, whose treatise 'De Trinitate' had been for six centuries the common property of Christendom. Undoubtedly St. Augustine had discerned in man's spiritual constitution, and even in the phenomena

---

[1] It may indeed be objected that the word *barbari* need not mean more than foreign. On the other hand it may fairly be doubted whether the word has not always carried with it a certain ethical flavour suggestive of outlandishness or boorishness. Thus Ovid sings of the open-mouthed savages who could not have appreciated his language, even had they understood it:—

'Barbarus hic ego sum ; quia non intelligor ulli :
Et rident stolidi verba Latina Getæ.'

And it is scarcely probable that the word should ever have lacked that flavour in the Latin of St. Anselm's days. I know of no case, with the exception of one presently to be noted, in which it can have meant no more than *foreign*, but of several, some of them amusing enough, in which it meant nothing less than *barbarous*. As regards our own country, St. Yves of Chartres once wrote to an Archbishop of York as follows:—'Benedictus Deus qui conversationem vestram lucere facit in tenebris barbaræ nationis' (Ep. 215).

The exceptional case to which I referred just now makes good rather than disproves my assertion ; so at least I think. It is where Rodulf Glaber in the preface to his History contrasts *orbis Romanus* with *transmarinæ seu barbaræ provinciæ*.

of the physical world, the bases of an inductive argument whence might be drawn corroborative proof of the verity that in God, who is One, there is such a threefold Personality as Divine revelation has made known to us. Undoubtedly, to borrow his own phrase, St. Augustine had found 'a certain series of trinities pervading the physical universe, whence ascending step by step and ever discerning a like phenomenon, he had crowned his work by seeking, and seeking not in vain, such an intimation in man's spiritual being of the supreme mysterious Trinity as we hope to find when we search after God.'[1] Undoubtedly St. Augustine had detected in the mind, the understanding, and the will of man in relation to what is outside of him, and as regards himself in his consciousness of his own existence, his experimental knowledge of self, and his love of self, a certain adumbration of the mystery that He to whose image man was created is personally Three whilst essentially One. But, by way of philosophical argument, this was the utmost that he had done. Anselm's pupils, however, had sufficient penetration to perceive that the discursive remarks which that argument had suggested to their lecturer were more than the mere *scholia* of a skilful commentator, and better than the mere deductions of a practised expositor, and that, not satisfied with elucidating revealed dogma by what man knows of himself and sees in the outer world, he was striking out an entirely new *à priori* path, and elaborating an argument which, starting from our conception of what the Supreme Being must necessarily be, compels us to own in Him such a Trinity of Persons as revelation has made known to us.

And if they were charmed by the novelty and persuasiveness of his argument, they were also charmed by the philosophical method of which it was an illustration.

Whatever God has revealed is true, and faith accepts

---

[1] S. Aug. *De Fid. Trin.* lib. xv. cap. ii.

what God has revealed with an implicit credence which disdains all idea of any need of demonstration to establish its credibility. To think such demonstration necessary were to set out for Olympus provided with poles and ropes and the other usual appliances for the support of tottering edifices, in hope of making the mountain so firm as not to shake and topple over before the first person who should stumble at its base.[1] Nevertheless, true though it be that the subject-matter of revelation has no need of demonstration by the efforts of reason, yet, inasmuch as reason as well as faith is the gift of God, it is inconceivable that the legitimate deductions formed by the one should be at variance with the facts recognised by the other; so that reason rightly exercised plays her proper part in suggesting the credibility of what is already believed, in exhibiting and elucidating its correspondence with her own deductions, and thus in justifying and making good its claim on us. Her office is *probare*.

Maurice, therefore, and his fellows, fascinated by the charms of a method as new in scientific theology as the Baconian method and the Newtonian were subsequently new in other domains, and fascinated with the enchantment that only comes from intellectual certitude, entreated their master to compose for their perusal an essay elaborated in illustration of it.[2] They begged him, that is to say, to compose an essay

[1] S. Anselmi *De Fide Trinitatis*, cap. i.

[2] It was to be an *exemplum meditandi de ratione fidei*—that is to say, a specimen of the method of thinking out a thing for oneself, the specific object being to show that the assumptions of faith and the deductions of reason on the given subject-matter are in harmony with each other. If it be objected that my explanation of St. Anselm's Latin phrase is verbose, I reply that St. Anselm's Latin is only too happily concise, and that I prefer verbosity with truth to concinnity with a false impression. I cannot translate the phrase word for word and say that the treatise was 'an example of meditation on the reason of faith.' The treatise is not a meditation; much less is it a treatise on the reason of faith. Such unfaithful fidelity of rendering does much mischief both to scholarship and to theology. Not all *conversatio* is conversation; not every *nudus* is naked; *memoria* is not in every case memory, nor does *meditor* always mean I meditate. When Tityrus practised on his reed his employment was a *meditatio*, but it certainly was not a meditation. The scientific search after the cause of the perturbation in Jupiter's

in proof of the position that the dogmas of revelation coincide with the à *priori* conclusions of reason. The chief subject to be handled in this essay was the Being of God.

Anselm refused their request, and persisted in refusing; but in the end their importunities vanquished him. 'I yielded the less unwillingly,' he says, 'as hoping that my efforts would not be known beyond our own limited circle, and that these my brethren growing tired of the treatise as a thing of little value, it would come to be neglected and forgotten. For I only too well know that if it was hard to put a stop to their persecution of me, it was harder still to comply with the terms of their request.'

But the document had not been long written before he saw that no such fate awaited it. First one, then another claimed permission to read it; and slowly the number grew of enthusiastic students who had weighed each phrase, pur-

---

orbit was not a meditation, but it might not improperly be called a *meditatio*. When St. Anselm calls his work an *exemplum meditandi* he means to say that it is a sample or specimen of the thinking-out method - let me be forgiven a very barbarous phrase—of the thinking-out method as opposed to the customary dialogue; a specimen, that is to say, of the way in which a man may solve an intellectual problem for himself in the silence of his own bosom. The treatise is no more a meditation—as the word meditation is usually understood—than it is an oratorio.

And St. Anselm himself explains the word *meditandi* in the sense which I assign to it; for in the opening of his subsequent treatise, the *Proslogion*, he says that he had written this *in personâ alicujus tacitè secum ratiocinando quæ nesciat investigantis*.

Nor is the subject of the treatise the 'reason of faith,' whatever those words may mean; I allude, as before, to Dean Church's rendering of the Latin. Its subject is the Being of God; and the words *de ratione fidei* are designed to describe not by any means its subject, but its method, its plan, its design. The subject might have been original sin or some other; but, provided only that the treatise were written *in personâ alicujus tacitè secum ratiocinando quæ nesciat investigantis*, it was an *exemplum meditandi*; and, provided that the author's object were to show how exactly the deductions of pure reason are in harmony with revealed truth, it was an *exemplum meditandi de ratione fidei*.

Let me add that my interpretation of the words *exemplum meditandi de ratione fidei* is at once justified and illustrated by Eadmer's account of the work; and Eadmer was no mean Latinist. 'Fecit quoque libellum unum quem Monologium appellavit. Solus enim in eo et secum loquitur, ac tacitâ omni auctoritate Divinæ scripturæ quid Deus sit solâ ratiòne quærit et invenit; et quod vera fides de Deo sentit invincibili ratione sic nec aliter esse probat et astruit.'—*Vita*, cap. iii. § 25.

sued each argument from premises to conclusion, and regaled themselves to heart's content on the nameless poetry with which, as in mountain ranges bathed with hues from heaven, its severest and hardiest passages are all aglow. They had been too well schooled, first by Lanfranc and then by Lanfranc's greater disciple, not to recognise much at least of its worth; and rare was the day on which some one of them might not be observed poring with intent pale face over its clearly-written page, heedless of all besides and captivated by its sublimity of idea, by its concinnity of reasoning, by the majestic ease and gradual victorious march of the constituent divisions of its argument, by its pomp of terminology, its lucid diction, and, more enthralling still, that strange but indescribable melodiousness of thought and phrase which marks none but the choicest exploits of human genius, and convinces the reader of the *exemplum meditandi de ratione fidei* that an author who could thus think and write must have thought and written to the minstrelsy of those

> solemn troops and sweet societies
> That sing, and singing in their glory move,

and enjoy the vision of God face to face.

Others, too, there were who, touched by the growing enthusiasm, and proud to know that to one of their own community had been reserved the praise of striking out paths of thought as sublime as they were new, craved permission after they had read the essay to copy it for their own use, and so in the author's phrase 'condemn it to notice.' He withstood their request with practised resolution; but there is a point in such contests beyond which resistance is not only unjust, but unwise. The treatise had been of service to his brethren in confirming their faith and informing their reason; why, then, should they not be allowed to make more intimate acquaintance with it? And if, in consequence of his too persistent refusal, defective or interpolated copies should ever obtain a surreptitious currency, the blame would be attributed to him, and not without reason, of any damage that might thence accrue to the orthodox cause—a cause which was dearer to him than life, and was at that time assailed by very able and very vigorous opponents.

Maurice, too, at Canterbury was plying him with a ceaseless artillery of letters, all charged with two requests most passionately urged, one of them in some sort an alternative to the other; and Maurice, who chief among his pupils had prompted him to essay the *exemplum meditandi de ratione fidei*, but leaving Le Bec before it was finished, had not as yet enjoyed its perusal; Maurice, who finding in the *agrestes et illiterati monachi* about him nothing to compensate for the patrician refinement, the philosophical elevation, and the saintly sweetness of his friend at Le Bec, had exhausted, but exhausted in vain, all his powers of entreaty, persuasion, and *finesse* to bend a prelate resolved to detain him where he was; Maurice, who to console his old master for their separation, intermitted nothing of the drudgery of school days long past, in case that master should have left anything untaught; Maurice, who to please him, and give token of an undying affection, occupied his leisure hours in reading all the Latin classics he could seize, or else in copying for him medical treatises of Hippocrates and Galen full of unmanageable Greek words, and encumbered with unintelligible glosses; Maurice, who had so many and such incomparable claims on Anselm's regard, had reason and justice on his side when he prayed that if there was indeed too little hope of his ever returning to Le Bec to read the treatise, he might at least be allowed to have a copy of it.

The Prior of Le Bec, however, well knew that if he allowed a copy to remain in any custody but his own, duplicates would soon see the day; and yet—for he believed that there were passages in it which might be misunderstood or misrepresented—he questioned whether harm rather than good, or rather, whether harm as well as good, might not come of its publication, and was more than half inclined to destroy it once for all. This was a grave perplexity. He resolved, therefore, as on another critical occasion fifteen years before he had resolved, to consult the one man living in whose judgment he implicitly confided, and to send a copy of the *libellus* across the Channel so soon as that *singularis consiliarius* who was just then in Rome should return to Canterbury.

CHAPTER VII.

CONSECRATION OF THE NEW BASILICA: THE 'PROSLOGION.'

FOUR years had well-nigh passed since the peaceful All Saints' Eve on which Herlwin and his monks took possession of the new church, singing their *O beata Trinitas*, when, in the early autumn of 1077, a whisper flew through cell and cloister that the *summus pontifex*, or, as he was sometimes called, the *apostolicus*,[1] of the people beyond the sea was at the gate. So he was, but scarcely in his character of *apostolicus*; for, on rounding the spur of the hill that overlooked the monastery from the west, he had slipped the episcopal ring from his finger, and, forgetful of his rank, was already within the precinct and hurrying forward to greet the abbot. Herlwin, eighty-two years of age, was an infirm and

---

[1] These designations, although applied *par excellence* to the successors of St. Peter in the See of Rome, were not confined to them. The *summus pontifex* of a province is its archbishop; of a patriarchate, its patriarch; and of Christendom, the Pope. Thus in Folcard's *Life of St. Bertin*, Wido, Archbishop of Rheims, is termed *summus pontifex* and *summus præsul*. As to the term *apostolicus*, there is, of course, a sense in which it is applicable to any bishop; as when St. Odo, on his elevation to the see of Sherborne, is termed by his biographer *pastor apostolicus ovium Dei*, or when Halinard, Archbishop of Lyons, is thus described:—

'Factus apostolici consors et compos honoris,
Duxit apostolicam factis et nomine vitam.'

Then, again, there is a restricted sense in which it is used of the occupant of a *sedes apostolica*, and it was in some such sense that it was applied to an Archbishop of Canterbury. St. Odo after his death appeared and sent a message to his designated successor. 'Nequaquam pallium patriarchatûs sanctæ Dorobernensis ecclesiæ obtinebis, nec unquam in apostolicâ ejus sede sedebis.' Canterbury was an *apostolica sedes* for a reason analogous to that which had made the see of Alexandria a patriarchate. Its founder was sent to our shores direct by the Pope. What St. Peter had been to St. Mark, that was Gregory the Great to St. Augustine of Canterbury.

bent old man, and no match for his friend in agility, though Lanfranc had seen as many as fourscore summers. Ere, therefore, the abbot could throw himself upon the ground before the great Primate of the Britains, the great Primate of the Britains was already falling prostrate before the abbot, who laid hold of him and arrested the homage, himself to experience the like treatment as he in his turn tried to pay his reverence to the illustrious prelate. A long and touching contest ensued—struggle is the very appropriate word employed by Milo Crispin, the prelate's biographer—a contest which was only compromised when each of the old men fell upon the other's neck and kissed him. On entering the cloister, Lanfranc, again in pleasing contempt of the conventionalities of a very ceremonious age, took his seat on the long stone bench which ran round the walls facing the quadrangle, and, looking as much at home and as much like his old self as if he had not been directing the destinies of a kingdom for seven years, won the hearts of all by calling to him first one and then another, first of the older men his ancient friends, and then of the younger ones who were children when he was prior, and finding a few appropriate words to say to each. The very *nutriti* were not forgotten—those wondering round-eyed little oblates, miniature monks in miniature hoods, who had been given or bequeathed to religion by men and women hard bested by the naughty world and desirous for their offspring of a happier lot than their own. In the refectory, too, the great prelate edified no less than in the cloister by taking his place as monk amongst the other monks, instead of accepting the seat of honour due to his rank, and by drinking from the same cup and eating from the same dish as they did. And when it was time to go into choir he refused to have the episcopal chair prepared for him, but went into Anselm's stall, playfully observing that he had not resigned his old office and was prior still. Prior Anselm was probably absent on one of the many errands imposed on him of late by the abbot's inability to leave the monastery.

Herlwin had long since resolved that none but Lanfranc should consecrate his church; and now that a not unimportant obstacle to the attainment of his wish had been removed by the irremediable illness of the Archbishop of Rouen,[1] he found his guest more than ready to accede to the petition, provided only that his business with the King were first transacted.[2] On resuming his journey the prelate left behind him a bounty sufficient to keep the community in food for a fortnight, and hurried on to Court, whence there soon came a messenger announcing Monday, October 23, as the day appointed for the consecration, and presenting to Herlwin another of Lanfranc's unnumbered testimonies of attachment to his old home, the *unde fieret*, the means for discharging the incidental but inevitable expenses of so important a solemnity.[3]

Gilbert Crispin, a member of the community, and subsequently Abbot of Westminster, has described the events of the day with a fervour and a suppressed emotion that can only be appreciated when we recollect that he belonged to a family which yielded to none in its respect for the Abbot of Le Bec ; that he had himself worn the habit at Le Bec in his very childhood ; that his widowed mother, the Lady Eva, dwelt in a house near to the monastery, whose inmates she affectionately called her children; and that his father had lived a benefactor of the house, had died a member of it, and

---

[1] John of Avranches, Archbishop of Rouen, had had a paralytic seizure in the summer, and was speechless. Le Bec was in his diocese. Since the repartition it has been in that of Evreux.

[2] Lanfranc had left Rome, I imagine, as soon as might be after the Feast of SS. Peter and Paul, and approaching Normandy late in August, had made for Brionne, on the chance of finding the King there. Not finding him there, he without dismounting rode on to Le Bec, whence, after a short stay, he proceeded to Rouen.

[3] St. Stephen's Abbey Church at Caen was consecrated on September 13, and Bayeux Cathedral, as it would seem, soon afterwards. Lanfranc was present on both occasions.

lay buried beneath the cloister which witnessed the procession of monks, abbots, and bishops on that memorable occasion.[1] Of bishops there seem to have been five in addition to the principal officiant. One of them was Odo, a legitimate son of the Conqueror's mother, the astute, ambitious, grasping prelate who had held an episcopal see almost from boyhood,[2] and was now *vicedominus* of the conquered kingdom, and Earl of Kent as well as Bishop of Bayeux; another was Gilbert Fitzosbern, of Evreux,[3] a tall man with a long neck, whose peculiarity of figure had won him the *surnom* of the Crane; then there were Robert of Séez[4] and Arnold of Le Mans, of whom little is recorded; and, last in seniority, the agreeable and philosophical Gilbert Maminot, recently appointed to Lisieux,[5] a prelate who diced, hawked, and hunted by day, to the scandal of monks, and only of monks, but who by night sat up to watch the circling sweep of the constellations and trace the mysterious journeys of the planetary stars, and on occasions such as the present played his part with a dignity and a recollectedness sufficient to modify the harsher judgment provoked by his devotion to fashionable sports. Besides these there were a troop of eminent churchmen from every part of Normandy, the most distinguished laymen of the duchy and their wives, and contingents of every order, from France, from Brittany, from Maine, from England, who either swelled the innumerable crowd of spectators or helped to prolong the varied and festive procession that made the circuit of the monastery before entering upon the greater solemnities of the day. One great personage was absent, it is true; the Conqueror

[1] The Marquis William had received the habit of St. Benedict on his deathbed. He must have died in the year 1074, not many months after the removal of the community to their new convent. His remains were still in the cloister toward the close of the last century, and I have a shrewd guess as to their present resting-place.
[2] Appointed in Bayeux in 1049.
[3] Appointed to Evreux in or about 1069.
[4] Appointed to Séez in 1070.   [5] Appointed to Lisieux in 1077.

was unable to assist at a ceremony which attracted all his duchy, and Gilbert Crispin quaintly but not unwisely suggests that Heaven might have been jealous had the monarch shared its joy, meaning to say that since Le Bec was not a ducal foundation, and since its *monasterium* had been slowly and laboriously constructed from the hardly won savings of the *pauperes Christi*, the presence of the sovereign would have been but inharmoniously in keeping with the consummation of an enterprise which the King of kings had manifestly taken under His own special protection. Gilbert Crispin's ideas of propriety were no doubt shared by the prince himself, who sent his apologies for not appearing, and by his queen, who was only present by the 'suitable largess of her bounty.'

The very elements favoured the great event; not a wreath of mist sullied the calm transparency of the soft October sky, and round about the grassy precinct of the fresh, hard-cut architectural pile the variegated and melancholy splendour of the forest foliage gleamed with the peculiar iridescence so familiar to the admirers of our autumnal landscapes. Long before the ceremonies began that dewy sward had been invaded by a multitude whose numbers[1] and whose untutored enthusiasm can only be appreciated by such of us as have witnessed like festive celebrations in provinces on the Continent where ancient manners flourish, and where popular taste, popular sentiment, and popular fervour are by nothing so much gratified as by those ecclesiastical functions in which the lowest prove as keen an interest, and take as unquestioned a share, as the

---

[1] We are informed that when Urban II. in 1096 consecrated a church at Anjou, it seemed as if the fulness of the world (*amplitudo orbis*) had flown into the place. The crowd which some few years later assembled to witness the consecration of the new cathedral at Laon was estimated at two hundred thousand persons—an exaggeration perhaps, but, if so, an unconscious one. It is only those who have lived and moved outside our island that can form a just idea of these immense concourses.

very highest. But when the procession at last emerged from the cloister, and all that Le Bec and all that ecclesiastical Normandy could boast of gravity and pomp, of dignity and splendour, came slowly into view, the half-barbarous and astonished crowd vented their delight, their wonder, and their devotion in murmurs that swelled anon into a tumultuous hubbub and drowned even the trained full-throated voices of the monks of Le Bec and their numerous brethren of the cowl. The wonder was that none of those good people were trampled to death, and that their graceless though not irreverent zeal did not throw processional chant and processional sequence alike into irremediable confusion. When, however, they perceived that the long double file of religious were already entering the house of prayer by its great western doorway, their enthusiasm escaped all bounds, and crosiered abbots [1] and mitred bishops [2] were so jostled and crushed that when they at last forced their way into the church they were not more thankful than surprised to have done so with bones unbroken. But no sooner had the Archbishop crossed the threshold than, entering at every inlet and carrying all the doors off their hinges, the invading torrent poured impetuously in, till positively it could pour no longer, for the very sufficient reason that no physical effort could find room for a single human being more in the stifled and stifling mass of men, women, and children that filled nave, aisle, transept, chapel, and sanctuary of the Church of Our Lady of Le Bec. Happily no one was injured.

Of the altars awaiting consecration after the performance of the other prescribed ceremonies the Archbishop of Canterbury ascended the principal, one being assigned to

---

[1] These had no mitres, unless indeed the Abbot of St. Augustine's, Canterbury, was one of them. He was as yet the only mitred abbot in Christendom, in virtue of a privilege granted by Alexander II. Even at Cluny the mitre was not worn until 1088.

[2] As to the proper dress for a bishop at the consecration of a church, there is a curious letter extant from Lanfranc to Archbishop John of Rouen (Ep. 13).

each of the inferior prelates, so that the quaint and august, because exceedingly ancient, rites of the *consecratio altaris* were begun simultaneously in six several parts of the building.[1] But those rites are so numerous, so varied, and so intricate that each of the officiants, unable to proceed *pari passu* with any of the rest, was fain to resign himself to the vociferous fervour of those round about him, of monks and clergymen gathered from all quarters and mutually unknown, of laymen of rank who knew the psalter and its chant less or more imperfectly, and of people of the baser sort, whose untutored throats were all that was required to improve the fierce rivalry of six distinct and independent groups of singers into such a discordant and afflictive chaos of keys, notes, tones, and cadences as we may well believe had never yet been known in the history of mankind. Nay, more: inasmuch as each group—such was their anxiety to hear their own song and not those of the other five which were distributed beneath the echoing roofs—sang with ever-growing energy, the constituent members of each were not long in falling out among themselves, and at last 'scarcely one of the singing crowd could hear his own voice,' for the more mercurial amongst them, in sheer ecstasy of physical excitement and devotional rage, sang they cared not what so long only as they sang, in utter disregard of that particular part of the function which their efforts might have been supposed to elucidate. The monks of Le Bec, indeed, to whom the church belonged, who had carefully practised their chant, and whose souls were penetrated with a joy that claims all our sympathy, seem to have been distributed about the several altars, with the design of maintaining vocal un-

[1] As the church had been in use since the autumn of 1073, there must already have been several consecrated altars in it. I imagine that three altars had been in use from the first, so that the full number was nine. A tenth was, I believe, added some fifteen or sixteen years later, in honour of St. Nicholas, in a chapel specially built in his honour and surmounted by a tower. The chapel, that is to say, occupied the ground floor of the Tower of St. Nicholas.

animity; but they were no match for their uncontrollable guests and, worsted in a too unequal contest, vented their overcharged hearts in silent showers of emotion, so that 'whilst others sang aloud with the voice of joy and gladness they, fixing their whole hearts' intent upon the Lord, poured forth to Him, and only to Him, the lone melody of their tears.'

The enthusiasm only abated when the miscellaneous crowd of earls and knights and noble dames, of monks and villeins, of children and their shrill mothers, of canons and hedgerow priests, left the church. But the day's work was not yet ended; indeed, the most trying part of it for Herlwin, who had been dangerously ill a week before, and had by sheer nervous effort risen to the exertions of the morning, were yet to begin. Not only in the refectory, but in every available room of the convent, in outlying tenements, in distant farms, at Bonneville and at Le Parc, tables had been set and furnished for all who might choose to partake of the abbot's hospitality. Those whose rank entitled them to more pretentious cheer than the rest vowed—doubtless in obedience to the quaint etiquette of the time—that their host had almost overdone his preparations for them; and for many a long day was it said that never had Easter dinner or wedding feast equalled the profusion of Herlwin's bounty on that memorable occasion. From morning till deep night did relay after relay of religious, some known to a few, some unknown by all, sit down at the groaning boards; from morning till deep night did the indefatigable host with the exigent refinement of his nature busy himself for the comfort of each and all. 'How are they getting on?' 'What do they say to it all?' 'Is there enough for them?' Such were his questions of the servants, who had a busy time of it indeed 'and could not stay for a moment in one place.' The answers to the last of these questions was always the same; there was still enough, enough and to spare. Then would the old man say to himself, 'Quid retribuam Domino pro omnibus quæ retribuit mihi?' 'What shall I render to the Lord? What shall I render to the Lord?' 'And so saying he rendered in thanksgiving all he had to give—that is to say, tears, the sacrifice of tears, the offering of a thankful heart to God for all His benefits.'

The morrow was a day of needful repose for the community, and chiefly for Herlwin. But what was the surprise of all when on the Wednesday morning the Archbishop announced his intention of taking leave of them! 'They all burst into tears, and there was no consoling the little ones; he therefore hurried off as quickly as possible, hoping their sobs might cease at least when he was well out of sight.'

Abbot Herlwin gathered up strength and courage to accompany his friend for some seven or eight miles of his journey.[1] It was a pensive and sacred hour—the last hour of mortal intercourse between those two men, men widely different in race, and wider still in their early opportunities for mental culture; the one bred for the schools, the other made in camps, but heroes both of them, and both most truly wise; since each had in the flower of his manhood relinquished at a call from Heaven what was to him the proudest realisation of youthful dream. And ever since that chill morning when the two men, the one in poverty and the other in nakedness, were so strangely thrown together in their sublime endeavours to live to Him 'who pleased not Himself,' each had learnt to value the other at his proper worth. But although, after so many years of sacred attachment, their last hour was a sad, it was a happy one. The heart of each swelled to think that the last 'Good-bye' would be presently said; but all of natural emotion that it proved was tranquillised and hallowed by the assurance of a not distant reunion, never to be interrupted. So that when the moment came to say it, each did his part, if with choking voice, yet with eyes

[1] *Duo milliaria.*

heroically mastered; and each, when anon he turned to cast a long last lingering look at his friend, comported himself as those do who sorrow, but who sorrow not without hope.

Thus soothed and fortified, Herlwin pursued his way home. He reached the margin of the valley, and looking down upon his monastery, scanned its massive walls, its long-drawn roofs, its solemn tower, proofs and records all of them of Lanfranc's genius, Lanfranc's generosity, Lanfranc's love for his *paupercula mater*;[1] and, round about, the turfy lawn, torn and trampled by the crowd of the previous Monday. What severance from his friend of friends could not do, thankfulness to the Power that had so beneficently watched his life now did. He hurried home and sought his room, and, sinking into a chair, gave vent to all the cataracts of his soul, crying through his tears, 'Nunc dimittis servum tuum, Domine, in pace; quia viderunt oculi mei. Yes, mine eyes have seen what I earnestly craved and ever prayed of Thee that I might see before I died. Thou hast fulfilled my desire; now will Thy servant go to Thee whenever it shall please Thee.'

'Then he kept silence, but the flood of tears he could by no means restrain; until the brother that spoke with him, unable to bear it any longer, was fain to introduce some other topic.'

The good brother changed the subject. Let us follow his example.

To revert, then, to the history of the *exemplum meditandi de ratione fidei*. Such evidence as we possess justifies the conjecture that Anselm would gladly have submitted the work to Lanfranc's inspection; or, rather, since the prelate's vision was impaired by age, would gladly have read it to him, while he was a guest at Le Bec; but that the abrupt termination

---

[1] I borrow this phrase from the Lire codex, which says of him, 'Non est immemor factus suæ pauperculæ matris, sed quoad vixit eam sustentavit, aluit et honoravit vehementer.'

of the visit made this impossible. He therefore sent the treatise after him to Canterbury, accompanied by a letter, in which, asking him to decide its fate, he said :—

'I have prefixed no title to it; for, to say the truth, I have not thought it worthy of being dignified with a name of its own. So, then, if you judge it well that I should have written what I have written, whilst approving it pray give it a name and hand it on to Dom Maurice. . . . But if it cannot bear your examination, do not return me the copy I send you, neither give it to him, but commit it to one or other of the four elements, and destroy it either by burying (in earth), sinking (in water), burning (by fire), or scattering wide (in air). But, whatever your judgment may be pleased to decide, I beg you to apprise me of it, that the copy I have kept may meet with precisely the same fate as that which I have sent you,' &c.[1]

At the same time he wrote a letter to Maurice, and a letter to the younger Lanfranc, who had now been some little time at Canterbury, recalled thither, as it would appear, on account of his health. In the former he sends his remembrances to two young gentlemen, secular clergymen, from Caen, Dom Vitalis and Dom Roger; and in the latter to a Dom Guido, a friend of the Archbishop's nephew, and kinsman, it may be, of the other Guido, young Lanfranc's old companion in travel and in religious profession.[2] In which case this second Guido was an Italian, and may have come from Italy in the train of the Archbishop in the summer of the current year, 1077. As to Vitalis and Roger, it is easy to surmise what had taken them to Canterbury. They must have gone there either to seek admission into Lanfranc's monastery of Christ Church, or else to ask his advice in the choice of a religious home. There seems to have been a

[1] *Ep.* i. 63.   [2] *Epp.* i. 65, 66.

curious interchange of postulants and of professed monks between Le Bec and Caen from 1063 to 1070, and subsequently to 1070 between Le Bec and Canterbury; for when Lanfranc left Le Bec for his new monastery he took three at least of its monks with him, and perhaps even regarded St. Stephen's Abbey as a colony from his own old home; and we certainly know of one—doubtless there were more—whom he sent thence to Le Bec. And whereas at Canterbury Prior Henry, Dom Herlwin, and Dom Maurice were *alumni* of Le Bec, Le Bec had received protégés of Lanfranc's in the second Osbern, in young Lanfranc, and in the elder Guido. There were two reasons for this transference of quite young men to the Norman house, and of others already formed thence to the English. The new civilisation had gained an ascendency at Le Bec which was denied to it at Canterbury, and Anselm was in nothing more successful than in the education of young men at the period of their adolescence. There was a *rationabilitas*, a reflectiveness, a craving for intellectual sympathy, or at least for intellectual response, in his nature, which seems to have rendered him happier in his treatment of young men than in that of children; a craving too for the fidelity and depth and steadfastness of affection which we seek in vain from wayward boyhood. He was not fond of teaching mere lads, but with the hearts of young men, struggling against self and ambitious of sanctity, his own ever beat in unison. He used to compare adolescence and early manhood to wax when in its fittest state for receiving an impression. 'If the wax is too soft, or if it is not soft enough, it reproduces in a very unsatisfactory and imperfect manner the device engraved on the seal; but judiciously choose a moment at which its condition is blended both of soft and hard, press your seal upon it then, and it receives the device in all its fulness of form and sharpness of outline. So is it with the stages of human life. Take a man who has spent all his time from infancy on to gloomy old age in the business of this vain world, a man who savours of earthly things and is thoroughly set to an earthly hardness; treat with him of spiritual things, talk to him about the exquisite charms of Divine contemplation, try to teach him to penetrate heavenly mysteries; and you will soon find that, so far from penetrating them, he cannot even see what you set before him. And no wonder; your wax is set; the man has not spent his time on this sort of thing; he has been schooled in other pursuits entirely. On the other hand; take a mere boy, unformed in age and intellect, and unable to distinguish between right and wrong; discourse as you will about this sort of thing, he will not understand you; no, not even you. And for a good reason. The wax is too soft; it runs: it cannot possibly take the engraving on the seal. Whereas a young man holds the middle place between the two, being happily blended of hardness and softness. Undertake to teach him, and you will be able to mould him as you wish. Such is my experience; hence my peculiar interest in young men, and my care to root up all the seeds of evil in them; that, being in time adequately instructed in the practices of Christian virtue, they may be transformed to the model of spiritual maturity.'

But, however, Vitalis and Guido soon found their way from Canterbury to Le Bec, whilst Roger remained behind. But Anselm could neither understand nor bear the delay, for, Herlwin being by this time helpless from palsy, the responsibility and the joy of alluring the choicer spirits of his acquaintance from the world to the cloister, was henceforth to be his own. He therefore addressed the following letter to his young friend; he was soon to write many such to others:—

'To his beloved, desired, hoped for, and expected Roger, the brother Anselm whom he loves: what is the more pleasing choice to God, and the more conducive to his own good, may he prudently seek and perseveringly adhere to, and happily set in practice.

'That which we have confided to the holy design of God alone I dare not decide by my own will. Still, I may give expression to my desire. I am fretted by your delay, and tormented by my long-protracted expectation of you. My heart cannot, will not forget what, I will not say you certainly promised, but what you certainly foretold me—that I might look forward to your returning and remaining here. And certainly what you said was said in all seriousness. Truly may I say that my eyes have failed for your word, saying, When will you comfort me?. Oh, let me not be deceived, for I have hoped in you; let me not be put to shame, for I have expected you; let not those be astonished nor let those say whom you have sent as the firstfruits of your ingathering and the pledge of your coming, let them not say, Why have you urged others to a home whither you have disdained either to lead the way or to follow? Especially when they came here all the more gladly and have been all the more gladly received by us in the hope of your soon following them. Oh, may the Lord direct your way in His sight! oh, may He direct your heart, and so give you according to your own heart and confirm all your counsels!'

Things have so much altered in the world, in some respects for the better, in some for the worse, that it is doubtless much more difficult to us than it was to Anselm's contemporaries to place ourselves precisely at his *point de vue*, and appreciate an appeal like this at its true worth; but of the sincerity and fervour of the appeal there cannot be a shadow of a doubt, and that sincerity and that fervour are only to be measured by Anselm's estimate of the transcendent merit of the true monastic life. If, however, we cannot learn or cannot realise that estimate, we may at any rate recall the fact that purity of morals was almost unknown outside the cloister; and the picture drawn by this very Roger of Caen in his 'Carmen de Contemptu Mundi' of the precariousness of domestic virtue is simply frightful. Anselm's appeal was not unheeded. The Roger whose name stands immediately after Guido's [1] is that of the poet, Roger of Caen.

But enough to have noted these names. For the *opusculum* has not been committed to the flames, or to earth, or to water, or to air. On the contrary, the Archbishop of Canterbury has written to the Prior about it; and the latter, after making a few, perhaps unimportant, alterations in it, has sent a fresh copy to Canterbury, accompanied by a letter to his *singularis consiliarius*.

Before the summer of 1078 the 'Exemplum Meditandi de Ratione Fidei' was a published work; but it bore no name, and may be almost said to have borne no title.[2] Several years were to elapse before it should be known first as the 'Soliloquium de Ratione Fidei,' and shortly afterwards as the 'Monologion of Abbot Anselm,' or more simply still 'Anselm's Monologion.'[3]

Whilst he was prosecuting the speculations embodied in this work, it had seemed to him that it might be possible to discover a short and simple argument, which should supersede the Platonic mode of proof therein adopted, and which, while establishing the eternity, the omnipotence, the omnipresence, the goodness of God, and the rest, should show that He is not endowed with these attributes as though participator of qualities exterior to Himself, but that they all have their absolute existence in Him, and that in Him they are not

---

[1] The name of Vitalis is the hundred and twenty-ninth; then comes a Bernard, then Guido, then Roger of Caen. Only four other professions were made before Herlwin's death in the August of 1078.

[2] I have had the happiness of seeing, handling, and collating a copy of this the first edition of the work. Its only title is *Exemplum Meditandi de Ratione Fidei*.

[3] That is to say, *Monologion, liber Anselmi*. Thus is the Jumièges copy entitled.

many, but one perfection. An original and bold idea, hitherto without parallel in the history of the human mind, and one which, as he used to say, reduced him to great straits ('quæ res, sicut ipse referebat, magnam sibi peperit difficultatem'); for his tension of thought prevented him from taking either food, drink, or sleep, and, what was more distressing, distracted and worried him at matins and the other offices. Food, drink, and sleep, indeed, were of slight importance to him; what alarmed him was that his quest of an argument in proof of the existence of the Supreme Being should mar the homage he paid Him. But the thing he sought eluded all his efforts; he seemed to be employed in an utterly hopeless enterprise, and he at last made up his mind to banish an idea which he suspected must be a temptation from the enemy of souls. But the more he laboured to get rid of the prepossession, the more rudely did it come back to him;[1] the more he struggled to keep it aloof, the more importunately did it assail him; and his labouring and jaded brain had no repose until one night at matins,[2] when, in the very agony of his effort to ward it off and follow the office undisturbed, suddenly the light broke in upon him; the argument he had sought displayed itself clear and bright to his mental vision, 'and his inmost soul was deluged with unspeakable joy and gladness.' As he stood in his stall in the sombre gloom of the scarcely illuminated choir, his large white hood drawn over his head, none observed his emotion, or saw the tears that rolled down his thin ethereal face, or dreamed that he, their prior, had descried and grasped a proof of the existence of God which should henceforth throughout all time compel the wonder and admiration of our race.

[1] *Magis ac magis* is Eadmer's phrase in the *Vita* and his own in the proem to the *Proslogion*.
[2] '*Inter nocturnas vigilias*.' Not 'in the night watches' (Dean Church), but during the office of matins, which comprised the *nocturnæ vigiliæ*.

A NEW ARGUMENT DISCOVERED.

His ecstasy was scarcely over when it occurred to him that others might be gratified to share the discovery; and as morning brightened up the cloister he traced upon his tablets [1] an argument of which this is a summary: The fool in saying there is no God shows himself a fool; for God is that than which a greater cannot be conceived; and since existence, unbeginning, unending, absolute existence, is a necessary factor in the idea of a being than which a greater cannot be conceived, God necessarily is.

The argument, not sketched thus in outline, but deduced and developed much as we now see it in the second, third, and fourth chapters of the 'Proslogion,' having been committed to the tablets, Anselm handed these to one of the community with instructions to take strict care of them. After some days he called for them, but they were not to be found; whereupon on fresh tablets he wrote out a second sketch, and entrusted the precious charge to the same guardian as before, but with special directions for more careful custody. The zealous and appreciative brother stowed them away in as safe a part as might be of his bed: a monk's bed was a sacred receptacle, to which only the prior and himself had access. But what was his dismay on finding them next day scattered about the floor of the dormitory, and their coating of wax dispersed in innumerable fragments all

---

[1] The tracing upon tablets was termed *dictatio*. The difference between *dictare* and *scriptitare* was the difference between a foul and a fair copy; and it was usual to make the former on tablets, the latter on parchment. Thus, when Osbern, the intrusive Abbot of Evroul (Orderic, ii. 96), had resolved to send to the Pope and ask his blessing, he bade Witmund, a clever monk, write on tablets a rough copy of a respectful letter to Alexander II. (*supplices litteras dictare*), which a young man named Bernard, a *nobilis antiquarius*, was to copy out carefully on parchment (*diligenter scriptitare*). Thus Lanfranc, excusing himself to a friend for the infrequency of his letters, says, 'tot impedimentis subjicio, tot animi rancores . . . . sustineo, tot calamitates . . . . conjicio, ut perrarò dictandi seu scribendi facultas detur' (Ep. 16); and St. Anselm, writing to his uncles, makes *dictatio* the office of the *stylus*, not the *calamus*. 'Utinam in legendo epistolam meam sentiant avunculi mei quem affectum in *dictando* eam testantur oculi mei; velociter enim fuit in ipso initio animus meus lacrymas exprimere quam *stylus* meus litteras imprimere' (*Ep.* i. 18).

over the room! He picked up the broken framework, collected the bits of wax, and carried the forlorn wreck to Anselm, who put them together as an antiquary might the débris of a shattered epitaph in the catacombs, and succeeded, though barely succeeded, in redintegrating their legend. It was now high time to take more jealous precaution, for a little carelessness might doom his few sentences to oblivion, 'and in the name of the Lord, he ordered them to be transferred to parchment. Eadmer speaks with enthusiasm of the little scroll (*parvulum volumen*),[1] modest in compass, but invaluable in its weight of thought and subtilty of speculative effort. Unquestionably a new chapter was opened in the history of human thought when the contents of that little scroll were first made known. It bore no name, and carried the simple but sublime inscription 'Fides quaerens Intellectum.' Several years were to elapse before, in obedience to legatine authority, he was to prefix his name to it, entitling it 'Anselm's' or 'Abbot Anselm's Alloquium de Ratione Fidei.' At a shortly subsequent date he designated it more briefly 'Anselm's' or 'Abbot Anselm's Proslogion.'[2]

---

[1] A scroll, not a leaved book. Thus Orderic (ii. 100) calls a *rotulus volumen*. A certain Abbot of St. Evroul had a very long scroll on which he inscribed the names of his monks, and lower down the names of their deceased fathers, mothers, brothers, and sisters. It was kept near the altar, where it was customary to say, 'Animas famulorum famularumque tuarum quorum nomina ante sanctum altare tuum scripta adesse videntur electorum tuorum jungere digneris consortio.' But once a year this list of names, which he now calls *volumen*, was unrolled (*dissolutum*) and spread across the altar (*super altare palam expanditur*). I conclude, therefore, that the proper meaning of *volumen* had not been lost in the eleventh and twelfth centuries, and that we must eschew the faithless fidelity that would translate *parvulum volumen* 'modest volume.' The *Proslogion* was first of all written on a scroll of parchment. Is that scroll to be found? Or can Anselm in his humility have destroyed it? Or has it perished otherwise?

[2] We have two letters to Hugh, Archbishop of Lyons, the latter of which gives some information about the titles. In the first he says, 'Quod in titulo opusculorum nostrorum nomini nostro addidi nomen *abbatis*, non ideo feci ut personam monstrarem honoratiorem, sed ut nominis excluderem aequivocationem.' In the second he says, 'Precor ut .... illud quod in ipsis titulis positum est, scilicet *de ratione fidei* velut superabundans recidentes, illum quem *Monoloquium* nominavi *Monologion* vocetis; et alterum non *Alloquium* sed *Proslo-*

These two essays, though not the earliest composed, were the earliest published of his works. As philosophical treatises they are unquestionably his most remarkable; and the author of the only authentic portrait of him which I know has happily expressed the contemporary estimate of their value. On either side of the saint there stands a disciple; one holds a book, the other a scroll. The book is the *libellus* once timidly sent across the strait to Lanfranc; the scroll is the memorable *volumen* on which had been transcribed from broken fragments of wax the first *à priori* argument in proof of the existence of the Supreme Being which human genius had as yet constructed.

gion tituletis; et secundum titulorum correctionem finem præfatiunculæ minoris libelli quæ de eisdem titulis loquitur emendetis' (*Epp.* ii. 11, 17). Archbishop Hugh was elevated to the see of Lyons in 1085.

The Jumièges copy is entitled *Proslogion, liber Anselmi.* I have also found a copy entitled *Alloquium,* and one in which survives the first designation, *Fides quærens Intellectum.*

CHAPTER VIII.

THE LAST DAYS OF ABBOT HERLWIN.

AT Cluny, in the middle of the floor of the infirmary, there was an outlined space reserved for a very pathetic purpose. It was there that the monks of Cluny, each in his turn, died. When a monk was seen to be in his agony this space was covered with carpet of sackcloth, on which were sprinkled ashes in the form of a cross, and the sufferer, lifted from his bed by the nurses, and laid thus on sackcloth and ashes, awaited his end. 'How else should a Christian die,' asked St. Martin, 'but in sackcloth and ashes?' Meanwhile the community flew with all haste to the infirmary—only in case of fire or death might a Cluniac monk quicken his step from a sober walk—gathered round the dying man, and sang psalms and litanies in his aid till he expired. When St. Odilo was near his end he fell back in his bed insensible; the brethren caught him in their arms, the sackcloth and ashes were hastily spread, and, thought to be even now expiring, he was laid upon them. But he recovered consciousness, and asked where he was. 'My lord, you are on the sackcloth and ashes,' said Brother Bernard. 'Thanks be to God,' was the reply. 'Are the children here, and all the brethren?' They were all present, he was told. 'Whereupon noting the cross that stood at his feet facing him, he fixed his eyes on it, moving his lips to say a last silent prayer, and then without any convulsion closed his eyes and was at rest.'[1]

And the Carthusian order, whose origin dates from the

[1] Migne, cxlii. 912.

close of the eleventh century, perpetuated this usage of death upon the floor, but seem with characteristic severity to have dispensed with the sackcloth. 'We laid bare the pavement,' says the biographer of our own St. Hugh of Lincoln, 'and sprinkled blest ashes on it in the form of a cross. He, too, blessed the ashes, and then bowed down his head and prayed in silence. And we, lest on his last day he should not hear divine service sung through to its end, began compline. We sang as far as the place of the psalm "He shall cry unto Me, and I will hear him : I am with him in trouble ; I will deliver him, and will glorify him," when he made us a sign, and we laid him down upon the ashes. But we continued singing, only a little faster than before ; and he, with a face all peace, serenest peace, began to breathe more slowly, until, as the choir were beginning the canticle of Simeon, he yielded his spirit into the hand of his Creator.'[1]

Nor was it religious orders only who observed the custom of lifting the dying from their bed and laying them on the ground. Waso, a secular Bishop of Liége in the middle of the eleventh century, when near his end was importuned by the surrounders to let them lift him from his bed, 'as is always done to a dying Christian.' 'Do not weary yourselves in vain,' he replied ; 'I shall depart to-morrow. To-morrow in God's name help me.' They waited till the morrow.[2]

Godehard, a Bishop of Hildesheim in the tenth century, had a servant who fell ill when the prelate was himself near his end. The poor young man was sent home, whither a message followed him from the Bishop, 'Put your trust in the Lord, my son, and be comforted, for the time draws near, and you and I will go home together to the land of eternal joy.' A few nights after, during the very early hours after midnight, the Bishop died, and the bells were set tolling. The lad awoke and asked the meaning of this. 'They are ringing

[1] Migne, cliii. 1104. [2] Ibid. cxlii. 761.

for matins,' said his mother with pious mendacity. 'Why do you deceive me?' he cried; 'why do you keep back the truth? My dear master is going to heaven, but alas! alas! he forgets me and leaves me here! Arise and lift up your hands and hearts, and commend his dear soul to the mercy of God, and entreat him to think of me.' And then he raised his eyes in longing heavenward, and cried, 'O holy prelate and kind father, by Him to whom you go I pray you have a care for me; leave me not here behind, for often have you promised me that I should go home with you.' His friends, stupefied with sorrow, obeyed the poor lad's behest, and then, turning their eyes towards him, saw that the vital spark had fled. They lifted him from his lowly pallet and laid him on the floor, and stanched their tears, happy to know that he had gained his heart's desire.[1]

But not only in episcopal palaces, in religious houses, and under the smoky rafters of poor men's cottages was this traditional use observed; those even who died under no other covering than the blue sky were consigned in their last moments to the lap of earth. St. Emmeram, the Apostle of Bavaria, had been hacked almost to death by order of a pagan tyrant south of the Danube; when, deprived of feet, of hands, of ears, of eyes, of tongue even, his disciples carried him off from the scene of torture in a waggon, hoping that he might die at Ascheim; but ere they could reach the place he cried to them with what voice he could to let them know that his hour was come. They were crossing a meadow three miles from Ascheim. They immediately lifted him from the waggon and laid him on the grass, where he expired.[2]

And the like had recently happened in the summer of 1077, not many miles from Le Bec. Hugh, Bishop of Lisieux, grandson of Duke Richard I. and cousin of the late Duke Robert, was at Pont l'Evêque when he received his sum-

---

[1] Migne, cxli. 1195. [2] Ibid. cxli. 982.

mons to depart hence; but, wishing to die under the shadow of his own cathedral, which he had built in great part and finished during his pontificate, caused himself to be carried thitherward in a litter. He made the journey attended by a convoy of clerks and distinguished laymen, but was seized with the pains of death ere he could reach Lisieux. His bearers carried him from the road to a grassy sward [1] hard by, lifted him from the litter, and laid him on the turf, where he passed away under the warm splendour of a July sky.

When the Archbishop of Canterbury, on the 25th of October, 1077, had hastened his departure from his old home, it was evident that the excitement consequent on the consecration of the church was too much for his friend the abbot. Herlwin had been seriously, even dangerously, ill a week before the ceremony, and only rose equal to the emergency of the occasion by a strain upon his reserved strength, for which he was now to pay dearly. The paroxysm of tears to which the old man gave way, on returning home after he had set forth the Archbishop on his journey, was soon followed by symptoms of paralysis. The limbs lost all their powers, 'and long before the anniversary of the consecration his prayer was granted him.' On Monday, the 20th of August, 1078, he took to his bed; he was convinced that his end was near, and said so. The shadow of death fell like a pall upon the house; its inmates moved about like men stupefied; their hearts were breaking; 'they could not eat, and sleep forsook their eyelids.'

On Wednesday, the 22nd, the abbot asked for the absolution and the other consolations of religion accorded to the dying.

His wish was communicated to the brethren in chapter; whereupon the prior, the father sacristan, and four lay brothers retired to the church, and returned after a few minutes in the

---

[1] A cross was erected on the spot where he died. M. le Prévost says (*O. V.* ii. 309), 'On pense que cette croix devait être placée dans le lieu qui porte aujourd'hui le nom de Pré-l'Evêque.'

following order: first, a lay brother with the holy water, then another carrying the cross, then two more with candles, behind them the father sacristan with the *oleum infirmorum*, and last of all Anselm, in alb and stole, carrying the maniple in the book. As they passed into the vestibule before the chapter-house the whole community rose and followed them to the sick man's room, singing the seven penitential psalms. But in truth theirs was very sorry singing, and the prayers that followed as they stood round about the bed of their dying father could scarcely be heard for the sobs that rose from many an overfraught heart. When the paralysed sufferer tried to say the *Confiteor* he could not articulate the words, and burst into tears; but the will was taken for the deed, and by the time that the brethren had concluded their own confession he had controlled himself sufficiently to say the words of the absolution. Then one by one the flock he had gathered round him—old men, young men, children—passed by his bedside; each gave him the sacred kiss, each received his blessing. He would gladly have addressed them all when this was done, but he had strength left for nothing more than to beg their prayers and receive extreme unction.

The three days and three nights that followed were days and nights of sorrow such as has seldom been surpassed. The time was spent in prayers and uncontrollable distress, and when the brethren said office it was hard work to get through a psalm without breaking down, for if one of them looked another in the face the forlorn expression that he encountered was only too true an index of his own woe.

During this interval the dying man had an indefatigable attendant in Abbot Roger, who had left his own charge at Lessay, so as to be near his old friend at such a time. Roger had lived with him in the early days at Bonneville forty years ago, and none could supply the place peculiarly his own in this emergency; but, since when a monk was dying there must be two in attendance, the second place was Anselm's. On the night of Friday, the 24th, Anselm slipped into the room, unobserved, as he imagined, so as to be ready in case the end approached, and sat himself down out of sight of Herlwin. But, at the first stroke of the bell for matins, the patient roused Abbot Roger, saying, to his surprise, 'Awake the prior, to say matins with us.' At daylight he begged that all the canonical hours of the day might be said in his hearing. This was done, and then, as knowing that he must soon pass away, he begged to be fortified with the most holy viaticum. Abbot Roger hurried to the church, the community remaining in and about the sick chamber; but, strange to say, on opening the *eucharistia*[1] he found that it was empty. His consternation may easily be imagined, but much less easily his joy at the wonderful providence which interposed in this extremity. It happened that a priest who was saying mass for Herlwin was already holding the Sacred Host in his hand, and on the point of communicating. Abbot Roger approached him and craved a portion,[2] which he carried and gave to Herlwin. But the

---

[1] The *eucharistia* was the vessel in which the Sacred Mysteries were reserved, and was probably suspended over the altar. The following from Matthew Paris (*H. M.* s. a. 1140) may interest some of my readers:—'Rex interea Stephanus missam in tantâ solemnitate devotus audivit; ubi cùm de more cereum regio honore dignum Deo offerens manibus Alexandri episcopi imponeret subito confractus est et exstinctus, quod regi contritionis signum fuit. Cecidit etiam super altare eucharistia cum Corpore Christi, rupto filo, præsente episcopo, quod regi ruinæ prognosticum erat.'

[2] In this there was no material irregularity. What Abbot Roger received was termed, at any rate in the diocese of Rouen, the *viaticum morientis*; it is the '*alia media pars*' of the following rubric of the Roman Missal : '[Sacerdos] accipit Hostiam, frangit eam super calicem per medium .... ex parte quæ in sinistrâ remansit frangit particulam .... aliam mediam partem .... ponit super patenam.' In case the dying person for whom mass was said desired to communicate, this *alia media pars* was reserved and carried to him after the mass ; if not, it was consumed during the mass. John of Avranches, Archbishop of Rouen, who was still alive at the time of Herlwin's death, writes as follows in his *Liber de Ecclesiasticis Officiis* : 'Tertiam [partem] viaticum si opus fuerit, in patenâ usque ad finem missæ reservet. ... Tertiam quæ remanet in altari vocat Sancta Ecclesia *viaticum morientis*. ... Si autem opus non fuerit, tertiam sacerdos, vel unus ministrorum accipiat.' I imagine, though I cannot feel sure, that the following passages, one from the Life of St. Odo of Cluny, the other from that of St. Gerald of Aurillac, allude to this custom : 'Cum venisset ad

sobs and tears of Herlwin's children were more than he could bear, and by signs and scarcely articulated sounds he bade them withdraw into the cloister as soon as he had communicated. There they lingered through the woeful day, awaiting his departure. Whenever the door of the room was seen to open all flew towards it in nervous terror, fearing that he was gone and expecting what they feared. Often in the course of the day he would say to Abbot Roger, 'What are they doing? Why do they delay? What is their reason, think you, for not coming?' who answered as we do at such times, not in the speaker's sense, but in another, and said, 'What do you want? They are in the cloister; they are praying for you; they will come as soon as you wish.' Then the sufferer was silent for a space, when again, and with greater agitation, he cried, 'Why do they delay? Why do they not come?' But whom did he mean? asked his friend; who were they that delayed? Herlwin's last word had been spoken; the question had no answer, as indeed it needed none.

The sun sank behind the hill, and the chilly mist was already gathering in white folds all up the valley, before the poor monks consented to retire into the church and sing vespers. Whilst the last echoes from the choir were yet floating through the gloom, the silence of the sick chamber suddenly deepened. Another minute, and Herlwin was stretched on ashes; another, and there was great joy in heaven!

The monastery had already been besieged by a miscellaneous crowd—such a crowd as in those days always came together when an abbot of singular piety was known to be dying; and, as soon as the bells began to toll, tried, in their impatience to wait till the necessary offices had been shown to the dead, to force their way into the cloister. But this they

---

Sanctum Paulum missam celebravit eique Corpus et Sanguinem Domini viaticum tribuit;' 'Quidam de sacerdotibus missam concitus celebravit atque sacrosanctum mysterium attulit.'

were prevented from doing. When the body of Herlwin had been duly composed in the *apparamenta* of his order and abbatial dignity, a procession of sad and sober pomp passed into the choir of the church, carrying their precious burden and singing, 'Subvenite, sancti Dei, accurrite, angeli Dei, suscipientes animam ejus; Offerentes eam in conspectu Altissimi. Suscipiat eum Christus qui vocavit et in sinu Abrahæ angeli deducant: Offerentes.' The outer doors of the church were now thrown open, and the sacred fabric was soon filled with mourners, who, untutored in the expression of their grief as of their gladness, kept noisy possession of it night and day until the rites of entombment were concluded.[1] In those rites several of the foremost churchmen and laymen of the province participated, and to Gilbert, Bishop of Evreux, was reserved the honour of consigning to a grave in the middle of the chapter-house one in whom more conspicuously, perhaps, than in any other of his time had been illustrated the victory of a higher law over what the world held dearest. Forty-four years had passed since Herlwin, the flower of Norman chivalry, tore himself from the court of Gilbert of Brionne, and he had been abbot for forty out of the forty-four.

[1] Herlwin's death took place on what we should call August 25; but, since he died at nightfall and after the conclusion of the offices of that day, the ecclesiastical morrow had commenced, and he was accordingly said to have died on the 26th. Thus St. Hugh of Cluny, who passed away on the evening of April 28, 1109, is reputed to have died on the 29th; and St. Hugh of Lincoln, who expired on the evening of November 16, 1200, 'brevi intervallo post solis occasum,' is commemorated on the 17th. Archbishop Theobald's death is thus recorded by Robert of Torigni (s. a. 1161): 'Teobaldus archiepiscopus Cantuariensis secunda feria Paschæ obiit.' Monsieur Léopold Delisle observes upon this (vol. i. p. 333), 'D'après ce passage, Thibaud serait mort le lundi, 17 avril 1161. Gervais de Cantorbéry met cette mort au 18 avril 1161.' I feel sure that there is no real discrepancy, and that the Archbishop must have died after vespers. It is in precise analogy with this that Roger of Hoveden asserts St. Hugh to have died on Thursday, November 16, although his anniversary was, as he knew, kept on the 17th. There is an apparent discrepancy in the *Life of Leo IX.* which may be explained by a knowledge of this fact. I refer to the date xiii. Kal. Jun. in the account of the prelate's arrival at Toul, an event which took place, according to modern computation, not on the 20th, but on the 19th of May.

A stone of black marble marked his resting-place, 'a memorial of his good deeds; an enduring memorial for his children, that when they meet to confer together on their spiritual employments they may have presented to them the thought of one who left courts to become a monk, forsook the world to lead a supernatural life. . . . I refrain from describing the grief of his bereaved children. . . . If indeed he need our prayers, may God grant eternal refreshment to his soul.'

Providence has ever watched over the relics of his mortality. The chapter-house was rebuilt in 1140, but he slept on undisturbed; and though storm and tempest have over and over again laid low the adjoining church in ruin, and angrier foes than they stripped its shrines of their costly coverings and robbed them of their costlier contents, have even swept its sacred vessels sacrilegiously away and stained its altars with the blood of its defenceless owners; although once, when the danger was greatest, cloister and dormitory were demolished, that what remained might be the better protected with ramparts and trenches, yet the chapter-house stood unhurt, and Herlwin still slept on undisturbed beneath his tombstone of black marble. Year after year—unless perchance when hindered by the disasters that followed upon English invasions of Normandy under Edward III., Henry V., and Elizabeth—the monks of Le Bec kept Herlwin's anniversary, with sombre pomp at first, but as the ages rolled on with gradually lessened signs of grief and gradually heightened signs of joy, until in the seventeenth century upon each twenty-sixth of August his tomb, which by this time had been raised from the pavement and set on six small pedestals of jasper, was covered with a carpet of cloth of gold, all the altars of the church were decked as for a festival, and, except that mass and office were the mass and office for the dead, greater pomp was not displayed at Christmas, at Easter, or at Pentecost than on the anniversary of Herlwin. At last, in the year 1706, permission was obtained from the

Archbishop of Rouen to replace the 'Missa pro Defunctis' by the 'Missa de SS. Trinitate.' Not satisfied with this, the fathers obtained leave to expose their founder's remains to the public veneration, and on July 7 in the year 1707, the grave was opened and its sacred spoils brought to sight. Corruption had spared the flesh of Herlwin.

In 1714 the place of his reinterred remains was marked by a stone of exquisite white marble in place of the black one. What eventually became of it—for it escaped unhurt at the dissolution of the abbey in 1792—will perhaps never be known; but there is a story afloat that its last office was that of a kitchen table in a neighbouring farmhouse, that it cracked and was thrown away. It bore the following inscription:—

HIC JACET
PRIMUS HUJUSCE MONASTERII CONDITOR ET ABBAS
VENERABILIS HERLUINUS
PRIMARIÆ INTER NORMANNOS NOBILITATIS
PATRE ANSGOTO, MATRE HELOIDE, IN PAGO BRIONENSI NATUS
INTER ARMORUM STREPITUS SUMMÂ CUM LAUDE
INTER AULÆ ILLECEBRAS SUMMÂ CUM INTEGRITATE VERSATUS
ABJECTO MILITIÆ SECULARIS PALUDAMENTO
CHRISTO DEINCEPS MILITATURUS
AB HERBERTO LEXOVIENSI EPISCOPO HABITU MONASTICO INDUITUR
ET UT CHRISTUM HABERET HEREDITATEM
BONORUM SUORUM CHRISTUM INSTITUIT HEREDEM
QUOS AGROS QUONDAM POSSEDERAT DIVES
HOS COLUIT PAUPER COLUIT ET JEJUNUS
UT CIBUS FIERET PAUPERUM
ET LABORANTIS SUDOR ET FAMES JEJUNANTIS
LABORES DIURNOS NOCTURNIS LEVABAT PRECIBUS
UT CUM VIRTUTUM STUDIIS STUDIA LITTERARUM CONJUNGERET
LITTERAS QUADRAGENARIUS DISCERE NON ERUBUIT
ET BECCENSI MONASTERIO LITTERARUM APERUIT GYMNASIUM
IN QUO PATERNÆ PIETATIS ALUMNOS ET HÆREDES
ECCLESIARUM PRÆSULES CANDIDATOS
LANFRANCUM, ANSELMUM,
PLURIMOSQUE ALIOS SUI SIMILES DISCIPULOS
AD OMNE VIRTUTIS OFFICIUM SUIS INFORMABAT EXEMPLIS
ABBAS VIRTUTI SIMILLIMUS
QUI PLENUS OPERIBUS BONIS
MORTEM OBIIT VII. KAL. SEPT. AN. D. MLXXVIII.
ÆTAT. LXXXIIII.

PATRI DE SE OPTIME MERITO
ÆTERNUM HOC PIETATIS MONUMENTUM PP.
MONACHI BECCENSIS CONGREGATIONIS S. MAURI
ANNO D. MDCCXIV.

As to the chapter-house, it, like the church, was rased to

the ground in 1809; and to this day there is not a corner of road, or street, or lane, or bridge within a mile of the tower of the Abbey of Le Bec that has not some exquisite fragment of carved mullion or of tracery for its curb stone. The very pigsties of the peasantry are constructed out of fragments of the church and chapter-house of blessed Herlwin's venerable abbey.

And what of blessed Herlwin's[1] remains? The story is a short but a consolatory one.

In the August of 1792 the curé of the adjacent *bourg*, a place which owes its existence and its prestige to Herlwin, and after Herlwin to Anselm, obtained leave from the directory of the Department of the Eure to transport the body of *le bienheureux Hellouin* from the recently deserted chapter-house to another resting-place. On Saturday, October 13, 1792, the massive and enormously weighty coffin of stone in which it reposed, and still reposes, was exhumed, and then slowly and laboriously dragged to the parish church of Le Bec Hellouin, where on the following day all that was mortal of the founder of Le Bec was committed to a new grave.[2] May the kind angels that have during eight centuries defended his ashes from insult prolong the same tutelary charge till the day dawn when those ashes shall revive!

[1] This is his proper designation. He is never mentioned at Le Bec save as *le bienheureux Hellouin*.
[2] An authentic account, hitherto unpublished, of this translation will be found in the Appendix.

Book III.

St. Anselm Abbot of Le Bec

CHAPTER I.

ST. ANSELM ABBOT-ELECT OF LE BEC.

THE monks of Le Bec, some hundred and twenty in number,[1] were seated round about their chapter house.[2] The prescribed psalms and prayers had just been recited, and they now awaited with some eagerness, it may be with some misgiving, the issue of a conference, the prospect of which had during several days contested with their tears for Herlwin every spare moment of their time. Herlwin's grave lay there in the middle of the chapter house; his tenantless chair stood at its upper or eastern end. Who was to fill it?

It devolved upon Anselm, as prior, to open the deliberations; but he had no sooner spoken than one of the elder monks rose and proposed that the prior himself be elected abbot. Anselm, who was less surprised than disconcerted, obeyed, nevertheless, with all promptitude the guide which now, as ever, presided over his conduct, and without waste of words set forth severally and clearly the various reasons which constrained him to decline the honour.

And what were those reasons? Eadmer observes an exasperating silence, not only upon this particular, but upon others, which we may think ourselves only too fortunate to learn from alien or accidental sources. It is not Eadmer who informs us that, after finally but most reluctantly yielding to

---

[1] Not more, I should say, than a hundred and twenty. A hundred and thirty-seven names had been inscribed since the establishment of the house; and by this time there had certainly been thirteen removals, whether by death, preferment, or emigration, and there may, of course, have been a few more.

[2] The chapter-house was pulled down some sixty years later to make way for a larger one, which subsisted till the present century.

his brethren's obstinacy, Anselm paid no homage to the sovereign when he received seizin of the abbey; or that he refused to fill the abbot's chair, to take his place in the abbot's stall, or even to touch the abbatial crosier, until he had been consecrated; or that the ceremony of consecration was postponed for nearly six months after the election.[1] These three facts had in Eadmer's day a significance which it is scarcely possible to exaggerate, and on which, for that very reason, this is not the moment for dwelling; nevertheless, his passing them over as he does provides us with a conjecture in explanation of his silence as to the motive of Anselm's refusal to accept the abbatial dignity.

But let us follow Eadmer's account so far as it leads us.

The Prior's brethren in religion were sufficiently staggered by the multiplicity and variety of his reasons, by the gravity of some, if not all, of them, and by the ability and earnestness with which they were enforced, to adjourn their deliberations. But the penetrating eye of their victim soon perceived that, if their judgment had faltered, their will gave no sign of consenting, and forthwith he felt the first pangs of such distress as he had never known before, and little dreamt that he should ever know again. Chapters were held on several

[1] We are indebted for these facts to the following account printed by Dom Bouquet from a MS. in the National Library at Paris:—

'Operæ pretium puto mandare litteris his qui sunt et qui futuri sunt post nos quo ordine et quâ libertate Beccensis Ecclesia constat ab initio. . . .

'Hic vir (Herluinus) nobilis genere et moribus postquam decessit, monachi illius, qui jam cœperant adolescere in bonitate et religione, prudentiam pastoris amissi retinentes, cautis consiliis in omnibus se providentes, Deo se primum commendaverunt, orationibus et jejuniis obnixè pietatem illius postulantes ut dignum pastorem eis proponere digneretur. . . .

'Electione peractâ innotuerunt hoc scilicet suam electionem principi Willelmo. . . .

'Princeps vero Willelmus cum honore et gaudio suscepit eum abbatiamque ei tradidit donatione baculi pastoralis, sicut mos est illius regionis, nec ab eo requisivit ullum hominium. . . . Sed Anselmus nullo modo consensit ut baculum portaret nec aliquid agere volebat nisi quantum in prioratu faciebat. Quapropter monachi acceleraverunt negotium ut benediceretur. . . . Gislebertus Ebroicensis episcopus peregit hoc opus in ipsâ Beccensi ecclesiâ, . . . vii. Kal. Martias. Dom Bouquet, *Recueil.* xiv. 270.

successive days, the Prior evermore reiterating his reasons, and his auditors opposing evermore to each argument, as it dropped sententious and irrefutable from his lips, the proof armour of an imperturbable obstinacy, until things came to a dead lock; as well they might, if one of Anselm's reasons was what I believe it to have been. But of this presently. The days came and went, but each day in its turn brought additional intensity to a mental torture which Anselm's monks, much as they might pity it, unanimously refused to relieve; chapters were convened and dissolved, but each chapter left him in worse plight than it found him, till, pushed to the very brink of despair in bootless quest of some way of escape, he was at last compelled to avow to himself that there remained but one desperate alternative; still there was one. The electors were deaf to reason; might it not be possible that they would listen to persuasion?

But the electors had, on their side, grown implacable; their patience was utterly exhausted, and the last moment for persuasion was irrevocably flown. They assembled once more, therefore, but this time, as it would seem, under the presidency of the cloister prior, and then once for all requested their victim to have done with objections which they knew by heart and were tired of hearing, and to yield instantly to their unanimous decision. This was rough treatment for so sensitive a nature as Anselm's. He burst into tears, and, with a cry that harrowed every heart, fell on his face upon the floor, praying and conjuring them in the name of Almighty God, and by the bowels of their compassion—if human hearts they had—and as they hoped for the mercy of God, to take pity on him and stop short here, and quit him of such a burden. But they had themselves endured much more pain than they had chosen to betray; emotion begets emotion; and therefore, but to his infinite dismay, they all did as he had done—fell prostrate as one man from their benches round about the chapter house, and so, in that posture of utter abasement, pleaded that it was the abbey that needed pity, they that needed pity; that surely the common good was not nothing to their prior; and that, after all, since they were many and he one, it were ill to sacrifice the many to the one and save self at the expense of others. The let-loose emotion of a hundred and twenty men could scarcely be easy to withstand; but, weighted with an argument like this, it was all but irresistible. Indeed, the argument is so precisely in Anselm's own style, and so absurdly like some of his own perfectly logical but semi-mathematical appeals, that one would dearly like to know who invented it. It was a *hunc suo sibi gladio* with a witness. Anselm's agony of distress is not to be described, and none of the participators in that strange scene seem to have retained a coherent recollection of what followed; whilst Eadmer, like a true artist, stops short abruptly.

But did we imagine that it was what the biographer styles the dogged affection and affectionate doggedness of Anselm's monks which won them the victory we should be much mistaken. Anselm had in him a capacity of obstinacy and resources of immobility which would have left him master of the field after a hundred such encounters, and the religious of Le Bec had neither themselves, nor their doggedness, nor their devotion to the prior to thank for their ultimate victory. Their ultimate victory, I say; for Anselm's was not an unconditional surrender. The success they hailed at this memorable meeting early in the September of 1078 was not finally assured them until late in the succeeding February.

Here, then, let us pause to note the concluding passage of Eadmer's account:—'At last the affectionate doggedness and dogged affection of the brethren, who desired to bear the yoke of the Lord under Anselm's government, won the day; but another and incomparably the greatest factor in their success was the injunction once laid upon him under obedience by Archbishop Maurille, on no account to refuse to carry the burden of any higher preferment that might hereafter be imposed on him. For, as he used to protest, he would never have consented to be made abbot but for the constraint of this injunction. It was by violence such as this that he was made abbot, and with due honour consecrated at Le Bec.'

Now, upon a careful examination of the whole account, it becomes abundantly clear that Anselm's more than obstinate refusal was inspired from the first by something else than that natural diffidence which the prospect of grave responsibility is apt to engender; for, had that been all, the obligation to obey Archbishop Maurille's very sacred injunction would have overcome his reluctance and aversion very much sooner than it did. Had that been all, he would, when the proper moment came, have exclaimed, 'Onus rejicere non audeo,' as he had done twelve years ago, and submitted, if unwillingly, yet without needless parade. The truth is that these scenes in the chapter house do not so much recall his distress in the metropolitan's presence twelve years ago, as anticipate his terrible anguish fifteen years hence at the bedside of William Rufus; and suggest by their very resemblance to the later episode the presence to his conscience of some serious doubt as to what might be his duty under present circumstances; those circumstances being, presumably, such as Archbishop Maurille had not in his time contemplated. The account reads like the record of a mental conflict, which could not have resulted from a less cause than the incidence of new conditions sufficiently grave to qualify even Anselm's estimate of the obligation to obedience which had been so solemnly laid on him by the Archbishop. Nor have we far to seek for the unforeseen circumstances and the new conditions. Gregory VII. had now worn the tiara for five years, and had quite recently, under pain of excommunication, forbidden laymen to give, or ecclesiastics to receive, investiture by the crosier; so that Anselm might well entertain a scruple lest what had been condoned in Archbishop Maurille's day might now be open to reproof as indefensibly similar in form to the condemned usage; I mean the *exterioris abbatiæ potestatis traditio* by means of a pastoral staff. Well might he question whether, even in a case like this, even in a case where the election had been scrupulously regular, utterly uncontrolled, and absolutely unanimous, and where the most unfavourable criticism could find no excuse for dreaming that Duke William, in handing a crosier to the newly elected abbot, would either be consummating a simoniacal contract or giving effect to a pretension to feudalise the Church—well might he doubt whether, even under conditions such as these, he could in conscience allow himself to take part in a ceremony which bore the semblance, at least, of disobedience to supreme spiritual authority.

For he not only withstood the unanimous choice of his monks, but prolonged his resistance to the very verge of a grave fault—conduct which it would be difficult to explain but by the presence of some such serious obstacle as a scruple of conscience.[1] How but thus are we to explain the earnest trial of

---

[1] The election of the fourth Abbot of Le Bec elucidates so remarkably that of Anselm, in its differences no less than in its resemblances, that I am fain to notice it at some length. On the death of Abbot William de Montfort, Boso, the favourite disciple of Anselm's old age and prior of the abbey, was chosen successor. He refused the election on the ground of ill health, and remained inflexible until the Archbishop of Rouen and the Bishop of Lisieux appeared on the scene, when the monks, once more resorting to the form of entreaty which seems usually to have been deemed final and irresistible, threw themselves upon the ground at his feet; but all to no effect. The Archbishop now interfered and required him under obedience to consent, but in vain. The thing, he said, was impossible; his health was unequal to the burden, and, besides, there were in his case grave moral impediments which rendered him unfit for it. 'Are you a monk?' cried the astonished and scandalised Archbishop. 'I trust so,' was the modest reply. 'Very well, then; even if you had murdered twenty men in your time I would not let you off, seeing as I do the feeling of the house towards you.' The horrified Prior rejoined, 'Twenty men! Why, I never killed one.' But there was another kind of murder in the background, and he must out with it. Taking aside the two prelates, he informed them that the Pope—Paschal II., I suppose—had once forbidden him ever to do homage to a layman, and that obedience to the Archbishop was thus rendered impossible. Eventually the King waived his claim to the homage, and Boso was consecrated.

every expedient for slipping the burden from his shoulders ('Quod ipse omni studio subterfugere gestiens'), the many and various reasons laid before the electors ('multas et diversas rationes ne id fieret'), his mental torture on their refusing to entertain them, and his dismay as to what to do next ('anxiatus est in eo spiritus ejus et quod ageret ignorabat')? How but thus can we account for the protraction day by day of all these endeavours, of all this anguish, of all this resourceless quest of a way of escape? What else can explain the final scene—the flood of tears, the heart-rending sobs, the appeal to his brethren's bowels of compassion, and much more that Eadmer had not the heart to set down in writing? All this can scarcely be otherwise interpreted than as the desperate effort to escape of a man reduced to two such grave alternatives as overt disobedience to the explicit and personal injunction of an immediate spiritual superior and seeming rebellion against as explicit a prohibition, albeit a general one, from the supreme pastor of the Church.

He used to say in his old age that it was Archbishop Maurille's peremptory injunction, and nothing else, which won his monks the victory. It would be more correct to say that they owed their triumph to the accuracy of his theological instinct.

And now that he had yielded he was the last man in the world to give scandal by refusing to comply with usages that admitted of a favourable construction, or to anticipate disaster by embroiling the spiritual and temporal powers of Normandy

---

So much for the conflict of obediences to Pope and Archbishop. But there is more to say. Boso had disobeyed his monks before he disobeyed his bishop. The word is scarcely too strong, and I employ it purposely.

No sooner was the difficulty composed than he protested to his monks, 'I wish you to know that from the moment that I perceived your unanimous love for me, if I had known that I must die on the spot, I would rather even then have died than fail to obey your will with all promptitude, but that I feared to offend God.'

Boso was a true monk, and well knew the meaning of monastic obedience. So was Anselm; and he must have had good reason for his conduct.

in a quarrel which might prove in the event to have been raised on a false issue.[1]

His exultant monks lost no time in informing the prince of Anselm's election. William was on the point of moving his court to Brionne, and deferred the grant of the temporalities until he should be at his island castle on the Risle, but was no sooner there than he sent three of his barons—Roger de Montgoméri, Roger de Beaumont, and Guillaume de Bréteuil—to Le Bec to ascertain if the election had been unanimous.

Men like these, men who have mingled in the battle of life in portions of the field where the light fell fullest and in moments of the struggle when passion was most fierce, are often only too glad to pass half an hour in a monastery, and watch, it may be with moistened eye, such intercourse as was that of Anselm with his monks. Roger de Montgoméri, a famous statesman and as famous a benefactor of religion in his own country, had by a life of devotion deserved well of the Conqueror when in 1066 he acted as his vicegerent in Normandy during the invasion of our island, and now enjoyed titles derived from Chichester, from Arundel, and from Shrewsbury. Roger de Beaumont,[2] who was to be invested some years hence with the famous Castle of Brionne itself, and after all end his days in a cloister, can scarcely have been a younger man than Roger de Montgoméri; for his great-nephew, William de Montfort, Anselm's successor in the abbacy, was already in or near his twenty-fourth year.

---

[1] He may, however, have sent to Rome, and I believe that he did. He would never have yielded but that seizin is a very different thing from investiture, and seizin by a crosier from investiture by a crosier. But although his good casuistry had reconciled the apparent conflict between his two obediences, nothing would be less unlikely than that he should insist on the postponement of his consecration until he knew that his conduct had been approved by the Pope.

[2] Curiously enough, Roger de Beaumont had a kinsman who was at this moment living under Anselm as professed monk—his wife's brother, Count Hugh of Meulan. Hugh had retired from the world in 1077, and was the last—or, if not the last, the last but one—to take the habit under Herlwin's administration.

William of Bréteuil was the youngest of the group, but cannot have been the least favourably disposed to the Abbey of Le Bec if he only inherited that affection for it which had inspired his father, William Fitzosbern, to save it from ruin on a memorable occasion a quarter of a century ago. Within a somewhat shorter interval he was himself to find his bed of ashes within its walls.

The three barons paid their visit, made their observations, culled, no doubt, a hint or two from the monks about the abbot elect and his frame of mind, and then, after a decent delay, took leave and rode back to Brionne. They had paced the cloister, breathed a sigh for Herlwin in the chapter house, conversed freely with not a few members of the community, and ascertained, beyond the need of words to certify it, how complete at once and how spontaneous was the attachment of all of them to Anselm. Half of those men were younger in religion, and for the most part younger in years, than their incomparable prior; but the elder half, inasmuch as the last professed amongst them had worn the cowl for some nine or ten years before the prior's profession in 1060, were for the most part well advanced in years, and must, from the interesting fact just mentioned, have formed quite a distinct 'set' from the junior moiety of their body. This elder half belonged to the old days of the mud-built cottages down stream, and well remembered the chagrin at the foreigner's early preferment which had so sadly tried some of them; but they remembered better still the patient obstinacy of his unfailing love through many years, and, recalling the episode of his supernatural affection for Osbern, knew the story by heart how, when the grave closed over the poor lad, their old jealousies were already and for ever disenchanted, their old ferocities already and for ever subdued, their old hatreds already and for ever extinguished, and how, during the last five years, each of them and all of them, drawn, charmed, and vanquished by a purity, an elevation, and a gentleness so rare as his, had found in him the depository of their dearest hopes, the director of their holiest endeavours, and the guide of their common journey to a common home.

Such was the report given by William's barons. The prince partook of their enthusiasm, and, charmed to learn that the abbot elect was thus loved, sent them back with a request that he would repair without delay to Brionne, bringing with him a few of his religious. The message revived all Anselm's alarms; but the encouragements and entreaties of his monks lent him heart, and, accompanied by a few of them, he set out for Brionne under the escort of his three noble friends.

No sooner were Anselm and his religious in the royal presence than William's eye rested on the central figure of the group, and his countenance—the countenance so often described as one whereon a terror-striking majesty sat unweariedly enthroned—instantaneously changed to an expression of gentleness which had erst been deemed impossible. The astonished attendants stood with riveted gaze, watching the two men. Unquestionably there was more royal blood in the subject than in the prince. But it was not Anselm's innate and unconscious dignity of mien that made the terrible and unbending king of men thus incline to him with modest courtesy, and thus speak to him as equal to equal, tone and manner both inviting him to say all that was in his heart to say. On the contrary, William's demeanour was the homage of a great moral power to a greater, and the outcome of one of the noblest elements in his own character. He no sooner saw than he interpreted the brow on which contemplation had set her soft but indelible imprint; the features refined in their natural lines, but chastened by long discipline into a type of countenance rarely seen here below; and the eye that looked full on him clear and calm, the witness and the spokesman of a pure conscience and a true heart. Need he demand fealty from such a man? The fealty was there. Or homage? He had paid it himself; why require it back again?

The Conqueror made no secret of the pleasure it gave him that so singularly gifted a subject had been chosen to adorn by his genius and his piety a chair which the heroic virtues of its first occupant had already made illustrious. It was, therefore, with more than ordinary satisfaction that he next proceeded to give him seizin of the temporalities of the abbacy by presenting him a crosier.[1] This, being touched by Anselm, was handed back to its owner, a bishop, no doubt, or abbot, who happened to be in attendance, and not improbably the prelate upon whom it now devolved to put him in corporal possession of the abbey by installation.

If the formality of the crosier bore an unhappy, albeit accidental, resemblance to the condemned usage of investiture, the succeeding ceremony involved no such inconvenience; and the prelate, who now returned with the abbot elect to Le Bec, encountered no reluctance when, upon entering the church, he proposed to set him in Herlwin's vacant seat in the choir.

The monks can scarcely have been idle in the interval; and, if we could but lift the curtain of an inexorable oblivion, we should probably discover that they had employed their industry in fitting to the iron crook[2] of Herlwin's disused crosier a staff of wood newly turned and polished. But, if so, their labours were premature. To touch a crosier at

[1] As I shall have to refer to this incident on a future occasion, I will in this place do no more than quote the following passages from Orderic :—

1. 'Dux autem .... præfato viro, qui electus erat, per cambutam Ivonis episcopi Sagiensis *exteriorem abbatiæ potestatem tradidit.*'—ii. 69.

2. 'At ille .... [Mainerio] per pastoralem baculum *exteriorem curam tradidit*, et prædicto antistiti, ut ea quæ sibi de spirituali curâ competebant suppleret, præcepit.'—ii. 126.

[2] If the Jumièges portrait may be trusted, the *fastigium* or crook of Herlwin's crosier can scarcely have been of ivory, or indeed of any kind of bone. I shall revert to the subject towards the close of this book.

Brionne, as he might have touched a sceptre, a walking-staff,[1] or any other object which habit or caprice might employ in token of a civil conveyance, was one thing; but to wield Abbot Herlwin's crosier, and to wield it at Le Bec—where, unless it meant nothing, it meant spiritual jurisdiction—was quite another thing. The latter he, therefore, refused to touch, as he persisted in refusing to exceed in any other particular the limits of privilege which he already held as prior.

[1] 'Ipse quoque Ansoldus decimam quam Hersendis soror ejus in mariagio habuerat et B. Mariæ reddiderat .... per virgam quam in manu [manum?] Johannis monachi et presbyteri tradiderat, concessit.'—*O. V.* ii. 449.

CHAPTER II.

ABBOT ANSELM'S CONSECRATION AND FIRST VISIT TO ENGLAND.

THE ceremonies observed at the consecration of an abbot, simple as they may be, are at once so various, and so entirely dependent for their moral effect upon the unchangeable liturgical forms into which they are engrafted, that it would be as difficult for modern pen to give a short and efficient description of them as it had been supererogatory in a writer of the twelfth century to do more than record the mere fact of such a solemnity in order to revive mental impressions as familiar to his readers as to himself. But, if by this time we have formed a just estimate of Anselm's character and of the affectionate reverence it had conciliated within the precinct of his convent by the spring of 1079, we have what is, after all, of greater value than any such account; for we know what must have been his own emotions, and what those of his household, as he and they took their respective parts in the eventful function performed in the Church of our Lady of Le Bec on the twenty-second of February in that year.[1] The Archbishop of Rouen being disabled by illness, the office of celebrant[2] devolved upon the prelate who had in the previous summer committed to the earth all that was mortal

---

[1] The feast of St. Peter's Chair. Why was this day chosen for the ceremony? Or rather, why had five months been allowed to elapse from the day of the final election, and, as I suppose, four months and a half from the day of installation?

[2] The fragment printed by Dom Bouquet (xiv. 270) errs in saying that Rouen was 'absque pastore.' Archbishop John was not dead, but speechless from paralysis. He lived till the ninth of the following September.

of Herlwin; the high-born and stately Gilbert, Bishop of Evreux.

The Church of our Lady of Le Bec had been arrayed in all its splendour; the walls glowed with Lanfranc's tapestries, and the altar shone with jewels and damask, the gift of one of the most illustrious of the assistants at the ceremony. A widow since early in the January of 1074, the interest which the Lady Eva took in all that concerned Blessed Herlwin's monastery was in great part a bequest from her husband, William Crispin, who had died in the religious habit, and now slept his long sleep in the adjoining cloister.[1] She and hers unanimously accorded Anselm such honours as were held due to the eldest son of such a house as theirs. She was his mother, he was her son, and one of his brothers by adoption had recently carried letters for him to Aosta, and not improbably another and more private communication still further south.[2]

Besides this lady and her family there were in the church, no doubt, representatives of the best houses of Normandy, eager to offer their congratulations to the new abbot, eager to crave his blessing, eager, too, to minister something in mitigation of a distress which for six months had pressed very heavily upon him and his community, and of which I shall say something in the next chapter.

We have seen that his reluctance to accept the abbatial dignity was a suggestive precursor of the troubles which were to befall him after the lapse of fourteen years; and it is a curious circumstance that he was scarcely consecrated before

---

[1] The year of William Crispin's death is ascertained from the *Nomina Monachorum*, the month and day from an extract from the necrology of Beaumont-le-Roger in the National Library at Paris (Latin, 13905.) This document has under 'Januarius, 6 idus O[biit] I^{us} (*i.e.* primus) Will. Crispinus monachus nostræ congregationis.' The date, therefore, of William Crispin's death is January 8, 1074.

[2] *Epp.* i. 18, ii. 9, 26.

For an account of this family the reader will be pleased to consult the fragment *De nobili genere Crispinorum*, appended to D'Achéry's edition of *Lanfranc*.

he made acquaintance with the very country in which those troubles were to have their theatre. The earliest important event of his abbacy was a journey which he made to England for the double purpose of visiting the monastic estates and of offering his respects to the Archbishop of Canterbury.

Never as yet had Anselm adventured the waves. Twenty years ago from the ramparts of the Castle of Avranches his wondering eye had for the first time scanned the broad ocean and gazed on the lustrous purple of the tides that wash the Côtentin; and it is just possible that from the Castle of Boulogne he may subsequently have measured the silver streak that severs the chalk cliffs of Kent from the seaboard of Picardy; but he was as yet a stranger to the perils of the deep—perils which, though neither few nor imaginary, were multiplied and exaggerated by his adopted mother and by his children in religion, who, so far from allaying that lady's apprehensions, seem to have enhanced them by their own.

Taking leave, however, of the tearful and agitated dowager and of his own tearful and agitated monks, Anselm set forth upon an expedition which had been the subject not only of his prayers and of theirs, but of the prayers of tenants, and of friends and neighbours both far and near, ever since it was first contemplated. He was attended by the proper companions of such a journey, and by Dom Girard, whose knowledge of the language, the customs, and the topography of Flanders qualified him to act as guide to the port of embarkation. The name of that port still survives in Wissant, an inland hamlet lying between Boulogne and Calais; for, thanks to the slow operation of natural causes, the ancient harbour has long been choked by its own white sand, and deserted by the sea, whose tides now ebb and flow four miles away to the west.

And a like fate has befallen Anselm's landing-place, since the Portus Lemanis of the Roman occupation, changed by the eleventh century to the name of Lympne, has long been deserted by the briny wave, which now breaks on the low shore of Romney marsh at the distance of well-nigh a league from its ancient limit.

Nor is the next stage in the Abbot's journey unrecorded. On the Via Lymenæa, the Roman road that ran from Lympne to Canterbury, there stood in Roman times a military station, superseded in early Saxon period by a residence of the Kings of Kent, and subsequently by the archiepiscopal manor of Lyminge. The hundred of Moniberg, or Nuniberg, in which Lyminge stands, recalls by its name the convent for nuns established there by no less a person than St. Ethelburg early in the seventh century. There, too, was Ethelburg buried on the thirteenth of December, 647; and there, in a spot to this day indicated by an arched buttress of singular aspect, her body still reposed in the year 1079.[1] The Archbishop was at the manor house awaiting his visitor, who on the following day wrote thus to his monks :—

'*Dominis et fratribus dilectissimis in Beccensi cœnobio Deo servientibus frater Anselmus, servus et conservus eorum semper sanctè vivere et sanctæ vitæ premium percipere.*

' Knowing, and knowing but too well, how truly anxious you in your love for me are to have news of my safety and well-being, I dare not distress you with any delay. On the day that Dom Girard, soon after sunrise, took leave of me

---

[1] In 1085 her relics were transported by Lanfranc to the Hospital of St. Gregory, recently established by him at Canterbury.

The following extract from Lambarde's *Perambulation of Kent* will interest, and may possibly entertain, some of my readers :—' I read in the *Annals of St. Augustine of Canterbury* that Eadbald (the sonne of King Ethelbert, the first christened King of Kent) gave it to Edburge, his sister, who forthwith clocked together a sort of simple women who, under her wing, there tooke upon them the Popish veile of widowhood.' And again, 'Lanfranc, the Archbishop . . . . translated the olde bones of Edburge from Lyminge to Sainct Gregorie's, and verified in Papistrie the olde maxim of philosophie, " Corruptio unius generatio alterius " (The corruption of one is the generation of another).'

The monastery of Lyminge was recovered to the See of Canterbury by Archbishop Lanfranc : 'Monasterium de Liminge cum terris et consuetudinibus ad ipsum pertinentibus.'

on board ship, the Divine protection answered your prayers by landing me in the middle of the afternoon on the shores of England, after a prosperous voyage, in which I suffered none of the inconveniences that afflict so many when at sea; and by bringing me in the evening into the society of our lord and father Archbishop Lanfranc, who gave me a hearty welcome in his manor of Lyminge; on the morrow of which events I pen these lines, hoping thus to satisfy your desire, and at the same time to urge and exhort your pious industry to burn with unceasing ardour and make ever fresh progress. As a brother I entreat, and as a father I admonish you, so to make it your study to live together as monks and religious, as that when you are blessed with the reward that awaits your endeavours I may have some share in the blessing. May Almighty God by His own dear care preserve you from all ill, and show His mercy upon you by still granting you all good, both in body and soul. Tell Lady Eva, our mother, the news, which, equally with you, she is longing to hear of her eldest son; and ask her to pray that, as her prayers, together with yours, have gained me the favour of a prosperous departure, notwithstanding all your fears, so they may obtain for me the further grace of a joyful return to your joyful midst.'[1]

The journey of the Archbishop and the Abbot from Lyminge to Canterbury was not without its proper interest. The two had not thus ridden together for twenty years; not since the memorable occasion when, had the elder friend bidden the younger turn anchorite then and there in the forest, he would have been obeyed.

At that time Lanfranc had already attained his grand climacteric, whilst Canon Anselm of Aosta was a young clergyman of six-and-twenty. The latter is now in the maturity of his manhood, and, although it is several years

[1] *Ep.* ii. 9.

since the former told off his full tale of fourscore, the grand old man is nevertheless vigorous enough at this very moment in all his magnificent endowments both of mind and body to give hope of an administration continued for an entire decade longer.

At that time Anselm was doubting whether to turn hermit, monk, or hospitaller; now, not only is he a famous abbot, he has by his transcendent gifts of soul and intellect compelled the unique homage of his prince, won the passionate devotion of his spiritual children, and in spite of himself achieved immortality.

At that time Lanfranc, the prior of an obscure and poverty-stricken mud-walled monastery, was laboriously striving by daily drudgery to procure funds for the erection of a new church; now, Primate of the Britains and patriarch of the *orbis transmarinus*, he has, with princely resources at his disposal, rebuilt St. Augustine's Cathedral Church at Canterbury; and now, even now, as they near the solemn pile, its bells ring forth wild welcome to him and to his guest.

On dismounting at the gate of the precinct of Christ Church, Anselm was confronted by its peculiar pomp. Prior Henry, his old friend from Le Bec, stood in the gateway, attired in cope of rich embroidery and bearing in his hands a Gospel-book heavy with goldsmith's work and encrusted with gems; on either side of the Prior stood a monk, one holding holy water and the other a censer; whilst behind these latter, and extending in two lines to the great western door, were the rest of the community, all of them arrayed in copes or dalmatics, except the choir boys, who wore tunicles. As soon as the Archbishop had offered holy water and incense to his guest, and the latter had kissed the book of the Gospels, a psalm was intoned, and the procession filed into the cathedral.

I need scarcely say that the eastern limb of the basilica contained the sanctuary, the apsidal termination of which was made additionally venerable by the quasi-patriarchal throne of St. Augustine; that the three easternmost bays of the nave were enclosed so as to form the monks' choir, and that the western entrance to this enclosure was surmounted by a colossal cross, on which hung a figure of our Divine Redeemer. On the pavement in front of this crucifix, and thus in the middle bay of the nave, carpets had been spread on which the visitor was to kneel in silent prayer before entering the choir; and like preparations had been made on the first ascent of the sanctuary, where again he was to spend a short time in devotion before entering the cloister.

But he was impatient to acknowledge the compliment paid him in a reception which seems very greatly to have surpassed in splendour and magnificence all previous solemnities of the kind; and was without delay conducted into the chapter house, which adjoined the cathedral, lying between its northern and eastern limbs, and there set in the seat of honour. When all had taken their places, a lesson of Holy Scripture was read before him; and then there was deep silence. Every ear was strained to catch the first tones of a voice about the fascination of which Dom Maurice had had so much to say; and of all the eyes fixed on him none were more eager than those of an acute and observant lad, English by name and birth, who was resolved to make notes of the sermon. His name was Eadmer.

The discourse, introduced by a few words of direct and formal acknowledgment, was characteristically Anselm's, in form cold and analytical as Aristotle, in meaning and purpose warm and sympathetic as himself; and as it seems to have been a sample of the method now for fifteen years employed by him at Le Bec, a method designed to prove that the deductions of right reason are in precise harmony with the maxims of Divine wisdom which lie scattered over the pages of Holy Writ, I venture to think that the reader will be pleased to make acquaintance with so much of it as Eadmer contrived to remember and record. I cannot, however, help thinking that, if the young monk had been at the time conversant with Anselm's method, he would have taken care to make note of the text which it was designed to elucidate. The subject was charity, and the illustrious expositor endeavoured to convince his audience from considerations suggested to us by our reason (*rationabiliter*) that he who bestows a kindness on another is in a higher moral state (*majus aliquid habet*) than he who receives it. 'He that does a kind thing makes God his debtor, not so he to whom it is done; for how is God made my debtor by my receipt of a favour from you or from anybody? If, therefore, it be a better thing (*majus*) to have that whereby God makes Himself a debtor, than that whereby He does not, then, since God makes Himself a debtor for kindnesses done, but not for kindnesses received, it follows that he who bestows is in a higher state than he who receives a kindness.

'Again, he that receives attention from another has the benefit of the good office, nothing more; he has played his part, and it is over. For example, he receives an estate, a benefice, a dinner of ceremony, or some such civility; but the other, after he has rendered the good office, still keeps the kindness that inspired it.

'And of this, my reverend brethren, we have an instance ready to hand in our mutual relation at this moment. You have granted me the favour of a kindly office; it is a kindly office, I say, which you have lavished on me. I have received it, and already it is a favour past; but the charity that prompted it, and which is so pleasing to God, still remains and dwells in your heart. And is not an abiding good a better thing, in your judgment, than a good by its very nature transitory?

'And, besides, if—and I will not deny it—by reason of your kind office towards me, there has been some growth of charity in my own breast, even this will redound to your reward, since it is to you that I owe so great a good. . . .

'If, then, we pay proper heed to these considerations we shall, I am sure, rest convinced that we have greater reason to congratulate ourselves when we are kind to others than when others are kind to us. All do not take this into their consideration, and hence many rather desire to be loved than to love.'

But it was not enough for Anselm to be the guest of the monks of Christ Church; he wished to be their brother. He therefore seized the earliest opportunity of craving the privilege of *fraternitas*. Prostrating himself in the customary manner upon the floor of the chapter house, he made his request to the Archbishop in these words: 'Peto per misericordiam Dei et vestram et omnium istorum seniorum societatem et beneficium hujus monasterii.' The request was granted in the following formula: 'Omnipotens Dominus concedat vobis quod quæritis, et ipse præstet vobis consortium electorum suorum.' He then rose and advanced to the Archbishop, who presented to him the Book of the Rule as the symbol of fraternal communion, saluted him with the customary kiss, and then seated him at his side, now no longer a friend, but a brother, and a sharer in life and after death of the prayers and good works of the monks of Christ Church. At the conclusion of the chapter each of the monks in his turn greeted him with the holy kiss.

This first visit of his to Canterbury was singularly well-timed, and was followed by happy results. Had he come a few years sooner, his awed and fascinated hosts would scarcely have been ripe to profit by the severe and exalted standard of monastic holiness which was to be recognised in all he said and did. For Lanfranc, on his arrival in 1070, found in the monks of Christ Church a community sadly fallen away from the ancient English piety. 'They amused themselves with hunting, with falconry, with horse-racing; they loved to rattle the dice; they indulged in drink; they wore fine clothes, studied personal appearance, disdained a frugal and quiet life, and had so many people to wait upon them that they were more like fine gentlemen than monks.' Such had they been nine years ago. 'But Lanfranc, skilled in the art of arts, the government of souls, and knowing well that habit is second nature, though bent on reforming, did his work with prudence, and, plucking up the weeds little by little, sowed good seed in their place.'[1] And now, though many of them dared scarcely hope to reach, all could at least appreciate and admire, however remotely, Anselm's exalted ideal of the religious vocation; for many of the things which he said surprised by their novelty, no less than edified by their fervour, and the pictures of the monastic state which he drew, sometimes in sermons in the chapter house, sometimes in conversations in the cloister, dazzled and amazed them, not so much by their strange unlikeness to the life once led in the Christ Church cloister, as by their exhibition of a type of existence which they had hitherto deemed unattainable here below:—

> Thrice blest whose lives are faithful prayers,
> Whose loves in higher love endure.
> What souls possess themselves so pure?
> Or is there blessedness like theirs?

But all these eloquent addresses of Anselm's had the characteristic peculiarity of his first discourse to them in the chapter house, and although designed for the heart were recommended to the understanding by a *rationabilis facundia* which was to be of service to the Archbishop himself as well as his monks before the visit had come to a close.

The name of a predecessor in the See of Canterbury, put to death by the Danes in 1012—I mean Archbishop Elphege—had been proposed to Lanfranc for canonisation; or rather, Elphege having been already canonised by the *vox*

---

[1] William of Malmesbury, *De Gestis Pontiff.* lib. i.

populi, Lanfranc had been asked to set his name in the calendar. But the acute Lombard hesitated to style him saint simply because he had lived a good life, or martyr because he had died a violent death. St. Cyprian's maxim, 'Non facit martyrem pœna sed causa,' had by this time been only too much neglected, not only in our own country, but in others. Thus in the Flemish monastery of St. Bavon the relics were honoured of an 'Adrianus martyr,' of whom there seems to have been no more to say than that he had been 'à latrone interemptus,' and those of a 'Sanctus Livinus episcopus,' concerning whom there was little knowledge, if any, beyond the circumstance that he had been 'à viris malignis interemptus.' No one would begrudge the crown of sanctity to Meinrad, the hermit of Einsiedeln, but surely his contemporaries erred in assigning him the palm of martyrdom simply because he died at the hand of assassins; and, however good a child the young Saxon king St. Edward may have been, no theologian would pretend that his eternal crown is adorned with the martyr's jewel for no other reason than that he was prematurely hurried to it by the treachery of his step-mother.

But the case of Archbishop Elphege was not quite the first of its kind. St. Mayeul, the famous Abbot of Cluny, was once, in the course of a journey home from Rome, captured by Saracens in the mountainous country below Mont Genèvre. The enemy required a ransom for him and his companions, and asked if he had the means at command for paying one. He replied that he had nothing of his own, and wished for nothing, but that he had tenants with no lack of real and personal property. Thereupon they fixed their price at a thousand pounds of silver, and despatched a messenger to Cluny, who bore a letter from the abbot himself containing these words: 'Nunc verò, si placet, pro me et his qui mecum sunt capti, redemptionem mittite.' The money was raised and the captives liberated. Now, if Mayeul had chosen to die rather than resort to his tenants for assistance, would he thereby have merited the title of martyr? By no means. Yet there can be no doubt that the general voice of the age would have assigned it to him. But by Lanfranc's time the uninstructed prodigality of the popular complacency had gone to such lengths that the admirers of Elphege, whilst promoting his canonisation, took no account of one of the most important elements in his case; and, though they mentioned another, did so incidentally and without any suspicion of its real value; for, as I have said, it was in their estimate a sufficient title to martyrdom that a good life should have been crowned with a violent death.

'Whilst he was engaged in these reforms and had Anselm under his roof, a friend and brother of one mind with himself, he one day said to him, as they were engaged in conversation, "Our English friends here have made themselves some saints, but when I come to think, as I sometimes do, about the subjects of this devotion as pourtrayed by those who pay it, I find it hard to free my judgment from some doubt as to their claim to beatification. Here in this very see, where by God's providence I am now set, one of them now sleeps his long sleep, Elphege by name; a good man, undoubtedly, and in his time Archbishop of Canterbury. They account him a saint, but they do more; they number him amongst the martyrs, although they acknowledge that he was put to death, not for the confession of the name of Christ, but because he refused to pay a price for his life. The pagans who, to use the English idiom, were envious[1] at him, and haters of God, having taken him prisoner, nevertheless, out of reverence for his person, allowed him the alternative of redeeming himself, and demanded of him an enormous sum of money for his

[1] *Æmuli.* The word 'envy' is still used in some of our counties in the sense of spite, grudge, resentment. In the sixteenth century this employment of the word was classical. 'I was envious at the foolish;' 'Be not thou envious at the wicked doers.' Lanfranc's words are worthy of note:—'Cum illum, *ut verbis utar Anglorum,* æmuli ejus . . . . pagani cepissent.'

ransom. But, as it was impossible for him to procure the amount without having recourse to his vassals, some of whom would thus have been impoverished, and others, perhaps, reduced to shameful beggary,[1] he elected to lose his life rather than to keep it on such terms. Now, my brother, I am anxious to hear your opinion upon this."'

The picture of two such men in council, the unaffected condescension of the one, the unfrightened humility of the other, their dignified familiarity and well-yoked skill, constitute one of the prettiest of Eadmer's vignettes.

'As one man of penetration engaged in conference with another, Anselm replied to this appeal in clear and luminous phrase, as follows:—" There can be no doubt that he who does not hesitate to die rather than commit even a slight sin against God would be infinitely more ready to die rather than offend God by some grievous sin; and, of course, to deny Christ is a more grievous sin than that a lord of the soil[2] should for the redemption of his life put his vassals (*homines*) to some temporary distress by a heavy drain on their purse. But this lesser thing Elphege refused to do. Much more unlikely, therefore, would he have been to deny Christ, had the infuriated crew urged him to do so by threatening him with death. Thus it clearly appears that holiness of an admirably high type held possession of his soul, since he chose rather to resign his life than, regardless of charity, to scandalise his neighbours. Far from him, therefore, was the 'Wo' which the Lord threatens to him by whom scandal comes."'

Thus much, then, for St. Anselm's opinion as to the claim advanced on behalf of Elphege to the designation of Saint. He was more than good, as Lanfranc avowed—he was

[1] William of Malmesbury (*Gesta Regum*, lib. ii.) says, 'Ipse patriarcha sanctus et reverendissimus vir Elfegus abductus et in vinculis tentus ad extremum cùm rusticos suos expilare ad se redimendum cogeretur et abnueret lapidatus et securi percussus, animâ cœlum glorificavit.' He was put to death April 19, 1012.

[2] 'Terrenus dominus.'

heroically good; and he was heroically good, not in refusing to claim the aid *ad corpus redimendum* which the custom of the age gave him the right to require of his vassals, but because, the ransom required being enormous, he chose to die rather than give scandal by consenting to its exaction. What follows relates to the second and graver question, Was Elphege in the strict sense of the term a martyr?

'Nor is he, in my opinion, unworthy of a place among the martyrs who, as we know on perfectly veracious testimony went to meet his death for a justice so heroic in its elevation. For blessed John the Baptist, who is venerated as a martyr first and foremost, and reputed such by the common consent of the Church of God, was put to death not for refusing to deny Christ, but for refusing to hush truth in silence. And what difference is there between dying for truth and dying for justice? Furthermore, inasmuch as, by the testimony of Holy Writ, as it little needs to tell your Grace (*vestra paternitas*), Christ is Truth and Christ is Justice, he who dies for justice and truth dies for Christ; and he who dies for Christ is by the Church esteemed a martyr. Now the blessed Elphege died for justice precisely in the same way as the blessed John died for truth. Why, then, should any of us doubt of one more than of the other that his death was a veritable and a holy martyrdom, since death was encountered from a like motive by each? It seems to me, my reverend father, that—so far at least as I understand the case—this argument is a good one; but if you think otherwise, I refer it to your wisdom to set me right, and recall me from my conclusion, and to instruct the Church of God and show her what is the most fitting view to take in a matter of such importance.'

The Archbishop was convinced. He had not been wanting in piety to the saints of his new country, to St. Ethelburg, to St. Dunstan, to St. Oswald, to St. Aldhelm; but he seems, in pursuance of Anselm's argument, to have conceived a sudden and enthusiastic devotion for his heroic predecessor. Not only did he cause an accurate history of the life and passion of St. Elphege to be compiled, but had the story set to music, to be read and sung in his cathedral;[1] and the Proper of the Saint's mass was not improbably the production of no other pen than his.[2]

If the monastery of Le Bec could at this moment boast as many as two estates in the west of our island, those estates lay at Winchcomb in Oxfordshire, and Brixton Deveril in Wilts; if only one, then Anselm's longest journey in his tour of inspection must have been to the former of these places. But an expedition, whether into Oxfordshire or into the more distant county, involved several pauses both in going and returning, and doubtless afforded, not only to deans and abbots, but to the great vassals of the Crown whose houses lay on the road, an opportunity of inviting the blessing which they felt sure would attend the residence, however short, of such a guest under their roof. As warm a greeting awaited the Abbot of Le Bec at a baron's castle as in the guest chamber of a monastery; and in one no less than in the other he fascinated and won the hearts of his hosts by the effortless sensibility which renders a refined and elevated nature all things to all, and the broad-hearted love which knows how to consecrate the courtesies of human converse to highest and holiest aims. To those who were not monks he made himself as if he were not a monk, that so he might win to the

---

[1] All this was done by Dom Osbern, who was, if not then, yet at a later date, Precentor of Christ Church, and has been described by William of Malmesbury (*Gesta Regum*, lib. ii.) as 'nulli nostro tempore stylo secundus, musicâ certò omnium sine controversiâ primus.' It would almost appear that Osbern was not at this moment at Canterbury. He was sent over to Le Bec in 1073; but I cannot be certain how long he remained there. I think, however, that he can scarcely have returned to England before 1081, when he probably replaced Dom Maurice, who had by that time been sent to St. Neot's (see *Ep.* iii. 5). Seven or eight years at Le Bec under Anselm must have done much for the style in composition so much praised by William of Malmesbury.

[2] See Appendix. By a decretal of Alexander III., in 1181, all causes of canonisation were henceforth to be submitted to the Holy See.

'perfect life' of the cloister both secular canons and men whose salvation was imperilled by an undue attachment to their state as denizens of the world. And though the ideal he propounded was severe, his hearers invariably listened to him with a zest that bespoke a hunger and a thirst to which none had hitherto thus ministered; such was his clearness of method, such his fascination of manner, such his purity and singleness of purpose. The more illustrious the rank of his hosts, the more hearty was the welcome which they accorded him; and Eadmer seems to remark of this his first visit to England what in course of years was undoubtedly the fact, that there was neither earl nor countess who did not deem it a loss of merit not to have shown some kindness to Anselm, or made some offering to God in the person of His servant.

But Le Bec had estates in Surrey, one at Tooting and another at Streatham [1]—both of them the gift of one of the foremost of the Conqueror's barons, whose name it would not be proper to pass over in silence.

It was not long after Herlwin's retirement from the world that his friend Gilbert, Count of Brionne, fell a victim to the vindictive rage of a family whose resentment he seems to have made it his business to provoke, and left behind him two little boys, Richard and Baldwin, who were at once carried by their tutor into Flanders and placed under the protection of Duke William's future father-in-law. Upon his alliance with Matilda, Duke William restored them to their native country, where, by the gift of Bienfaite, Orbec, and other estates, he made them only too imperfect a compensation for the loss of their paternal inheritance, the noblest portion of which, the Castle of Brionne and its domain, was now in his own hand; but some thirteen years later he rewarded Richard's

---

[1] 'The two manors seem to have been (subsequently) consolidated, and to be what is now called the Manor of Tooting-Bec, being Upper Tooting, which is in the parish of Streatham.'—Manning's *County of Surrey*.

services on the field of Senlac with a grant of land in the conquered kingdom. Now the proper domain of Brionne reached to the distance of a *milliarium Brionense* from the castle in all directions; and the story goes that Richard de Bienfaite, ascertaining by actual survey the exact length of the *milliarium*, had the measuring line transported from Brionne to England, and there traced round about his new stronghold at Tunbridge just such a circle as had determined the lost domain.

But attachment to home was not all that Earl Richard had inherited from Gilbert of Brionne; and, if he had given the manors of Tooting and Streatham to his father's favourite monastery during its founder's lifetime, one of his earliest acts under the new administration was, in conjunction with Rohais, his countess, to dedicate to religion Richard, the youngest of his five sons. This young gentleman, affectionately called a *monachus parvulus* by the good abbot, will reappear in the course of the history; and all that I need meanwhile say about him is that some time after his profession at Le Bec he was sent back to England to lead the religious life under Dom Maurice in the first priory which the mother house seems to have established in our island, the Priory of St. Neot, in Huntingdonshire; and that in the year 1100 he was nominated Abbot of Ely.

We learn from the Ely archives that, shortly after the Conquest, Gilbert of Clare—an error, I presume, for Richard Fitzgilbert of Clare—laid claim to property at Neotsbury which really belonged to the Abbey of Ely, and ousted the monks in residence, with the exception of three, who, invincible by famine or violence, held dogged possession of it until they were transported to Le Bec to be replaced by a colony from that monastery. They must have held out, I imagine, from 1069 to 1072; and I think their names were Osmund, Allard, and Ruard.[1] Be this as it may, Anselm in

[1] The story of these three men's heroic obstinacy is to be found in Drysdale's

1079 paid a visit to his Huntingdonshire priory, where he opened the shrine which contained the relics of the saint, and, removing a small portion of them for his own monastery, relocked the chest and took possession of the key.

His return to Le Bec was accelerated by most interesting news, the news of a vocation to the religious life for which he had long hoped and prayed.

Dom Rodolf, treasurer of the Cathedral of Beauvais, belonged to a corporation of secular ecclesiastics who practised with but indifferent zeal the virtues which became their order, and were already converting their prebends into hereditary benefices transmissible to their illegitimate offspring. Rodolf's youth had thus far served as protection to his innocence, and it was Rodolf's youth which had now for some time pleaded with Anselm to snatch him, if snatch he might, from reach of the contagious influences which so closely beset him. Rodolf seems to have been appointed treasurer to the society for no other reason than that it was his fortune to be the son of one of those great noblemen who had it in their power to convert great ecclesiastical preferments into sources of livelihood for their children; and, so far from dreaming of the cloister, responded with eager zest to the solicitations of the world until the summer of 1079, when he paid a visit to Le Bec, nobody quite knew why. As, however, he was taking his departure, an irresistible impulse seized him, and, exclaiming that he was resolved to become a monk, he sent away his horse in charge of an attendant, went back into the cloister, insisted on being allowed to remain, and soon displayed so vivid an anxiety and so mature a fitness for the religious life that before the news could be carried to England his hair had been shorn to the fashion of the Crown of Thorns and his canon's dress exchanged for the dirty-white frock of the novices of Le Bec.

Monasticon and in Gorham's *History of St. Neot's*. The latter work contains a letter of Anselm's, not published elsewhere, about the shrine of St. Neot.

Apprised of his conversion, the overjoyed and thankful abbot wrote to him from England in the following terms:—

'*Frater Anselmus, dictus abbas Beccensis, suo olim amico desideratissimo, nunc domino et fratri et filio charissimo, novo Christi militi Rodulfo; per contemptum terrenarum et falsarum divitiarum adipisci cælestes et veras divitias.*

'Glory be to God on high, who on earth gives men good will, whose high right hand has, according to my desire, turned the will of my dear and longed for child from a world, which in the event does no good to any and very much harm to all who love it; turned it from the vain world to very truth, the truth which never hurt any and is good to all who seek her. I speak to you in this short letter, dearest to my heart, you whom my conscience tells me I long to see more than all mankind, and to converse with face to face more than with any living mortal.[1] For I know the devil's malignant spite; I know how he chafes with rage to find that you have slipped from his hands—ay, slipped from his lips. And hence I am sure that he will in many ways try to befool you. The service of God which you have chosen is, he will tell you, a grievous burden, and his own service in the world's love, which you have renounced, a delightful one. So that . . . . . my soul within me will have no rest until my eyes shall see my desired one, and my mouth speak to my dearest child, and my heart strengthen my new comrade to withstand the darts of the devil.

'Therefore I beseech Almighty God, who has withdrawn you from the love of the vain world, and His most holy Mother, who, on your flying to her, has taken you under her protection, to keep you safe from any shaking of your resolution. And I beg you, through Him whose

---

[1] '*Plus quam alicui in terrâ viventi.*' A reservation not improbably inspired by his immortal love for Osbern.

grace inspired you to take it, to allow no crafts and no suggestions of the enemy to alarm you. For that enemy tries to annoy you, that he may conquer and rejoice over you; but God permits this that you may have a claim to the crown your victory shall win. . . . The Lord preserve you from all evil. Amen.'

Returning to his monastery without delay, he at an early date received Dom Rodolf's profession, and, soon afterwards, if not on the same occasion, that of his *monachus parvulus*, Dom Richard. It must have been about this time that he professed Baldric, his future prior; and, before many weeks had passed, a great-nephew of Roger de Beaumont presented himself at the gates of the abbey, craving admission to its cloister; I mean William de Montfort, whose home on the Risle lay at no great distance, and who was one day himself to become Abbot of Le Bec.

CHAPTER III.

ABBOT ANSELM IN HIS CLOISTER: HIS SECOND VISIT TO ENGLAND.

THE summer of 1078 had been exceptionally hot and dry; no rain fell in all the north-west of Gaul, and a drought ensued such as filled men's hearts with the gloomiest forebodings.[1] Herlwin passed away just as the heat was at its worst; and scarcely was he gone when a sudden rise in the price of provisions showed Anselm and his monks, or might have shown them, how grave was the general apprehension.

The following season was scarcely less unpropitious to the fruits of the earth, and by the anniversary of Herlwin's death the prospects at Le Bec were exceedingly gloomy.

Meanwhile, however, the new abbot and his monks had purchased some plots of land at a price which told seriously on their resources, and had followed up the sublime improvidence by a second. One of the bells of their church was cracked, and another refused to ring in tune with the rest of the peal. They therefore took them down, and set about converting them into a large tenor, when, finding that the metal was insufficient, they purchased with pious haste and

---

[1] I am indebted for these facts to an MS. preserved in the public library at Orleans, *Clarii Floriacensis Chronicon.* I do not know if it has been printed. 'Anno m. l. xx. viii. Hoc anno totum tempus æstatis nimis calidum sine pluviâ fuit, unde multi fuerunt territi.' This throws light on a letter of Anselm's to Archbishop Lanfranc, in which he gives some account of the distress. That letter (*Ep.* ii. 1) is not given in full in the printed editions.

The *Chronicle of St. Hubert*, with which I have made acquaintance since the preceding note was written, and on which that note throws some light, seems to imply that the drought of 1078, like the terrible cold of the previous winter, extended from end to end of Europe.

at great cost what was wanting to complete their work. Michaelmas came, the Michaelmas of 1079; the tithe corn was paid in, their own harvest was housed in the granary at Le Parc, and then the frightful truth burst on them that they had neither food nor money to last them till All Saints' Day. Darker and yet darker loomed the coming woe, when, as even now they felt the keen tooth of famine, there came a present of twenty pounds from Lanfranc to avert the calamity. But those twenty pounds were swallowed up and disappeared, just as the first shower after drought sinks into the thirsty earth and vanishes; and before many days the poor men were for a second time at their wits' end. It was in this or some other such conjuncture—for the crisis recurred more than once—that when treasurer from his empty chest, bursar from his empty larder, sacristan from his unprovided sacristy, flew to the prior in pale quest of help, he imperturbably replied, 'Trust in God, and I feel sure He will supply all our wants,' and so resumed his occupation. That very day, or early next morning, word was brought that barges from England laden with provisions—beans and oats, if nothing better—had come up the Risle and were moored at Pont-Authou, waiting to be discharged. But after a few weeks treasurer, bursar, and sacristan appeared as before, not doubting that within four-and-twenty hours a hundred hungry men would be sitting in the refectory at empty tables. 'Trust in God' was the quiet rejoinder, and before the next setting sun some baron or other great personage was announced, who, bringing with him a bag of money, had come to crave the *confraternitas* of the community; and once more they escaped starvation.

Despair could never refuse to breathe again when once the poor monks knew that their abbot had uttered his omnipotent 'Trust in God.' 'Trust in God,' he said another time, and presently a rich postulant[1] was in the guest room, offering

[1] The rich postulant to whom Eadmer alludes was probably William de

himself and all his worldly goods to the service of God under the patronage of Our Lady of Le Bec. And so they were saved again.

The fascination was complete; and the Abbot's children in religion revered at a wondering distance an elevation and a repose of soul which had their source in intimate sustained communion with the Fountain of all good.

In the midst of these troubles, and on the first of December,[1] Anselm had to appear before the King[2] in a lawsuit which concerned the monastery. His Norman neighbours would seem to have been somewhat perplexed by his notions of justice, and, failing to comprehend his distaste for the sharp practice which was at once so familiar and so dear to themselves, to have mingled some little amazement with the respect which those notions could scarcely fail to command. They were astonished to find that he would never allow his tenants to compass a dishonest object under cover of legal right, override the decalogue by a congeries of *coutumes*, or convert the chief of the cardinal virtues into a synonym for the legerdemain of pettifoggers. But if a case came into court in which Abbot Anselm believed that right was on his side, his conduct was still more perplexing. Then, whilst the opposite side plied arguments deemed miracles of forensic skill by a crowd of approving auditors, who, after following with rapt attention the cunning intertexture of legal threads, watched with growing applause the apparition of the design, as little by little it stood forth to view—whilst all this went on, Anselm, 'not troubling himself about that sort of thing, would discourse to any who chose to lend him a hearing out of the Gospel or some other part of Holy Scripture, or set forth

---

Montfort, who was professed in 1079 and succeeded Anselm in the abbacy. He was a great-nephew of Roger de Beaumont. I have already mentioned a brother-in-law of Roger de Beaumont as having been professed in 1077.

[1] *Ep.* ii. 1.

[2] Not, of course, in his quality of King of England, nor in his quality of Duke of Normandy, but as Count of Brionne.

something for the forming of good manners; or if he had no one to listen to him, sweetly reposing in heart's purity, would drop asleep.' So he slept, and then, when the other side had finished, awaking, would listen to a briefly worded summary of the argument. Enough: he rose, spoke a few short phrases, and even as he spoke the showy tissue unravelled of itself and fell to threads.

This is no idle praise. Lanfranc had some years before broken down before the cunning of the Norman *coutumiers*; and it may even be that Anselm's pleadings in the county court of Brionne, no less than his discourses in his own cloister at Le Bec, were the first harbingers of a brighter day, those for lawyers as these for theologians.

The relentless demands made upon him by a minute, unflagging care for the intellectual and moral development of his children in religion one by one may account in great measure for the scantiness of biographical detail which characterises this portion of his history. For, delegating the external business of the house to the prior and others whom he could trust, he made the walls of the cloister, so far as he might do so, the limit of the sphere in which his energies were exercised; and, if we could only contrive to think of him for a moment as one of those scholarly recluses who seem unable to live, or move, or breathe beyond their own dear academic bounds, we should perhaps forgive the spite which has told us almost nothing of his life for so long an interval. But he was no such recluse, and we must be satisfied with the sorry consolation of reflecting that even had a dozen anecdotes survived of this period, we should still have the hopeless task before us of guessing at the strange spell he wielded over his monks and at the intimacy of his converse with the unseen world.

One night the sacristan,[1] who slept in the church, and whose duty it was to call up the house for matins, walked forth into the cloister, there, no doubt, by stellar observation to

---

[1] His name stands eightieth on the list.

ascertain the hour, when, as he passed by the chapter house, he opened the door and looked in. There stood the abbot, his arms outstretched in prayer, and his whole form enveloped in a sphere of dazzling light. Dom Riculf—for that was the sacristan's name—had never known him in the chapter house at such a time, and, besides, had no doubt that he was in bed. In order, however, to assure himself that what he had seen was illusory, he went up into the dormitory, expecting to find Anselm there. The abbot's bed was empty. He came down and went again to the chapter house. Anselm was there, undoubtedly; but the luminous globe had vanished. Riculf's story seems to have excited no surprise, only curiosity as to the meaning of the portent.

Nor have we the advantage of a voluminous correspondence in our review of Anselm's administration as abbot; for fourteen letters written between the years 1079 and 1092 can scarcely be expected to yield an adequate account of so long a period. Still, some of these fourteen letters are simply inestimable, for they afford us a glimpse, not indeed of Anselm's cloister, but of Anselm's heart, and such a glimpse as makes us jealous of the men he loved. The following was written shortly before he set out on his second journey to England, an enterprise undertaken, as I believe, in the year 1083:—

'To his loved, his loving, and his longed for William, brother Anselm, styled Abbot of Le Bec. May he love not the world, nor the things that are in the world, but enjoy the love of God, and give God his love.

'I begin by styling him my loved and my loving one, in reply to the request he makes of my love.

'A soul dear to my soul has, through the medium of a letter all flagrant and all fragrant with affection, asked me, as token of my affection, for a letter of solace. What is sweeter or more agreeable to affection, or what greater solace has it, than affection? How, then, can I better solace you in your love for me than by writing to tell you that my soul's love for you is such that my heart will know no consolation, and my longing for you be all unappeased, unless I have you for my own? Truth to say, when you ask me for my affection with such fervour and such importunity of affection, you do more than incline me to love you; you oblige me to long for you. Your affection for me makes you crave my handwriting for your comfort; mine for you makes me desire your presence for my joy. So, then, if you do not wish to do violence to my heart, satisfy the longing you have taken such pains and made such effort to kindle.

'O dear soul, how can you tell me that you love me, and yet suffer my heart to break from love of you? If the same flame burns in you as burns in me, then your soul and mine must needs be melting with one and the same desire. But how can you really wish for my affection without returning me your own? Be not cruel, therefore, to your soul and mine; but come and console your soul and mine.

'And when you leave your city be like Lot. Look not back. Look ahead and learn the way forward; look not behind, but forget the way back. So, with the apostle, shall you forget the things that are behind and reach forward to those that are before.

'Now I tell you what I mean, and I tell you frankly. Come, and let our lives be spent together, if you really wish us to be a consolation to each other. I might, my dearest friend, adduce to you numberless places of Holy Writ which exhort you to despise the world and its concupiscence, if you were not already familiar with them. But do not forget that if we are passing through the false it is only that we may reach the true. Love not the false if you would have the true. . . . I am going to England before the middle of Lent, and hope to return at Whitsuntide. . . .

'May Almighty God prevent all your wishes and all your actions with His counsel, and further them with His help, friend of mine, dearest to my heart.'[1]

During this his absence in England two kinsmen of his, Haimo and Raynald by name, came to Le Bec in quest of him. Their precise relationship to the saintly abbot cannot, I fear, be ascertained; but the most probable conjecture would make them sons of his second cousin, Amadeus II., Count of Maurienne and Aosta. They were not, however, the first relations by blood who had sought him out. When he was as yet prior a cousin, Dom Folcerad by name, and son, as I imagine, of Count Gerard of Ensheim, came to Le Bec begging to be admitted a member of Herlwin's community, but, whether because his own abbot refused to give him up or because Herlwin declined to receive him, was obliged to wait for better days. He came at last, however, and came, I suspect, as soon as ever Anselm was free to receive him. This, I make no doubt, was the first name inscribed amongst the *nomina monachorum Becci* after Herlwin's death.[2]

---

[1] *Ep.* ii. 25.

[2] The only name of Anselm's professed monks which is lost to us is that of the first (No. 138). It is just possible that, now that I know what to look for, I should see traces of the word Folceradus had I an opportunity of examining the codex. But it gives me a very lively satisfaction to be able to say that I am convinced that the missing name is that of Anselm's kinsman.

Folcerad, in the time of Anselm's priorate, was a monk—where I cannot say, perhaps in the very convent into which Anselm in his boyhood had himself sought admittance. He came to Le Bec to see his kinsman, and spared no effort to obtain release from his present home and country, so as to live under Anselm's rule, but in vain. William the Conqueror wrote twice to the good man's temporal ruler, probably the Count of Maurienne and Aosta, and Herlwin wrote twice to his abbot, but in vain. He went back in the company of a Dom Rodulf or Rudolf—the Rodulf or Rudolf, I suspect, who accompanied Anselm from Aosta when he left his home (No. 70). My own opinion is that Herlwin was not very zealous in the business (*Ep.* l. 46). Be that as it may, some time afterwards there came a verbal message from Dom Folcerad's abbot consenting to his monk's migration; but Anselm, mistrusting it, wrote to him to ascertain the truth. He does not in his letter represent himself as abbot; and, what is still more remarkable, makes no mention of Herlwin; but speaks in general terms of the *abbates* of Le Bec—or we should say, 'the abbot, whoever he may be.' 'Si ergo Deus posuit in corde

And, besides Folcerad, there was another kinsman, a certain cousin Peter, whom Anselm remembered as quite a little boy in the old days, and who seems no sooner to have heard of his succession to the abbacy than he hastened to submit himself to his rule. It is his name, I imagine, which stands immediately before that of William de Montfort.

But to return to Haimo and Raynald. The Abbot was in England when, in the spring of 1083, they found their way to Le Bec. On hearing of their arrival he wrote:—

'When I heard, souls dearest to my soul, that you had come so far to see me, I cannot tell you how my soul was deluged with joy, how the blossom of my hope for you expanded, how my desire after you, always ardent, broke out into flames of impatience. Already, my dearest cousins, do my eyes long to see you face to face, already do my arms stretch forth to clasp you, and my lips are impatient for your kiss, and all that is left to me of life yearns to have you for companions, that my soul may rejoice with you in the fulness of the joy of the life to come. . . . Hope alternates with prayer, and prayer with hope, that He who has brought you so far will finish what He has begun according to my desire. But meanwhile my desire urges me on; my heart from its fulness compels me to speak. O taste, my dearest loved ones, O taste and see that the

---

vestro ut præfatum filium vestrum sub abbatum ejus regimine penitus concedatis' (*Ep.* ii. 20). I suspect, therefore, that this letter of Anselm's was written after Herlwin's death and before his own consecration.

It may be asked, however, Did Folcerad really change his monastery after all? A very pertinent question, to which I am happy to be able to give a very pertinent answer. In *Ep.* iii. 25 Anselm, then Archbishop of Canterbury, writes to Dom Boso, 'Domnus Folcheradus consobrinus noster . . . . olim factus est monachus Becci.'

Now it is evident that he had not been living at Le Bec for some time; and Boso is presumed to know nothing of his ever having done so. He must, therefore, have left before 1089, when Boso made his profession.

We must, therefore, find him a place somewhere before No. 261. And as every place but No. 138 has some other name, his must be No. 138, just where Anselm's letter (ii. 20) to his abbot would have led us to expect to find it.

Lord is sweet! for how sweet He is you can never know so long as the world is sweet to you. . . .

'O how my love for you struggles for utterance! how it longs to shape itself into words! but no words will do. How much there is it wants to say, but my time is too brief and my sheet too small. Do Thou speak for me, O good Jesus; speak to their hearts, else the ear hears in vain; speak to them; tell them to leave all and follow Thee; promise them that when Thou comest to judge they shall sit with Thee and judge with Thee. . . . If they hold to the world, what grief and sorrow will be mine! I am writing too much, but a love past bound compels me. My loved and longed for, farewell; and stay where you are—stay never to go. Let me hear of your good beginning before I come, and when I come find you there.'[1]

One scarcely knows which the more to admire in all this —the writer's enthusiastic devotion for a life of sacrifice and penance, or his tremendous pathos of affectionate appeal to the hearts he longs to win. The *dic, O bone Jesu, cordibus eorum* is the perfection of written rhetoric.

Meanwhile he was growing uneasy about his friend William. William was a man of war; William's brother had gone to the land of the Orient to do battle with the infidel, and William was all eager to follow him and fight by his side. But Anselm's unearthly love for a soul so dear rebelled against this, and he wrote him a letter, the full beauty of which can only be discerned upon comparing it with its predecessor, written before he started for England. Its very superscription resumes the strain of plaintive desire with which the first missive ended, and the two ideas of affection and longing which ran through the first are here worked up into a passage of delicious melancholy. But this is suddenly arrested; remonstrances and reproaches take its place, then after a

[1] *Ep.* ii. 28.

while the cry of desire is heard again, and the whole ends in a melody of hope.

'Such is the affection for your soul, O loved and longed for, with which is has pleased Almighty God to enthral me, that, between her yearning for your salvation and her fear lest your salvation be imperilled, my own soul will not rest. I am tormented day and night on your account. And, blessed be God, may He yet take from you your hatred of your soul, as He has given me this love for it. Bear with me, dear friend; bear with me, for I love you. . . . Love for your soul urges mine, and her love for you will not suffer mine to let you hate that soul, the love of which is part of herself. . . . You, my dearest one—love grieves to say it, but grief loves to do so—you—may God forfend it—you are the enemy of a soul that is dear to mine; you are the enemy of your own soul; for he that loves iniquity hates his soul. Believe me, it is iniquity upon iniquity whither you are hurrying with such eager zest, my loved one. It is iniquity upon iniquity to which the world's headlong torrent is bearing you away, my desired one. Yes; war with all its cruel riot, what is it but iniquity? And the vain world's ambition is nothing but iniquity. And the never-satisfied greed of empty goods and hollow honours is all iniquity. And it is after these—ah! I see him, and, ah! how I love him and long to hold him back— I see him hurrying away, and the cunning foe deludes him on. O God, lover and rescuer of souls, let not the enemy carry off Thy servant!

'You say, my longed for brother, "It is not these things I love, but my brother who is involved in them; and I am all impatience to be involved in them with him, that I may help and shield him." Oh woe! Oh woeful grief of the woeful error of men! Why, mortal, why do you not rather say, "I love not these things, but Christ my God; and so

I flee away from them, and hie me to Him, that He may help and shield me." What! When you hear the crash of a world falling on your brother to his destruction, why do you do despite to the call of Christ, and run away to be crushed at your brother's side? How is one dying man to help and shield another? How can one worm help and shield another? How can you save your brother from being crushed and confounded? Tell me, my brother, while you are helping and shielding him, who will help and shield you? Will God do so, the God whom you take less pains to follow than you do to follow your brother? . . .

'Have done with the Jerusalem that is; it is no vision of peace, but of disaster. Leave alone the treasures of Constantinople and Babylon—they are only meant for blood-stained hands—and set out on a pilgrimage to the heavenly Jerusalem, the vision of peace. There shall you find treasures that are prepared for those that do not despise them.'[1]

Enough. The letter did its work; William's name stands immediately before Haimo's, and the Abbot must have professed the two soon after his return to his monastery. Not for nothing had he poured out his soul on parchment.

Nor was it only or chiefly in writing that he knew how to make such heart to heart appeals. It was by the instrument of speech that he worked the most wonderfully upon others; and the *dic, O bone Jesu*, in his letter to Haimo and Raynald recalls a similar phrase in a story recorded concerning Dom Boso.

This young man, the son of honest parents near Rouen, had already gained distinction as a profound and acute thinker, when, at the age of twenty-three, and in the year 1089, he found his way to Le Bec in quest of the

[1] *Ep.* ii. 19.

Abbot's assistance in solving some metaphysical problem which he could neither unravel nor dismiss from thought. The heedless youth did what so many had already done—fell a victim to the fascination of the Abbot's sanctity, and soon returned to the wooded valley and the convent by the babbling beck. Nor only so; he brought with him an elder brother and a younger, whose names together with his were soon entered on the boards.[1]

At once fervent and punctilious in the discharge of a monk's primary duty, the divine office—or, as it was otherwise called, Divine service, the service of the Lord, God's work—Boso soon won the special regard of Anselm, and rewarded his care of him by a rapid growth in virtue and an unremitting application to intellectual pursuits. The enemy of souls, perceiving this, assailed him with some terrible temptation, which, after threatening him with distraction for some days, brought him at last covered with shame to the feet of the Abbot. He told the whole story. Anselm listened, turned on him a look of ineffable sympathy, said three words, 'Deus consulat tibi,' and dismissed him. In a few moments the tumult ceased, the clouds vanished, and light and peace resumed their reign. Boso never forgot the 'Deus consulat tibi;' and as he told the story, or at least as Eadmer tells the story for him, it would seem as if he had no more to say. But others inform us that he was no sooner gone than the Abbot flew to the church, and, stretched at the foot of one of the altars, poured forth the prayers and tears that obtained for the poor youth the grace of this instantaneous and permanent cure.

We owe the preservation of this story in its two forms to two accidents. Boso knew Eadmer towards the close of Anselm's life, hence the one; and, as in time he became Abbot of Le Bec, it was proper to write his Life when he was gone, hence the other. But, after all, Boso was only one

[1] 260, 261, and 262 in the *Nomina Monachorum*.

of the many who—most of them young, innocent, enthusiastic; some, like Oliver Talvas, in middle life and not unhurt by the world; a few decrepit and weary of life—had recourse to him, the greater number to find rest with him; some few, as it would appear, to turn away irresolute or defer till it was too late. One of these last, though indeed he may have been professed elsewhere, was a certain Henry, to whom the following lines were written:—

'However much glory, my dear friend, you may have acquired in the world, ponder on its end, and in that end ask yourself what profit is there, and what reward? And, on the other hand, think how bright is the hope of those who tread the world's glory under their feet. Perhaps you reply that monks are not the only people that are saved. Nothing could be more true. Still, who are in the surer and higher state, those who try to love God only, or those who wish to link two loves together, the love of God and the love of the world? But perhaps somebody will say that the monastic state is not free from danger. He that says this, why, ah why, does he not think what he is saying? Think, rational soul, think and say, is it reasonable counsel, seeing there is danger everywhere, deliberately to linger where the danger is greatest? Certain it is that if he who tries to have no other love than God keeps his resolution to the end, his bliss is secure; but if he who chooses to love the world does not give up his resolution before the end, his bliss is either lost or uncertain or impaired. . . . But many say God is more angry with a sinning monk than with another man, because his fall is greater. Nothing can be more true, so long as the monk remains in sin. But be sure that, when he comes back repenting, God clasps him in the embrace of a kinder and more intimate love if he returns to his old resolve than one who is not a monk and does not make the same resolve. ... If, then, it is better for innocent souls to come to the monastic life than to stay away, and for the penitent to return to it than to remain aloof, why do you delay? Should you be taken out of this life whilst you are hesitating, your loss would be irreparable. Ah, my dearest friend, much could I tell you of the height and security, the repose and joy, of the monastic life, but that would make my letter too long; but come, come quickly to so great a good, for by no other good will you more effectually attain your highest good. I have known more than one promise and then delay; and death has removed them, and they could not complete the work which none but themselves hindered them from doing, could not even begin what they were purposing to do. I greatly fear this in your case; but God avert it from you, my dearest friend. Farewell, and do not delay.'[1]

Henry's name is not in the list of Anselm's religious.

But this letter reminds me that he had a way all his own of illustrating to his novices the characteristics, the difficulties, and the merits of the monastic state; and one of the tenderest of his many quaint similitudes is that in which he compares a monk to one who has made oath of fealty to an earthly superior. Should he have the misfortune to fall into sin, his very profession was a pledge to him of the Divine commiseration. He was like the vassal who could say to his offended lord, 'My lord, I confess that I have done very wrong and that I am bound by my promise of fealty. But, since I am sorry for the wrong, must I fare worse than those who have refused you their fealty and have offended you besides? The reason why I wanted to be your servant was that, should I ever do wrong, you, instead of judging me as a stranger and another's, might correct me as your own.'

[1] *Ep.* ii. 29.

How can we think but with envy of the hundred and sixty monks, conquests through fifteen years of a love so exquisitely gentle, so heroically strong? Happy indeed should we have been had it been ours to see the play of those refined and sensitive features, to hear the intonations of that eloquent voice, and to prove the sympathy that drew so many, old men, young men, children, to share his supernatural life of penance, labour, and prayer. Happy, thrice happy, they who were so blest!

CHAPTER IV.

DEATH OF WILLIAM THE CONQUEROR—SUCCESSION OF WILLIAM RUFUS.

WHEN, in the summer of 1087, William the Conqueror was carried mortally hurt to Rouen, he made it his chief care to prepare for another world. Anselm was summoned to Court, and a lodging provided for him near the room where the King lay. But scarcely was he there before he in his turn fell suddenly and dangerously ill. Complete repose was declared necessary for him, and he was carried across the Seine to his priory at Sotteville, or, as it was then called, *Hermentrudis Villa.*

The Conqueror's life was drawing to its close, and if, as we review that marvellous career, we seek for something which shall be in keeping with his reverence for Anselm and his desire for Anselm's aid in this emergency, our search will not be all in vain. His zeal for the reformation of manners among the secular clergy ; his resolution that great ecclesiastical preferments should not be debauched by men of scandalous life ; his munificent endowment of religious houses and the encouragement he offered to the like generosity in his barons by legal confirmation of their numerous and ample donations to sanctuaries of piety and learning—these all exhibit William the Conqueror in a more welcome light than measures of severity forced upon him by his acquisition of the crown of England and acts of cruelty suggested by his determination to ensure his hardly won conquest. But, after all, these measures and these acts, in so far as they deserved condemnation, were deplored by their author himself, deplored explicitly, unreservedly, and publicly before he passed away; and it is in any case worthy of reflection that the Norman conquest was mercy itself as compared with all previous invasions of our shore, and chivalry itself, both in its pretensions and in its acts, as compared with some at least that have succeeded it.

Formed by nature to govern others, and skilled in the art of governing, William the Conqueror was surpassed by no prince of his age in the due use of such moral appliances as are not beneath the dignity of a ruler who is other than indifferent to the respect of his subjects. His majestic mien and quelling glance were no symptoms of rebellion against that Divine Kingship of which his own was but a faintest shadow; they were rather the appropriate accessories to a grandeur and strength of character which distinguished him from his predecessors in the duchy, and to a true nobility of soul wherewith nature had marked him out as the first of his race to wear the crown of royal sovereignty; and his subjects wondered that a prince in many respects so unlike the Charlemagnes and the Alfreds of a past age and the Roberts and Edwards of his own, a prince who never wrote hymns or wore sackcloth, should, nevertheless, be so devout, so chaste, and, in the general tenour of his life, so mindful of his own responsibility, so mindful of the majesty of God. An instance of this last characteristic may not be out of place here.

It was some time after his conquest of England that, penetrated with a profound respect for the Cluniac reform which at Jumièges, at Fécamp, and in the monastery of St. Ouen had already done much for Normandy, he not only wished it to be extended into our island, but craved admission into its *societas*. His request was granted; and contemporary writers tell us that when the monk who had acted as his proxy in the business was ushered into his presence, he instantly rose from his seat, doffed his head gear, and bowed himself to the ground with as much reverence as if an angel had come to him from heaven. His lords stood dumb with surprise, deeming it a strange thing that the neck that rarely bent should be thus humbled. But when the monk had retired, and they were already set on asking why, without any visible reason, why before a mere disciple of St. Benedict who carried in his hand nothing that could claim such homage, he had thus lowered his royal majesty, 'Wonder not,' he said, 'that I bowed down so reverently; for the occasion obliged me to do what I judged suitable to it. Never as yet have I received such a boon as this. Think not that even when the crown of this realm was given me I received an honour that may compare with this. All things that I possess here below will have an end as surely as they had a beginning; they were given me, and I shall leave them all behind. But heaven and its glory are eternal, and of heaven and its glory have I now received an earnest in being united with the sacred society of Cluny.'[1]

The church of St. Gervais, on the western outskirt of the city of Rouen, possesses an historic interest to which the vulgar herd of English travellers are appropriately indifferent. Deep buried below its choir and accessible by means of a trap-door and a precipitous flight of steps, there lies a subterranean structure, whose architectural peculiarities suggest some church in the Roman catacombs. It is the cradle of the Church of Normandy. In it St. Mellon was buried; in or over it were long preserved the relics of St. Gervasius sent from Milan by St. Ambrose himself; and although its

[1] Migne, clix. 923. The account adds that in acknowledgment of this favour the Conqueror presented the abbot and monks of Cluny with a cope nearly all of gold; scarcely anything was to be seen in it but gold, or amber, or patterns in pearl wrought into the texture, or rows of precious stones; and it had a fringe of little gold bells all along the lower border. The Queen on the same occasion sent a chasuble, so stiff by reason of its magnificence that it could not be folded.

metropolitan honours had been transferred to a church within the walls of Rouen long before the eleventh century, still the venerable crypt was not forgotten, the Conqueror's grandfather committing its custody to a colony of monks from Fécamp, who built their choir over it. In no more appropriate spot, then, than this priory of St. Gervais could a Christian Duke of Normandy wish to breathe his last sigh; and it was by his own desire that, when the noise and tumult of Rouen had grown irksome to him, William the Conqueror was transported thither. There, as Orderic informs us, Gilbert, Bishop of Lisieux, Gontard, Abbot of Jumièges, and several other prelates, made unremitting efforts and took most anxious pains for both the spiritual and the bodily welfare of the sufferer. The bishop was none other than the Gilbert Maminot who consecrated one of the altars at Le Bec in 1077; the abbot was a Cluniac monk, and, amongst the great Churchmen of Normandy, second only to Anselm in reputation for sanctity. No doubt he had been summoned to supply Anselm's place.

As the prostrate prince surveyed the chamber, his keen and practised eye, made keener by suffering and informed by illumination from the eternity he was nearing, read the thought that was uppermost in the hearts of the men that hung about him. When was the near, uncertain, perhaps terrible, future to begin? His children were haggling over the partition of crown, coronet, and dowry; his barons trembling for the fate of their fiefs; his chaplains forecasting the advent of an unprincipled successor. We may not, and dare not, doubt that Gilbert and Gontard did their best, the one for his body, the other for his soul; or that the latter was bold enough, strong enough, tender enough, to turn a deaf ear to the coming storm and attempt the supreme endeavour of taking that lonely soul into his charge and bearing it company, tranquil and undisturbed, to the bourn of the cleansing fires. To die alone is Heaven's behest for each of us; but it was the peculiar lot of William the Conqueror to be deprived of the one man in Normandy, who, as he knew without the faintest shadow of a doubt, possessed all the heroism, all the tenderness, and all the wisdom that were required to vanquish to the very uttermost the attendant trials of such a change as the present. And as he lay there racked with the fierce pain of his inner wound, he let his thoughts fly evermore to his friend down at Sotteville, and missed no opportunity of evincing an attachment that had in it all the intimacy of a fraternal love. Whatever of choicest fruit for the assuaging of his thirst, or of carefully prepared delicacy for keeping up the spark of life, was brought to the King, he sent half of it across the Seine to Abbot Anselm.

On Wednesday, the eighth day of September, his two sons, William and Henry, were summoned to the sick room. There the dying prince, after taking such order for the distribution of his dominions as he deemed best and wisest, indited a letter to the Archbishop of Canterbury, in whose hands the destinies of England were soon to lie, and causing it to be sealed with his royal and ducal seal,[1] handed it to the elder of the two, and bade him take ship for England without delay. Whatever reluctance William the Red may have felt in obeying such an injunction was overcome by the fond parent, who kissed him, gave him his blessing, and hurried him away.

The pain which had tortured the royal sufferer relaxed its grip at evening, and yielded to the dull anodyne of mortification. Gilbert Maminot knew the meaning of this, and whispered it to Gontard; but bishop and abbot deemed it wise to postpone the administration of the last rites till the morning, and prepared to keep watch. All through the

---

[1] The seal need not be described. Abbot Herman of St. Martin's, Tournay, writes like one who had seen it. 'Guillelmus duos principatus obtinuit, existens comes Northmannorum et rex Anglorum, ita ut in sigillo suo ex unâ parte sederet super equum ut comes, in aliâ super thronum cum sceptro ut rex.'

night the attendants, now slumbrously awake and now fitfully dozing, were undisturbed by start or cry of pain. A waxen torch cast its mellow flicker on the walls of the room, and by the lessening of its bulk marked for any who might languidly regard it the steady lapse of the monotonous hours, for no bell rang for matins in the adjacent church; all was hushed and kindly still. And who shall say how the sufferer was employed? Yesterday he made a full and detailed avowal to children and attendants of the errors of a career eventful from the first. Is memory now reweaving all this chequered panorama? Or does he regretfully yearn for the friend who has been so strangely taken from him? Or is it Anselm's midnight hymn that he is mentally reciting?—

> Light that shinest through the gloom,
> Offspring of the Virgin's womb,
> Roll the darkness all away,
> Clothe us in Thy glorious day.[1]

Or is he already entering on those mysterious regions where some subtler faculty than the thought that frames itself in speech is called into exercise; regions where sight and knowledge are evolved, of which present sight and present knowledge are but a rudimentary beginning? Who shall say?

The day broke; the growing light recalled him from his

---

[1] 'Lux quæ luces in tenebris
Ex alvo natus Virginis,
Nostram noctem nos exue,
Diemque tuam indue.

'Maria Dei thalamus,
Posce te venerantibus,
Virtutibus ut splendeant,
Quos reatus obtenebrant.

'Gloria tibi, Domine,
Nato de Sanctâ Virgine;
Regnanti, victo funere,
Cum Patre et Sancto Spiritu.'

There are eight such pairs of verses, each pair followed by the same doxology. They are assigned to the several ecclesiastical hours, compline included.

reverie; the great bell at the cathedral down in Rouen began to toll, and the sound floated up through the clear air, soft and full. He asked what it meant. 'Sire,' was the reply, 'it is the bell for prime at St. Mary's.' 'Then he raised his eyes to heaven in a transport of devotion, and, stretching forth his hands, exclaimed, "To my Queen, God's holy Mother, Mary, I yield myself; and may she by her holy prayers reconcile me to her dearest Son, our Lord Jesus Christ."'

The arms dropped upon the coverlet, and the jaw fell. He had not received the last unction, and his attendants had made sure that God would not let him die without it. This was a premonitory seizure, but certainly not death. And so, taken off their guard, they did what they had been rehearsing—lifted him from his couch to stretch him on the floor, for only thus might a Christian die—when, even as they did so, the truth flashed on them. Terrible always, he was worse than terrible in this new mood of his. They had thought him their consecrated dying king; it was an unanointed corpse they were handling!

Panics like these are instantaneous, and in an age like that were irresistible. Bishop, abbot, and earl quailed under the shock, and, their reason overborne by dismay and horror, flew from the chamber of the dead![1]

William Rufus was at Touque when the news overtook him. Accompanied by Robert Bloet, a chaplain of the late King's, he crossed the Channel and made with all speed for

---

[1] This seems to me to be, on the whole, the right account of an event which has by some writers been invested with additional and unnecessary horror, and it is supported by Eadmer's words, 'mox ut in terram spiritum exhalaturus positus est.' Orderic's rhetorical apostrophe has been somewhat overcoloured by Dean Church in the process of transference from Latin into English. *Spoliatus* is not exactly 'foully stripped;' and the time that elapsed before the composure of the corpse for burial was not two solar hours, but the interval between prime and terce, during which the monks, uninformed of what had happened, were in the chapter house. And certainly I can find no authority whatever for the Dean's assertion that 'the servants stripped the very corpse.'

Canterbury, where he found the Archbishop. The news well-nigh broke the heart of the venerable prelate; but he recovered self-possession with more than the energy of ninety years, and soon addressed himself to the task that now devolved upon him.

England was without a king. Whom, then, were the bishops and barons of England, with the concurrence of the Primate, to elect for their sovereign? Or whom, if elected without the Primate's concurrence, would it soon be his duty either to accept as worthy or to reject as unworthy of the crown? The Conqueror's letter, much as Lanfranc might respect its contents, could not release him from the obligation of proposing, or, if not of proposing, then of accepting, the most eligible candidate for the throne. His choice lay between the Conqueror's three sons, Robert, William, and Henry. Robert was the eldest, William had been recommended to his preference, and Henry could boast that he was born in the purple.

As to the Conqueror's refusal to make an absolute bequest of the crown, it might well have been dictated by prudence, even if piety had failed to suggest it; for the bishops and barons, if old constitutional usage was to be observed, were entitled to lay claim to its disposition, and the theory was not as yet obsolete that Kings of England were the elected rulers of their people.[1] Physical inability to take the field, intellectual incapacity for personal government, or moral unfitness to be the leader of Christian men, would be certain to entail such results as human wisdom, at least in England, had not as yet contrived means for averting. The clergy, therefore, and the nobility would not be likely to neglect their immemorial rights; and amongst the former body there was one whose judgment as to moral fitness was pretty

---

[1] Not, that is to say, set up by a clique, nor even by the citizens of London, but solemnly chosen by a *bonâ fide* election, in which the lords spiritual, the lords temporal, and the commons took their legitimate part.

sure to be accepted with an implicit confidence. Occupant of a chair more ancient than the throne of England, and depository of an authority whose limits stretched far wider than the boundaries of the realm, the Archbishop of Canterbury was the most influential and most powerful of all prelates in Christendom, with one obvious exception; and it would even seem as though long use had given the successor of St. Augustine of Canterbury the same sort of prerogative in the election of Kings of England as was enjoyed by the Sovereign Pontiff in the election of Kings of Germany. It need not, therefore, surprise us to learn from Eadmer that without Lanfranc's consent it was impossible for William Rufus to become King of England.[1]

Lanfranc hesitated. Henry's supporters, if indeed he had any, must have been too few for him to concern himself much about that prince, and the choice lay between Duke Robert and William the Red. Robert may have been vain, silly, worthless, and sure to involve his subjects in misery; but William the Red might prove heartless, headstrong, and despotic; and, after all, the separation of the kingdom from the duchy was a contingency not to be thought lightly of by men who in that case would find themselves the vassals of two rival lords.

But Lanfranc had misgivings in the moral order as well as in the political; and so persistent was his reluctance to consecrate the Red Prince that the latter, rather than lose the prize which already seemed to be escaping him, was fain to promise, under oath, others swearing with him as his sureties, that, should he be made king, he would in everything observe justice, equity, and mercy throughout the realm, defend the peace and liberty of the Church against all men

---

[1] 'Lanfrancus, sine cujus assensu in regnum adscisci nullatenus potuit' (clix. 361c). Thus Orderic's account of the illegitimacy of Harold's accession is not only that he was not duly elected, but that he was consecrated by an archbishop who had been suspended by the Pope—not only, that is to say, was Harold an intruder; the sacred oil had been poured on him by an intruder.

THE NEW KING.

and in all things, and invariably comply with the Archbishop's precepts and counsels.[1]

It was not, therefore, until the nineteenth day after his father's death that William Rufus was consecrated King of the English.

The first act of his reign was in keeping with the generosity of his early, if indeed it did not presage the prodigality of his later, years. He threw open the royal treasury at Winchester, and bringing out to the day its accumulated hoard, gave to some of the chief ecclesiastical establishments ten golden marks, to others six, and five silver shillings to every *ecclesia villæ*. He further sent into each county the sum of a hundred pounds for distribution among the poor, and displayed his piety towards his fond, and perhaps too partial, father by lavishing precious stones, as well as the precious metals, upon his sepulchral monument at Caen.

William of Malmesbury, whose praise is perhaps elegance of style rather than severe accuracy of record, gives the fol-

[1] This was a gratuitous promise made to gain the Primate's consent, and must not be confounded with the coronation oath. The latter was, no doubt, identical with that taken by the Kings of England before the Conquest. What that was may be learnt from the following transcript from Archbishop Robert's *Benedictionarium* preserved at Rouen :—

'*Incipit consecratio regis.*

'*Rex autem cum consecrandus fuerit de conventu seniorum ducatur per manus à duobus principibus ad basilicam, choris interim hanc antiphonam cantantibus, duobus tamen episcopis initiantibus*, Firmetur manus tua et exaltetur dextera tua, justitia et judicium preparatio sedis tuæ, misericordia et veritas precedent faciem tuam. Gloria, p. et f. et s.s. *Reveniens ad ecclesiam prosternat se coram altari et ymnizetur* Te Deum Laudamus. *Quo ymnizato erigatur de solo et ab episcopis et plebe electus hæc triplicia jura ei servaturum promittat:* Hæc tria populo christiano et mihi subdito in Christi promitto nomine, in primis ut ecclesia dei et omnis populus christianus veram pacem nostro arbitrio in omni tempore servabo ; aliud, ut rapacitates et omnes iniquitates omnibus gradibus interdicam.; tertium, ut in omnibus judiciis equitatem et misericordiam precipiam ut mihi et vobis indulgeat suam misericordiam clemens et misericors deus qui vivit et regnat.

'*His peractis omnes dicunt* Amen.
Hic sequantur orationes ab episcopis,'
&c. &c. &c.

lowing account of William Rufus:—' He was conspicuous for a hauteur of character, which in the lapse of time degenerated into excessive harshness. The change was slow and gradual, and so stealthy was the inroad of vice into his bosom that virtue was already driven out before he himself perceived the change. The world was long in doubt as to what turn, what permanent direction, his character would take at last. At first, and while Archbishop Lanfranc was still alive, he shunned all that was wrong, and men hoped to find in him the very pink and model of a king. Upon the Primate's death the balance hung for a while all too equally poised, and dipped irresolutely, now on the side of virtue, now on that of vice; but in the latter part of his reign the love of good waxed finally cold in him, and an undergrowth of ill ripened quickly and grew to seed. More than this, he was not so much liberal as a spendthrift, his pride was a supercilious disdain, and his severity degenerated into cruelty. May I venture, *pace majestatis regiæ*, not to conceal the truth? The truth is, he feared God but little, and men not at all. . . . In his more public intercourse with others he held himself erect, his face swelling with importance; his eye flashed threateningly, and you stood pierced by its glance; whilst, affecting a rigour that was not his own, he made you tremble as he spoke, so fierce was the tone of his voice. So far as we may venture to conjecture, the apprehension of straitened means made him unduly fond of lucre, and suspicion of other men's unfaithfulness unduly prone to severity. At table and in his private intercourse he was easy and agreeable; he was very fond of raillery, and knew how to veil the recital of his own peccadilloes under the disguise of such a graceful verbiage as at once mitigated the odium of the offence and diverted the attention of his hearers to his skill in innuendo.'

Such is William of Malmesbury's account in the 'Gesta Regum.' In the 'Gesta Pontificum,' however, he so far rectifies it as to give us to understand that the hopeful period of William's reign came to a close immediately, or almost immediately, upon his settlement in the throne, some seven or eight months after his accession, and not on Lanfranc's death—in the early summer, that is to say, of 1088, not in the early summer of 1089. And this more accurate statement tallies with that of Eadmer, who informs us that a change in William from good to ill, and all that that change implied and involved, accelerated Lanfranc's end; not that Lanfranc's end invited William to swerve from a course of rectitude hitherto pursued. An occasion presented itself—what occasion I shall have to enquire when the proper moment comes for doing so—on which the Primate, perceiving that the youthful prince had ventured on a policy irreconcilable with the promises which had secured him his crown, took him to task in mild and temperate phrase. William at once flew into a passion; his face turned from red to crimson; his tongue, always too large for his mouth, became unmanageable, and he spluttered out the words, 'Who can keep all his promises?' The dignity with which Lanfranc, now more than ninety years of age, received this affront disinclined the royal boor to attempt a second; and a second might have tried too sorely the reticence of the gentlemen about him. From that day forward, therefore, he, with sidelong glance of apprehension, tempered some of the excesses to which the desire of his heart was prompting him; but it was remarked that he never again had a kind look for his monitor.[1]

[1] 'Non rectis oculis super pontificem intendere volebat.' One would suppose at first sight that these words mean 'was never again able to look him in the face'—that is to say, from shame—but the passages I am about to quote seem to discourage the idea that he had grace enough left for shame. The first is from Eadmer (clix. 514), who in his account of his own troubles in Scotland says that the king of that country, being thoroughly out of humour with him, took all possible means for annoying and injuring him, and could neither look at him *recto oculo* nor listen patiently to what he wanted to say. The second is from a letter of St. Thomas of Canterbury to Alexander III., in which he quotes the following words of the King: 'Ipse (filius meus) vos tantâ affectione diligit ut aliquem inimicorum vestrorum recto lumine nequeat intueri' (*Ep.* 25). In each of these cases the notion conveyed is that not of shame, but aversion.

Disappointment, grief, and anxiety soon fretted away the Primate's attenuated thread of life. '*His pertæsus non moras longas in luce traxit.*' Enfeebled by slow fever, he consulted the physicians, who prescribed a remedy which, if it failed to cure, would very probably kill, and then, fortified with confession and the life-giving Body and Blood of our Divine Lord, resigned himself for better or for worse to the rude skill of the age. It had been misapplied. He passed away on the 28th of May, 1089,[1] and was buried in his magnificent cathedral in front of the great crucifix.

No sooner was Lanfranc's death announced to the King than he divulged a scheme, the audacity of which was as yet without precedent in the history of our country. Its author, Renouf by name, was the son of a woman whose crimes and talents were by her scandalised and wondering contemporaries ascribed to intercourse with the enemy of mankind. To the fiend, too, as they believed, was she indebted for the loss of one of her eyes, but not before commerce with a low-born, inconspicuous priest in the Bessin had destined her to immortality as mother of the most audacious, the most versatile, and the most unscrupulous of miscreants.

Renouf's education, wherever obtained, had not been of the highest order, when, as yet a mere boy, he found his way to the purlieus of the ducal court of Rouen; but in volubility of speech and readiness of resource he possessed natural endowments which, recommended by a handsome face and figure, soon compensated for this deficiency and made him the admiration and the envy of the grooms, the lackeys, and the footmen amongst whom he lived.

---

[1] I believe a doubt has been raised as to the day of the month on which he died. The date I have given is confirmed by the necrology of Beaumont-le-Roger —' *V. Kal. jun. D. Lanfrancus archiepiscopus.*'

His tomb was opened in 1158; witness the following (Cod. Lambeth, 585): '*De Inventione Lanfranci.* Lanfrancus archiepiscopus in tabulâ plumbeâ ponderosâ valde inventus, in quâ à die primæ sepulturæ suæ intactis membris mitratus et spindulatus usque in illum diem jacuerat annis videlicet lxix, et aliquot mensibus, ut in gornalio habetur,'

Choosing the clerical profession as his avenue to place, he in course of time obtained a footing at court, where he carried himself so arrogantly to the gentlemen employed about the King that the first suitable *sobriquet* would be sure to cling to his name. To Robert le Despenser belongs the felicitous invention of the word Flambard, and Renouf now gloried in a surname. His first preferment seems to have been the deanery of Christchurch Twynham, which he held till the year 1088, when, being made a King's chaplain, ample opportunity was afforded him for unfolding to his master designs the execution of which soon convinced the world that his nickname had been invented by a prophetic inspiration. 'In very sooth, cries Orderic, 'he was an *ardens flamma*; he brought in new ways that cruelly crushed hosts of people and turned the Church's momentary songs of joy into wailing and sorrow.'

Taking the Domesday survey for his source of information, he carved off from all lay estates, whether in English hands or Norman, so much of them as might be in excess of a certain area, and doubled or even trebled[1] the sum total of the revenue derived from the tax on land throughout the country by the double process of raising the assessment per hide beyond its legal limit and of fictitiously augmenting the number of taxable hides through the employment of a reduced standard of superficial measurement.

There is little need to say that many rich men were impoverished and many poor men utterly ruined by these measures, or that many a little holding which had been handed down from father to son through long years was confiscated to the Crown, and its wretched occupant mercilessly evicted, either because the soil refused to yield the exorbitant charge or because the cultivator was unable to procure it from

[1] W. M., *Gesta Regum*, § 314; O. V. iii. 313. I should, perhaps, say trebled; for William of Malmesbury's words are 'duplum adjiciebat.' The little I have to say on this subject will be found in the Appendix.

other sources. Prayers, remonstrances, threats, were all alike wasted on Renouf. He quibbled, haggled, bullied, as circumstances prompted, and after quibbling, haggling, bullying, to his own heart's content, bore down at last upon his tired and disheartened victim with such a storm of invective as extorted what he wanted. But broken hearts and ruined fortunes were unimportant trifles to the Firebrand, who, on reporting his successes to the King, was applauded with a laugh and a chuckle, and the flattering avowal that there was only one man living who knew how to practise his talents thus, or who could snap his fingers at mankind and their hatred, provided only that he pleased his master.

Nor did Church lands escape. It was the ancient custom of our country that the revenues of a vacant abbey should be administered by the bishop of the diocese, those of a vacant see by the archbishop of the province, and disbursed in the relief of poverty, the building of churches, and other good works. But that practice had for some thirty years been superseded by another which committed such revenues to the custody of the sovereign, in virtue of the privilege of *advocatio* granted by Nicholas II. to the Kings of England; and, since the business of an *advocatus* was protection, not administration, the revenues were allowed to accumulate during a vacancy. Hence in the Conqueror's time not a penny was touched of the moneys that accrued to a church between its avoidance and the appointment of a new incumbent.

Now, what Renouf proposed was, to replace this *advocatio* by *dominatio*; in other words, to abolish the office of guardian of the temporalities and establish absolute lordship in its place. In short, Cæsar was to take from God the things that were God's, and render them to himself. The reader has not forgotten that William Rufus, on the convenient but questionable ground that no man can keep all his promises, had by this time tossed his precoronation oath to the winds. In those days of personal government the only effective check upon royal tyranny was conscience, and the only proper person to keep that check in working order was the Archbishop of Canterbury. But now there was no Archbishop of Canterbury. What, then, would happen next? And next? But this was not all. As if it were not enough that the assumption of absolute lordship over ecclesiastical property should be succeeded by its natural consequences, the needless prolongation of vacancies and the confiscation of moneys accruing during those intervals, two further contrivances were set in operation. The first of these was that the King should rack the rents by farming the various sources of revenue to the highest bidder; the second, that after prolonging the vacancy to the satisfaction of his caprice he should sell the succession.

Renouf had been William's chaplain since 1088; on Lanfranc's death he was made justicer of the kingdom, and he already enjoyed, in addition to this, the two offices of King's procureur and King's receiver, when on Whit Sunday, the 29th of May, 1099—*pace regiæ majestatis* be it recorded —he was appointed Bishop of Durham. His acknowledgment of the honour was the sum of a thousand pounds; but a thousand pounds could easily be spared from his enormous savings.

Seated in the chair of St. Cuthbert, whose distinctive characteristic it was to punish sinners upon their first offence with equal quickness and severity, our adventurer was for a season cowed into such a moderation of behaviour as no influence, human or divine, had ever as yet elicited. But no sooner had he, after a few very cautious essays, convinced himself that the saint's resentment might be provoked with impunity, than he relapsed into his own old ways, and even went to such lengths of impiety as to violate an usage which, in the opinion of his contemporaries, was more sacred than the revenues he had secularised or the shrines he had profaned; and it was the memorable distinction of Renouf that he dared to arrest, and with his own hands drag to punishment, the trembling wretch who had fled to his cathedral for benefit of sanctuary.

Upon the death of 'his own king' fortune for the first time frowned on him. One of Henry Beauclerc's earliest royal acts was to consign him to the Tower of London, where, however, in consideration, perhaps, of his episcopal character, he treated him with leniency and even kindness, and gave him a pecuniary allowance, which, with help from his friends, enabled him not only to live right sumptuously himself, but to give his wardens a daily invitation to dinner. It must have been either on the Feast of Candlemas or on the morrow, which in 1101 was a Sunday, that, having ordered an unusually copious banquet, he plied these gentlemen with wine until they were *admodum inebriati* and fell under the table. Now amongst his wine jars was one heavy, not with the exhilarating juice, but with a stout hempen rope. This he drew from its hiding place and tied to the mullion of the window; then, fastening the episcopal staff to his person, he got out of the window and let himself down. The rope was very rough, and he very heavy, so that the flesh on his hands was laid open to the bones; Orderic duly remarks that his lordship had forgotten to assume the episcopal gauntlets. But this was not all; the rope was too short, and so—but dear old Orderic must tell the story—'gravi lapsu corpulentus flamen ruit, et, pene conquassatus, flebiliter ingemuit.' But his accomplices had a good horse in readiness; he flew to the coast, took ship for Normandy, and landed safe and sound. His mother was less fortunate. That venerable sorceress sailed in another vessel, having in charge his money, his plate, and his other treasure. But her son's dignity failed to shield her from the infamy which she had incurred as the devil's confidant, and while the crew, neglecting their proper duty, tormented her for her witchcrafts, which were many, they were surprised by pirates, who seized the treasure but let her go.

Renouf at once became the life and soul of Duke Robert's enterprise against the new King of England. This service had an early reward in the preferment of his brother Foucher to the see of Lisieux; and on Foucher's death in 1102 he himself took possession of it in the name of his son Thomas, a boy of twelve, and for three years governed it *non ut præsul sed ut præses*.[1]

But I need not further pursue his history; and it may suffice to add that he was reconciled to the King soon after the battle of Tenchebrai, in 1106, and returned to Durham, where he died in 1128.[2]

To return, however, to the ten years that intervened between Lanfranc's death and Renouf's promotion to the see of Durham. The frightful traffic in sacred things inaugurated by William Rufus and his minister brought bad men, and none but bad men, to the fore; and public morality was at an end. 'Alas! alas!' cries the Wiltshire monk, 'in a few short years all was changed. There was not a man in office that had not dishonoured his place by purchase. In every clerk you saw some petty attorney, and priests were turned to publicans. Forgive the phrase; there was not, I mean, a parish priest who had not taken his cure of souls on farm. There was not a wretch, whatever his condition, not a miscreant, whatever his crime, who, let him but drop a whisper of profit to the royal purse, failed to obtain a hearing; and the bandit could get the halter loosened from his throat by offering the King money. The high tone of knightly prowess

---

[1] A younger boy had been secured the right of succession. Some interesting details of this scandal are to be found in the correspondence of St. Yvo of Chartres (*Epp.* 153, 154, 157).

[2] The famous crosier which he carried with him in his perpendicular escape from confinement—for I presume it to be the same—was buried with him. So much of it as in the course of more than seven centuries could waste had wasted, but its iron crook and ferrule were brought to light a few years ago.

was relaxed and lowered; and hangers-on at court, themselves living upon the substance of their rural dependents, devoured the poor people's little fortunes and took the food out of their mouths.'

William of Malmesbury wrote for royal readers, and for young ones. Nevertheless, such is the picture he paints, when, after turning from the public immorality to that of the court, he passes from this to the private life of some of its members, that I draw the curtain over it.

CHAPTER V.

ABBOT ANSELM'S THIRD VISIT TO ENGLAND.

As William the Conqueror sank to his end Anselm was already recovering from the illness that had kept him prisoner at Sotteville. He was thus able to travel as far as Caen for the funeral of his royal friend.

It may have been during this interval of convalescence that, whether in dream or in ecstasy matters not, he had a strange but characteristic vision. He beheld, and lo! a river swift and full. That river as it rushed along swept into its current all the unseemly residues of earth; and the further it flowed the muddier and fouler did it seem, till at last it showed no better than one vast turbulent drain. But on it rushed, and on, and sucked and carried off whatsoever lay on its banks; and men dropped in, and women; and high and low dropped in, and floated down and down, irreparably swept away. 'But how are they to live,' he thought to himself, 'and wherewithal shall they quench their thirst?' when a voice told him that they lived on the stream and relished their food. 'What!' cried he, loathing and horrified. 'Why, no man for very shame could bring himself to drink such noisomeness.' 'Wonder not,' rejoined his companion. 'What you see is the world, and the men and the women of the world drop into its current and drift away. But would you like to behold the true monastic state?' 'I should,' said Anselm; whereupon the guide set him in the quadrangle of a large and spacious monastery, saying, 'Look around.' He looked, and lo! the walls of the cloister round about were overlaid with glistening silver; a silvery radiance gleamed on him whichever way he turned; whilst the very turf, though it yielded to the tread and then redressed itself, and showed in every way a real sward soft and elastic, was yet turf of silver. And, besides all this, there was such a nameless sober grace and chastened gaiety about the spot that he was fain to cry, ' Here let me dwell.' To a true monk like Anselm there was an especially appropriate charm in such a scene; for, since heaven was his ultimate home, he must be content that his monastery, whose every detail was a symbol—the refectory of reading, the chapter house of self-discipline, the dormitory of contemplation, the oratory of devotion—that all this fabric of protection and enclosure set round about the tranquil sward, the *hortus conclusus* of the elect but unbeatified soul, should be transfigured to a beauty such as this. Not as yet might he behold the city whose streets are of pure gold, and all her gates pearls; and his fairest vision of the cloister could scarce be fairer than this silvery splendour. So he cried, 'Here let me dwell.' ' Be it so,' said the guide; ' but would you not like a glimpse of real patience?' ' I should indeed,' he said, for patience was his dearest aspiration; ' I should indeed,' he said; and, as he spoke, guide and vision vanished.

In the spring of 1088 Anselm paid his third recorded visit to England in his quality of abbot, landing on our shore on Mid-Lent Sunday, March 26. He came intending to ask the new King for a confirmation of the grants of land hitherto made to his monastery in our island, and hoped to obtain that favour at the general meeting of the peers at Easter. He would then inspect his estates and return to Le Bec for Whitsuntide.

But when Easter came he found but the shadow of such an assembly as might have been expected to gather round the prince and share the joys of his first Paschal coronation; for the turbulent and mischievous Bishop Odo had tampered with the barons, and already at Rochester, at Pevensey, at Tunbridge, at Arundel, at Shrewsbury, at Leicester, and at Norwich the standard of revolt was unfurled, or, where not unfurled, unfurling. The King, therefore, begging his visitor to wait till Whitsuntide, led his troops in all haste to Tunbridge, where, after a two days' siege, he received the submission of its defender, Earl Gilbert, the son of Richard Fitzgilbert. Six weeks later a campaign, as memorable as it was brief, was brought to a close under the walls of Rochester.

There is little need to say that the miscarriage of Bishop Odo's enterprise was mainly due to the indolence of the Duke of Normandy and to the help given William by his native subjects. But when the prelate and his adjutants, Eustace of Boulogne and Robert of Bellesme, on returning to Normandy, told the Duke who it was that had conciliated the King's clemency in their favour, the Duke must have been less than human did he not resolve to evince his gratitude to the counsellor who had so marvellously conjured William's resentment as that three such enemies as they should be permitted to ride forth from the gates of Rochester and to quit the island, not a hair of their head injured. That counsellor was Lanfranc.

There was a full court at Whitsuntide. William's unswerving adherents, such as Hugh of Chester and William of Warenne, were there to congratulate their master and themselves; whilst less faithful barons, such as Gilbert of Tunbridge and the Earl of Shrewsbury, were also there; for after their recent experience of a magnanimity that refused to punish, it would ill have become them to stay away.

During Whitsun week, or at any rate before the breaking up of the court, the Abbot of Le Bec wrote to his monks, telling them that he had spoken to the King on a subordinate matter of business, about which they had sent him a message, but that he had as yet no definitive reply to give them, and that he hoped to obtain the desired deed of confirmation, but hinting in the last sentence of the letter that it was just possible his return home might be slightly postponed. In the course of a few days, however, he left England, embarking, as I imagine, at Bosham, and carrying with him not only the King's charter of confirmation, but pleasing recollections of sympathy from one and all of the King's barons and regrets for a friend dearer and closer to his heart than any of them; for, if I am not mistaken, the brutal speech, 'Who can keep all his promises?' had just been made to Lanfranc, and the adieux of archbishop and abbot were saddened not only by the reflection that these were probably their last, but by an apprehension of the early incidence of some great disaster.

After a brief halt at Caen he set forth in haste, whither we know not. He had communicated the secret of his movements to the Abbot of St. Stephen's, but all that we can gather from his letters is that he was bent on some special errand somewhere in the kingdom of France, that he had scarcely discharged it when he was laid low with fever induced by mental anxiety, and that he scarcely regained his cloister before the middle of July.[1]

I shall have to recur to these incidents in a later portion of my work.

---

[1] 'Beccum ante festivitatem S. Benedicti . . . . videre non potui.' This *festivitas S. Benedicti* was not March 21, but July 11, on which day is celebrated the translation of the body of St. Benedict from Monte Cassino to Fleury.

CHAPTER VI.

LE BEC AND CANTERBURY AT THE CLOSE OF 1089.

'HERE let me dwell,' must have been his prayer when, on returning to Le Bec in the July of 1088, he once more found himself in the society of his monks. One of the youngest of them—youngest in profession, at least, for he had only worn the cowl for a month or two—was Baldwin,[1] erewhile *advocatus* of the diocese of Tournay and a man of political celebrity; whilst amongst the novices there were Hugh de Gournay, member of a family famous in history; and Odo, an old friend of the Abbot's and not improbably a native of Aosta.

And very soon others found their way to that secluded valley, for the most part young men who had no higher wish than to serve God under Anselm's direction and in emulation of Anselm's piety. Indeed, the prosperity of Le Bec—so far as the prosperity of a community may be gauged by its exterior accidents—must now have been very near its culminating point, for the number of professions during the next twelvemonth can scarcely, upon the most moderate calculation, have been less than twenty, and may, indeed,

---

[1] We shall see more of Dom Baldwin, but meanwhile I must observe that M. Le Prévost (*O. V.* iv. 14 *n.*) is mistaken in supposing him to have been a Norman. He was a Fleming, and the place whence he derived his surname was the Flemish Tournay, not a hamlet near Le Bec. The allusions to him in Abbot Herman's *Restauratio Abbatiæ S. Martini Tornac.* leave no doubt of this.

As to the other persons mentioned in the text, I must beg the reader to compare *Epp.* ii. 25, 26 and the *Nomina Monachorum*. The 'domina Basilia' mentioned in the second letter was the widow of Hugh de Gournay, a friend of the Conqueror's, and was at this time living near Anselm's monastery with the Lady Eva.

have risen to thirty; whilst, if the man be happy who, though burdened with responsibilities, has no cares; who, though poor, is no longer pinched by want; who, though great, has not yet an enemy; if he may be deemed happy whom Popes have summoned to share their counsels and kings to receive their confidences, and the products of whose genius, inspired with all the grace of youth and with all the vigour of manhood, are already set by the discerning side by side with those of the foremost guides of thought in bygone ages; if he be truly happy who in a time of conflict, of passion, and of tumult can thankfully avow that, though empires have been swept by political whirlwind and kingdoms ravaged from end to end by moral pestilence, the storm has not come nigh him, nor the plague approached his dwelling—if such a man be happy, then Anselm's happiness was at its flood between the summer of 1088 and the summer of 1089.

But when visions are at their brightest who shall say how soon they may be blurred? In the May of 1089 Archbishop Lanfranc went to his reward, and was followed in September by Gerbert, Abbot of St. Wandrille. The Conqueror, in the dying speech commemorated by Orderic, had mentioned Gerbert by name in the following connection:—' Never,' said he, ' have I dishonoured Mother Church; on the contrary, it has been the great desire of my life, whenever occasion might offer, to show her respect. Never have I made traffic of ecclesiastical preferments; and as to simony, I have always detested and kept clear of it. In the choice of dignitaries (*personarum*) I have tried to find out sound doctrine and meritorious life, and so far as in me lay I have entrusted the government of the Church to the worthiest men that were to be had. This my boast has its verification in such men as Lanfranc, Archbishop of Canterbury; Anselm, Abbot of Le Bec; Gerbert, Abbot of Fontenelle; Durand, Abbot of Troarn, and many others the teachers of this my realm, whose praise, if I mistake not, has extended to the very limits of Christendom. Men like these have been my companions in counsel; I have found truth and wisdom in their society, and it has always been a satisfaction and a pleasure to me to avail myself of their advice.'

But no such principle of action was to rule the Conqueror's successor in the duchy, who, being only a duke, soon displayed a melancholy pride in aping the offences of an emperor. No sooner was Abbot Gerbert dead than Robert Courthose, as though he were free to set aside the rights of the proper electors and to trample the best interests of their monastery underfoot, boldly adopted the imperial theory, threw canon law to the winds, threw his duty as a Christian prince to the winds, threw public decorum to the winds, and made known his resolution to give away the abbacy of St. Wandrille at Fontenelle to whom he would, just as he might have given a tenantless cottage or a tenantless field of his own to whom he would. What the Conqueror had treated as a public trust the Conqueror's son now treated as a private chattel.

Here was a change indeed; and to give that change effect, to transfer that change from the realm of theory to the realm of practice, only one condition was required. A vacant dignity was to be treated as a chattel, and all that was needed was a man to accept it as a chattel. And a man there was thus ready; and that man was a monk, a Benedictine, a nephew of the late Archbishop Lanfranc, and, cruellest of all, a child, disciple, subject of Anselm, Abbot of Le Bec!

On hearing the news Anselm wrote a letter to the Duke's unhappy accomplice, and sent it to him wrapped in a parchment cover, upon which was the following memorandum:—

'Brother Anselm, however unworthy, yet still Abbot of the Monastery of Le Bec, to Brother Lanfranc, monk of the same community. May he decline from evil and do good.

'I, Brother Anselm, under God the lover of your soul, your faithful adviser, and, by God's ordinance and your own election, your abbot, admonish you in the name of our Lord Jesus Christ; I counsel and I bid you read carefully this my letter more than twice or thrice; and, placing yourself in the presence of that strict Judge under whose eye you are, ponder well my words and my admonition. And should it chance that, whether from miscarriage or from your refusing to read it, some one else should do so, then in the name of Almighty God I charge him not to withhold salutary admonition from your soul, but on opening this premonitory injunction either to read it to you or to give it you to read, and then to unfold the letter itself and spread it out before you for you to read it for yourself from beginning to end; which if he refuse to do, may God require your sin at his hands, and so there may be no shifting of blame in the day of the revelation of the just judgment of God.'

This terrible *proœmium* must have ensured the perusal of the *ipsa epistola* which accompanied it—a cry of anguish arrested and set down in writing:—

'Before things were set in train for your receiving an abbacy, I said to you and to others, I said in private and in public, I said from my heart and with my lips, that I was unwilling you should do so; that I disapproved of such a course; that I did not advise it; that I should never require it; and that, were you ever to accept one without my express command, I should never assent to any bishop's giving you the *benedictio abbatis*. And yet I know not by what Divine judgment it was that I was kept in ignorance of the pain that awaited me when you should be in the very way for receiving such a gift. But when the mischief was done, then the terrible gravity of the thing fell on me like a thunderbolt and the awful judgment of God stood revealed to my view. I heard, and my bowels were troubled; I considered and trembled for fear; my heart was broken within me, and all my bones trembled. I felt how hateful a thing it was in the eyes of God and of all whom God has enlightened. So, I tell you, and I tell you sorrowing, that you first, and by means of you all our order, and most of all I, your abashed and sorrow-stricken father, and with me our Church, your mother, all of us are made a reproach to our neighbours, a scorn and a derision to those that are round about us; and to all that hear of it is a pattern set and an example given for the dishonour and the destruction of the Church of God; and in this our age and this our country you, you have made yourself the beginning and the beginner of it.'

Yes indeed, this is a cry of anguish, but it is more. It is a singularly valuable evidence that the plague which had so long afflicted the Empire had as yet been warded off from Normandy. 'You have made yourself the beginning and the beginner of the thing in this our age and in this our country.' He then proceeds :—

'Bear with me, my son, when I speak so seriously; I am not urged by passion sprung of hatred, but constrained by sorrow sprung of love. The afflicted brother longs to succour the brother he sees perishing; the trembling shepherd flies to snatch his dread Master's sheep out of the jaws of the lion; the father follows his poor son to call him back as he hurries on to hell. Oh! come back! come back to my bosom! Think well what you have done; probe well your inmost heart. You have cast away the counsel of the Eternal and held by evil counsel; for the Lord casteth away the counsels of princes, but the counsel of the Lord endureth for ever.'

In this last sentence is his only allusion to Duke Robert,

but it is intelligible enough, and is quite in the style of his letters generally, where every word is well chosen and has its own peculiar meaning.

'It is not Christ the Truth who has made you abbot, but your own cupidity, and the temerity of those who perceive not the things that are God's. Remember that he that entereth not by the door into the sheepfold, but climbeth up some other way, the same is a thief and a robber; and that the thief cometh not but to steal and to kill and to destroy.

'My son, you have not entered by the door, for you have not entered by Christ; not by Christ, because not by truth; not by truth, because not by rectitude; for no monk enters into an abbacy by rectitude who does not enter by regular election and by obedience.[1]

'Do not make excuses for yourself. You will say, "I have not entered by disobedience, for you did not forbid it." Be it enough that there was no rectitude in your act, since you did not enter by obedience. True, I did not say "I forbid it" or "I require you not to do it." I thought it enough for a reasonable man that over and over again I said, "My heart refuses, it disapproves; my mouth neither advises nor enjoins it, and never will enjoin it;" "should you ever receive an abbacy without my express command you will never have the Archbishop's blessing." A monk should not expect to hear a word of command when once he knows the wish or the advice of his abbot. Since, then, you have not entered by the door, the thing is too sad for me to say; but reflect, and say to yourself what name The Truth Himself gives you, and what it is that He says you have come to do.'[2]

---

[1] This sentence is worthy of the writer, for it contains an allusive reference to his lectures on Truth, which must have recalled to Dom Lanfranc happy days fifteen or sixteen years gone by.

[2] *Ep.* ii. 42.

The plague spot has at last appeared on the monk of a Norman monastery, and that monastery Anselm's. Abbot Anselm's vision of terrestrial happiness has faded. His discipline of patience will soon begin.[1]

But Robert's brother, the King of England, had already for some months been engaged on a far more daring flight, the logical outcome of the assumption that ecclesiastical preferments are the property of the prince; and his procedure upon Lanfranc's death must now engage our attention.

The monks of Christ Church were in the very agony of their bereavement when the jaunty and irrepressible Renouf, attended by a group of satellites, drew rein at the gate. He entered the cloister, and, blandly requesting that the necessary information might be given to his clerks, bade the latter draw out a schedule of the property of the see, both within and without the walls of the city. When these schedules were completed, and the simple faces of the English monks were still beaming with admiration of the Norman lawyer's conscientious accuracy and their guileless hearts invoking benisons upon a prince who would not suffer the sacred revenues of the see to be wasted during its vacancy, the royal chaplain in brief and clearly uttered phrase informed them that he thereby levied a duty upon their victuals, that he imposed a tax upon their lands, and, finally, that the whole property of the see of Canterbury was from that moment forward part and parcel of the royal demesne. Sentence of death all round would not have dismayed his listeners more, and, be it well believed, would have given them far less pain.

Henceforth not a bushel of corn, not a sack of beans, not a basket of fish was brought into the precinct but the *ad valorem* duty was charged upon it. The sacredest spot in our

---

[1] The personality of the younger Lanfranc is of slight importance compared with the facts that give the case its real interest. It may, however, be well to add that the *Chronicon Fontanellense* says he died in 1091, a statement which the learned editor of *Neustria Pia* has somewhat rashly called in question.

island was infested by the very scum of mankind, whose business it was to pry into granary, store-room, and kitchen; to march about the cloister as if it were their own; to issue orders here, to launch threats there, and to flaunt the royal impiety, the royal license, and the royal greed in the face of its distracted inmates. Discipline was soon lost in disorder; then discontent and discord broke loose; then the tithes, falling into arrear, came in at rarer and yet rarer intervals; then famine and beggary raised their horrid front; and, whilst some of the monks took to flight and sought shelter in other homes, those that remained remained to witness and to experience still more ruthless outrages and still more cruel woes.

Much of this misery was the indirect consequence of the royal confiscation; the direct results were more disastrous.

Hitherto the Christ Church rents had been mercifully assessed, had never been burdensome, had sometimes been little more than nominal. Not so now. Now, the King, having ascertained what each estate might be forced into yielding, let it *ad firmam* for twelve months to the highest bidder, provided the sum offered were in excess of the reserved rent. The contract, however, was not worth the parchment on which it was written, for the farmer was in danger of being outbidden at any moment, in which case he could only save himself by outbidding the outbidder. But this was only the beginning of troubles. At the end of the first year there was a general reletting of the estates by auction; at the end of the second there was another, at the end of the third another, and at the end of the fourth yet another. Hence untold sufferings—untold because ineffable. Oppressed and oppressing, men preyed upon their next poorer neighbours, and these in their turn on a still more unhappy class. The humblest were the first to fail, but others followed, and then others, the destructive tide rising with a steady fatality and engulfing layer after layer in the hierarchy of wealth; and the historian, himself a witness of what he records, grows more than eloquent when, describing the sufferings of the tenants, he tells how the desolation of their homesteads and their own hearts' misery surpassed one the other in woeful alternation under the cruel and still more cruel racking of their rents, how year after year the wonder grew that the winepress of extortion could be made to receive one squeeze more, and how mankind were made to learn by ghastly experience on what scanty sustenance the flame of human life could make shift to escape extinction.

Those who suffered the most by this cruelty were Englishmen, inhabitants of Kent, who had risen *en masse* in their sovereign's behalf a little more than a year before it began. It was their sweat, their blood, their life, that for five long years were converted into gold for the feeding of William's foreign mercenaries. He had the nation under his heel, and he meant to keep it there.

CHAPTER VII.

LE BEC AND BRIONNE IN THE SPRING OF 1090.

THE moment has come for recording an episode in the history of Le Bec which, whilst it ruffled the tranquillity of Anselm's spiritual family, can scarcely have helped to deepen his own.[1]

The reader has no need to be reminded that upon the death of Count Gilbert—an event which took place in the early days of the old monastery down stream, and before Lanfranc had come to make the name of the secluded beck illustrious— the young Duke of Normandy, at that time a boy in his teens, conferred the fief of Brionne upon his first cousin Guy, Count of Burgundy ; or that Guy made a sorry return for the favour, took arms against his lord, was defeated at Val-ès-Dunes, and, retiring to Brionne, shut himself up in his island fortress, where for two long years he baffled all the skill of his outraged besieger and capitulated at last in the year 1050.

On his kinsman's surrender Duke William took up the seigneury of Brionne, and was on many occasions the near neighbour first of Abbot Herlwin, then of Abbot Anselm.

It was during a period of retirement to his water-bound stronghold and the forest which, vocal with bark of fox and cry of partridge, overlooked him from close neighbouring cliffs on this side and that, that Duke William conceived his terrible resentment against Lanfranc, and then, taking shame to himself, went forth to meet the poor prior, who was ludicrously employed in stimulating the inactivity of the 'three-footed horse.' It was during another such that, when the beech

---

[1] The story is to be found in Bouquet, vol. xiii.

leaves were already mellowing to their fall, he paid his royal homage to Abbot Herlwin's newly chosen successor.[1] It was during yet another such that he for the first time listened to Anselm's pleading in court, and watched the growing wonder of his lords as they discovered that the orator was indifferent to the issue, provided only that justice were done.

When, however, Robert Courthose in 1087 succeeded to the coronet of Normandy, that prince conferred the seigneury of Brionne upon the aged Roger de Beaumont, who, after a short tenure of some two years, transmitted it to his son Robert, Count of Meulan, and not long afterwards sought repose from the fatigues of an active and eventful life in the abbey of Saint Peter at Préaux. But during the interval which elapsed between Roger de Beaumont's resignation of Brionne and his assumption of the religious habit an opportunity was offered him of displaying that diplomatic skill for which his name was famous. It was on this wise.

Soon after taking possession of Brionne, Robert of Meulan betrayed a wish to obtain the seigneury or *dominium* of the Abbey of Le Bec, a right which the Duke had reserved to himself when he gave the domain to Roger de Beaumont, and thus, like Gilbert of Brionne, like Guy of Burgundy, and like the great William, to be patron of the abbey. We cannot, I fear, learn when it was that he first gave the thought a lodging in his bosom; but there can be little doubt that he brought his scheme to light soon after the death of Archbishop Lanfranc, and still less that he hoped to win fresh favour with the King of the English by its successful execution. Anselm's name was already whispered as future Archbishop of Canterbury as early as the year 1090. Why, then, should not the wish of William Rufus have been confided to so trustworthy, so able, and so resolute a dependent

---

[1] I scarcely need remind the reader that it was not as Duke of Normandy but as lord of Brionne that the Conqueror in 1079 conferred the temporalities of Le Bec on the newly elected Abbot.

as Robert of Meulan as early as the fall of the year preceding? For Duke Robert's retention of the lordship of the land on which the abbey stood,[1] and of the patronage of the abbacy, might prove a grave obstacle to Abbot Anselm's removal. And if Count Robert was prompted by any motive in advancing his new claim, what motive more strong than devotion to the prince whose interests he had now for several years upheld with all the energy of his being? And if he had any end in view, what end more definite, and to himself more advantageous, than the removal, if so be he could effect it, of Abbot Anselm from Le Bec at that prince's bidding? And, yet again, the suspicion, whatever its intrinsic value, derives confirmation from two noteworthy facts —first, that Robert de Meulan precipitated, if he did not suggest or compel, his father's resignation of Brionne; and secondly, that the resignation took place either shortly before or shortly after the close of the year 1089.

The crafty Count then—it was said that his rival in the arts of management was nowhere to be found between Windsor and Jerusalem—began by attempting Anselm's ear through the intermediary of a confidential embassy—*tunc primùm, ut astutus homo, privatim aures Anselmi per nuntios expetiit.* Might he venture to beg, indeed suppliantly pray, that the Abbot would grant him the great favour he so devoutly coveted? What more natural, more excusable, and in its way more praiseworthy than so pious an ambition? Besides, the change he contemplated would make him, however unworthy to succeed, yet still the successor of men like Count Gilbert, Count Guy, and the incomparable prince lately taken from them, all of whom as resident neighbours had learnt how to grace their seigneury by augmenting the revenues of the monastery. And there were other ways in which a lord of Brionne might be of material service to a

---

[1] Dom Herlwin's abbey down stream had stood on his own *alodium*, which was just outside the *comitatus Brionensis*; not so the new abbey.

religious house situated on the proper Brionne demesne, which must necessarily be out of reach to a distant and non-resident patron. For example, it would be most agreeable to him to see the castle chapel served by fathers from the monastery. To all which the tranquil Abbot answered, 'To grant this is not within my competence; the abbey is not mine, but the Duke's, and as pleases him so will the issue be.' 'The Count makes no doubt,' said the messenger, 'that the Duke's consent will easily be had; all he wants is to ascertain your own wish on the subject, and to have your concurrence.' Abbot Anselm may not have been a good man of business, but his head was perfectly well set on his shoulders, as his answer proved. 'I have no power whatever to act in this matter, but I frankly tell you that, in my opinion, the Count is undertaking no easy task.' 'How?' exclaimed the interlocutor. The Abbot gave his reasons in detail, and the messenger, saying nothing—for he had nothing to say—bade a disconcerted adieu. His report of Abbot Anselm's *exposé* would seem to have taken Count Robert by surprise, for, says the chronicler, *obstupuit ad prudentiam viri.*

As to Abbot Anselm's monks, the news fell on them like a death knell. Their first impulse was to take the Duke into their confidence without delay. This saved them. 'By the marvels of God,' he shouted, 'what is this I hear? What tomfoolery is this? The Count of Meulan wants to take my abbey from me, does he? My favourite abbey, too! The traitor wants to steal it from me, does he? By the marvels of God, he shall have short joy of the grant I have made him.' As good luck or good management would have it, William Crispin, the son of Herlwin's friend the first of the name, William of Bréteuil, and Roger of Bienfaite, who, as grandson of Gilbert of Brionne and son of the long since evicted Richard, was the last man in the world to brook Count Robert's claim, now came upon the scene, and, venting their ire in a volley of terrible oaths, swore to recall

all that their respective families had ever given the abbey, should the Count in any manner of way get it into his seigneury, and concluded by discharging a round of abuse on the Duke himself for having been so simple as to hand over the key of Normandy to a man who was not to be trusted. Whereupon the monks, satisfied with the issue of their expedition, went home again.

After the lapse of a day or two Count Robert, who was quite in the dark as to the impression he had made on Anselm's religious, was announced at the abbey. But before the Abbot could reach the guest room, Dom Farman, who had worn the cowl for more than forty years and now held the distinguished post of cellarer; Dom Eustace, one of the best heads for business in the house; Dom Albert, the senior member, or nearly so, of the community; and Dom Robert, whom, I regret to say, I cannot identify, had flown through the cloister, borne on the wings of rage, and were already face to face with their visitor, of whom, in voices which they fondly thought they were controlling, they begged to learn what it was to which they owed the honour of his visit. He, practised mocker that he was, answered them just as if he were the best friend they had ever had and were quite unconscious that they were angry with him. This, of course, exasperated them; and, by the moment the Abbot was in the room, they were already favouring their visitor with a few sarcasms, against which his noble rank served as a very sorry defence. But the Abbot restored order, and then, seating himself, began, 'Count, you will never succeed in what you are taking such pains to accomplish. Our lord the Duke does not wish it, neither do the exalted personages on whose bounty we live; and, what is more than all else put together, their reverences my sons in religion will on no account agree to it. The Castle of Brionne has not come to you by inheritance; you hold it at the Duke's pleasure, and he will resume the grant whenever he pleases. But why should the battle be fought out here and by us? Find out what our lord and yours wishes, and rely upon it that his decision will be final and his injunction absolute.' But in Dom Eustace's noble bosom the storm was still raging; the Abbot's tact was lost on him; he was young; he was one of the junior set; his blood had not begun to cool in his veins; composure and soft words were not to his liking. So, starting to his feet and stretching forth his right hand towards the church, he cried, 'By this church, whose monks we are, I say that even if you, Father Anselm, and our prince the Duke of Normandy were to bring yourselves—a thing I cannot contemplate as likely—yet, were you and he to bring yourselves to say 'Yes,' we, the monks of Le Bec, would one and all of us quit its walls sooner than allow this thing. And as to you, my lord Robert, by this church'—he must have been much moved thus to break the rule of his order which forbade swearing—'by this church I swear to you that as long as I live, and the rest of us, on no account and by no contrivance shall the liberty of the Church of Le Bec be petticoated at your bidding.' The others now took up the parable, and only stopped short when the Count went away, which he did in high dudgeon; 'whose dudgeon the monks thought nothing of; all they cared for was to keep the independence of their church independent.'

In the course of a few days the seigneur of Brionne set out for Rouen; whereupon the monks, apprehending anything and everything from the vacillating character of Duke Robert, sent forth an embassy, who somehow stole a march on the Count—they must have kept a wakeful eye on his movements to do this—and arrived at Rouen just in time to apprise the Duke of his approach; when in he came. 'Ah, Lord Robert,' said Courthose with a chuckle, 'how goes it with you and the monks of Le Bec?' Disconcerted at the sight of the white Benedictines, he replied, hanging his head, 'As well as may be. Whatever you order them to concede,

concede they will.' 'Thou liest,' roared the prince, 'out and out, thou liest! By the marvels of God, never was emptier thought than thine, that I should be such a simpleton as to give my abbey up to thee.'

But enough of this. The embassy returned to Le Bec, satisfied to think that Count Robert's hopes were now finally crushed; but they were, I suspect, mistaken. He seems to have made one more effort to get what he wanted, and they can scarcely have told their story at home before the schemer, under pretence, it may be, that the value of the seigneury of Brionne was materially lessened by the subtraction of so good a piece of patronage as the most famous abbey in the duchy, had already set up a claim for Ivri, a fortification at one time held by his father.[1] 'I gave your father more than a fair equivalent for the stronghold of Ivri in the noble Castle of Brionne,' said Duke Robert. 'I do not allow it to have been an equivalent,' was the rejoinder. 'What your father gave my father, that I want to have. Otherwise, by St. Nicaise,[2] I will do you a displeasure.' This speech cost the Count dear; he was thrown into prison, and Brionne entrusted to Robert of Bienfaite, son of Baldwin of Meules and thus a grandson of Count Gilbert's. It was now that Robert of Meulan invoked the intercession of his father, and so well did old Count Roger ply his arts that the captive was before long at large again. Sire and son now approached the feeble prince, and by the instrumentality of a 'huge heap of money' induced him to recall the recent grant to Count Gilbert's grandson. The latter not unnaturally refused to give up what he called his heritage to anyone but the Duke; and in the course of the next Whitsun week—the Whitsun week, that is to say, of 1090—when a fierce summer's sun was already flaring down its meridian blaze on the surface of the Risle, he found

[1] Orderic, iii. 337.
[2] There was, I imagine, even then a church to St. Nicaise at Meulan.

himself and his fortress suddenly surrounded and close invested by Duke Robert and the two allies that had bought him into their service. The siege, thanks to a device which seems to have won some applause at the time, was of short duration. At a little distance from the edge of the cliff which at that point overlooks the left bank of the river a detachment of the enemy erected a forge, lighted a fire, plied the bellows, threw their arrow-heads and javelin-heads into the glowing embers, and then, just as the day was at its hottest, discharged one general simultaneous shower of pointed and red-hot missiles into the lichen-mantled roof of shingle which served as a protection to the hall of the castle. A poor protection. Before the deluded defenders knew what had befallen them their dwelling-place was wrapped in flame. By sunset all was over. Then Robert of Meulan entered into possession of the ruin, but took care henceforth not to molest the monks of Le Bec with a claim for which he had paid so dear. As to that claim and its object, whatever be the reader's estimate of the suggestion which I have advanced, a personage has in any case now made his *début* upon our pages who will have before long to appear again. He was a servant with two masters; and if it be too much to say that he loved the one and hated the other, it is certain that he held to the one and despised the other.

And yet why not hate Duke Robert? Duke Robert had thrown him into prison. Could he be expected to pardon the indignity?

CHAPTER VIII.

ROSCELIN'S HERESY: ABBOT ANSELM'S FOURTH VISIT TO ENGLAND.

THE trials which befell Abbot Anselm in the scandalous preferment of the younger Lanfranc, and in the designs of the Count of Meulan on his monastery, were accompanied by a third.

In the year 1080 or 1081 a novice bearing the name of John received the habit of St. Benedict at the hands of Anselm. He was a Roman by nationality and a clergyman of the Lateran, but had already spent some time in the society of the canons of St. Quentin at Beauvais. In the course of some six or seven years a still older inmate of Le Bec, Dom Fulco, or Foulques, a native of Beauvais or its neighbourhood, was raised to the episcopal chair of that city, and had not long been established in it when some of the canons, hoping thus to get rid of a man whose life was a rebuke to them, declared that his father had bought him the bishopric, and that he must be deposed. Foulques was summoned to Rome, whither he went attended by Dom John, whose knowledge of the people and city of Beauvais, of the clergy and court of Rome, and of the road that lay between the two places, rendered him a suitable companion for such a journey. When, however, the canons of the Lateran beheld their ancient clerk adorned with the tonsure and clad in the garb of a Benedictine, they lodged a complaint against the Abbot of Le Bec for having made a monk of him; and it was not without difficulty that he obtained leave to accompany the bishop on his homeward journey, under promise of returning to the

Pontifical Court by a certain date.¹ This was in the summer of 1089, the year of Archbishop Lanfranc's death.

But scarcely had Dom John reached Beauvais before he heard of a strange report about his abbot. The famous Roscelin of Compiègne was giving out to the world that the late Archbishop of Canterbury had assented to a certain heretical thesis of his concerning the Holy Trinity, and that Anselm actually held the opinion enunciated in it. Dom John, strangely staggered by such a rumour, wrote to Anselm, who sent him in reply a short philosophical exposure of Roscelin's fallacy, and announced his intention of treating the subject at greater length.²

But this was not all, for, hearing that a council had been summoned to meet at Soissons, he wrote a letter to his former disciple, the Bishop of Beauvais, which he begged him to submit to the assembly. It contained the following passages:—

'As to myself, I hold what we confess in the Creed when we say, "I believe in God the Father Almighty, Creator of heaven and earth;" "I believe in one God, the Father Almighty, Maker of heaven and earth;" and, "Whosoever will be saved, before all things it is necessary that he hold the Catholic faith." These three professions of Christian faith I believe in my heart and confess with my mouth, as being quite sure that whosoever denies any of them, and in particular whosoever asserts for truth the blasphemy which I hear Roscelin has attributed to me, be he man or be he angel, is anathema; and I further say, so long as he persists in this impiety may he be anathema, for he is not a Christian at all. If he be a baptised person bred among Christians, he should by no means be listened to; no account of his error should be asked of him; no account of

---

¹ 'Ante exactum à præsenti quadragesimâ annum' (B. Urban II., *Ep.* 23). The letter was written on August 1, 1089, so that the *præsens quadragesima* was the Lent which preceded the Feast of the Assumption.
² *Ep.* ii. 35.

our truth should be accorded him; and as soon as his treason against the faith is ascertained past doubt he should either anathematise the poison he has belched forth, or else be anathematised by all Catholics unless he repent. . . . Our faith is to be defended by arguments from reason against the infidel, but not against those who profess to glory in the name of Christian. It is only right that the latter should be required to hold unimpaired the promise made in their baptism, and only reasonable that the former should be convinced how unreasonable they are in contemning our belief. It is a Christian's duty to attain to understanding through the avenue of faith, not to go to faith through the avenue of understanding, or if he cannot understand, then to fall from faith. When he can understand, let him rejoice; when he cannot, then let him adore what he fails to grasp. I beg you to take this my letter to the Council.'

Meanwhile he began his treatise, throwing it into an epistolary form, but had not gone far in it when he heard that Roscelin had recanted and that the heresy had no adherents. He therefore laid the unfinished document aside and thought of something else. We will do the same.

In 1090 an accession was made to the Le Bec property in England in the gift by Gilbert, Earl of Clare,[1] of a church belonging to his castle at Clare, in Suffolk. This church, which was well endowed, had hitherto supported seven secular canons; and these, or so many of the complement as there might be, were now to change their habit and their profession; but Anselm, who was the proper person to give the one and receive the other, refused to come to England.

After some little time the same sort of thing occurred on the western side of our island. The King's cousin, Hugh

---

[1] Son of Richard Fitzgilbert, lord of Bienfaite and Tunbridge; grandson, therefore, of Count Gilbert of Brionne, the defender, that is to say, of Tunbridge in the siege of 1088.

Earl of Chester, had on his estate a church in which the body of the royal virgin St. Werburg had for two hundred years reposed, and which was served by a body of secular canons, apparently thirteen in number. This corporation the Earl wanted to convert into a religious community, and begged Anselm to effect the change; but Anselm, as in the previous case, refused to set foot on our shores.

The summer of 1091[1] seems to have been just such a summer as that of 1078. The corn crops failed from drought; the black harvest followed in its turn; then came dearth of food from end to end of Normandy; and then, when Anselm's monks hoped for food, as heretofore in bad times, from their English estates, their hopes were disappointed; for those estates were suffering from the royal extortion, and from the royal extortion there would be no redress so long as the Abbot refused to visit England and with his own eyes see what was going on. He persisted in refusing.

The truth is that a whisper had for some time flown about our island, and passed thence to the duchy; a whisper which, though it caused him no concern, it would be indecent, as he felt, to pretend not to have overheard. He was now nearly sixty years of age, of a physique far from robust, in a frail and variable state of health; and his letters and other sources of information place it beyond doubt that by temperament and predilection he courted repose and calm, that secular business was worse than distasteful to him, and that the merest dream of removal to a sphere of turmoil and unrest would have been as alien to the bent of his thoughts as to his tastes and habits. Eadmer, indeed, assures us—and we can easily understand him —that Anselm's entire being was so set and moulded to the monastic model, that the sheer impossibility of removal from the cloister was in his estimate as absolute a fact as any axiomatic truth. The cloister was the theatre of all his forecasts, as it was the limit of all his tranquil hopes here below;

[1] See *Chron. S. Stephani Cadom.*, in Michel's *Chroniques de Normandie.*

and I will venture to declare that never on unfrequented granite isle did limpet cling to its rock with more serene unconsciousness than the Abbot of Le Bec to a home whose every inmate was bound to him by an intimate love strong as death. He never dreamt even of the possibility of preferment; and it cannot be too often repeated that his refusal to enter England was prompted, not by an apprehension that the primacy might be offered him, but by dread of giving scandal.

Meanwhile the Earl of Chester fell grievously ill, and sent a very different message from the first. Anselm must come, and come quickly; he must come, not as abbot but as confessor, and in his quality of spiritual physician succour and heal a stricken sinner. Hugh was an old friend of his, probably his oldest friend in Normandy; for the two must have made acquaintance three-and-thirty years ago at Avranches. 'And if,' so concluded the message, 'a fear about the archbishopric keep him back, I protest by my faith that there is nothing whatever in the flying rumour. And, *per hoc*,[1] let the holy Abbot know that it ill becomes him to be kept back by nothing when that nothing prevents his helping me in my great and grievous need.' Still this appeal was unavailing; for Anselm feared that other people, who had not Earl Hugh's opportunities of feeling the royal pulse, would be as likely as ever to take the scandal he was so loth to give. The poor Earl, however, was not to be baffled, for Anselm's was the only bosom on which he could lay his throbbing head and pour out all his heart's secret; so he sent, for the third time, not now a message, but a letter dictated by himself, all eloquent with the touching unrestraint of the second person singular, so difficult to transfer unspoilt into English. 'Know well,' said the document, 'that if thou come not, never all through the life eternal wilt thou have such repose as not to feel an everlasting pang for not having come to me.' The

---

[1] *Per hoc*, a kind of oath. This sort of thing was quite the fashion. Other instances will occur in the course of the history.

reply to this appeal was not unworthy of the casuist who had spoken in the case of Elphege. 'I am hemmed in all round. If I go to England an unworthy suspicion may, as I fear, find place in somebody's mind, and I shall be thought to have gone to canvass the archbishopric. If I stay away I shall violate that brotherly charity which we are bidden to show not only to a friend, but to an enemy. And if in the case of a foe violated charity be a sin, what is it in the case of a friend? The Earl of Chester has certainly been from days long since gone by my intimate familiar friend; and my friend, as he says, is now in want of me. In necessity is a friend proved. If, then, for fear of the unfair opinion which some men may possibly form of me, I do not help my friend in his necessity, I incur a sin of my own of which there can be no doubt by way of obviating a sin in others of the commission of which there is a doubt. I therefore, commending myself and my conscience to God—a conscience free from all ambition of earthly honour—will set forth under the watchful eye of His holy love to do what my friend wishes. *Cætera ipse Deus agat.* And may He for His mercy's sake keep me by His grace free from all hindrance that comes of secular business.'

As soon, therefore, as the anniversary of Abbot Herlwin's death was over—for the day was kept with great solemnity—he set out for Boulogne, where he wished to call on the Countess Ida, but where, this business done, he was compelled to prolong an irksome delay till wind and weather should permit him to embark without probability of shipwreck.

Now during the interval of time thus passed at Boulogne his monks did what they thought a very clever thing. On recalling all that their abbot had said about Earl Hugh's first, second, and third summons, and still more the speech in which he had announced his intention of going to Chester, it occurred to them that he must quietly have resolved not to visit any of their English estates, but to quit the island as soon as might be after seeing his penitent; and that the phrase *cætera ipse Deus agat*—or, as we should say, 'I leave the rest to Providence'—may not have borne the meaning which they in their eager delight at the thought of the proposed voyage had all too inconsiderately put upon it. Whilst, therefore, he was still lingering at St. Ulmar's, he was surprised by a message which informed him that, unless he wished to be branded with the sin of disobedience, he must attend to the interests of his community in England before presuming to return to his monastery.

If celestial beings are capable of so humble a pleasure as amusement, the angels who presided over the good men's deliberations must have smiled as they watched them thus innocently plan their own discomfiture.

On the seventh of September, then, Anselm embarked, silent and preoccupied, and attended by two of his monks, Dom Baldwin of Tournay and Dom Eustace. The former of these was a man of the world and of business, and the latter seems to have been well acquainted with the condition of the Le Bec property in England.

They landed at Dover, and mounting horse, reached Canterbury just as evening hung forth the moon. But when Anselm alighted at the gate of Christ Church a scarcely suppressed murmur surprised his ear; for, whether it be that some most trifling yet profound coincidence had just been noted, or that some fiery wonder even now flashed in prophetic hint across the sky, or for whatever reason, the monks in the precinct and the congregated citizens who had come to learn who the visitor was insisted on acclaiming him as their future archbishop. He was abashed and disconcerted, and hurried on into the cathedral. The still and pensive hour shed through the venerable pile an influence all too well in keeping with the forlorn condition of our country. Discerned yet scarce discerned through the deepening twilight, massive column and sweeping arch and storied ceiling filled his soul with an exquisite pathos, and presently he lay stretched on Lanfranc's grave below the crucifix, shedding tears of regret at his own loss and of anguish at the spectacle of the woe of the mother of Christianity in this our land. 'How doth the city sit solitary that was full of people! The mistress of the isles is become as a widow, and the princess of provinces set under tribute. . . . The enemy hath put out his hand to all her delectable things; for she hath seen the spoiler enter into her sanctuary.'

Compline was said by such of Lanfranc's monks as still remained, and then strict silence continued through the night. But on the conclusion of prime [1] next morning Anselm surprised and astonished his afflicted hosts by taking leave of them. It was a great day, the Feast of the Nativity of the Blessed Virgin, and they were in great trouble. Why, then, leave them so soon? But he was deaf to entreaty; he wanted no more acclamations; he must escape notice. So he went.

He seems to have fixed upon Westminster as his first resting-place, in which case the Court cannot have been far distant; and as an established usage no doubt forbade him to enter England for the inspection of his estates without, as a preliminary duty, paying his respects to the King, he lost no time in doing so.

Upon his approach to the palace such marks of satisfaction were evinced as the evil counsellors of William Rufus would have found some difficulty in checking, even had they deemed it decent to rebuke a reverence which they must have been less than human not themselves in some degree at

---

[1] Eadmer says *summo mane*. I justify my interpretation of the phrase by the following passage from Abbot Hermann's *De Restoratione Abbatiæ S. Martini Tomacensis* :—

'Summo mane, finito capitulo . . . . vestem clericalem deponunt et monasticam . . . . suscipiunt, ita ut cum matutinos et primam ritu clericali cantassent jam tertiam . . . . cantaverint.'

least to share. But if any such were there, they skulked appropriately and naturally out of sight, and left the first greetings to a group of gentlemen who hurried to the vestibule to give him welcome in the King's name, and express their own joy at beholding so revered and so unexpected a visitor.

If Abbot Anselm's appearance at such a place as the royal palace had now become did not revive in William's courtiers those hopes for the future of England which had now for some time been set aside, it must at least have recalled to them those happier, purer, brighter days in a no distant past when he was wont to receive a less ostentatious, because a more cordial, welcome than that which now awaited him in the Throne Room. In those days royal sovereignty owned and honoured the Divine law as its rule and model; in those days royal greed, not yet grown insatiable, left a few things sacred in the land; in those days royal lust was an unknown phrase; in those days in this palace of Westminster decent custom stood sentinel to human frailty, modesty could pace the corridors without alarm, and a man like Anselm was not out of place. But now the royal palace was a very lazar-house of moral ill; the flimsied veil of shame had already been scornfully cast aside; and the anointed sovereign of a Christian people himself gave example to his courtiers of a icense and a debauchery for which names are not to be found. It was a strange place for such a visitor.

As Anselm's guides conducted him to the chamber of presence the King of England assumed a part more than royal; stepped from his throne, advanced to the door, and after overwhelming his visitor with kisses—God save the mark!—took him by the hand, conducted him to his own couch, and, bidding him be seated, sat beside him. The Abbot, with good breeding as exquisite as it was all his own, yielded to treatment for which a lifelong knowledge of the ways of courts scarcely, perhaps, afforded him a precedent, and sustained for some minutes a lively and agreeable conversation with the sovereign. But he cannot have been simple enough to think that such a welcome from such a man was a spontaneous outburst of respect and affection. What, then, can have been its motive? Let us pause a moment to conjecture.

Years ago, when Anselm was as yet prior of his monastery, an incident occurred which must have served to fix the direction of the general hopes of England in regard of him. On retiring to rest—whether at night after matins or at midday for his *siesta*, remains uncertain—he found a gold ring in his bed. Many questions were asked, but no clue could ever be obtained to the mystery. Of course we who live eight centuries after the event know, each one for himself and diversely from everyone else, how that ring found its way there, and dissolve into fits of merriment at the serious mention of so insignificant and so contemptible an episode. But when Lanfranc heard of it he said, 'Mark my words: that man will some day be Archbishop of Canterbury.' Now this presage and its interpretation cannot have remained a secret; the story must have been told at a hundred firesides; William the Conqueror must often have pondered over it with mingled wonder and pleasure; the Red King must over and over again during the last three years have reflected on it with some perplexity, and the Red King's barons kept hope alive on it during that interval; so that, absurd as it may have been in the Conqueror, the Red King, and the Red King's barons to waste thought upon such a trifle, it would be absurder still in us to disdain all notice of it in the present connexion. For presages like this commanded a religious respect in the eleventh century, and so sacrilegious an offender as William Rufus, powerless to exorcise the thoughts which it suggested, must have been convinced that, long as he might keep the archbishopric vacant, Anselm would live longer, and that, brief as might be the residue of Anselm's life, the season of the Church's widowhood would be briefer, and, unless he repaired the wrong, more brief still his own tenure of the royal throne of England.

But Anselm was a Norman subject, and it would be wise, by way of averting a very evil omen, to keep him in England, now that a favouring chance had brought him there.

Avarice, however, was in the Red King, if not a more powerful, yet a more urgent motive than even superstition.

Everything was by this time venal, and if his barons were —as indeed they were, if only in their own interest—anxious to have an Archbishop of Canterbury, there was now an opportunity for inviting them to offer a price for the luxury they craved.

On the whole, then, the most probable account of the extraordinary reception thus given to the Abbot of Le Bec is that William Rufus meant to say to his barons, This is the man whom the King delights to honour; let me have a fair price and he shall be your Archbishop.

Can Anselm have suspected this? Not improbably. For having come to Court to make suit for his abbey, he seems to have changed his intention before he had been many minutes in the King's company.

After some little time, then, spent in conversation he intimated that he would like to confer in private with the Royal Majesty. Baldwin and Eustace and the gentlemen in waiting all retired; the door closed; the prince and the monk were left alone, sitting together. The saint fixed his eye upon the sinner. It was time that a word should be said about the domestic morals of the royal household, of a palace by night studiously wrapped in darkness, and by day scandalous in the manners and the garb of some of its inmates; about the comments which all classes of the King's subjects were passing upon a moral debasement of which it was only too probable that he himself had sounded all the depths. William grew very red, but, unable—such was the overmastering authority of his monitor's rebuke, and such the sweetness of his monitor's manner—to vent chagrin in rudeness, broke out into a constrained laugh, declared his inability to stop other people's tittletattle, and awkwardly suggested that it was beneath the elevation of Anselm's nature to believe all he heard.

Anselm, having thus done his duty by the son of his late friend [1] and by himself—for this was not the way in which to court preferment—retired and left the prince to commune with conscience.

On reaching Chester he found the Earl out of danger, remained with him for some days, and returned to Westminster early in October.

The secular concerns of his abbey now engaged his thoughts; but on presenting his petition to the King for a relaxation of the enormous taxes which Renouf Flambard had levied on its English estates, he failed to obtain redress, and was desired to wait till Christmas. But he need not be idle, for Roscelin, who had made a fictitious recantation of his heresy at the Council of Soissons,[2] was again disturbing men's minds. He therefore sent to Le Bec for the unfinished treatise on the Incarnation which he had thrown aside, and prepared to devote his leisure to its elaboration.

[1] The date of the interview is not recorded, but it may have taken place on the 9th of September, the anniversary of the Conqueror's death. Indeed, nothing could well be more probable than that it did.

[2] See *Ep.* ii. 51. There is some uncertainty as to the date of the Council of Soissons. I imagine it was held in the spring of 1090. The compilers of the *Histoire Littéraire de la France* are strangely mistaken in setting it as late as the beginning of 1093; for the letter in which St. Anselm speaks of it as an event already some time past can scarcely have been written later than the middle of October 1092.

CHAPTER IX.

AN INTERVAL OF SUSPENSE AND ALARM.

WHEN the Court assembled at Gloucester in the month of December, the thought of the patriarchal throne at Canterbury so long left tenantless had already inspired the King with an alarm which he was careful not to betray to his barons.

William Rufus was no atheist. On the contrary, it was one of the worst features of that bad man's character that, although he recognised the designs of Divine Providence and acknowledged the scrutiny of Divine Omniscience, he yet beheld in those designs nothing better than the cunningly laid plans of an adversary who meant some day to outwit his manœuvres, and in that scrutiny nothing better than the watchful gaze of a foe who meant some day to execute vengeance on his affronts; so that his faith in an Infinite Being, minutely interested in him and his concerns, was but another name for intimate consciousness of his own revolt against God and intimate fear lest the Divine forbearance should not hold out for ever.

It is just possible that upon assuming the seigneury of the Canterbury estates he was as much frightened as gratified at the thought of Renouf's audacity, and contemplated with shrinking alarm the first pecuniary product of that miscreant's impiety. Let it have been so in the summer of 1089; by the winter of 1092 every sentiment of respect, of decency, of awe, had long ago disappeared before an insatiable avarice; and nothing but craven fear, whether of Divine wrath or of human indignation, could now compel him to renounce a sacrilege which had lost all terrors of its own.

But how long might he delay? If the growing displeasure of God were in anything to be discerned it was in the aspect of the political horizon. And he scanned that horizon with some alarm. In Flanders the death of Robert the Frisian [1] had a few weeks previously left the succession to a second Robert, a prince of capacity and courage who was not unlikely to give the Conqeror's favourite son the full benefit of an animosity which he had shared with the Frisian against the Conqueror himself. But this was not all. Henry Beauclerc had quite recently secured a footing in Normandy,[2] and Henry was the dread of William Rufus no less than Robert Courthose; for their father had prophesied that, outliving William's tenure of the crown of England and Robert's tenure of the coronet of Normandy, he would in due time make both crown and coronet his own; and the astute Henry, seconded by such a man as the new Count of Flanders, would prove a very different foe from the indolent Robert represented by the late Count of Boulogne. How, then, avert the omen but by propitiating that Divine resentment of which it was the indication? And how do this but by repairing the great sacrilege of his reign, and furthering the manifested will of Heaven, in regard of the archbishopric of Canterbury? Henry was Divinely destined to be King of England; Anselm was Divinely destined to be Primate; and there was only one

---

[1] Robert the Frisian, Count of Flanders, died October 4, 1092.

[2] The importance of this event could scarcely be overrated. Orderic records it thus:—'Anno ab vic. Dom. 1092 . . . . Henricus . . . . Danfrontem auxilio Dei suffragioque amicorum obtinuit, et inde fortiter hæreditarium jus calumniari sategit. Nam idem dum esset junior non ut frater à fratribus habitus est, sed magis ut externus exterorum auxilia quærere coactus est, et quinque annis' (i.e. from the moment of his father's death) . . . . 'admodum fatigatus est. Tandem Donfrontani nutu Dei ærumnis tam præclari exulis compassi sunt et ipsum . . . . sibi principem constituerunt' (iii. 384). And again, 'Henricus frater ducis Danfrontem fortissimum castrum possidebat et magnam partem Neustriæ sibi favore vel armis subegerat' (iii. 475).

remedy for the fear already stirred within him by this double conviction.

Still he was wary enough not to let fear disarm discretion. It might be possible to conciliate, if not the friendship yet the neutrality, of the new Count of Flanders; and, inasmuch as the numerous leases under which the Canterbury domains had been distributed would not determine until Midsummer, he might well keep his reflections to himself for some months to come, by all means, however, detaining Anselm in England and awaiting the chance of a pecuniary bid from Anselm's friends.

Meanwhile how were the King's barons employed? The almost hopeless hope recently revived in the hearts of the Canterbury monks of once again beholding a Primate who should be the mouthpiece of the nation, its leader, and its guide, and the bond at once and centre of the public interests,[1] was already taking with William's barons the form of an inchoate and timorous resolve. This was not much, it is true, but it was something, and more could scarcely at that moment have been expected of them. Their fiefs and titles were the reward of services rendered five-and-twenty years ago, and the first man among them who should rouse the royal ire might, as the reward of his courage, soon behold fief escheat to the Crown and title vanish into air. On the other hand, dangerous as it might be for one man to speak, they felt that the time was approaching when all of them must act; unless, indeed, some political chance should limit the capacity of a tyranny which at this moment knew no bound. Three years ago the prince had appropriated the most sacred of all sacred properties in the land; last summer he had committed a like iniquity at Lincoln;[2] next year he might do the same with some other diocese. And what would be the end of it all? Might a Christian

---

[1] 'Os omnium, vexillifer prævius, umbo publicus.'—W. M., *De Gestis Pontiff.* lib. i.

[2] Remigius, Bishop of Lincoln, died in the May of 1092.

king in a Christian land be suffered to extirpate Christianity by way of filling his purse and feeding his mercenaries? Was it altogether inconceivable that, having asserted and enjoyed the liberty of thus treating ecclesiastical property, he should, under the convenient term of *consuetudo*,[1] claim a like liberty with the next military fief that fell vacant, and after ruining the estates sell the succession to some stranger to the prejudice of the heirs? But this was not all.

By protracting thus inordinately the vacancy of the see of Canterbury the Red King had violated a sacred constitutional usage, and, indeed, had thrown the constitution out of gear. For what the Sovereign Pontiff was to Christendom as an all-compelling power ordained to uphold right against force, to shield the weak from the oppression of the strong, and to oblige sinners to listen to the threats and tremble at the sanctions of Divine justice, that, in his proper sphere and within limits ample if clearly defined, was the Archbishop of Canterbury to the King and people of England; and the occupants of the Chair of St. Peter at Rome, their own incommunicable privilege apart, recognised and owned so accurate a copy and so plenipotentiary a representative of themselves in the occupants of St. Augustine's chair at Canterbury as to call them the popes of a secondary empire.[2] Had Constantine relinquished the capital of his empire in favour of St. Sylvester? Ethelbert relinquished Canterbury in favour of St. Augustine, and retired elsewhere, symbolising by that act the recognition of his accountability to that power of whom St. Augustine, by the mission given him by Gregory the Great, was within his realm the representative.[3] The old metropolitan church at Canterbury

---

[1] I hope in a subsequent chapter to have something to say on this word *consuetudo*.
[2] *Apostolicus alterius orbis*. I shall have something to say about this on a more proper occasion.
[3] 'Hic (Ethelbertus) Cantuariam regni sui caput et sedem regiam S. Augustino jure regali dedit.'
[4] 'Prædecessor noster Gregorius constituit . . . . metropolitanam et primitivam

had been a copy of the Lateran basilica at Rome.[1] The Archbishop of Canterbury was, in virtue of his office, the legate of the successor of St. Peter. As recently as 1049 Leo IX. had given witness to the tradition of centuries by confirming the rights long enjoyed by the Primate of Britain of taking rank at Rome immediately after the seven cardinal bishops.[2] It was the prerogative of the Archbishop of Canterbury to confirm or to annul the election to the sovereign dignity in our island as it was the Pope's to confirm or to annul the like in Germany. And if none but the Pope might crown an Emperor of the West, none within our shores save the Archbishop of Canterbury might presume to crown a King of England.[3]

It would, perhaps, be impossible to form an exaggerated estimate of the religious prestige with which the Chair of St. Augustine was invested by the whole universal people of England; difficult it certainly is, under the altered conditions of our age, to conceive an adequate idea of the political importance of its occupant; and if the spiritual grandeur of the see of Canterbury was the only adequate measure of the scandal which the Red King had now for three years and a half given to England and to Christendom, the dignity of its occupant as a great power in the constitution was the only adequate measure of the political wrong which for three years and a half he had inflicted on his people.

---

sedem in civitate Dorohernio ubi caput totius gentis Anglorum à diebus paganorum habetur.' Boniface V. to Abp. Justus.

[1] And called 'ecclesia Christi' because St. Sylvester had given a like dedication to the Lateran basilica. The Vatican basilica had its copy in the Church of St. Peter and Paul, afterward at St. Augustine's.

[2] 'Addidit etiam præfatus episcopus nobilitatem Anglicæ hierarchiæ exponere quod, scilicet, Cantuariensis præsul apostolicâ auctoritate Romæ assidere debeat sanctæ Ruffinæ pontifici .... Quæsitum est in decretis et inventum ibique papæ atque omnium assensu corroboratum.' Goscelini Cant. Mon. *Hist. Translat. S. Augustini* [Migne, clv. 32].

[3] William the Conqueror was, I know, crowned by two apostolic legates in the year 1070, but this was an exception which proved the rule. There was at that moment no Archbishop of Canterbury.

POLITICAL FUNCTIONS OF THE PRIMATES. 317

There cannot be doubt that whilst by immemorial custom the *proceres*, *principes*, or *primates* of the realm acted as counsellors of the King, the Archbishop of Canterbury was his monitor. It was theirs to advise the Crown as to the material administration of the kingdom, police, taxes, defence against invasion, and the rest; it was his to inform and direct the conscience of the sovereign whenever material interest and moral obligation might come in contact, and, by the sanctions of Divine law, to check the first symptoms of indifference to the interests of the subject. There was no public opinion, no press, no parliament; and even had there been, the theories of which public opinion, press, and parliament serve in these days as the illustration had not as yet found a lodging in the wildest of fancies. Once chosen, the sovereign must not only reign, but govern; and he was expected to govern, not in conformity with human law dictated from below, but in obedience to Divine law as interpreted by its proper expounders, and in emergent cases by the Primate, who held towards him the relation of father to son, and whose authority over his conscience was the only official check against despotism known to the age. Bad kings had chafed against the check, but there it was; so that when Lanfranc, suspecting what might happen, required William to swear that in all things he would obey his admonitions, he only reduced an ancient usage to a formula; and when Anselm, always happy if sometimes quaint in his similitudes, represented King and Primate as two oxen coupled by the same yoke, the theory was accepted without challenge; nor, indeed, would it have been advanced without the justification of fact.

Hence it can scarcely be unreasonable to suppose that thirst for gold had not been William's only motive in so long refusing to let Lanfranc's empty throne be filled, and that lust of power had urged him thus rudely to break a prescription which princes less audacious would have been content slowly to enfeeble,

Good reason, therefore, had the *primores regni* for alarm, as they gathered around him at Gloucester at the close of the year 1092. He had already for nearly four months detained in England the man whom they wished to see adorned with the archiepiscopal mitre, but had not said one syllable about Canterbury. This was scarcely fit conduct for a Christian king. He was fast forfeiting the name of Christian.

Happily, however, they had good reason to indulge a sentiment more potential than that of alarm. This was the eleventh occasion—or might have been, if it was not—on which, during the space of three years and a half, they had assembled without a president; but it was perhaps the first on which they felt that they could no longer suffer themselves to be thus deprived without forfeiting their self-respect, and without betraying one of the most precious of their rights as the constitutional advisers of the Crown. We know not what had on previous occasions been said about the vacancy of the archbishopric and about the confiscation of its revenues, but may reasonably presume that, keeping the two subjects distinct, the prelates and barons, however indisposèd or disinclined to discuss the latter, had not for an instant forgotten that it appertained to them to discuss the former, inasmuch as their constitutional right to a share in the election of the Archbishop of Canterbury imposed upon them the corresponding duty of providing that the vacancy of the primatial see be not causelessly and unreasonably prolonged. If it was in his quality of territorial lord that, abusing the privilege of *advocatio*, William had taken the archiepiscopal estates into his seigneury and appropriated their revenues, he was in his quality of King bound to consult his Council upon the appointment of a new Archbishop; and, whether or not the assignment of the Canterbury revenues during the vacancy appertained to the realm of *consuetudo*, there could be no question that the ancient law of

England empowered the *magnates regni* to advise the King as to the person most fit to play the part of *pater patriæ*.

And the moment had at last come at which it would have been worse than foolish and worse than wicked to neglect the assertion of their right. For if the King had hitherto excused his delay by the failure of the Count of Meulan to secure the patronage of Le Bec, and by the refusal of the Abbot of Le Bec to visit England, they were now already complaining to each other that it was time they should own the King was trifling with them, time they should ascertain what it was he meant, time they should make, if only a timorous and inchoate resolve, yet, at the very least, that.

But it was evident that they must be exceedingly cautious, inasmuch as, however disinclined to betray their electoral responsibility or relinquish their electoral right, it would be of little use in asserting the one and claiming the other to make a demand they could not enforce; a difficulty rendered all but hopeless by the fact that, William having hitherto refused to acknowledge the Pope, any reference they might make to the Holy See would only be a provocation to him to throw himself into the hands of the heterodox party.

My own belief, then, is—and I hope to justify it in a subsequent part of the narrative—that, sending privately to Rome for advice, they postponed all formal action in the business to Easter, entrusting themselves meanwhile to the mercy of Heaven, and resolving to let the King know at least thus much: that, in their opinion, it was now high time to appoint a new Archbishop.

After some considerable discussion this resolution of the prelates and barons took a form with which the statement of a grievance would have been incompatible, and thus a singularly prudent one; still, a form which would let the King know how close home their grievance had come to them, and thus a singularly suggestive one; above all, a form which, appealing as it did to the royal conscience, was a singularly admonitory one. They one and all approached him, and 'with suppliant entreaty'—so says Eadmer—'begged their lord the King,' that he would 'allow prayers to be offered throughout all the churches of England that God would vouchsafe to put it into his heart, by the appointment of a worthy pastor to the Mother Church of the kingdom, to raise her up from her fallen estate, and through her others.' He was 'somewhat indignant' at the proposal, but with all the tact of a good governor gave the permission craved, adding, however, with a scornful laugh, that, let the Church pray as she might, he should not desist from doing precisely what he pleased; 'for,' said he, 'no man's prayer shall ever change my will.' The remark was received quite as a matter of course, and the *primores regni* retired from the presence.

Anselm, who was probably the guest of the Abbot of St. Peter's at Gloucester, and who must have overheard all the gossip concerning the Court with no other hopes and no other fears than such as he had entertained on previous occasions when sent to England in the interests of his abbey, regarded this extraordinary incident with all the interest of a Churchman indeed, but with the same sort of personal unconcern as would in these days be evinced by a foreigner casually landed on our island upon the eve of a general election. His friends at Le Bec had been quite right, he thought; the best informed men in England had now for four months said nothing to him to justify the faintest suspicion that preferment awaited him in their midst; and if he had himself instinctively and as of course made no allusion to the Canterbury scandal, the Earl of Chester who was cousin to the King, the Bishop of Rochester who knew all about Canterbury, the Abbot of Westminster who had no dearth of political information, can scarcely have been thus utterly uncommunicative, except as knowing that any rumour which might once have disturbed him was a vain one, or as being indisposed to make needless allusion to an unwelcome subject.

And if anything could have deepened his security, it was what happened next. The bishops on whom it devolved to order the *modus orandi* for the relief of the Church of Canterbury from her long and unprecedented widowhood and woes, asked him to undertake the charge; and thus, as he himself could on no account have asked such a service of any man whom he conceived to be, whether wittingly or unwittingly, a candidate for the primacy, his conviction that the prelates, like the barons, had simply overlooked him was, if confirmation were possible, confirmed.

So strange a request from wearers of the mitre took him by surprise; but there is a point beyond which resistance ceases to be humble, and he was at last fain to yield. As soon, then, as the *modus orandi* he suggested had been set forth, the Court broke up, and bishops, barons, and abbots went each his way, the only unanxious man of them all being Anselm. He was as one in the centre of a cyclone.

CHAPTER X.

ST. ANSELM'S APPOINTMENT TO THE PRIMACY.

THE King seems to have been enjoying the pleasures of the chase in the royal park of Alveston, a richly wooded property carved out of the Forest of Kingswood and commanding an extensive view of the valley of the Severn, when, about the end of February, Abbot Anselm, his tour of inspection being now completed, waited upon him to take leave.[1] But William desired him to postpone his departure,[2] and he retired to Arle, a manor in the parish of Cheltenham belonging to St. Peter's Abbey at Gloucester.[3]

Shrove Tuesday fell this year—the year 1093—on the 1st of March; and it was on or about that day that one of the peers happened in the course of conversation to remark to the King, 'We do not know a holier man, I am sure, than the Abbot of Le Bec, Anselm. He loves nothing but God, and it is as clear as noonday that his heart is set upon nothing here below.'

---

[1] In 1088 he had allowed himself about five weeks for his round of inspections. The business at Chester, arrears of work elsewhere, and not improbably visits to new estates, would now add two or three weeks to the five. And he had said in the autumn (*Ep.* ii. 51), 'Reditum nostrum ante quadragesimam non spero futurum.'

[2] This is a noteworthy fact. Eadmer says (clix. 363), 'Detentus est in Angliâ fere mensibus quinque. . . . Post hæc in Northmanniam regredi volens negatâ à Rege licentiâ copiam id agendi habere non potuit.'

[3] I confess I speak without absolute certainty. The county historians seem to have nothing to say that can help me. The *History of St. Peter's, Gloucester,* says, 'Ethelbaldus rex Merciorum dedit Deo et Sancto Petro Gloucestriæ. . . . viginti hidas terræ in villâ quæ vocatur Alre;' but all that I can get from Bigland (*County of Gloucester,* i. 312) is the following about Arle Court: 'Attached to the ancient structure was a chapel, now destroyed, on a beam of which was a date, 1250. Here likewise is a medicinal spring.'

For six months had William Rufus preserved a sullen and tormenting silence about his captive; but the tenor of this remark, and its manifest sincerity, surprised him into speech. It was like the happy accidental touch that sets a spring in motion, and lo! valves unfold, and the treasured hoard lies all displayed. His tongue was unloosed; he could restrain himself no longer. 'No, indeed?' he asked with a sneer, 'not even upon the Archbishopric of Canterbury?' 'Not even upon that; certainly not,' was the curt but respectful reply. 'Such at least is my conviction, and there are many who share it.' 'I tell you what,' cried the flushed and excited prince, 'he would come clapping his hands and skipping for joy, and would fling himself into my arms, if he had the slightest hope of being able to aspire as high as that. But I swear by the Holy Face of Lucca [1] that just now neither he nor

[1] I need scarcely say that this was the Red King's usual oath. 'The object by which he swore .... was the Face of our Saviour on a very ancient crucifix of cedar, said to have been carved by Nicodemus himself, and to have been miraculously brought to the city of Lucca in 782, where it is still preserved with the greatest care and veneration in the chapel of the Holy Cross in the ca'hedral. "Il volto santo di Lucca" has always been highly prized by the inhabitants, who have even stamped it on their money. Four of their coins, dated 1725, 1735, 1749, and 1766 .... are figured in Bonneville's *Traité des Monnaies*, Paris, 1806.'—Note by the Rev. J. Griffiths in his edition of Inett's *History of the English Church* (ii. 134).

Copies of this venerable relic are not wanting. I remember to have seen one at Naples; but I have a curious fact to note. Some four hundred yards from the prætorian gate of the city of Aosta is an archway erected in honour of Augustus and in commemoration of the defeat of the Salassi. That archway is called Saint Voult, and numberless local charters preserved from the Middle Ages make mention of it under the name of *sanctus vultus*. There can be no doubt of the origin of the name, for a very ancient crucifix still stands in the vault of the arch. I cannot tell the age of this crucifix; it did not occur to me when I was at Aosta that I should have to write a note about it; but I make no doubt that it either is or has replaced a copy of the venerable relic at Lucca. Such copy of that venerable relic adorned the archway, I suspect, in the early days of Anselm; and if so it may have been Anselm to whom William Rufus was directly or indirectly indebted for so much as he knew about the 'Holy Face of Lucca,'

Gervase of Tilbury gives the following account (*Otia Imperialia*, xxiv.):—

'Est alia in linteo Domini figura expressa quæ ut in gestis de vultu Lucano legitur hoc suum habuit initium. Cùm Dominus Redemptor noster exutus vestimentis suis in cruce penderet .... mater ejus et aliæ quæ cum eâ erant citò euntes emerunt linteum mundissimum tam amplum et extensum quod toti Crucifixi corpus

any other man shall be Archbishop but myself.' This outburst frightened the interlocutor dumb ; and the exasperated monarch, whose eyes, owing to a caprice of nature's in the colouring of the iris and a mixture of whites in the cornea, glared hard and frightful at times like this, repeated the oath and cried, 'By the Holy Face of Lucca, neither he nor any other man shall be Archbishop but myself!'

Those words reached Heaven. Scarcely were they spoken when the speaker fell suddenly and alarmingly ill. But none were more alarmed than he. At last the hand of God had touched him! And was this God's answer to the prayers that he had sneered at?

As he was carried in all haste to Gloucester the news flew on the wings of terror from end to end of England, and by the morning of the following Sunday[1] bishops, abbots, tenants-in-chief, were crowded in and about Gloucester Castle, waiting for the curtain to fall on a career once bright, indeed, but of late despotic without bound and sensual beyond the reach of words. Eternity was nigh at hand, and a soul so sadly bested must not be let go into eternity as it was. It was a crisis of salvation or of damnation, and they implored him to think of his dearest interests, to have pity on himself, to open his dungeons, to set his captives free, to forgive his debtors—ah! how many a tale of woe and of broken hearts had those poor debtors to tell!—to restore their liberty to the

operiebat pendentis de cruce; cùmque deponeretur apparuit totius corporis effigies in linteo expressa, ad cujus similitudinem et exemplar Nicodemus vultum Lucanum effigiavit.' He then goes on to give the history of the journey of the *volto sacro* from Jerusalem to Lucca.

The Père Longueval says of this crucifix, 'Le Christ est représenté attaché à la croix habillé, comme on le voit en effet dans plusieurs anciens crucifix, et que le peuple nomme pour cet effet *S. Godelu* ou *Vaudelou*, par corruption de *S. Voult, de Lucques* (*Hist. de l'Eglise Gallicane*, tom viii. p. 66).

[1] I suppose the King to have been taken ill on the morning of Shrove Tuesday. York lies a hundred and fifty miles from Gloucester 'as the crow flies,' so does Rochester; and the greater part of England is within a much shorter radius. Most, therefore, if not all, of the bishops must have been on the move by Thursday morning; and most, if not all, of them can have had little difficulty in reaching Gloucester by Saturday night. They had forty hours of daylight for their journey.

churches he had enslaved, their proper pastors to the charges let out on hire, and above all to set free the see of Canterbury, a see 'the oppression of which,' to borrow their own phrase, 'had reduced the religion of Christ in England to the level of a deplorable degradation.' Thus did they beseech him.

What took place thereupon Eadmer does not inform us. Suffice it to say that after an interval—how short or how long an interval matters not—the sufferer in an ecstasy of terror cried out for Anselm. It was his impious speech about Anselm and the archbishopric that had provoked the thunderbolt; and now the long-nursed conviction that his own temporal welfare was inextricably involved in Anselm's preferment arose and overpowered him, and, questioning whether life could hold out till the Abbot's arrival, he insisted on his being summoned.

The bearer of the message, breathless and agitated, broke rudely in upon the sacred *rêveries* of the abstracted recluse, who, as having no immediate interest in the affairs of the realm, had not been apprised of the King's illness, and hurried him off in hot speed to receive the last sigh of the royal sufferer. When he entered the sick chamber, first one and then another anxiously begged to know what he thought the best course to be taken for the salvation of the sinner. 'Tell me,' he said, 'what you have yourselves advised him to do.' The answer was satisfactory, and he resumed, 'It is written, *Incipite Domino in confessione*; hence it seems to me that he should first make a good confession of all the offences against God of which his conscience accuses him, and unfeignedly promise amendment for the future, should he recover; and when he has confessed, then let him give orders that what you have advised be immediately set in execution.' The bishops thereupon requested him to receive the confession, and approaching the sick man, told him that Anselm was there, and advised his resorting at once to the sacrament of penance.

The sufferer, racked by the memory of sins which even now held him quivering on the brink of endless woe, and by a bodily torture which even now seemed severing his immortal from his mortal part, acquiesced. The room was cleared; the priest and the penitent were left alone.

When summoned again into the sick room, the *primates regni* perceived that the expression of anguish had disappeared from the King's face. God had spoken to him through His minister; he had listened to the voice, and all that now devolved on him was to make public reparation and public promise of amendment. In the presence, therefore, of the nation, thus represented round about his bed by the lords spiritual and temporal of the realm, he frankly and explicitly engaged his royal word henceforth, should he be spared, to govern his life by mansuetude and justice; and handing the sacred rod of sovereignty[1] to the bishops, begged them to go and lay it in his behalf on the altar of the church appertaining to the castle.[2] But he did more.

I need not remind the reader that the dying prince—he thought at least that he was dying—had been exhorted, before Anselm's arrival at the castle, to liberate his captives, to forgive his debtors, and to put an end to the public evils of which he was the author; but it is particularly worthy of remark that the solemn act which is now to be described contained no explicit promise of the reparation of the Canterbury scandal and others of like character. The very terminology of such a promise might have involved the discussion of questions with which it would be cruel to disturb the last moments of a dying man. Nevertheless, if anything could

---

[1] 'Virgam emendationis indicem per episcopos . . . . super altare vadem mitteret.' It was a *virga*, not a *virga pastoralis*. The *virga* was one of the royal insignia. The insignia were the ring, the sword, the crown, the sceptre, the rod. I say this on the authority of Archbishop Robert's *Benedictionarium*, the priceless relic of Anglo-Saxon England preserved in the public library at Rouen. To have had what was not his own laid as a pledge on the altar would have been absurd.

[2] I have no doubt whatever that the *ecclesia* of the various accounts is the church, or chapel, of Gloucester Castle.

bind the King's conscience to repair those wrongs it was the act now to be performed, and with a conscience thus bound he might resign himself without fear into the hands of his all-merciful Creator.

Whilst the venerable procession of the bishops left the room, carrying the dove-crowned ensign of royalty to the altar, a clerk was instructed to draw up an edict in which the sovereign proclaimed three acts of indemnity and pledged himself to as many principles of government. All his prisoners whatsoever were thereby set at liberty, all debts due to him irrevocably cancelled, and all offences hitherto committed against his person consigned to lasting oblivion. The document then went on to promise good and holy statutes to the King's subjects, the inviolable observance of law, and such a strict enquiry into wrongs and abuses as should be a terror to evil-doers generally.

The contents of the parchment were now read to the sick man, who, amidst tears of joy and exclamations of thanksgiving from the charmed and affected bystanders, commanded the great seal to be affixed to it. Never, never had they known a conversion at once so sudden and so sincere. God's chastisement had done its work; the stricken sinner had turned, and he should live. Henceforth they had a good king and a great one; and oh! might God long preserve him to them![1]

The penitent had relieved his conscience, had complied with the requirements of his confessor, and had inaugurated a new era. Anselm's task was done; and Anselm was already retiring, when some well-meaning persons in the company suggested that now was the time to raise the common mother of the realm from her long widowhood, by appointing her a pastor. With all his heart, said the King from his pillow; indeed, it was the very thing that he was thinking about.

[1] 'Gaudetur a cunctis, bendicitur Deus in istis, obnixè oratur pro salute talis ac tanti regis!'—Eadmer.

But who was to be appointed? All depended on him. He must speak the word.

So then the dying prince, dying till this last effort broke the spell and gave him back to life, drew himself painfully up in the bed, and supporting himself on his elbow faintly said, pointing to the Abbot of Le Bec, 'That is the good man I choose, Anselm.'

The name 'Anselm' was instantly caught up, and passed from mouth to mouth; a confused hubbub, partly murmur of approval, partly cry of benediction, resounded through the room; prelates and barons dropped instinctively aside, and there, amongst them but now no longer one of them, there, stark with amazement and pale as the dead, stood Anselm!

He neither moved nor uttered sound, till some of them, advancing with intent to lead him to the King's bedside for investiture of the archbishopric, recalled him to self-control. But he refused to receive investiture of the archbishopric, protesting that for many reasons such a thing was out of the question. Whereupon the bishops, leading him apart from the crowd, began, 'What are you doing? What do you mean? Why attempt to baffle God? You see that the law of Christ is almost a dead letter in England. Everything has fallen into confusion. There is no abomination that is not rampant. We and the Church it were ours to rule have fallen into danger of eternal death through this man's tyranny. You see all this, and yet when you might come forward and help us you scorn to do so. Strangest of men, what are you thinking about? Where have your senses gone?'

Yes, indeed, what was he thinking about? He was thinking about things little dreamt of in their state theology, if indeed he was thinking at all, and if his senses, as they suspected, had not forsaken him.

'In the oppression of the Church of Canterbury,' they continued, 'we are ourselves all crushed and destroyed; that

Church cries out to you, that Church in her distress craves your help for herself and all of us; and yet you care nothing for her liberty, care nothing for our recovery, refuse to share your brethren's toil, and only seek your own selfish, indolent ease.'

'Bear with me,' he remonstrated in his turn, 'bear with me, and listen. It is all quite true, I own. Your trials are many, and call for relief. But reflect, I implore you. I am already in the decline of life¹ and quite unable to endure the toils of place. How then, when I cannot do my own proper work, am I to do the work of all the Church all over England? And, more than this, my conscience bears me witness that ever since I have been a monk I have shunned secular affairs; never have I been able to apply myself to them to my own satisfaction; there is nothing in them pleasing or attractive to me. Therefore let me have repose, and do not employ me on what I never liked, lest harm come of it.'

'No, no,' they replied; 'accept the primacy of the Church, and never fear. Show us the way. Tell us, teach us what to do, and we will engage to follow you, and obey you, and carry out your injunctions to the letter. Busy yourself with Heaven for us, and we will arrange your secular concerns for you.'

'Impossible, impossible,' he interrupted; 'I am abbot of a monastery in another kingdom, with an archbishop to whom I owe obedience, a temporal prince to whom I owe subjection, monks to whom I owe all the counsel and help I can give them. I cannot break with my monks without their leave, nor set myself free from my prince's seigneury without his permission, nor shake off the yoke of obedience to my archbishop, if I would save my soul, without his release.'

'All that is a light matter; their consent will easily be got.'

¹ *Grandævus.*

'No, not at all,' he insisted; 'what you want will never be.'

They were out of patience, and laying hands on him dragged him to the sick man and reported his obstinacy. Tears came to the King's eyes. 'Anselm,' he said, 'what do you mean? Why hand me over to the torments of eternal punishment? Remember the friendship my father and mother always had for you, and you for them. By that friendship I implore you not to let their son perish body and soul. Sure I am that perish I must if I end my days with the archbishopric in my seigneury. Help me therefore, reverend father, and take out of my hands a pontificate for the keeping back of which I am sore confounded, and fear I shall be worse confounded through eternity.'

The bystanders were greatly moved, but Anselm, inexorable even to an appeal like this, instead of yielding, began to make excuses—what we are not informed, still—to make excuses to the sufferer. Conduct which they deemed so unworthy of himself, so unworthy of the occasion, so cruel to a dying man, made the bishops angry. 'What madness has come over you?' they cried. 'You are disturbing the King and killing him outright. You see him dying under your eyes, and are not afraid to ruffle him by your obstinacy as he dies. Know this, that all the turmoils, and cruelties, and crimes that henceforth shall afflict our country will be set down to you, if you this day do not, by accepting the pastoral care, prevent them.'

This was a frightful menace. What could he do? Whither could he turn? Gladly, he used to say, would he then and there have died. Who could help him? Baldwin and Eustace were standing by. He turned to them and said, 'Ah, my brethren, why don't you help me?' Eustace could not speak; Baldwin, the better tutored of the two in self-control, so far mastered his emotion as to say, 'If it be the will of God, who are we that we should rebel?' but burst into tears as he spoke, and blood flowing from his nostrils showed what the effort had cost him. 'Your staff is soon broken,' said poor Anselm.

But if Abbot Anselm was in extreme distress, the King was in an agony of terror to find that his expostulations were all in vain, and bade the entire company try what entreaty could do. But before bishops, barons, abbots could obey, Anselm was at their feet. He could not, would not consent.

This exasperated them; they were furious at his obstinacy and ashamed of their own weakness. 'The pastoral staff!' cried a voice. 'The pastoral staff!' cried all the rest. They caught him by the right arm, and, some dragging and others pushing, got him close to the King's bed, and there held him wedged. The King offered him the crosier, but he kept his hand closed and refused to touch it. The bishops, now thoroughly maddened and set upon winning their game if even by main force, tried to open his clenched fist, but to no purpose, although he was so hurt by their roughness that he cried out for pain. At last they succeeded in unlocking his forefinger, but, even so, before they could use their advantage it was closed again and dug into the palm. That thin white hand was never to be opened without the consent of the owner.[1] The bishops, therefore, applied the crosier to it and held it there, whilst barons, abbots, and courtiers, serried in thick crowd, bore them and him away in the direction of the church. As they went a voice sang out, 'Te Deum laudamus;' the clerical members of the moving mob immediately caught it up, yelling forth its sacred periods with the uncurbed fury of so many mænads; whilst the pale and frantic monk, struggling, but struggling in vain, to get free of them, cried, 'It is nought that ye do! it is nought that ye do!' and the convoy of laymen shouted, as they scuffled along, 'Long live the Bishop! Long live the Bishop!'

It would appear that as soon as the bishops had, by

[1] See *Epp.* iii. 1, 2.

religious ceremony as solemn as their excitement permitted, done all they could to ratify the royal appointment and relinquished their hold on their captive, they made it their business to apprise him of one or two circumstances of some importance. Anyhow, at whatever moment informed, informed he very soon was—

First, that, little as he thought it, he had been a prisoner for the last six months, and that the King, from the moment he found him in his power, had resolved to detain him in England, so as sooner or later to raise him to the primacy.[1]

He was further informed that their royal master had resolved to compel Duke Robert's consent to the promotion. For the Duke was, as we have seen, particularly tenacious of his patronal right in respect of Herlwin's monastery; was, in his own way, as proud of Abbot Anselm as his father had been before him, and might be expected, from the very considerations which had engaged William to secure Anselm's person, to strain every nerve to recover his possession of him.

He was, in the third place, informed that as far back as Christmas communication had been made with Rome on the subject of the protracted vacancy, and his name mentioned as the object of the national choice.[2] So that, whilst the King without his knowing it had kept him prisoner for the last six months, they in their turn, the lords spiritual and temporal of the realm, had, for many weeks at least, indulged the settled hope that he would ere long be granted them as the answer to their prayers for an archbishop.

But more than all this: he now knew something else of which it is high time that I should apprise the reader.

The message which brought him from Arle to Gloucester

---

[1] There can, I think, be no doubt of this. He must have written to Le Bec for his unfinished treatise against the heretical *theses* of Roscelin in the October of 1092 (*Ep.* ii. 51); and it would seem from the text of the *De Incarnatione Verbi* that at that time he was already *ad episcopatum captus et retentus* (Migne, clix. 262).

[2] *Ep.* iii. 3.

Castle was, whether purposely or not, so worded as to blind him to certainly the principal, and perhaps the sole important, reason for which his presence was required. It bade him 'come in all haste to the King, to support and strengthen him by his presence before he should die;' and he must naturally have supposed that the King wished him to hear his confession. But it is more than probable that he would not have been summoned at all had it not already been decided to promote him to the primacy; and if Eadmer, whose task it was to show things as Anselm saw them, was too good a dramatist prematurely to inform the reader of a fact carefully concealed from Anselm until the very last, we must not therefore refuse to accept the overwhelming evidence supplied us from other sources of information. The reflecting reader can scarcely have failed to note that in his aside with the bishops in the King's bedchamber, Anselm spoke as holding them rather than the prince responsible for the trouble that had come upon him. And very properly. The fact is that they and the temporal peers had solicited and obtained a *congé d'élire* at the earliest possible moment; had solemnly and unanimously elected him; and, after presenting his name to the King, who was only too willing to ratify their choice, had summoned him from Arle, if for no other purpose yet at any rate for that of his appointment to the primacy.

King and kingdom, bishops and barons, *clerus* and *populus* had elected him. How was he to escape?

The only questions likely then and there to occur to him were—Had the election been regular? Did the King really think that he had given him investiture of the archbishopric? On the first question the less said the better, as he discovered in the sequel. As to the second, whatever the King might think, Anselm had his own conviction. To give and to receive are distinct and separate acts; to offer and to accept are distinct and separate acts; and investiture is a game at which two are to play, or it is nothing. He had not been invested, and the King knew it. Confining himself, therefore, to this fact, and avoiding whatever might harass the King's repose or fret his temper, but contriving to mingle words of comfort and prophetic cheer with what he felt it his duty to say, he was no sooner permitted to leave the church than he went straight to the patient's chamber, and, standing by his bed, said, 'My lord King, you will not die of this illness; hence I wish you well to understand how easily you may undo all that has just been done. I have not consented, nor do I consent, to its being deemed a valid proceeding.' The King's reply has not been recorded; perhaps he said nothing, for if Anselm's fortitude half an hour ago had set him thinking, Anselm's prudence now set him wondering; and, like the Count of Meulan on a memorable occasion, *obstupuit ad prudentiam viri.*

On his retiring from the King's presence the bishops and the entire peerage took care, in recognition of his new honour, to show the way. As soon as he found himself alone with them he paused and addressed them as follows:—' Do you really know what mischief you are planning? You are for yoking to the plough a poor weak old ewe by the side of an untamed bull. And what will come of it? Not only untamed, but untamable, the savage bull will drag the poor sheep right and left over thorns and briars, and, unless the poor thing disengage itself, will dash it to pieces. Where then will be her wool, her milk, her young? She will yield none of them and will be worthless. And why? Because you heedlessly yoked together the sheep and the bull. The plough is the Church, as when the Apostle says, "You are God's husbandry, God's building." In England the two best steers of the herd are set to draw the plough and trace the furrow—the King and the Archbishop of Canterbury. The King's business is with temporal justice and material rule, the Archbishop's with Divine instruction and spiritual government. One of them—I mean Archbishop Lanfranc— is now no more; and the other, dragging the plough after him at will, has displayed the wildness of a bull that nothing can tame; and yet you want to yoke me with him—a feeble old ewe with a mad bull. Surely I have made my meaning clear to you. Think who it is that you are coupling me to; think, and give up your scheme. For if you do not, I tell you what will happen. Instead of my yielding you the wool and the milk of the Word of God, and lambs for God's service—you may not think it, but what I say is true—the King's cruelty will first wear me out and then with many wrongs completely crush me; and the delight some of you for a moment feel at the thought of your own relief from trouble, when once you find that the accustomed counsel and hoped for help are no longer to be had, will, to your dismay, be turned into utter misery. And the next thing that will happen will be this—you will live to see it, I assure you—the Church you are taking such pains to raise from widowhood will fall into widowhood again with her pastor still alive. And who will have to bear the blame but you, who so inconsiderately have coupled together a ferocity like the King's and weakness such as mine? And when he has got me under him, and there is not one of you that dare face him, then to his heart's liking will he worry one and all of you.'

As he said these words the composure he had forced himself to assume gave way before an only too true vision of the future. He burst into tears, and signing to them to leave him to himself, sought his lodging.

In the solitude of his chamber he now surveyed and studied the appalling panorama, counted the woes he should live to endure, and with prophetic certitude rehearsed the part he was to play in each moving scene. But while his spell-bound fancy was thus engaged there grew into the vision forms and faces dear to him, and dearer than even he had thought. The future disappeared; he was looking at the past; he was at Le Bec again!

Enough, enough. He has not recorded details too sacred for our impertinent gaze. All we know is that, after some time, he was seized by a paroxysm of emotion which endangered life and reason. His wailings brought people to the room, who, horrified at the alteration in his features, ran for holy water, splashed him with it, and gave him to drink of it—a remedy rarely tried, but tried especially in cases of demoniacal possession or of frenzy.[1]

The paroxysm passed away, but he was changed from what he had been. The tension of nerve and the subsequent collapse left their mark on him. A strangely rapid failure of sight was one memento to him of that terrible day; and henceforth he was an old man.

All this took place on Quadragesima Sunday, the sixth of March, in the year of grace a thousand and ninety-three.

[1] A knight *mente captus* was once brought to St. Odilo of Cluny for healing. 'Misertus itaque homo Dei tantæ calamitati et condolens gratissimæ juventuti cum fratribus in terram ante altare Sancti Petri prosternitur, psalmis insistit, patrocinia sanctorum cum litaniâ requirit ; deinde surgens ad vexatum accedit *aquâ sanctificationis aspergit, bibere cogit*, et sic recedere permittit.' The man was cured.- *S. Odilonis Cluniac. Abb. Vita* (Migne, cxlii. 933).

A similar case occurs in the history of St. Hugh of Cluny. 'Tunc sanctus, misericordiâ motus, aquam afferri præcepit, quam precibus sacris et benedictionibus præsignavit, acceptoque cochleari *ter de aquâ illâ in ore mulieris orando infudit.*' - Migne, clix. 921.

CHAPTER XI.

THE LAST DAYS OF ST. ANSELM'S ABBACY.

ANSELM had prophesied truly. Six weeks from the day on which the Red King lay quailing on his bed of anguish the Red King was well enough to hold his usual Easter Court at Winchester.

But meanwhile he became only too painfully conscious that in his hour of helplessness and terror he had belied his reputation for wariness and caution by establishing a precedent the remote consequences of which even he could not exaggerate. And who was to blame? Often and often did the convalescent ask himself the question as he lay tossing on his couch. Yes, who was to blame?

The reader has not forgotten that when the bishops and barons were readmitted to the royal bedchamber after the King had made his confession to Anselm, the sick man caused one of the sacred ensigns of his royalty to be carried forth and laid upon the altar of the adjacent church in attestation of his resolve henceforward to live a life of clemency and justice. In that there was no great folly, and had that been all he could have borne the remembrance of the critical day without alarm. But what could have possessed him that he should execute a document which bound him to give the people good and holy laws, to respect their rights, to avenge their grievances? To break a verbal promise or a verbal oath was an offence trivial and usual, but to violate the terms of a written contract made venerable by the impress of the great seal of the realm, were a crime which the estates of the realm might refuse to condone. Holy Writ itself was scarcely more sacred than such an instrument; and what might not his barons some day require of him in virtue of it? How great, then, and how gratuitous had been his folly! Great, because what he had done once he might be called upon to do again; gratuitous, because in the annals of the English Crown no such charter had ever as yet seen the light. Indeed, indeed, he had established a very perilous precedent, and I suspect that William Rufus knew better than a remote posterity the value of the parchment engrossed in his behalf, marked with his sign, and sealed with his signet on the day when at Gloucester he lay quivering in the hand of God. We owe Magna Charta to the document in virtue of which Henry I. in the year 1100 won the crown of England; but I question whether that document would have been executed save for the earlier edict drawn up at Anselm's instance on Sunday, the sixth of March, in the year of grace 1093. That precious and primordial charter of our liberties has perished; there was every motive for destroying it. But, in an age when precedent reigned unquestioned and omnipotent, it was precedent enough that such an instrument should have had existence; and I am much mistaken if amongst the names which adorn the annals of our freedom the first place of all should not be claimed for the pious and unassuming monk who, before adorning the throne which was after the lapse of a century to be filled by Langton, thus forestalled and anticipated Langton's exertions for the protection of the people of England against the despotism of an alien dynasty.

Still, great and gratuitous as was the folly with which the convalescent prince reproached himself in having thus by parchment, sign, and seal given his subjects a hold, however uncertain, upon him, his indiscretion had not stopped there. Had it done so he might have been content to await its consequences; but, alas for him! the charter contained other clauses, whose operation he already felt, and felt in a diminished exchequer. This was the greatest grief of all. Alas for him! the loss of so much pelf was the grief that came the closest to his heart; and, alas for him! Renouf the Firebrand was by this time at his side. 'Incredible folly!' cried the prince. 'Incredible!' echoed his diabolical adviser. And who was to blame for it? Who? Yes, who? Not Anselm, for any other good confessor would have laid on him the very same injunction; nor yet the bishops and abbots, who, whilst Anselm was yet on his way from Arle, urged him to do this very thing, forgive his debtors and release his prisoners for debt. No, no; the fault was not theirs; it was not a human fault at all; but the fault—scarce does the pen dare to write the words, and yet they must be written—it was the fault of One whom he, the anointed king of a Christian people, now no longer owned as a Father who chastises where He loves, but as a mean vindictive Foe that had basely frightened him, to take advantage of his fright and to subtract so many pounds, so many shillings, and so many pence from his exchequer.

From the moment this horrible thought took possession of him—and Renouf the Firebrand was at his side to give it emphasis and energy—from that moment all was changed. From that moment the good angels who had been hovering sadly over him fled sorrowing away, and the banished demon returned, accompanied by seven worse, to take possession of him.

Unprecedented woes now scourged England. Such prisoners as had not been set free in obedience to the King's edict were by his command not only detained, but set in stronger hold and laden with heavier irons; such as had, were pursued and reconsigned to their dungeons; the fictitious debts forgiven and the vexatious suits let drop were exacted and pursued afresh by a miscreant minister whose justice was all unjust and to whom mercy was an undreamed-of attribute; and as men watched the Firebrand now coldly scanning the first doubtful apprehension of his victim, now gleefully studying the anguish that accompanied the extortion of the victim's uttermost farthing, the avowal broke from one and all that their old miseries had been very blessings in comparison with the new. Nor did they deem amiss; for the Firebrand was the proper agent of a prince to whom it had by this time become a light thing to crush out hope from the hearts of his people and as light a thing to harbour every evil principle within his own.

It must have been at Easter that the good Bishop of Rochester, who had been the chief prompter of the King's too brief repentance, took occasion to admonish him, now that his health was better, to live circumspectly and to God. 'Know this, Bishop,' he cried, 'that never, by the Holy Face of Lucca, shall God have good for evil out of me!'

Strange and horrible phrase! It was to prove the keynote of his remaining life. '*Never shall God have good for evil out of me!*'

Let us now resume the thread of Anselm's history.

His appointment to the primacy rendered it unseemly that he should be permitted to reside any longer at Arle. Chosen by King and kingdom [1] to be the spiritual head of the *alter orbis*, he must henceforward reside on one or other of the archiepiscopal manors until such time as he should take possession of his church and see; and the royal sufferer gave order accordingly, requesting the Bishop of Rochester to act as *major domo* to him. It probably formed part of the official functions of the Bishop of Rochester to do so; in which case the King's injunction may have had special reference to a difficulty which had never as yet occurred in like case. Gundulf might take his dismayed and unwilling friend—Archbishop as all called him, Abbot as he called himself—

---

[1] The words 'à rege et regno' occur with sufficient frequency in the accounts of elections to the primacy to render it probable that they were a formulatic phrase.

take him to Hayes, to Harrow, or to Lyminge, and usher him into a suite of rooms which had not been occupied since Lanfranc was last there; but then the house was *de facto* not Anselm's, but the King's; and Anselm was, so to speak, a guest under his own roof. Nor was this all. The archiepiscopal estates had been let at an exorbitant rent to farmers, who must now for some months to come be allowed to make the most they could of every flock of wool and every ear of corn, and the Archbishop elect must therefore buy, or Gundulf must buy for him, the food and raiment needed for himself and such retinue as necessity or custom had set to wait upon him. But whence was money to be had? For every penny of toll and other direct revenue accruing from the day of Lanfranc's death had been diverted to the King's purse.[1] Not only, therefore, was Anselm, so to speak, a guest in his own house; he was, so to speak, a pauper on his own land; and it may have been to meet this difficulty that the royal invalid supplemented Anselm's appointment to the primacy by the immediate transference to him of the *alodium* of St. Alban's, and thus of such customary revenues as the Crown had hitherto derived from the lands belonging to that abbey.

When we last saw the poor Abbot of Le Bec he was in his lodging at Gloucester, bereft of self-control, almost of reason; dosed and splashed with holy water; woe-begone and broken-hearted. From Gloucester he was, as we have seen, conveyed by Gundulf to one of the archiepiscopal manors, but not before that prelate had written the monks of Le Bec a letter, the very first sentence of which told them all. That sentence was, *mutatis mutandis*, the formula set forth in the Pontifical for presenting a bishop elect for consecration:—

---

[1] 'Rex Willelmus junior in regiâ villâ quæ vocatur Aluwestan vehementer percussus infirmitate civitatem Glovernam adiit, ibique per totam quadragesimam languosus jacuit. . . . Sed Anselmo nil de archiepiscopatu præter id quod rex illi dari jusserat accipere licebat quoad tributum, quod post Lanfranci obitum singulis annis inde acceperat persolveretur.'—*Memoriale Fr. Walteri de Coventrid.*

'You know, my dearest friends, for how long a time the English Church has been like a family without a father, like a flock without a shepherd, and bereft of all paternal consolation. But God has in mercy turned and listened to the sighs of the orphans, the groans and wailings of the widows, the prayers of His faithful, and vouchsafed at last to visit and console them with His grace. Thanks to the working of God's unspeakable power, our lord the King of the English has, by the counsel and request of his peers and on the prayer and petition of clergy and laity, entrusted Abbot Anselm with the government of the Church of Canterbury. We owe this without doubt to the all-merciful work and ordinance of God. So, then, we humbly desire and earnestly beg you, as our most dearly beloved brethren, to lay aside all sadness and all heart-burnings, if any there be, and abstain from opposing the Divine will, the Divine work, and the election of good men, but rather to give thanks to God and to acquiesce with joy and willingness in what has taken place.

'There is another thing which I am bound to tell you. It may perhaps be possible to oppose the thing for a time; to undo it will in the long run be out of the question. I tell you the truth when I say that notice and the intention of this thing have already travelled far, and have by this time no doubt reached even the Apostolic See. Take wise advice, therefore, and charitably do without reluctance what without doubt you will sooner or later do.[1] Farewell.'

---

[1] 'Utimini igitur sapienti consilio, et per charitatem facite sine dilatione quod quandoque facturi estis sine dubitatione.' I wish I could be quite certain about the precise moral force of *dilatio* in this sentence. The verb *differre* has two meanings. It seems when followed by an infinite always to indicate refusal. Thus Hugh of Flavigny says of some one who refused to go to the funeral of a certain abbot, 'ad patris ire distulit exequias' (cliv. 397A); Rudolf Glaber, concerning St. William's refusal to swear fealty to the Bishop of Vercelli, 'omninò quod hortati erant facere distulit' (cxlii. 706A); William of Malmesbury (*H. N.* § 42) of a like refusal here in England, 'distulit fidelitatem dominæ facere;' and St. Odilo of St. Mayeul's obedience to a Divine intimation, 'parere non distulit' (cxlii. 949A). And I should say that it has the same meaning when

All were now agreed that nothing more might, could, would, or should be done before Easter; and so soon as the King was known to be out of danger the peers spiritual and temporal took each his leisurely departure from Gloucester Castle. As they did so the muse, with appropriate but exasperating indolence, laid aside style and tablet, disdaining to record anything further concerning Anselm for the next six weeks.

Then, when the Court was already assembled at Winchester, a strange thing happened—in good grammar a *miraculum*; in good theology, if I err not, a miracle.

The pensive and contemplative Abbot, the Bishop of Rochester, and Dom Baldwin of Tournay were in their lodging in an outskirt of the city of Winchester, when one night a neighbouring roof of thatch caught fire. The flames spread rapidly around, devouring everything; and the dwelling that sheltered the three monks was already invaded by people intent on saving its furniture, when the mistress of the

---

used absolutely, as when St. Anselm on being asked to do a thing refused (W. M. 1496A).

When, however, *differre* governs the accusative of a thing it seems to signify delay or postponement, as when the Conqueror postponed certain formalities till he should be at Brionne, 'concessionem atque donationem distulit usque dum veniret Brionium' (Bouquet, xiv. 270). This, too, seems to have been the meaning given by Conrad the Salic to the word when he refused to let some causes stand till he should have been consecrated, 'constantis est nequaquam differre quod aptè fieri valet' (cxlii. 1229D).

If, however, the accusative be of a person, not a thing, it is sometimes at least, if not always, susceptible of the meaning 'to put off,' and when we say 'he put the man off,' 'distulit hominem' (clvi. 907B).

What, then, does *dilatio* mean? Does it mean refusal, or postponement, or, in some vague way, putting off? Guibert of Nogent distinctly calls St. Bruno's refusal of a bishopric a *dilatio* (clvi. 855D). Eadmer, on the other hand, must mean 'delay' when he says of William Rufus, 'qui cum regni fastigia præripere gestiret et Lanfrancum .... non omninò consentaneum inveniret, verens ne dilatio suæ consecrationis inferret ei dispendium cupiti honoris' (clix. 361B). I am on the whole inclined to think that Gundulf purposely employed a word which on the face of it indicated the idea of delay, but was susceptible of another and stronger interpretation. The official notice from the King must have reached Le Bec soon after this letter from the Bishop of Rochester. We shall never know what it was like, I fear.

house desired them to touch nothing; she had no fear, she said; so long as Archbishop Anselm was there she and hers were safe. Overhearing this, Dom Baldwin repaired to Anselm and begged him to lend his help to their hostess. 'What can I do? What assistance can I render?' was the courteous and considerate enquiry. 'Go out,' said the Fleming, 'and make the sign of the cross before the flames; God might perhaps keep them back.' 'For me? No such thing.' Baldwin was silent; he had an idea of his own, and thought it prudent not to repeat what their hostess had been saying. Meanwhile the angry element came roaring on, and was soon so close as to make them seek safety in flight. But no sooner were they out in the stifling air than, before he had time to check them, Gundulf and Baldwin had seized their friend's right hand, and were making the sign of the cross with it in face of the conflagration. In an instant the globes of flame collapsed and expired, leaving a house which they had seized half consumed.

Easter Sunday fell on the seventeenth of April. Ten days later—that is to say, on Wednesday, the twenty-seventh [1]—the King by the following document conveyed the temporalities of the see of Canterbury to the Archbishop elect.

'Willielmus Rex Angliæ episcopis comitibus vicecomitibus ceterisque fidelibus suis Francis et Anglis, salutem. Sciatis me dedisse Anselmo archiepiscopo archiepiscopatum Cantuariensis ecclesie cum omnibus libertatibus et dignitatibus ad archiepiscopatum Cantuariensem pertinentibus et sake et soke on stronde et on streame on woden et on felden tolnes et beames gridbrech hamsokne forstalles et infangencthcves et flemenefremthe et omnes alias libertates in terrâ et mari super suos homines infra burgos et extra et super tot theines quot ecclesie Christi concessit Edwardus Rex cognatus meus. Volo etiam ut monachi

---

[1] Bartholomew Cotton (*Historia Anglicana*) supplies us with the date. 'Anno gratiæ m. xc. iij. v. Kal. Maii rex Willelmus Dorobernensem archiepiscopatum Anselmo . . . . concessit.'

ecclesie Christi Canturie pariter habeant in omnibus terris et tenementis suis omnes predictas libertates in terrâ et mari in aquis et viis et in omnibus aliis locis que ad eos pertinent in tantum et tam pleniter sicut predicti ministri exquirere debent. Portum etiam de Sandwico et omnes exitus et consuetudines eis concedo et confirmo quas Odo Biocensis episcopus et Cantie comes eis concessit et cartâ suâ confirmavit et nolo pati ut aliquis hominum se intromittat de omnibus rebus que ad cos pertinent nisi ipsi committere voluerunt nec Francus nec Anglus.'[1]

The first of the attesting signatures is that of William of Saint-Calais, Bishop of Durham, the second that of Gundulf, Bishop of Rochester. The former was soon to prove himself the most virulent of Anselm's enemies, as the second was already known to be the most devoted of his friends.

Custom had no doubt assigned a term within which Duke Robert must either grant or refuse the request for letters dismissory which the King had sent him immediately after the election; and, could we but ascertain that the term was one of forty days, we might conclude that a deed like this, executed fifty-two days after the election, was executed in rejoinder to a recently received rejection of that request, and in attestation of the King's resolve to have his own way. I have no proof to offer in corroboration of this idea, but I think it a highly probable one.

Be that as it may, Duke Robert's was not the only unwelcome despatch which had by this time been placed in the King's hand; for the Archbishop of Rouen was unwilling to resign the most distinguished churchman of his province, and

[1] I give this document as I find it in the printed editions. A copy preserved in the Cottonian Collection (*Titus*, c. ix.) presents some slight variations in spelling. On the sixth line, however, it gives 'archiepiscopum' instead of 'archiepiscopatum'; and concludes thus, 'Portum etiam de Sandewico et omnes exitus et consuetudines ex utrâque parte eis concedo et confirmo sicut rex Cnut eis antea dedit et codicello suo confirmavit. Domos etiam et omnes consuetudines in villâ de Sandewico eis concedo et confirmo quas Odo,' *et cætera*.

the monks of Le Bec were struggling to regain their abbot with a fervid intensity which only too faithfully betrayed the poignancy of their regret at having ever obliged him to visit their English estates.

How, then, was the King of England to subdue this threefold recalcitrancy, and with it Anselm's?

The poor Abbot, indeed, seems to have protested that the election could not stand, since the Christ Church monks had had no part in it; a technical but forlorn objection, to which the Christ Church monks themselves most eagerly replied— such at least is the obvious inference suggested by an extant letter from one of them [1]—that they had not been refused their proper part in the election; that nothing but unavoidable necessity had obliged the lords spiritual and temporal to choose a primate without their concurrence; that their own hopes in his regard, hopes indulged ever since Lanfranc's death, had long been notorious; and that, had they been represented at Gloucester on Quadragesima Sunday, they would have seconded the choice of the *proceres regni* with still more joyful acclaim than that with which they had greeted his arrival in our island on the seventh day of the preceding September.

Thus foiled, and thus reduced to a bare *nolo episcopari*, to which every power and every party in the kingdom refused a hearing, he was left to fight it out with the King unsupported by one solitary adherent, for his allies were all in Normandy. The issue was simple enough. 'I will not be Archbishop of Canterbury,' said the slight, pale, and attenuated monk. 'You shall be Archbishop of Canterbury,' rejoined the robust and rubicund prince as a sinister expression played in his terrible eye. He had found out Anselm's one weak point; he had singled out that point to attack; he meant to carry that point.

As to the triple alliance beyond sea, William had no need

[1] *Ep.* iii. 2.

to concern himself about the Archbishop of Rouen, who would give little trouble if let alone until other opponents had been disposed of, but turned his more serious thoughts alternately to Duke Robert's council chamber and to the chapter house of Le Bec. He had been at peace—nominal peace—with Duke Robert for a year or two, and the only proper way of punishing that prince's refusal to surrender Abbot Anselm would be to precipitate an inevitable renewal of hostilities; but that might not be done until he should have secured the alliance, or at least the neutrality, of the Count of Flanders; not, that is to say—for so the event proved—before the end of July; and meanwhile Robert Courthose was out of harm's reach. If, however, the monks of Le Bec could be made to yield, the Duke's mortification on finding himself betrayed by his favourite monastery would be a delightful subject for the royal heart to muse upon, and the thought of dealing a moral infliction of the kind was all the dearer inasmuch as whatever the material damage it might be in the power of the sword to inflict was already bespoken in another quarrel.

By the time, therefore, that the deliberations of the council at Winchester were terminated, the King had already resolved to aim specifically at two objects—the breaking of Anselm's obstinacy and the breaking of the obstinacy of Anselm's religious.

The next month, that of May, is barren of record; and, indeed, the muse may have found nothing to chronicle. The King was biding his time, and Anselm in England, and Anselm's monks in Normandy, were anxiously awaiting that relief of their common trouble which they saw that only Heaven could send.

But rumour was by no means idle, and, as though there were not already reasons enough why the King should be set upon forcing Anselm's acquiescence, supplied the quidnuncs with another. It was incredible, so they argued, that even the combined influences of superstition, of jealousy, of self-will, and, though last not least, of respect, however reluctant, for the rights of his peers, should have kept the King so long firm to his resolve, had not his master passion been in league with them. During the four years just ending he had been making of their Jerusalem a heap of stones, and it was incredible he should now suddenly surcease, except to enthrone himself upon the ruins. Anselm, they continued, was a man of contemplation, study, and prayer; his heart, and mind, and soul, and strength were all set on God; as to secular cares and the world's business, he shunned them all; and as to money, houses, or lands, school himself as he might for a few awkward weeks to master the condition of the temporalities of the see of Canterbury, when once the mitre should sit easily on that ethereal brow, the sublime intellect within would sicken of the tedium of bending to commercial details infinitely trivial, would soar indignant to her ancient sacred speculative heights, and would count it shame henceforth to waste her energies on a tenement, a manor, or a fief. And meanwhile, they continued, the King would contrive, encroaching here, pilfering there, confiscating at a third point, under pretext of consuetudinary right and under cover of judge-made law, to secure to himself little by little broad lands, houses, and revenues, which thenceforth would remain in royal hands till the crack of doom.

All this gossip found its way to Canterbury; but some of the Christ Church monks shook their heads, and said they scarcely took so gloomy a view of the future. Meanwhile the thirteenth week from the election had ended, and it was Whit Sunday. A day or two, and King and council were at work again; Anselm trembling for his fate, his monks at Le Bec trembling also. A fortnight more, and Lanfranc had now been dead four years. A few days more and the leases of the Canterbury lands began to fall in, first one, then another. And then, then, then, men learned what the cunning prince had all along been planning; and Anselm, poor

Anselm, heard what was even now a-doing, recalled the King's sinister glance at Winchester, and in his anguish cried out, in the words of the anguish of a Divine Exemplar, 'If it be possible let this chalice pass away from me.'

I know not how to gauge the cruelty of the blow. Perhaps the cruellest thing about it was that it was dealt at the most sensitive part of Anselm's nature, and that the royal miscreant who dealt it gloated over the smart he caused with all the keen satisfaction of a man who had carried the infliction of moral anguish to the perfection of a science. Kinsman of the prince who could punish Herlwin by ruining his poor dependents, and son of the prince who could punish Lanfranc by burning the corn of his innocent and helpless friends, William Rufus knew perfectly well what he was doing when he pressed the vice of extortion tighter down than ever on every tenement of the Canterbury property. After a day or two of breathing time, a day or two of hope, every occupant of the Canterbury domains found himself suddenly crushed under demands that he could scarcely satisfy and live—the horrors of that opening fifth year have been compared to the evisceration of a criminal who had already undergone the doom of being flayed alive—and the only answer vouchsafed by the royal myrmidons to the cries and tears and maledictions of the woe-begone victims was, that the fault was Anselm's; that the lands had been conveyed to him, that he had refused to take them up, but that if he chose to do so all would be well. And Anselm was the man who had so delicately seized the golden grain in the character of Elphege, the dread of doing harm to souls; Anselm was the man who had risked grieving his sick friend at Chester from the same dread, the dread of doing harm to souls. Whither, then, whither could he turn with all this misery set to his charge? Whither, whither could he turn, when the very monks of Christ Church, who had almost worshipped his name, made themselves the vehicle of a thousand reproaches? 'Reflect,' they wrote to him, 'reflect, dear friend. These are the murmurs launched at you:—"Is this the man we were so glad about? Is this the man all the world has been talking about? Why, he has played us false. He has destroyed our souls." And know this: there will be no end to it so long as you hold out.' 'O Omnipotent God,' they even dared to write, 'whoever it be that has set this obstacle in Anselm's way, may he be anathema among men.' Whither, then, whither could he turn? Only to Him who knows all our griefs and counts all our tears, and pray that, unless it were impossible to the Uncreated Wisdom to whom is no impossible, the thing he so much dreaded might be averted from him.

Whilst he was thus writhing from the first blow another crueller than it succeeded; a threat, and no less a threat than this, that, unless he yielded, the monks at Le Bec should learn the meaning of the phrase royal retribution. What! Were the estates in England that had kept the poor men from starvation to be escheated? And when war broke out, which would happen soon, were fire and sword and engine of destruction to turn Le Bec into a voiceless wild? Yes, that was the meaning.

This broke him. After miracles of prudence and fortitude prolonged through four months of struggle against hopeless odds, there was nothing for it but surrender, and he despatched Dom Baldwin to Le Bec with a letter, part of which needed the bearer's *vivâ voce* exposition to elucidate what lay between the lines, for such embassies were beset with danger; whilst part was intelligible enough without interpreter. It contained the following passages:—

'As to their election of me, or, in plain words, their forcible seizure of my person, I have thus far resisted as best I could; but now, willing or not, I am forced to own that day by day the judgments of God hedge me in closer and closer, thwarting all my efforts; and I am at last convinced that there is no conceivable and no possible way of escape, and that neither I nor anyone else can any longer oppose the royal resolution without doing a grievous general harm both to the bodies and the souls of others, and without provoking the wrath of God. The truth is that I am vanquished by the strong arm not of man, but of God, against whom there is neither prudence nor fortitude; and am satisfied that all that remains for me to do, now that I have prayed as best I might, and striven as best I could, that, if it were possible, this cup might pass away from me undrained, and I have seen my prayer cast out and my efforts broken, is to turn at last to God and cry, "Nevertheless not as I will, but as Thou wilt." . . . Things have come to this—and I own the hand of God in all— that I must accept one of two alternatives: either to be of service and use to you and many others, or, from no lack of will, but from sheer want of power, to be of no use or service, whether to myself, to you, or to anyone.

'But if, by holding out, you make me choose the latter of them, you will by so doing cause my old age to be dragged out and worn away in a grief that nothing can medicine, so great and manifold will be the consequent evils; evils, let me add, which will seem to be attributed to you, and to me even, by those who do not at this moment apprehend them.'

The full meaning of all this will never be known.

But enough. Victory was with the King.

In reply to the letter just quoted Anselm's monks sent their heart-broken abbot a letter of release indeed, but a letter so full of emotion as to be scarcely fit for the King's perusal; and well it was for them that, whether by accident or from precaution, their courier was not intercepted upon landing in England. There were scalding words in that letter which would have ruined them had an unfriendly eye beheld it. Alas for us, though, that Anselm should have destroyed it! But he did well.

He wrote back, therefore, entreating them to send two letters, one to the King, the other to himself, and added :—

'I strongly advise you in your letter to the King to do what really is the right thing. Let him see that you are not so much thinking of your own will as submitting to the will of God; and be careful not to forfeit the royal favour by your manner of expressing yourselves. Without that favour you cannot exist, and wilfully to forego it would be worse than useless—would ruin you, and ruin you utterly. Do not do that; do not by so doing charge my heart with a fresh load, for it is already freighted beyond its strength.'

These admonitions require no comment.

As to the Duke's letter to Anselm, there would seem to have been that in it which the charity of the recipient obliged him to consign to oblivion. Robert was very sore; indeed, so sore as to allow his chivalry the dishonour of dropping bitterness into Anselm's wounds by an insinuation the cruelty of which would, he knew, give infinite pain. But if he was the Red King's brother he was the Conqueror's son, and taking shame to himself as the fit of chagrin passed off begged forgiveness of the wrong.[1]

Archbishop William's letter is extant in the 'Historia Novorum,' and Anselm's care has preserved us the final answer of his monks.[2] On receiving news of the Duke's consent and the Archbishop's, so runs the latter document, they

---

[1] 'Gratiâ Dei faciente dominus noster princeps Northmannorum misit mihi litteras plenas magnâ benignitate et excusatione sui, si quid aut credidit aut dixit de me aliter quàm decuit amore meo et dolore de amissione meâ cogente ob meam ad archiepiscopatum electionem.'—*Ep.* iii. 15.

[2] Their letter to the King must have perished like so many other documents which one would give anything to be able to recall to existence.

assembled in chapter, and there gave, each by each, and each in his turn, as the president called upon him by name to do so, their several opinions. Those opinions were as various as the terms in which they were expressed. 'One party,' it continues, 'although deeply grieved and much moved at the thought of your unparalleled and tender love and devotion to us, yet, urged by the fear of God, whose all-wise providence they believe to have brought the thing about, willingly concede what is asked, and do so for the honour and advantage of the Church of God and in accordance with your advice. The other party adhere to their own more enthusiastic judgment, and think it more trustworthy than your own; they think it a better judgment, and, urged by love of you, adhere to it so obstinately as utterly to refuse on any account to yield to the persuasions of any of their brethren whether older or younger. Which side outnumbers the other, or which outweighs the other by the collective wisdom of its constituent members, Dom Lanfranc,[1] who was present at the chapter, and saw and heard all that was done and said, will give you a very full and sufficient account. We give you this brief and succinct recital of what has taken place because the bearer presses us to do so. May Almighty God dispose your life in His good pleasure, and preserve it long to the common benefit and joy of His faithful people. Amen.'

Some three weeks after the despatch of the letters dismissory from Le Bec, and early on the morning of Monday, the fifteenth of August, the well-known and anxiously expected form of Dom Girard might have been seen riding down the silent and

[1] The author of *Neustria Pia* (p. 170) would seem to think that this was the Lanfranc who was intruded into the abbacy of St. Wandrille's in 1089. The *Chronicon Fontanellense*, on the other hand, declares that the intruder died in 1091. If the Lanfranc of this letter was really a monk of Le Bec, then he was the Archbishop's erring nephew; but we have no proof that he was, and he is rather described as a witness of the proceedings than as a participator in them. For surely it is far more likely that there should have been another Lanfranc somewhere than that the Fontenelle chronicler should have made so grievous a blunder in his dates. Can he have been a Christ Church monk?

dew-drenched valley of Le Bec. He must have ridden all night, aided through the space between twilight and twilight by a moon then at her brightest, and was charged with a burden the carriage of which had not been unattended with risk from surprises on the way. That burden was not indeed the pastoral staff of Anselm, but that without which the pastoral staff was valueless; the *ipsissimum insigne* of the abbatial office; the carved crook, that is to say, of what material formed I know not, except that it can scarcely have been of ivory, with which his staff had been surmounted.[1] It had once been Herlwin's; for nearly fifteen years it had been Anselm's; but on that sad morning, even though a grace clung to it such as once clung to the residuary mantle of the prophet, it was to Anselm's children now no more the symbol of his paternal, gentle sway, but the announcement of an irreparable loss and an inconsolable orphanage.

At the conclusion of prime all proceeded to the chapter house, and in a few minutes Dom Maurice, our old friend to whom we owe the 'Monologion,' was reading to them as best he might a letter which Dom Girard had delivered to the prior on arriving. It contained the following passages:—[2]

---

[1] Milo Crispin, writing of Anselm's successor at Le Bec, says, 'Beato abbate Anselmo in Angliam translato et abbati facto *cujus fastigium virgæ* prædictus Willelmus .... suscipere meruit.'
And the *procès-verbal* on the opening of Herlwin's coffin in 1707 describes the crosier as *n'ayant pas de bout recourbé*.
I hope I have not been presumptuous in drawing a very obvious inference.
If the Jumièges portrait may be trusted—I, for one, have no doubt that it may—the *fastigium virgæ* can scarcely have been of elaborate workmanship. It had been used by Herlwin, and may have been of bone. Bishop Sicard of Cremona gives the following description of the crosier in his *Mitrale* (cxiii. 79D):
'Hic ergo baculus ex osse et ligno conficitur, quæ crystallinâ vel auratâ sphærulâ conjunguntur. Os superius recurvatur; lignum inferius ferro acuitur, modicè tamen retunditur. Os et lignum arte rasili poliuntur.'

[2] There is another letter (*Ep.* iii. 10) on this subject, addressed to the Bishop of Evreux, which I would most earnestly commend to the careful attention of the reader. I dare not spoil it by giving extracts from it; and it is, I fear, too long for insertion *in toto*. The writer in one passage seems to allude to his director. Who that director was we have, I fear, no means of knowing.

'I hear that there are some [1]—who they are God knows—who either feign of malice, or suspect of ignorance, or are urged by an unthinking sorrow to assert, that I am not so much forced into the archiepiscopate by religious necessity as drawn to it by corrupt greed of power. I do not know how I can assure them of the secret of my own conscience in this thing, if they are not already satisfied of the truth from my past life and converse. I have worn the monk's habit for full three-and-thirty years, three of them without preferment, fifteen as prior, fifteen as abbot; and all the good men that have known me during all that period have been kind enough to think well of me from no effort on my part, but from the goodness of God; and those who have known me best and closest have been kindest of all in their good thought of me, and none of them has ever witnessed any act of mine whence he could conclude that I took pleasure in being set over other men. What am I to do, then? How shall I drive off and crush this false and hateful suspicion, lest it hurt the souls of those who erewhile loved me in the love of God, by lessening their charity; or lest it hurt the souls of those whom any advice or any example of mine, how worthless soever, might else have profited, by making them believe that I am worse than I am; or lest it hurt not only the souls of these but those of others who do not know me and may hear this report, by setting a bad example before them for imitation? O God, Thou who knowest all things, I do not justify myself by the scrutiny of Thine own strict judgment,

But, indeed, the whole group of extant letters written on this occasion should be carefully studied. They are *Epp.* iii. 1, 4, 7, and iv. 116.

[1] This refers to Duke Robert; not of necessity to any but he, for it was usual with St. Anselm to employ the plural for the singular when he did not wish to mention names. That any of Anselm's monks should have thus spoken is simply incredible. The Dean of St. Paul's says (p. 184), 'There were some (of the monks) who whispered complaints of his ambition and self-seeking.' He had neither the one nor the other; and in the whole of the correspondence there is not a syllable to be found in justification of the Dean's assertion.

because Thy great apostle, though he said "*nihil mihi conscius sum,*" yet added immediately, "*Sed non in hôc justificatus sum, qui autem judicat me Dominus est.*" And that simple and upright man who feared God and shrank from evil, to whom, by Thine own witness, there was not the like on this earth, said, "*verebar omnia opera mea.*" But as my heart reads my conscience I read it out before Thee, O my God, that all who peruse or hear this letter may know without misgiving that I am writing it in the light of Thine eye.'

The reader will forgive me for interrupting him. What follows is not so much part of the letter as a transcript upon parchment of the saint's examination of conscience in the presence of Almighty God, and thus one of the most solemn passages, if not the most solemn, in his whole correspondence.

' Thou, Lord, seest, and be Thou my witness, that I do not know, as my conscience tells me, what love of anything which Thy servant, a despiser of the world, ought to despise, it is that can be attracting me to consent to become an archbishop or binding me to such consent ; and that, could I only do it without violating that obedience and charity which I desire, since they are Thy gift, to keep for Thy sake, I would rather live a life of service and obedience as a simple monk under the rule of a prelate than be lord over others, or be set above them, whether to guide their souls or to support their bodies, or than gain any earthly dignity. Thou seest, and be Thou my witness, that, as my conscience tells me, I know not how I can without sin break myself loose from the firm resolve of those who have elected me,[1] and that fear of Thee and the charity

---

[1] These words make it clear enough, for they are written under circumstances of most deep solemnity, that Anselm had been duly elected. This, however, has been denied. The reader will find a note on the subject in the Appendix.

and obedience which I owe to Thee and Thy Church so compel and bind me that I dare not persist in opposing their pious prayers and the strong desire they have evinced. O Lord, if my conscience deceives me, show Thyself to me, and correct me; and, whether it please Thee that men's enterprise in this their election of me succeed or that it fail, lead me in Thy way, and I shall walk in Thy Truth. O Lord, Thou seest my conscience; be Thou therefore my Witness to those who think ill about me, and show it to them, lest they harm their own or another's soul in judging of it amiss.'

The writer now resumes his letters, and, addressing himself again to his children in religion, proceeds as follows:—

'So now, my dearest brethren, you have heard all that my conscience has to say about my quest, or my dread, of the archbishopric. And if I knowingly lie to God, I know not to whom I am to speak the truth. And if, notwithstanding what I have just said on this subject, calling upon God to bear me witness, anyone should, either by direct phrase or by suggestive hint, miscommend me to another, I think that God will be with me against him, and will answer to him for me; but I will comfort myself meanwhile in the testimony of God. . . . I add a few words for your comfort. My dearest brethren, I pray you not to be distressed above measure at our separation. Let not your hope be in man, but in God, because if I have been of any good to you it was not my doing, but His. Many, almost all, of you came to Le Bec on my account, but none of you took the habit at my instance, nor did you make your vows to God in the hope of any reward that I could give. From Him, then, to whom you gave all you had, expect all that you need. Cast your care on the Lord, and He will nourish you. Bend all your thought to the serving of Him, and He will

Himself take all your care upon Himself, and nourish you. . . . To our Lord Jesus Christ, and His kind mother Mary, and St. Peter to whom He committed His sheep, and to St. Benedict whose rule you profess, and to all the other saints of God do I commend you, my dearest brethren; and, by their merits and intercessions, may He who redeemed you be your Abbot and your Guide, and, when this life is done, bring you to reign with Him in His kingdom. There may it be mine to see you and rejoice with you for ever, through His mercy who is God blessed for ever. Amen.

'Many of you whom I have so dearly and affectionately loved that each was prone to think himself the best beloved are wondering why I do not write something to each of them as a souvenir of our friendship. The reason is not that I have forgotten them, but that there are too many of them. . . . All I say at present is, let them remember that my sole object in thus loving them was that they might love God and their own souls. They know it well; and what I desire of one and all of you, and beg, and admonish, and counsel one and all of you, is, do so still; do so, and my love of you can never be impaired. Choose yourselves a new abbot without delay. . . .'

Let us pause here. The story of Anselm's abbacy is ended.

Book IV.

ST. ANSELM ARCHBISHOP ELECT OF CANTERBURY.

CHAPTER I.

PRELIMINARY CONSIDERATIONS: ST. ANSELM'S ACCEPTANCE OF THE PRIMACY.

POPE GREGORY VII. died on the twenty-fifth of May, 1085; Archbishop Lanfranc died on the twenty-eighth of May, 1089. During the interval two Pontiffs, Victor III. and Urban II., mounted the Apostolic throne; but neither of them was ever recognised, officially at least, in England. How was this?

Shortly before his death, St. Gregory VII., when asked by the bishops and cardinals who stood about him to direct them in their choice of a successor, advised them to choose Desiderius, Abbot of Monte Cassino, a monk in whom the qualities of prudence and zeal were very happily blended, and who, besides holding the first rank among the cardinal priests of the Roman Church, was fortunate enough to enjoy the friendship and confidence of the princes of central and southern Italy. But, in default of Desiderius, they were without delay to select the first that could be had of three prelates whom the dying Pontiff now proceeded to name—the Archbishop of Lyons, the Bishop of Ostia, and the Bishop of Lucca.

Some weeks after Gregory's death the Pontificate was offered to Desiderius; but he refused the honour with so successful an obstinacy that no efficient efforts were made for his appointment before the following Lent. But, even so, and even then, fresh delays were interposed, and it was only on the Whit Sunday of 1086 that the clergy and people of

Rome, disregarding the Abbot's remonstrances, took him by force, and, with the cardinals at their head, carried him into the Church of Santa Lucia, at the foot of the Palatine, where they elected him Pope and gave him the name of Victor III. But he was not yet subdued; for, although he consented to wear the blood-red robe such as now distinguishes the members of the Sacred College, he would not allow himself to be decked in the auguster garment of white which constituted the distinctive dress of the successors of the Apostle; and, daring in the course of a few days to retract his concession, forbade the Papal cross to be carried before him, and announced his resolution of courting once more the seclusion of Monte Cassino.

An effort to carry him thence to Rome for coronation having been thwarted, in part by his own entreaties, in part by the approaching heat of summer, he had his own way for the remainder of the year and until the middle of the following Lent—the Lent of 1087—when on Sunday, the twenty-first of March, he so far yielded to the instances and prayers of Cenci, the Roman prefect, of the Roman nobles, and of most if not all of the princes and bishops of central and southern Italy, as to resume the discarded cross and purple. But, even so, he returned without delay to his monastery; and it was only on the ninth of May, and within a week or two of the second anniversary of the late Pope's death, that he at last received episcopal consecration.

He spent a week in Rome and then returned to Monte Cassino.

He came back to the Eternal City, it is true, in the following month, but only to find it in the hands of the Imperial faction, and the Feast of the Apostles was no sooner over than he sought the safety he needed and the solitude he loved in the territory of a friendly prince and in his own cloister.

In the month of August he opened a synod at Benevento, but before its work was done he was struck down by a malady which had for some time troubled him, and was carried at once to Monte Cassino, where, on the sixteenth of September, and after a pontificate of four months from his consecration, he expired.

Meanwhile a very strange account of the election of the Abbot of Monte Cassino to the Papacy had been spread abroad by no less a personage than the Archbishop of Lyons, who had for many years, and until the death of St. Gregory, sustained the supplementary dignity of Papal Legate for all Gaul. The Archbishop [1] declared that, arriving in Rome too late to witness the first election of Desiderius in the summer of 1086, he had followed him to his monastery, and there from his own mouth heard things which on no other authority would he have believed, besides a variety of scandalous stories about him communicated by trustworthy witnesses; that in the Lent of 1087 he had been requested by competent authority to join in choosing some suitable person as Pope, and had partially succeeded in thwarting the arts of the Abbot to ensure re-election, when the Abbot, who had meanwhile composed the reluctance of the official consecrator, procured consecration and slipped himself into the Papal chair. The Archbishop's story ends thus:—'After his consecration by the Bishop of Ostia he attempted to say mass at St. Peter's, but was struck by the hand of God *infra actionem*. Whereupon, acknowledging too late his sin, he abdicated the Papacy, and, summoning such of his monks as were about him, desired them to carry him to Monte Cassino, and bury him there in the chapter house with the obsequies proper to an abbot, not those proper to a Pope.'

Such was the story sent by the Archbishop of Lyons in or about the July of 1087 to the Marchioness Matilda of Tuscany. The truth or falsehood of its earlier portion is not of present importance; but that which it just now concerns us to notice, and to notice very carefully, is that, although

[1] Hugh of Flavigny in his *Chronicon* gives the same account.

Archbishop Hugh, writing in the summer of 1087, does not categorically announce Victor's death, he yet distinctly states that, being seized with a mortal illness within a few days of his consecration, Victor had immediately resigned the Papacy.

What rumours may meanwhile have reached England we have no means of ascertaining; but, unless Orderic [1] was in this instance exceptionally careless, that diligent historian cannot have been much more fortunate than the Archbishop of Lyons, for long after the event he declared that Victor was seized with diarrhœa on the sixteenth of May, seven days after his consecration, and that he died in the following August.

On the whole, then, we may fairly assume that within a week or ten days after Lanfranc heard of Victor's consecration a report reached him, certainly of Victor's serious illness, possibly of his death; in which case, apart from the obvious considerations that he was in England whilst the Conqueror was in Normandy, that he could not with decency discredit an account accepted by the Legate of that vast territory through which ran the highway from Rome to Canterbury, and that the Conqueror was even now languishing under a dangerous malady or dying of a fatal wound, and not in a condition to be troubled with conflicting or useless rumours, his only reasonable course was to await trustworthy information on the state of affairs in Rome.

And if the report of Victor's abdication in the middle of May, which, false as it was, reached Lanfranc by the end of July, was followed at the end of October by the report, false as it was, of Victor's death in August, there was nothing for him to do but to await the announcement of a successor to the vacant Pontificate. And even if on the receipt of the first false news he had sent immediately to Italy to test its truth, even so, his messenger could scarcely have reached Monte Cassino before the very day of the real death of Victor.

[1] *O. V.* iii. 306.

Let us now turn our attention more particularly to England.

There is good reason to believe that during the first six or seven months of the Red King's reign—he ascended the throne at the Michaelmas of 1087, at a moment when nobody could say whether or not there was a Pope for him either to acknowledge or to disown—his relations with Archbishop Lanfranc were on the whole pacific. He sought and acquiesced in the Primate's counsels on the outbreak and on the suppression of Bishop Odo's conspiracy; and, if a hint given by William of Malmesbury may be taken as guide, it was not until after the reconciliation at Whitsuntide that he betrayed any resentment against the Churchman, when, as is not improbable, it occurred to him, and occurred too late, that he would have done well to inflict a fine on his rebellious barons before receiving them back to favour; in other words, that he had erred, and erred to his own pecuniary damage, in listening to the Primate's counsels of mercy.

But what was the occasion, and what the date, of the first rupture between William Rufus and Archbishop Lanfranc? As to these, since, in the absence of certain information, we must be satisfied to make the most probable guess we can, we may, I think, assume it as likely that the occasion was the first of any gravity that next presented itself; for it is notorious that the wrath of the Red Prince was ever ready and ever swift; and further, that the occasion was the first of any gravity that next presented itself upon which the Primate would deem it his duty to remind the prince of the oaths he had taken; the first occasion, that is to say, upon which a difference would be likely to arise between them, not upon William's conduct as a man, but upon his conduct as King. For it was then that the memorable speech was made, 'Who can keep all his promises?'

William the Conqueror had imposed upon this country four pretensions inherited by him, whether in germ or in their fulness, from his forefathers, the Dukes of Normandy. One was that no one in the whole of his dominion should acknowledge a duly appointed Bishop of Rome as Pope except at his bidding ; another, that no one should receive a letter from the Roman Pontiff unless it had first been shown to him ; a third was that the Primate, when holding a general council of the bishops, should bid and should forbid nothing but in pursuance of the royal initiation ; the last was that no bishop might prosecute a tenant-in-chief, or a servant of the Crown, for incest, adultery, or other *capitale crimen*, or excommunicate or otherwise punish him for the same, without authorisation from the sovereign. These claims are distinctly set forth by Eadmer, and should be carefully borne in mind as we follow him page after page through the 'Historia Novorum.' Now, such was the state of England at the moment with which we are concerned, the Whitsuntide of 1088, that William Rufus and Lanfranc can scarcely have come into collision upon the third or fourth of these claims. The country was too distracted, and the King too uneasy, for Lanfranc to think of summoning a national council; nor was the Churchman likely to unsheath the sharp edge of justice when he had so recently quelled an insurrection by the blunter sword of mercy. Besides, news of the highest importance had just come from Rome—news of the election of a new Pope, Urban II.—and prudence informed him that, inasmuch as it is wise to confront grave difficulties one at a time, he must not anticipate and enhance an apparently inevitable trouble by provoking others which might well be left to slumber. Rumours of the election of Urban must have reached England early in May ;[1] and the Whitsuntide Court

---

[1] Urban was elected on the twelfth of March, 1088. He wrote to Lanfranc announcing his election on the tenth of April, twenty-nine days later. Allowing nine weeks for the journey from Terracina to Westminster, we may conclude that the letter was delivered about the twelfth of June.
A practised courier would perform the journey by land from Rome to Wissant in six weeks ; but the messenger sent on this occasion would probably require a

must have been in full session at the very moment when a letter from the new Pope, written at Terracina on the tenth of April, and forwarded in all haste from Canterbury, was delivered to the Primate. That letter was, I suspect, all that was needed to set the combustible temper of the King in a blaze. If Lanfranc read it without first showing it to the King, a royal *consuetudo* was violated ; if he showed it to the King before reading it, the King had something of some moment to say about the writer. Who was this Otto of Ostia that he should call himself *servus servorum Dei* when Guibert, Archbishop of Ravenna, had long ago been made Pope by the Emperor ? And even if one was as much Pope as the other, or if Otto were Pope and not Guibert, or Guibert Pope and not Otto, who and what was an Archbishop of Canterbury that he should dare to speak on the subject when, for England at least, the decision on such a matter was the personal prerogative of the King of the English, and of no other man ? It was thus that William Rufus spoke to Lanfranc's successor in the January of 1094. Can there be a doubt that he spoke thus to Lanfranc in the June of 1088 ?

On the whole, then, I suspect that this letter from Urban II. was the occasion of the rupture between William Rufus and Lanfranc, who, forecasting in an instant all the miseries that must ensue to England from the unopposed assertion of this new and monstrous claim, reminded the prince of the engagement in virtue of which he had received the crown. The prince's reply is too well known to be repeated.

few days more, and we may fairly allow seven weeks for the journey by land from Terracina to the shores of Picardy. Such, however, were the dangers which beset the road through Lombardy that the sub-deacon Roger would be likely to avoid the ordinary route, and make his way into Gaul by crossing the Mediterranean ; in which case we must add a few days to our seven weeks. And when he reached Wissant he was, not improbably, detained there by the very wind which carried Bishop Odo and his party back from England. I conclude, then, that the sub-deacon Roger can scarcely, even under favourable circumstances, have reached Dover before Whitsunday, and that in all probability he only landed in time to reach Westminster on the octave of the festival.

Lanfranc was checkmated, and it is hard to see what course of energetic action was now open to him.[1] Bowed down with length of days—for he had exceeded by more than a decade the longer span of life allowed to us by the Psalmist—the ancient prelate prayed as he had prayed sixteen years before, when things, dark as they might be, were brightness itself to the storm which he now saw gathering, and awaited his end. What sort of storm it was to be we shall see in the following pages; what sort of storm it was to be he divined, if any could divine. The only lever by which he could have checked the omnipotence of the tyrant's capacity for mischief had snapped in his hand, and there was no mending it. The King had now categorically declared that kings of England were not to be outdone by kings of Germany, and that no archbishop of his should obey the Pope save at his behest. What, then, could the old man do against the petulant youth? The lever had broken in his hand, and there was no replacing it by another. So he prayed as he had prayed sixteen years ago, 'that God would deliver his soul from her fleshly prison.'[2] He prayed as he had prayed, and by the next Whitsuntide the throne over which he had shed a new lustre stood vacant in Canterbury Cathedral.

We can scarcely, I repeat, be mistaken in assuming that

---

[1] There is a curious passage in Anselm's correspondence (*Ep.* ii. 44) which shows that between his departure from England after the Whitsuntide Court of 1088 and his arrival at Le Bec about the eleventh of July he had been into France—the kingdom of France, which lay south of Normandy. Such a *détour* on his way home can scarcely have been contemplated when he left Le Bec in the spring; and his way of alluding to it shows that there is something to be read between the lines. What, then, can have taken him into France? What can have happened in England to take him into France? What can have happened in England to hurry him away to France, where he seems to have spent the last week of June? I think I can guess. I suspect that Lanfranc, forbidden by the King to write to the Pope, sent Anselm in all haste out of the country charged with a letter or a message to some prelate in France, the contents of which letter, or the purport of which message, were by that prelate to be transmitted to the Pontiff. This is no fanciful guess. Anselm himself did the very same sort of thing some six years later when himself set in that very predicament.

[2] Lanfranc, Ep. 43.

the letter announcing Urban's accession reached England by the middle of June ; and were we only certain that the Firebrand had by that time been taken into William's closer confidence, and, further, that Lanfranc fell ill in the latter part of June, we might then, I think, accept the account which I have hazarded of the rupture between King and Primate as possessing the highest degree of moral certainty that can reasonably be desired for it ;[1] for it is scarcely conceivable that when once the Red King had resolved upon asserting the quasi-imperial pretensions[2] which were to give a distinctive character to his reign he should neglect his first opportunity of doing so.

To assert those pretensions and thus germanise England he had a most inviting instrument ready to hand in the first of the four *consuetudines* which Eadmer has described to us ; the *consuetudo* in virtue of which his ducal forefathers had claimed the right of taking the initiative in the recognition of a duly appointed Pope, pretending, as it would seem, that the disciplinary authority of the Holy See was meanwhile in their dominions void. Or rather, availing himself of this *consuetudo*, he converted it into something which was worse in degree and worse in kind as well, and, not satisfied with making England wait till he should recognise a new Pope, propounded it to be his right to impose upon his subjects as Pope for them whom he would.

But I am anticipating, and at present it is enough to

---

[1] Anselm's letter (ii. 53) in which he condoles with him on his illness must have been written soon after receipt of the news, but was not written (see *Ep.* ii. 44) until after the eleventh of July. The news, however, of Lanfranc's illness was accompanied, it would appear, by a request from him *de conducta Langobardorum* ; and if, as is probable, Lombards were wanted for the building of Rochester Castle (see the whole story in *Anglia Sacra*, ii. 329), we may assume that it left England within a few weeks after Whitsuntide. All tends to prove that Lanfranc fell ill soon after the receipt of the Pope's letter.

[2] 'Dicebat imperator sui officii esse quem vellet papam eligere nec erat alterius apostolicum etiam nominare. Rex Willelmus allegavit eandem rationem quod nullus archiepiscopus vel episcopus regni sui curiæ Romanæ vel Papæ subesset.' —Matthew's *Paris*, Hist. Major.

know that whatever doubt he may have affected to entertain as to the validity of Pope Urban's election was a flimsy pretence; for had he had a real doubt—a real and honest doubt—he would scarcely have allowed—as we shall soon see that he did—six years and a half to pass away before making a first effort to solve it.

On reviewing, then, the King's conduct during the interval between the first recorded breach of his oath in 1088 and Anselm's acceptance of the primacy in 1093, we see that the chief grounds of apprehension for the future are referable to three lines of conduct: first, the royal confiscation of the Canterbury revenues; secondly, the royal intolerance of the constitutional tradition which had made the Primate of Britain official guardian of the King's conscience; and thirdly, the royal purpose of weakening the relations with the successor of Peter, which had made the kingdom of England from its earliest days an integral portion of Catholic Christendom. In these three designs the Red King was abetted by as many privy counsellors—Renouf the Firebrand; Robert, Count of Meulan; and William of Saint-Calais, Bishop of Durham. These three men were the respective agents of his designs on the proprietary rights of the holder of the Archbishopric of Canterbury, on the constitution of the realm, and on the religion of the people of England.

Let us now resume the history of the Archbishop elect.

It was in the summer of 1093, and about the middle of July, that, bent into resignation to the will of Heaven, Anselm breathed forth his *fiat voluntas tua*; and it was during the first ten days of August that he despatched Dom Girard to Le Bec with the valedictory letter quoted in the last chapter. Between the two events, however, and about the end of July, he had an interview of some importance with the sovereign. But, strange to say, on the last night of the month a flaming meteor swept the firmament; and as it glid along the amazed beholders saw, or thought they saw, that it bore the form of a pastoral staff. What might that fiery crosier mean?

The interview took place at Rochester. The King had gone there, I imagine, to inspect the castle which Gundulf had undertaken to build for him five years ago, and was on his way home from Dover, where he had just held an interview with the Count of Flanders. And assuredly, if he had with him the text of some such treaty as was concluded with the Fleming a few years later, he must have been in high spirits, for, in that case, he had bought the Fleming's neutrality, or, should need be, the Fleming's active co-operation upon his next invasion of Normandy; and the Fleming was now his vassal, that vassal's *feudum*, fief, or fee being not land, but money, money drained from the broad lands of Canterbury. And Robert of Meulan—for the King was accompanied by that cunning statesman—must also have been in high spirits; inasmuch as he was by this time aware that the poor monks who once insulted and outwitted him, and the Duke who once swore so many oaths at him, had at last been forced to sign away their interest in their much-prized abbot.

No doubt it was into the room of state in Gundulf's great square tower that the Archbishop elect was ushered. How worthy of a king was that vast hall! What a height from floor to roof; how stately those columns; how cunning, how adroit, how bold the ornament of each sculptured arch; how cool the air; how luxuriously soft the light! Gundulf had so far allowed his genius to revel in its construction as to exceed the first estimate, to his own loss, by an added fifty shillings on every hundred; and quick brains and cunning hands from Lombardy had been engaged to realise his every inspiration. It was Anselm himself who had contracted with the Italians and sent them over to England. And here now stood Anselm. Here too stood the King.

Drawing the prince aside, so as not to be overheard, the monk addressed him as follows:—

'Sire, I am still of two minds whether or not to accept the primacy. Still, if I should see my way in reason towards doing so, there are one or two things I should wish you to do. Let me briefly state them to you.

'I desire that you restore free of suit or controversy all the lands which the Church of Canterbury, to the rule of which I have been elected, held in the time of Archbishop Lanfranc of blessed memory, and that you promise me right and judgment anent the other lands which that Church held before Lanfranc's primacy, but which, subsequently lost to her, are not yet recovered.

'Further, I desire that in things which appertain to God and our holy religion you trust yourself first and chiefly to my advice; and that, as I wish to have you for my earthly lord and defender, so you take me for your father in spiritual things and your soul's guide.

'Then as to Urban, the Roman Pontiff, whom you have not as yet acknowledged as Pope, whereas I both have acknowledged and do acknowledge him, and intend to show him all due obedience and subjection, I give you this hint in order to prevent scandal in the future. I beg you frankly to tell me your own mind on these subjects, that knowing it I may be the better able to shape my course.'

Whereupon the King called for the Bishop of Durham and the Count of Meulan, and requested Anselm to repeat in their hearing what he had just said. He did so, and received through them the following reply: 'I will restore you all the lands of which the Church of Canterbury was seised in Lanfranc's time precisely as they were then, but as to the rest I make no agreement just at present. However, in these and other things, I shall obey the dictates of duty, and confide in you accordingly.'

With these words the interview ended.

The King left Rochester and resumed his journey. On reaching Westminster he found that the long-desired letters from the Duke of Normandy, the Archbishop of Rouen, and the monks of Le Bec had arrived, and was soon on horseback again riding to Windsor.

The Bishop of Durham, meanwhile, was on another highroad, travelling in all haste to his palatine see, where he and the King of Scotland were to place the first stones of an architectural pile of unique and imperishable splendour. Alas that to so magnificent a creation should be associated so unworthy a name! A monk, in the first instance, at Saint-Calais, and subsequently Abbot of St. Vincent's at Le Mans, he was appointed to the see and palatinate of Durham in the year 1080; but, having joined the standard of the Bishop of Bayeux in 1088, followed that prelate into Normandy after the capitulation at Rochester, and was not restored to his honours until the September of 1091. Note him as he rides along; mark how he mutters to himself, and divine the scarce whispered scheme that he is weaving in a dark and sullen heart. Should he try to give it vocal form the right words would fail him, for not yet has he had time to think out his thought. Let him ride on, then; but mark him well.

I suspect that the King, upon reaching Windsor, found Renouf waiting to hear the news, and somewhat disconcerted that unjust justicer by his account of the Rochester interview. It certainly is worthy of remark that the only one of the three questions to which he had given an undiplomatic reply on that occasion was, notwithstanding his rapacity, the very question upon which the Firebrand was not at hand to advise him; as though there were something in Anselm's presence, something in Anselm's manner, that he could not rebel against or bear up against when left to himself.

But the imprudence must be rectified. Sending, therefore, to inform his illustrious victim that the necessary documents had come from Normandy, he implored him no longer to slight the unanimous wish of the kingdom evinced in his election to the primacy, and at the same time begged that he would be so good—he asked it simply as a favour and a token of friendship—as to excuse him from giving up some Church lands which after Lanfranc's death he had granted to vassals of his own, to be held by them as hereditary tenures. The two portions of the message were very prettily juxtaposed, with the coy hint peeping daintily out between. That hint was not to be mistaken. Bribes, plain vulgar bribes, were the order of the day; everything for the last four years had been subject of traffic, and what the King now wanted was something to compensate the loss incurred by his gratuitous disposal of the primacy on that awful day at Gloucester. He had done his utmost to force the archbishopric on Anselm; but now that Anselm had accepted or shown signs of accepting it, Anselm's opportunity had come for offering a kind of recognition which was by this time customary; and surely Anselm, who was both scrupulous and penniless, must appreciate the delicacy of a suggestion, compliance with which could not cause him inconvenience and need not give him scandal. But the simple Benedictine took a different view of the matter; he had no mind to rob his successors in the see of Canterbury, and, in reply, begged to be excused.

Now, then, he breathed again; now, then, he was at liberty; now, then, after five months of anguish, he had in quite an unexpected way escaped the terrible preferment, and the primacy of Britain would be sold to some one that could be found to pay for it; now, then—for he had by this time sent his crosier back to Le Bec—he could slip away unseen to some tranquil retreat, and pass the residue of his days in the estate of a mere monk; not ministered to, but ministering. So he dreamed.

Alas, poor dreamer!

The King, much nettled by the refusal of the Archbishop elect to surrender the coveted estates, entrusted the execution of his orders to the zeal and fidelity of the Firebrand, and moved his court to Gloucester, whither on the 24th of the month the King of Scotland, in accordance with an agreement made to that effect, came to take his share in a treaty of peace and alliance between the two realms. But the disdainful monarch refused to speak with him, refused to see his face, sent messages requiring that of him which could never in honour have been conceded, and then bade him begone. The Scot retraced his ineffectual steps, and, browbeaten and befooled, made for his native land.

Anselm, not informed of the King's humour, was still dreaming the fair dream so congenial to his temperament, when news came of the real state of things. He was not to escape so easily. Renouf was at work again; and when that is said the reader knows all. Already on some of the Canterbury estates rents had been racked from five to forty shillings, and they would soon be up to fifty. The King must have Anselm for archbishop, but the King must also have money for the archbishopric, and this was the King's way of getting it.

What, then, was Anselm to do? See all the old miseries afresh enacted and prolonged till Kent was a wilderness, or curtail a property that was not yet his own to the perpetual detriment of his successors?

In this emergency it was that the barons of England for the first time interposed—for the first time, not the last.

It may be that they were alarmed for the integrity of their own estates in no distant future; unquestionably they were stung to indignation by conduct which there was no word in their vocabulary to describe. Nor they alone; the whole nation was exasperated. And so the King, not yet given up to a judicial blindness, yielded, or affected to yield, to the general clamour.

By this time he was at Winchester. To Winchester, therefore, was Anselm summoned. Unfortunately for posterity, Eadmer was not there to record what was said by princes by prelate or by baron, or by the careworn and emaciated monk that stood there among them. Let it, then, suffice us to know that the King of the English in the presence of his peers not only relinquished, or pretended to relinquish, his claim to the recently disputed estates, but made such protestations of the good things he was going to do for the Church as at length elicited the final consent of a man who, whatever might be his own preferences, his own love for seclusion, or his own dread of publicity, of pomp, and of honour, had that in him which gave him courage, when once he clearly saw the Finger of God pointing the way, to go where that Finger pointed, even though in going he should have to walk through furnaces of fire.

Following, therefore, the precedent established by Lanfranc, a precedent doubtless approved by the legates who, being in England on the occasion, must have been cognisant of Lanfranc's act, he became the *homo* of the King; not indeed for the archiepiscopal dignity, as though it were derived from the Crown; nor for the archiepiscopal estates, as though they were resumable by the Crown; but for the enjoyment of those estates, inasmuch as the King, although not their *dominus*, was charged with their *advocatio*. 'More et exemplo prædecessoris sui pro usu terræ homo regis factus est.'

CHAPTER II.

FEALTY AND HOMAGE: ENTHRONEMENT OF THE ARCHBISHOP ELECT.

As performed between subject and subject, the homager being a layman, in our own country and in the fifteenth century, the ceremony of homage is thus described by Littleton:—' When the tenant shall make homage to his lord he shall be ungirt, and his head uncovered, and his lord shall sit, and the tenant shall kneel before him on both his knees, and hold his hands jointly together between the hands of his lord, and shall say thus: "I become your man (*je deveigne vostre home*) from this day forward, and unto you shall be true and faithful, and bear to you faith for the tenements that I claim to hold of you, saving the faith that I owe unto our sovereign lord the King, and shall lawfully do to you the customs and services which I ought to do at the terms assigned. So help me God." And he shall kiss the book.'

If, however, the oath of fealty was taken, but no homage made, the vassal stood before his lord, and holding his hand upon the book said, ' Know ye this, my lord, that I shall be faithful and true to you, and faith to you shall bear for the lands which I claim to hold of you, and that I shall lawfully do to you the customs and services which I ought to do at the terms assigned. So help me God.'

If the contracting parties were the sovereign and a subject the words 'of life and limb and of earthly worship' were inserted immediately after 'from this day forward,' and the saving clause after the words 'hold of you' omitted.

Keeping still to Littleton, I have to add two remarks.

The first is that when a woman did homage she did not say, 'I become your woman,' for 'it is not fitting that a woman should say that she will become a woman to any man but to her husband, when she is married. But she shall say, "I do to you homage, and to you shall be faithful and true, and faith to you shall bear for the tenements I hold of you, saving the faith I owe to our sovereign lord the King."

The second is, that when a man of religion did homage to his lord he did not say, 'I become your man,' &c., 'for that' —again I quote Littleton—'he hath professed himself to be only the man of God. But he shall say thus: "I do homage unto you, and to you shall be true and faithful, and faith to you bear for the tenements which I hold of you, saving the faith which I do owe to our lord the King."' Commenting on which passage, Coke observes, 'In the old books and records the homage which a bishop, abbot, or other man of religion doth is called fealty, for that it wanteth these words: "I become your man." But yet in judgment of law it is homage, because he saith, "I do to you homage,"' &c.

This distinction between laymen who became the King's men and clergymen who did homage seems to have subsisted early in the reign of Henry I.; for that sovereign, desiring to secure the succession of his son, convened the bishops, abbots, and *principes* of the kingdom for that purpose on the sixteenth of March, 1116, when, whilst the *principes* became the men of the young prince—*facti sunt homines ipsius Wilhelmi*—the Archbishop of Canterbury, the rest of the bishops, and the abbots promised that, should they survive the King, they would transfer the crown to his son, and not become his men, but do him their homages—*eique hominia facturos*. But more of this in another place. All that I here wish to indicate is that as far back as the year 1116 it seems to have been the usage that Churchmen should not make themselves the men, still less the liegemen, of the King.

There is no need to inform the reader that homage was of two kinds, simple and liege; but it may be well to remark that the character of the homage paid in any case does not seem to have been determined by the formula employed in making it. For (1) when in 1403 the Duke of Brittany made his homage to the King of France, the chancellor of that kingdom spake as follows: 'And now, my lord Duke of Brittany, as to the homage which you have done to our lord the King here present, he understands that the said homage is liege, because all the homages which his vassals make and give him, and especially the peers of France, one of whom you are, are liege homages;' and (2) Ducange quotes from the 'Registrum Feudorum Campaniæ' the case of a vassal who did not know whether the homage he had paid were simple homage or liege.

The scope and stringency, however, of liege, as distinguished from simple, homage, as far back as the beginning of the thirteenth century, may be gathered from the following declaration made in the year 1211 by Fernand, Count of Flanders, at the instance of his liege lord the King of France:—

'I Fernand, Count of Flanders and Hainault, notify to all that I am the liegeman of my illustrious lord Philip, King of France, against all mortal men and women ('contra omnes homines et fœminas qui possunt vivere et mori'), and that I have sworn to him that I will do him good service and faithful; neither will I fail him so long as he will do me right of his court. But should I fail of good and faithful service to him, I give leave to all my vassals, be they barons or be they knights, and to all communes, townships, and boroughs of my land, to be against me, and that to the utmost of their power they be for a help to the said my lord the King and for an injury to me. And I will and require that all the aforesaid, as well barons as knights, and the rest, swear and give this security to my lord the King. But should anyone refuse thus to swear, I would do him all the harm in my power; neither would I make peace or truce with him, save by the will and good pleasure of my lord the King, &c. . . . Done at Paris in the year of our Lord m.cc.xi., in the month of January, and on St. Vincent's Day.'

This document shows that the Count, whatever the formula employed, had done two distinct things—made himself the King's liegeman and taken an oath of fealty to him; and it shows that lord and vassal had each of them his duties. But it also shows into what a frightful engine liege service might be converted; for the judgment whether the vassal had kept or broken his engagement, was left, not to a just God who judges justly, but to a prince who might at any moment put almost any meaning he chose upon the words 'good and faithful service.'

I said just now that the Count of Flanders had done two distinct things—become the King's liegeman and taken an oath of fealty. But it would be more correct to say that on occasion of taking the oath of fealty he had become the King's liegeman. This is an important distinction, for it recognises the fact that the relation established by fealty is older than that established by homage. But more of this presently.

Turning, however, to our own country, not indeed as it was in the fifteenth century, but as it was from the end of the reign of Edward IV. back to, at any rate, the beginning of that of Edward I., we find that during that period, if not from a still earlier age, the writs of summons to Parliament exhibited a noteworthy distinction between the *magnates* and the *prælati* of the realm; for, whereas temporal lords were required to appear *in fide et ligeantiâ*, the bishops were called *in fide et dilectione*. The former class, that is to say, were *trusty and liege*, the latter *trusty and well beloved*; the former were *fideles et ligii*, the latter *fideles et dilectores*.

I am not aware that any attempt has been made to ascertain when it was that this usage was established of styling a clergyman the king's *fidelis et dilector* in contradistinction to the layman, who was his *fidelis et ligius*. Neither do I believe that any attempt has been made to ascertain when it was that he was said to make homage to the king (*hominium regi fecit*) in contradistinction to the layman who became the king's man (*homo regis factus est*). But whatever I may have to say on these two very interesting subjects must be deferred to a later page, for our present concern is with homage as distinguished from fealty.

Time was when the vassal or tenant was called the king's *fidelis*, the term *homo* being not as yet in use; as at a later period, the term *homo ligius* not being as yet in use, the vassal or tenant of the king was simply called his *homo*.

Now it is the legal relation of a vassal or *fidelis* to his lord which is set forth by the word *fidelitas, féaute, fealty*—his legal relation, I say, not his moral duty. And upon becoming the lord's *fidelis* he made, in virtue of that relation, a promise corresponding to it; the which promise, although it acknowledged and enunciated the duty of faith, or *fides*, received its name and description, not from that duty, but from the relation which had occasioned it; and was called, not a promise of faith or *fides*, but a promise appertaining to fealty or *fidelitas*. And when the promise was made under oath the formula employed was called not *sacramentum fidei*, or oath to bear faith, but *sacramentum fidelitatis*, that is to say, the oath taken by a man on becoming his lord's *fidelis*, or the oath proper to the vassal's relation of fealty to his lord.

But whereas the legal relation of *fidelis* to *dominus* was established by the promise—or the promise under oath—of fealty, that of *homo* to *dominus* was established not by a verbal promise, but by a symbolical act. To make himself the king's *homo*, the tenant or vassal—I am speaking of laymen—placed his hands within the king's hands. In Littleton's day he knelt, but it does not therefore follow that he had always knelt, or that, if he had always knelt, the kneeling was essential to the homage. In Littleton's days he said, 'I become your man;' but it does not therefore follow that he had always employed that or any other verbal formula; and I think that we shall be safe in assuming that when homages were first made they were made by the one and only ceremony of joining of hands. They may have been made kneeling, but, if so, the kneeling was a congruous accident, nothing more. They may have been accompanied with a form of words, but, if so, that form was a congruous adjunct, nothing more. This, I say, would seem to be the most probable account.

In other words, when a man became the *fidelis* of a king he established himself in that relation by pronouncing a form of words, whether with or without oath, which bound him to discharge the duties appertaining to it. But if the king, for whatever reason, desired to draw close and tighten that relation, the *fidelis* would, whilst he spoke the words, hold his hands within the king's, and the closeness and stringency of relation thus established was denoted by the phrase *homo*. He was the king's *fidelis*, it is true; but he was more than that, he was the king's *homo*.

Thus I am the king's *fidelis*, as I have been for many years, but when I this morning repeated my oath of fealty to him I held my hands within his, and by so doing became one of his *homines*. Yesterday I was his *fidelis*, but to-day I am more; I am his *homo*.

And now it is time to enquire in what the ceremony consisted by which Anselm, Archbishop elect of Canterbury, notified that his fealty to the King of the English was that not of a mere *fidelis*, but of a *homo*. That he knelt to show himself the King's man is inconceivable. For (1) the age would not have tolerated such an impropriety; (2) even seventy years later, when Adrian IV. wrote a letter of reprimand to Frederick Barbarossa, he accused him of no such indecency as that of making bishops go down upon their knees before him; and (3) neither in the Council of Clermont, held soon after the date of Anselm's homage, nor in that of the Vatican, at which Anselm was present to say all that he knew on the subject, was any other usage censured than that of making bishops and priests place their hands within those of laymen.

Standing, then, before the King, the Archbishop elect placed his hands between the King's hands, and made declaration of fealty; and that such *intromissio manuum*, without an accompanying form of words proper to it, was all that was needed for the doing of homage may be inferred from two passages in the letters of Bishop Yves of Chartres, himself a distinguished lawyer, in one of which he speaks of persons who had become his vassals *per manum et sacramentum*, i.e. by act of homage and profession of fealty, and in the other of archbishops who had done fealty *et per manum et per sacramentum*; whilst a diploma of Louis le Gros speaks of the obligation contracted by homage as one contracted *per manum*, and says nothing of a corresponding declaration.

To hold his hands, then, within the King's hands whilst pronouncing the formula of fealty was sufficient to make Anselm the *homo* of the King.

We must now enquire what, precisely, that formula may have been.

There are two letters extant from Archbishop Lanfranc to the Conqueror. One of them begins thus: 'Domino suo Anglorum regi Willelmo fidelis suus Lanfrancus, fidele servitium et fideles orationes.'

The other: 'Gloriosissimo domino suo Anglorum regi Willelmo fidelis suus Lanfrancus, fidele servitium cum orationibus.'

There is a formality in these addresses to the *dominus* from his *fidelis* which lends importance and interest to the words *fidele servitium* and *orationes*, for a presumption is raised by them that when Lanfranc 'made his fealty' to the

King he bound himself to (1) faithful service to him and to (2) prayers for him.

And if we examine Anselm's letters we find the presumption justified. Of fifteen letters sent by him to King Henry I. there is absolutely not one the superscription of which does not contain 'fidele servitium,' and either 'orationes' or 'fideles orationes,' and in a message of his to the King sent through Bishop Gundulf,[1] he commends himself to him with his 'fidele servitium'; 'fidele servitium domino et regi.' Nor is this all; in the body of his letters to the King he never fails to style himself the King's *fidelis*.

We may then, I think, conclude that Lanfranc and Anselm, on becoming, each in his turn, the *homo* of the reigning prince, engaged, each in his turn, to give the King *fidele servitium et orationes*. But more than this. The latter prelate in one of his letters to Henry I. calls himself 'fidelissimus animæ vestræ et corporis vestri et veri honoris vestri;' and that these words are a quotation from his promise of fealty to the Crown is rendered probable by the peculiar Latinity, and also by these two facts: (1) that Bishop Fulbert of Chartres, writing some ninety years previously to Richard the Good of Normandy, said 'nos .... animæ vestræ corporique vestro .... fideles sumus;' and (2) that the same prelate, who was a great lawyer, says to the Duke of Aquitaine, 'agnosco me perpetuum debitorem esse animæ tuæ et corpori tuo.'

Thirdly, there can be no doubt that the words 'fidele consilium et auxilium' formed part of the formula; but they will occur so frequently in the course of the following pages that I need say no more about them at present.

In St. Anselm's case, then, the profession of fealty contained the phrases (1) 'fidele servitium,' (2) 'fideles orationes,' (3) 'fidelis animæ vestræ et corporis vestri et veri honoris vestri,' (4) 'fidele consilium et auxilium,' and perhaps, as we

[1] *Ep.* iv. 35.

shall see later on, (5) 'fides et honor.' That the formula will ever be recovered is more than I dare to hope.

So much, then—alas that it should be so little!—on Anselm's profession of fealty, a profession made concurrently with the act which constituted him the King's man.

I shall not unduly anticipate what must be recorded in the sequel of this history if I pause to notice an obvious objection.

Why, it may be asked, should Anselm, who in 1093 put his hands within the Red King's, so obstinately refuse seven years later to do the selfsame thing to Henry I.? For two reasons. (1) The Holy See had in the interval forbidden such ceremonial act from bishops to kings; and (2) he knew too well the high value set on precedent by the princes of the Norman dynasty not to feel convinced that if the Christian interests of England were not to be placed, all of them, under the heel of the sovereign, the precedent of episcopal homage rendered to the prince must be broken, and broken without delay. The royal investiture of bishops meant, or might any day be made to mean, that bishops received their proper spiritual jurisdiction from the Crown. And, knowing this, Anselm would have been blind not to see that, the corporal ceremony of homage having now been superadded to the verbal profession of fealty, that ceremony might at any moment be made to mean that bishops were not only the men but the bondsmen, not only the servants but the slaves of kings, and in such wise the bondsmen and slaves as that even an Archbishop of Canterbury should be required to invoke the hatred and enmity of all mankind were he ever to swerve from it; for that was, as we have seen in the instance of the Count of Flanders, the manifest tendency of the institution known as homage.

The whole drift and current of the usage of investiture tended to encourage the heresy that princes were the depositories whence bishops were to derive their spiritual jurisdiction; and Anselm saw as clearly as his neighbours that the whole drift and current of the concomitant usage known as homage tended to convert princes who were, and rightfully enough, the *domini terreni* of bishops from *domini terreni* into *domini ligii*, and thus not only to change bishops, by means of the transitional estate of *homines*, from *fideles* into *ligii homines*, but to convert them from temporal subjects into spiritual subalterns.

To all this a very plausible rejoinder may be made; that what Henry required of Anselm in 1100 was, after all, only that which Anselm had given to the Red King seven years before, the title of *terrenus dominus* as distinguished from that of *ligius dominus*, and that, until evidence to the contrary be produced, we must believe the Primate to have been afraid of the fire before he had burnt his fingers, and to have cried out before he had been hurt.

This very plausible rejoinder would claim a reply were it only guaranteed by facts. But, alas! the guarantee of facts is all on the other side. It was because he had burnt his fingers that he was afraid of the fire, and because he had been hurt that he cried out. On the very morrow of his homage to William Rufus, that worst of men, resolved that his poor victim, who thought himself a servant, should find himself a slave and have the axe before his eyes from the moment in which he owned the jurisdiction of, not this or that pope, but the jurisdiction never yet called in question of the See of Peter, caused a document to be engrossed which fixed on him the brand of personal servitude direct and absolute. ' Hoc donum factum est die crastinâ quâ Anselmus Archiepiscopus meus ligeus homo factus est.' [1]

Had the Firebrand a part in this? Not improbably. He was one of the witnesses to the deed. Be that as it

---

[1] 'Inspeximus (Henricus VI.) etiam quandam aliam cartam ipsius progenitoris nostri in hæc verba: Willelmus rex Angliæ . . . . Sciatis me dedisse . . . . Hoc donum factum est die crastinâ quâ Anselmus Archiepiscopus meus ligeus homo factus est.'—See Dugdale, vi. 1271.

may, what was written was written, and the King had known his own purpose in causing it to be written. The basest and cruellest of tricks had been played, and the King had known his own purpose in playing it.

And now that we are again on the course of our journey we will push on at once for one short stage more.

As morning broke on Canterbury on Sunday the twenty-fifth of September, hope revived in the hearts of its inhabitants. The city was soon astir, for the new Archbishop was coming. He was met by a long procession of monks and clerks, who, with songs of joy scarcely audible above the acclamations of the delighted populace, led him to the venerable primatial church of All Britain. Nothing was spared to lend dignity and pomp to so auspicious an occasion; and when the Bishop of London conducted the thin, white-headed, but singularly handsome man to the foot of the throne, which for four years and a half had stood empty, and then, bidding him mount the sacred stairs, set him, dizzy and bewildered, in the augustest chair save one in Christendom, then, then from a thousand throats there sprang such jubilee of thanksgiving as smote the gorgeously tinted roofs of oak till they trembled and shook.

Was all this joy too full, or what? Scarcely had the spent echoes of the *Te Deum* subsided and expired when, insensible to every sentiment of delicacy, of pity, and of shame, Renouf the Firebrand marched blustering into the sacred place. The King had sent him; he was come to serve a writ on the new Archbishop. Men's blood boiled at the indignity. 'What,' they cried, 'might he not pass his first day in peace?' And, after all, as if the tyrant and his miscreant clerk had studied to aggravate indignity by insolence, the case was one of which the royal courts had by law no cognisance, for it lay within the jurisdiction of the spiritual tribunals. But Anselm was powerless against the King, and, auguring the future from the present, scanned and foretold the griefs he was to endure. On the threshold of a new life of service, set him to do by God, he stood, as Solomon says, in fear, and prepared his soul for temptation, 'knowing that all that will live godly in Christ must suffer persecution.'

APPENDIX

APPENDIX

APPENDIX TO VOL. I.

ANECDOTON A (pp. 28-33).

IT has been my happiness to light upon the following very valuable fragment in Cod. 499 of the Queen of Sweden's Collection in the Vatican Library. There can be no question as to its genuineness:—

'Vir Dei venerabilis Anselmus cùm adhuc esset puerulus, ut ipse postmodum referre solitus erat, litteris imbui valde desiderabat, parentesque suos ut ad scolam mitteretur assiduè exorabat. Unde divinâ providentiâ disponente ad hoc pervenit quod tanto mentis amore rogabat. Denique traditus est cuidam consanguineo suo ut eum attentiùs doceret, qui eum in domo suâ reclusit ubi studiosiùs doceretur, et ne evagando foras licentiâ à studio discendi præpediretur. Ubi dum diutius clausus haberetur pæne in amentiam versus est. Post aliquantum verò temporis reducitur matrique redditur. Puer inexpertam sibi clientium videns frequentiam expavit et omnium consortia fugiebat ac etiam aspectum declinabat atque interrogatus responsum non dabat. Videns hæc mater cum lacrimis exclamavit, Heu me miseram, filium meum amisi. Pertractans autem et recogitans apud semetipsam quid facto opus esset salubre reperit consilium. Præcepit itaque omnibus domûs suæ famulis et ancillis ut eum permitterent facere quicquid vellet nullusque ei obsisteret, immo si cui aliquid imperaret facere non differret, sicque ad priorem Deo volente rediit sospitatem. Cùm autem ad virilem pervenisset statum et religionis habitum suscepisset tantâ discretione erga omnes studuit se habere et quos regendos susceperat maximè juvenes tantâ lenitate in morum honestate informare sicut in se olim didicerat huic ætati convenire. Cui Dei gratia ita semper affuit ut nullus nostrâ ætate fuerit qui tam in hujusmodi dispensatione profecerit. Nam vita ejus et conversatio disciplina morum aliis extitit, sicut in libro vitæ ejus pleniùs invenitur.'

ANECDOTON B (pp. 89, 90).

The following account of Lanfranc's introduction to Herlwin is taken from an unpublished codex (96 Lat.) in the public library at Evreux. Internal evidence shows it to be the work of a monk of Le Bec who wrote early in the twelfth century.

The account of Lanfranc's adventure in the forest presents no material difference from that given in the 'Chronicon Beccense,' but what follows is very interesting:—

'.... Cui perquirenti ubi haberetur vilius terræ illius cenobium dictum est non longè abesse cenobiolum quoddam pauperrimum et despicabile, quod a quodam monacho nuper converso de seculo quoquomodo edificabatur qui dicebatur Herluinus. Quod ille audiens præpeti celeritate illuc advolat. Evenit autem divinâ prudentiâ, ut cum illùc veniret abbas persemet faceret furnum ad panes coquendos. Interrogat ille ubi esset abbas loci illius. Ostensus est illi ubi operabatur. Et cùm ad eum accederet forte abbas intraverat furnum. Qui accedens ad ostium furni, nondum enim desuper erat constructum, interrogat quis diceretur abbas loci illius. Ille statim respondit. Ego, sed hoc cur perquiris? At ille. Quia volo hîc monachus fieri, si Dei et vostra voluntas permiserit. Et abbas. Es clericus an laicus? Et ille. Clericus scolaris sum, genere Italicus, et vocor Lanfrancus. Tunc abbas, cui forte jam Deus aliquid de eo innotuerat, vel ad quem jam fama viri venerat, inclinans se ad os clibani, dixit ei, Ego in nomine Domini te suscipio. Ad hoc et ipse Lanfrancus inclinans se ad os clibani osculari voluit pedes ejus. Quod ille non permisit, nisi solùm manus. Statimque projiciens Lanfrancus indumentum quô amictus erat, cepit et ipse operari cum ceteris operariis et cum ipso abbate. Completo ad horam opere rediit abbas ad fratres; eisque innotuit voluntatem et desiderium clerici et ita communi consensu omnium regulariter recepit eum, tradens ei regulam ad legendum. Quâ perlectâ professus est se sub eâdem libenter victurum. Et non post multos dies stabilitatem suam ibi firmavit monachicâ professione.'

The account usually attributed, whether rightly or wrongly, to Milo Crispin makes Lanfranc a postulant at the beginning of the interview and a novice at the end of it, a circumstance which, in my humble opinion, throws a very grave suspicion on it. It may be divided into five parts, thus:—

1. 'What do you want?' ('Quid vis?') 'To become a monk' ('Monachus fieri volo').

2. The rule is shown to the postulant.
3. He reads it and promises to obey it.
4. The abbot grants the petition—*concessit ei quod petebat.*
5. Lanfranc kisses his feet.

The order observed on the reception of a novice was this :—

1. He was asked what he wanted, and replied that he wished to become a monk ('interrogatus quid dicat in his vel in similibus verbis petitionem suam facit . . . . '" Monachum fieri desidero "').
2. An account was given him of what monks have to do and endure.
3. He promised to bear all.
4. The abbot said, 'Nos . . . . concedimus . . . . quod requiritis.'
5. The novice kissed the abbot's feet.

Herlwin was an old soldier and the model of monks, and I shall never believe that he could do so irregular a thing as admit a postulant to the novitiate after the very irregular fashion with which he has been credited by Lanfranc's biographer; for few things could be conceived more out of harmony with the monastic spirit.

But, on the other hand, if the account given in the codex be true—and it is not, like Milo's, antecedently incredible—then Milo's mistake is easily accounted for. Herlwin said 'Ego suscipio te' in the sense of 'Come as a postulant;' for when Lanfranc fell at his feet he would not allow him to kiss them, as though he were already his spiritual subject. Milo, or those from whom he had his account, put a wrong meaning on these words; believed Lanfranc to have become a novice in the bakehouse; and, thus believing, foisted in the detail—a detail correct enough in its proper place— about the book of the rule, and made one complete but false story out of two.

Both in Milo's account and in the other the showing of the rule is made to take the place of the *vivâ voce* address customary on the reception of a novice. This is quite intelligible, for Herlwin's Latin was of a humble order. But the document was shown in the chapter house, as the codex describes; for it is not to be believed that Lanfranc can have read it through in so short a space of time as must have elapsed before prime, and it is scarcely conceivable that Herlwin should have been so punctilious as to make his postulant peruse that lengthy work and yet so forgetful of his own duty as to violate its spirit and its plain injunctions.

APPENDIX.

ANECDOTON C (Book III. passim).

The following list of monks professed at Le Bec from its foundation to the end of Anselm's abbatial career is taken from the codex which supplied me with the first of these *anecdota*. It has been of incalculable service to me :—

NOMINA MONACHORUM BECCI.

Dñs abbas Herluinus.
Walterius.
Herveus.
Baldricus.
Roscelinus.
Goscelinus.
Gausbertus.
Hugo.
Drogo.
(10) Rogerius abbas.
Adam.
Tedbaldus.
Ingerius.
Odo.
Albertus.
Ansgotus.
Odo.
Rodulfus.
Guilielmus abbas.
(20) Walterius.
Gotbertus.
Olricus.
Fulconius.
Osbernus.
Alveradus.
Turstinus.
Normannus.
Rodulfus.
Ascelinus.
(30) Fulcrannus.
Albuinus.
Anastasius.
Drogo.
Boso.
Lanfrancus archiepiscopus.
Rainaldus.
Bernardus.
Arnulfus.

Goscelinus.
(40) Herluinus.
Rainaldus.
Walterius.
Walterius.
Petrus.
Teodericus.
Raherius.
Ansfredus.
Albertus.
Rodulfus.
(50) Tedulfus.
Turulfus.
Durandus.
Ansgotus.
Balduinus.
Fulbertus.
Herunbertus.
Richarius.
Farmannus.
Gislebertus abbas.
(60) Benedictus.
Ricardus.
Isuardus.
Ricardus.
Robertus.
Guillermus.
Osbernus.
Gundulfus episcopus.
Anselmus abbas et archiepiscopus.
Hernostus episcopus.
(70) Rodulfus.
Frod . . . .
Ansfredus.
Mauricius.
Henricus abbas.
Osulfus.
Azo.
Bonizo.

Rodulfus.
Amalbertus.
(80) Riculfus.
Serlo.
Gillebertus.
Warnerius.
Milo.
Gaufridus.
Teodericus.
Ansfredus.
Harwardus.
Ricer abbas.
(90) Goscelinus.
Warinus.
Odo.
Henricus.
Walterius.
Osmundus.
Attardus.
Ruardus.
Osbernus.
Zulco.
(100) Lanfrancus.
Guido.
Hervaldus.
Giraldus.
Teduinus primus monachus novæ ecclesiæ.
[R]obertus.
Alannus.
Rodulfus.
Willermus.
Godefridus.
(110) Odo.
Chetellus.
Widimundus.
Hugo.
Drogo.
Girardus.

'NOMINA MONACHORUM BECCI.'

Bartholomeus.
Robertus.
Ursus.
Fulco episcopus.
(120) Haimo.
Walterius.
Gradulfus.
Restaldus.
Henricus.
Hermenfridus.
Warinus.
Franco.
Gislebertus.
Vitalis.
(130) Bernardus.
Guido.
Rogerius.
Anselmus.
Joh.
Ama.
Hugo.
Hugo.
Hucusque monachus primus abbas.
. . . . . .
Goso.
(140) Girelmus.
Adelelus.
Teodericus.
Rodulfus.
Guido.
Ricer abbas.
Walterius.
Baldricus.
Rogerius.
Osmundus.
(150) Hugo.
Achardus.
Gislebertus.
Willermus.
Robertus.
Martinus.
Teduinus.
Eustachius.
Rodulfus.
Guido.
(160) Vitalis.
Petrus.
Guilielmus, iij abbas.
Romanus.

Guarinus.
Salomon.
Adam.
Tezo.
Godefridus.
Walchelinus.
(170) Guimundus.
Robertus.
Geroldus.
Lanscelinus.
Robertus.
Dyonisius.
Gualo.
Johannes episcopus.
Andreas.
Rainaldus.
(180) Rainaldus.
Paulus.
Goscelinus.
Ascelinus.
Bernerius.
Petrus.
Odo.
Goscelinus.
Grumoldus.
Ivo.
(190) Willermus.
Lanfredus abbas.
Herveus.
Herveus.
Rodulfus.
Willermus.
Haimo.
Wibaldus.
Stephanus.
Gaufridus.
(200) Malgerius.
Willermus.
Gunduinus.
Gaufridus.
Fulco.
Albertus.
Ricardus.
Rogerius.
Robertus.
Hugo.
(210) Walterius.
Arche . . . boldus.
Albericus.
Rodulfus.

Hugo
Ricardus.
Ivo.
Willermus.
Gaufridus.
Ebremerus.
(220) Hugo.
Warinus.
Bernardus.
Herbertus.
Girboldus.
Aselmus.
Stephanus.
Ricardus.
Rainaldus.
Baluinus.
(230) Hugo.
Vivianus.
Ivo.
Hermannus.
Bernardus.
Hugo.
Willermus.
Odo.
Thestedus.
Johannes.
(240) Tebaldus.
Hildoardus.
Rodulfus.
Valo.
Walterius.
Warinus.
Ricardus.
Walterius
Rodulfus.
Rodulfus.
(250) Ermenfridus.
Hildebaldus.
Ivo.
Oliverus.
Girardus.
Anschitillus.
Ursus.
Rodulfus.
Rodulfus.
Tedboldus.
(260) Gislebertus.
Boso iiij abbas.
Rainaldus.
Walterius.

APPENDIX.

Hunfredus.	Ricardus.	Ilbodus.
Gislebertus.	Ricardus.	Hugo.
Walterius.	Anschitilus.	(290) Rainaldus.
Baldricus.	Odo.	Christianus.
Hugo.	(280) Gislebertus.	Willermus.
Rodulphus.	Willermus.	Warinus.
(270) Walterius.	Rainaldus.	Fulcherius.
Ricardus.	Walterius.	Vigerius.
Rodulphus.	Rodulfus.	Rainaldus.
Robertus.	Walterius.	(297) Seifridus.
Gaufridus.	Restaldus.	Hucusque monachus
Walterius.	Hugo.	ij abbas.

ANECDOTON D (p. 208).

THE ANNIVERSARY OF BLESSED HERLWIN.

It would be foreign to my purpose to expatiate on the havoc wrought on the suppression of the monastery of Le Bec—a long and painful story. Amongst the little that escaped destruction there have been preserved, perhaps as unworthy of the destroyer, three copies of a little sacristan's manual—a sort of kalendar of anniversary masses, and the like, proper to the community. They are preserved in the public library at Evreux. Conspicuous amongst the other directions contained in this 'Regula Becci' is the following, which I believe has never been published :—

'SEPTIMO KAL. SEP.

'Vigesimâ sextâ ejusdem mensis celebratur obitus venerabilis Helluyni primi abbatis ac fundatoris egregii nostri hujus cenobii becensis. Habet missam matutinalem ad majus altare chori cum collectis *Deus indulgentiarum*, *Singulariter*, *Miserere* et *Fidelium*. Tabula duplex in quâ procurat omnia cantor ut in præcipuis festis. Omnes in choro assistentes albis paratis revestiantur. Responsorium a tribus. Tractus ad quattuor dicitur. Quotquot sunt luminaria dum servitium agitur ardeant ut in solemnibus festis. Tabula chori aperitur. Altaria et tumulus non luctus sunt sed triumphi. Tapetum sericum cum aureis feliis contextum super sepulcrum sternitur. A vigiliis quæ pridie hujus diei solemnes dicuntur usque ad missam peractam ad sepulcri latera quod in capitulo est duo cerei jugiter ardent. Hæc dies solemnis est atque inter festa quatuor ad *Venite* commemorata in conventu. Mensa duplex est. Cantor legit de vitâ ejusdem. Diebus præcedentibus fit rasura. Quæ lectiones et responsoria ad vigilias dicuntur in tabulâ cantoris rubro scribuntur.

Duo habentur thuribula argentea. Non dicitur *Libera*. Quisquis sacerdos pro eo celebrat sub officio et oratione præcedenti. Tertiam psalterii partem dicunt novitii, monachi laici septem psalmos penitentiales vel centum *Paternoster* et *Ave Maria*.'

ANECDOTON E (p. 210).

THE TOMB OF BLESSED HERLWIN.

Not less interesting than the preceding extract is a singularly pathetic document preserved at the *mairie* of Le Bec Hellouin, a copy of which I have with some difficulty obtained. It is as follows :—

'EXHUMATION DU CORPS DU BIENHEUREUX HELLOIN.

'L'an mil sept cent quatre-vingt-douze, quatrième de la liberté, premier de la République Française, le dimanche, quatorze octobre, à deux heures après midi, on a célébré dans cette paroisse la translation du corps du bienheureux Helloin, premier fondateur et premier abbé de la ci-devant abbaye du Bec. On a transporté le même jour de l'abbaye dans l'église paroissiale une croix richement ornée d'un grand nombre de reliques ; comme deux autres reliquaires de forme de pyramides couverts d'une feuille simple d'argent, et deux autres reliquaires de bois d'ébène couverts de cuivre d'or.

'Le bienheureux Helloin naquit en Normandie l'an de Notre Seigneur neuf cent quatre-vingt-douze ; son père se nommait Angot, seigneur normand, et sa mère Héloïse, descendante des comtes de Flandres.

'En l'année mille trente-quatre, après avoir vécu et servi sa patrie environ pendant quarante ans à la cour de Gilbert, comte de Brionne, il fonda le monastère du Bec, et il y mourut en odeur de sainteté le vingt-six août mille soixante-dixhuit, et fut inhumé avec pompe et religieuse cérémonie dans le chapitre du monastère, dans un tombeau de pierre brutte d'une pesanteur considérable, avec sa croche en bois, ses brodequins et ses ornements sacerdoteaux. En mille sept cent sept, six cent trente et un ans après sa mort, on ouvrit son tombeau, comme il appert par son procès-verbal du cinquième jour de juillet, mille sept cent sept, ci-joint, qui constate qu'on a trouvé à cette époque son squelette tout entier sans la moindre marque de corruption ni dérangement d'aucun os, sa crosse intacte à sa gauche et ses brodequins seulement décousus ; lequel procès-verbal nous a été remis ès mains par le ci-devant prieur. Dans le mois d'août dernier le citoyen Marette, curé de la paroisse, sachant que l'abbaye du Bec, en vertu d'un droit de la seconde législature nationale, devait être évacuée par les religieux qui l'habitaient, présenta une requête au directoire du département de l'Eure, afin d'être autorisé à transporter dans son église le corps et le tombeau du bienheureux Helloin, qui reposait dans le chapitre de l'abbaye, avec partie des reliques les moins précieuses et (? des) ornements qui décoraient l'autel de l'église de l'abbaye dans les jours des grandes fêtes.

'Les membres du directoire du département de l'Eure s'étant fait un devoir d'accorder au curé toutes ses demandes fondées sur ce que les précieux dépôts restant dans une église supprimée ils seraient privés du culte qu'on leur doit et qu'on leur rend, il se fit autoriser par la municipalité du Bec et par les frères de charité qui ont bien voulu contribuer aux frais et travailler à cette exhumation. On ne parvint que le samedi, treize du présent mois, après beaucoup de travail et de fatigue, à tirer ce tombeau du sein de la terre où il était renfermé et couvert de la tombe de marbre, soutenue de quatre [1] petits pilastres, aussi de marbre, tels qu'ils sont dans l'église vis-à-vis des fonts baptismaux.

'La difficulté du transport, à raison de la pesanteur énorme du tombeau et la pluie qui tombait depuis un mois, détermina le curé à faire traîner le même jour—samedi—ce tombeau à force de bras depuis le chapitre de l'abbaye jusqu'à son église, où il arriva à cinq heures du soir et fut placé dans l'endroit destiné, orné décemment, environné de cierges, et y demeura exposé à la vénération des fidèles pendant toute la journée suivante. Pour exciter de plus en plus la foi et la piété des fidèles, on découvrit le dessus de sa tombe, et une foule innombrable de citoyens en rendant les honneurs dues à sa sainteté et à ses vertus fut témoin qu'il était encore dans le même état et la même situation où on l'avait trouvé en mille sept cent sept. Il demeura ainsi

---

[1] My copyist has certainly written *quatre*, not *six*; but I think that, misguided by his own experience, he has inadvertently made a clerical error. In the year 1791 there certainly were six pilasters under the stone; at this moment there are only four under the wooden slab which has replaced the stone in the parish church. Of course two of them may have been removed between the spring of 1791 and the autumn of 1792; but it is more likely that they disappeared with the stone. When that was removed I cannot say; nor can I find anyone who remembers to have seen it *in situ*. Doubtless the pillage was effected before the reopening of the churches for Christian worship. I quite believe the story of its having been converted into a *table de cuisine*.

exposé, couvert seulement d'un simple voile, depuis le samedi au soir jusqu'au dimanche après la cérémonie.

'Tous les curés circonvoisins avaient été priés d'assister à cette pieuse cérémonie, mais la circonstance du dimanche, et plus encore la continuité du mauvais temps, les empêchèrent de s'y rendre ; il ne s'y trouva que les curés de Saint-Taurin des Ifs, de Bosrobert et le citoyen Jovar, ci-devant procureur de l'abbaye du Bec. Le même dimanche, à deux heures d'après-midi, quoique la pluie tombât en averse, le clergé partit processionnellement pour l'abbaye, accompagné du citoyen Ansoult, commissaire du directoire du district de Bernay, des officiers municipaux du Bec en écharpes, des frères et sœurs de la charité et de Sainte-Barbe, avec torches et cierges. Le curé de Saint-Taurin des Ifs marchait sous le dais en surplis, étole et chape, accompagné des enfants de chœur en tuniques et le curé de la paroisse, aussi en étole, suivi d'un grand concours de peuple. Parvenus à l'abbaye, ils trouvèrent la croix et les reliquaires dont il est mention ci-dessus sur le grand autel. Après avoir chanté le *Veni Creator* et quelques antiennes et oraisons en l'honneur des saintes reliques, le curé de Saint-Taurin donna la bénédiction au peuple avec la croix, après quoi le curé du Bec donna à deux enfants de chœur chacun un reliquaire à porter, et se chargea des deux pyramides, qu'il porta lui-même, et la procession revint à l'église paroissiale dans le même ordre qu'elle était allé à l'abbaye au son des cloches. Arrivé à la paroisse, on déposa les reliques sur l'autel ; le curé monta en chaire et prononça une courte et pathétique exhortation analogue aux circonstances ; après quoi on chanta solennellement les vêpres et complies. Pendant le *Magnificat* le célébrant encensa la croix, les reliquaires et les autels, et fit aussi rendre les mêmes honneurs au corps du bienheureux Helloin, toujours découvert dans sa tombe. Après complies on chanta le salut, donna la bénédiction avec la croix, et on entonna le *Te Deum*, pendant lequel on fut au tombeau du bienheureux Helloin ; et à la fin, après l'avoir encensé, chanté quelques antiennes et oraisons et l'avoir invoqué comme un puissant intercesseur auprès de Jésus-Christ, on le couvrit d'une chasuble, et après avoir été recouvert du dessus de sa tombe on remit dessus la terre qu'on avait enlevée de vis-à-vis des fonts et maçonna la tombe dont il était décoré à l'abbaye, de sorte qu'il est ici comme on l'a vu depuis environ cent ans au chapitre de l'abbaye.

'Fait et certifié véritable par nous, prêtre, curé de ce lieu, soussigné, le dit jour et an que dessus.   MARETTE,

'Curé du Bec.'

The marble tombstone has gone—gone past recovery, I fear—but it was a modern substitute for the original, and, since its inscription has been fortunately preserved, its loss need not on its own account greatly afflict us. It has been replaced by a wooden slab of about the same size, adorned with a painting intended to represent Herlwin; but this is a modern concern and of no value. Dean Church in his 'Life of St. Anselm' borrows a somewhat misleading account of Le Bec from the pages of Mr. Freeman. Neither of those gentlemen can have been on the spot, and the 'effigy' of which the latter speaks has no existence.

I spent a few days in the exquisite little valley of Le Bec in the August of the eight-hundredth year after Herlwin's death. It was not my first visit; and I confess that I went there then only that I might prove the melancholy pleasure of being in such a spot on such an occasion. I need scarcely say that the oldest part of the monastery at the date of its abandonment was the chapter house; that the church, though far less ancient, was next to it in antiquity; and that the least modern structure next after the church was the bell tower, a detached and, fortunately, very massive piece of architecture. The cloister and other buildings were modern in style, as in date. Most of the latter have been allowed to stand; so, too, has the tower, thanks to the solidity of its construction, although its *flèche* has been removed. But of the church and—incomparably more deplorable to the antiquary—of the chapter house not a stone remains *in situ*. Still I could identify the site of Herlwin's church; I knew the site of his chapter house; I could people the surrounding sward with its sorrow-stricken crowd; and as the shadow of night fell, and silvery mists floated up the valley, I could say, ''Twas at this moment, eight hundred years ago, that this hushed and silent air was thronged with angels waiting for the soul of Herlwin.'

On the following day the curé of a neighbouring commune —for, sad to say, Le Bec Hellouin, although no inconsiderable village, has not its own priest—said mass in the parish church in honour of *le bienheureux Hellouin*. The attendance might perhaps have been more numerous than it was; but all who came—and they were more than ordinarily come even to a Sunday mass—had bunches of flowers, which they laid on the tomb. This had been adorned with a canopy of silk and with a cross and lighted candles. After the mass the priest and his assistants came down from the altar to the tomb, preceded by singing men in copes and a confraternity bearing their proper badge. Hymns were now sung and prayers recited, after which the nosegays were blessed with the usual ceremonies, to be presently reclaimed by their several owners. More than this could scarcely perhaps have been attempted under existing circumstances ; less certainly might have been done. This blessing of the flowers on Herlwin's tomb in the parish church of Le Bec was a custom observed annually until some few years ago, and seems to have been a perpetuation of one of the little traditional ceremonies observed in the olden days in the chapter house upon the recurrence of the twenty-sixth of August.

The *procès-verbal* drawn up on the occasion of the disinterment of Herlwin's remains in 1707 is quoted in Charpillon's 'Dictionnaire Historique de toutes les Communes du Département de l'Eure.' 'On trouva dans le sarcophage un corps revêtu d'une chasuble, ayant à sa gauche une crosse de bois et à ses pieds et jambes des pantoufles et des petites bottines. Le dit corps était dans sa situation naturelle, sans qu'aucune partie fût déplacée, quoique toutes les chairs fussent consommées ; la tête un peu recourbée, parce que le tombeau était trop court ; la mâchoire belle et les dents blanches ; les mains dessus la poitrine ; la crosse n'ayant pas de bout recourbé, peut-être à cause de la petitesse du tombeau. Une des pantoufles, décousue par le bout, laissait voir distinctement les doigts du pied.'

ANECDOTON F (p. 239).

THE PROPER MASS OF ST. ELPHEGE.

The following fragment of a mass of St. Elphege is preserved in the Vatican Library. Alas that there should be no more of it !

'custodiat. per dominum.

'PRÆFATIO.

'eterne deus. In cujus amoris virtute beatissimus martyr Elfegus hostem derisit, tormenta sustinuit, mortem suscepit. Quique ab ecclesiâ tuâ tantò gloriosior prædicatur quantò (per) sui devotionem officii bino moderamine effulsit. Ut in uno creditum sibi populum tibi domino deo conciliaret, in altero semetipsum in odorem suavi(ta) tis sacrificium offerret, in utroque filii tui domini nostri jesu christi fidelis imitator existeret. Qui pro omnium salute tibi æterno patri suo preces effudit et peccati typographum quod antiquus hostis contra nos tenuit proprii sanguinis effusione delevit. Et ideo.

'POSTCOMMUNIO.

'Grata tibi sint omnipotens Deus nostræ servitutis obsequia, ut illius interventu nobis salutaria reddantur pro cujus immarcessibili gloriâ exhibentur. Per.'

NOTE A (p. 1).

ST. ANSELM'S PEDIGREE.

§ 1. *On the Social Rank of his Parents.*

It was customary in the eleventh century to indicate the social position of a *nobilis* by the term *dignitas generis*; not by *nobilitas generis*, which embraced a higher, and therefore a narrower, area. To claim *nobilitas generis* a man must have been the kinsman, or at any rate the *affinis*, of a king; but, as there were no royal marriage acts in those days, and as the reach of canonical affinity was far more extensive than at present, the number of people who could claim *nobilitas generis* was exceedingly numerous. Still the difference between *dignitas generis* and *nobilitas generis* was distinct and well defined.

Nobilitas carnis, in its turn, covered a higher and narrower area than *nobilitas generis*, and included none but the blood relations of kings.

Nobilitas lineæ, again, was applied to none but the lineal descendants of kings, and I suspect none but lineal descendants in the male line; but of this I cannot feel certain.

Nobilitas natalium, if indeed the term existed—for I feel sure that I have seen it, although I cannot find it in my commonplace book—must have been used to indicate a person whose mother was royal as well as his father.

And the last and proper home of *nobilitas* was the prince himself, who was addressed as *nobilitas vestra*. So that the style *nobilitas vestra* was never given to a mere *nobilis*, as when your inferior calls you 'your honour;' nor to a peer, as when we say 'your lordship;' but only to the prince.

I will not weary the reader with a proof of this entire statement, but will content myself with subjoining a few passages in illustration of my general meaning.

St. Yves of Chartres was gently born, for he was 'nobili à sanguine natus;' but he distinctly assures us (Ep. 3) that he had not *nobilitas generis*.

That bishop himself, writing (Ep. 5) to the Countess Adela, says,

'Regius in excellentiâ vestrâ sanguis ex utrâque lineâ descendens nobilitatem generis in oculis hominum commendat.'

Duke Richard III. of Normandy, in his marriage contract with the daughter of the King of France, says, 'Hæc omnia tibi . . . . transfundo, ut, juxta nobilitatis tuæ lineam dotata . . . . mihi jungaris.'

And the epitaph on the tomb of Queen Matilda, the consort of Henry I., was :—

> O regina potens, Anglorum linea regum,
> Scotos nobilitans nobilitate tuâ.

I take these instances at haphazard out of a large number, and I do so in illustration of my meaning, not in proof of my position; for that would require a dissertation, which would be more than appears necessary in the present connection. For the word about which I am concerned is not *nobilitas*, but *nobiliter*.

At the very opening of his 'Life of St. Anselm' Eadmer says, 'I shall say a few words about the family and character of each of his parents, that thus the reader may have a sufficient idea of the origin and root of that which in due time was so illustrious in him whose parents they were destined to be. His father's name was Gundulf, his mother's Ermenberg. Both of them, in the world's phrase when it notes social rank ('juxta sæculi dignitatem'), were *nobiliter nati*, and lived at Aosta in a style proper to the *nobiliter nati* ('nobiliter conversati sunt'). They were not *ignobiles* in rank ('divitiis'), but unlike each other in character.[1]

All, then, that Eadmer says about their origin is, that they were *nobiliter nati*; of their rank, that they were *divitiis non ignobilis*; and of their state, that they lived *nobiliter*. In other words, the fulfilment of Eadmer's somewhat verbose promise about the origin of Gundulf and of Ermenberg is comprised in two words—*nobiliter nati*.

What, then, does *nobiliter natus* mean? What is the technical and conventional sense which the eleventh century attached to it?

Like *nobilitas* in the phrases I instanced just now, it is not the correlative of *nobilis*, but relates to a far higher and far smaller circle than that of *nobiles*.

---

[1] I think, however, that the right reading must be, not 'ambo divitiis non ignobiles, sed moribus ex quâdam parte dissimiles,' which reads like a false antithesis, but 'ambo divitiis non impares, sed moribus ex quâdam parte dissimiles.' But be the right reading what it may, it does not appertain to my present enquiry. *Divitiæ* denotes rank, not property, as when we talk conventionally of the 'rich and the poor.'

If I wished to say, in eleventh-century Latin, 'He behaved like a gentleman,' I should eschew such a phrase as *nobiliter egit*; but if I wished to say, 'He played his proper part as a king,' *nobiliter egit* would be precisely what I wanted.

But the question I wish to answer is, What sort of people were Eadmer's *nobiliter nati?* What sort of people were his *nobiliter conversati?* Of all the rings in the social target, which ring were they? Were they the children of kings, and none else; or the lineal descendants of kings, and none else; or the blood relations of kings, and none else; or was the idea of royalty, after all, not a necessary factor in its meaning?

Has it, however, a precise meaning of its own? Such a phrase as *nobiliter copulata* may, by the borrowed light of the context, mean 'royally married;' but if there were no context what would it mean? I think its own proper meaning is 'like a prince,' 'in princely fashion,' and the like, not 'nobly.' Thus (1) Rudolf Glaber (iii. 4) says of a certain Hervé who clearly belonged to the *haute noblesse* that, *ut generosioribus mos est*, he was *nobiliter educatus*. (2) The biographer of St. Mayeul tells us of that famous abbot who was 'præclaro stemmate natus,' 'clarissimis natalibus ortus,' 'ex utroque parente geminâ nobilitate coruscus,' 'de nobilissimâ prole,' and 'Gallicanâ generositate conspicuus,' that, *sicut generosioribus mos est*, he was *nobiliter educatus* (cxlii. 652). (3) Archbishop Lanfranc, writing to Queen Margaret of Scotland, says of her that she was 'regali stirpe regaliter progenita, regaliter educata; nobili regi nobiliter copulata' (cl. 549). (4) St. Anselm, in his superscription of a letter to the bride of the King of Denmark combines the adverb *nobiliter* with *regia nobilitas*, as follows: 'Venerabili dominæ, regiâ nobilitate, sed nobiliùs morum probitate, pollenti.'

If, then, *nobiliter educatus* be a term properly applicable to none but the *generosiores*, and if kings and queens can be said to be *nobiliter copulati*, people who are described as *nobiliter nati, nobiliter conversati* must certainly be members of the higher nobility, and may certainly be royal.

I now turn to another phrase, *mediocritas natalium*. For William of Malmesbury writes thus of St. Anselm: 'De Anselmo est sermo, qui, in Augustâ civitate oriundus . . . . mediocritatem natalium in clarissimam famam face virtutum suarum extulit.'

What, then, is *mediocritas natalium?* Clearly not the birth of a mere *mediocris*, any more than *nobilitas natalium* is the birth of a mere *nobilis*; but probably the next best thing of its kind after *nobilitas natalium.* The man who was sprung from a line of princes had *nobilitas lineæ*, whatever his mother may have been; but I believe that he needed what was called *æqua prosapia* to give him the still higher distinction of *nobilitas natalium.*

Suppose, however, that a child's mother were the lineal descendant of kings, but not his father; would he have *nobilitas lineæ ?* By no means. The mother has it, but not the child, because the father is not royal. Has he *nobilitas natalium ?* No; because, although the mother that bare him was royal, he was not born in the purple. What, then, is his state? His state, as I believe, is that of *mediocritas natalium.* I cannot prove my contention, I confess; for although I have been for now several years on the look-out for the phrase, I have only found one other instance of its occurrence, and that instance is not productive of much definite information. Still that instance is so far confirmatory as that it renders it probable that there were degrees of *mediocritas natalium.* A royal father gives you *nobilitas lineæ*, whatever your mother may be; and what you receive from him, that you transmit to your children. But not so with a royal mother, your father not being royal. You and your sister have in that case *mediocritas natalium*; but if your sister marries non-royally then her children have in their turn a modified *mediocritas natalium.* It is in some such way as this that I am disposed to account for the qualifying adjective in Guibert of Nogent, whose father was *claris bene naturalibus propagatus*, and who renders especial thanks to God for his own *bona mediocritas natalium.* His father, I mean, was a member of the higher nobility, but his maternal grandmother, or maternal great-grandmother, was royally descended in the male line. Had his mother been thus descended, he would have, I apprehend, taken care not to put in a qualifying adjective, and would have thanked God simply for his *mediocritas natalium.*

If, then, this guess of mine be correct, St. Anselm's father was not royal; not, I mean, royal by lineal transmission of royalty from father to son. Still he was *generosior.* I at one time thought that he might be descended from King Berenger II., but I cannot find that Berenger II. had any granddaughter or great-granddaughter, resident at least in Italy or married to a Lombard husband; and the conviction that, if he had been a grandson or a grandson's son in the male line of Berenger II., his son would have been described as possessing *nobilitas natalium*, or at any rate *nobilitas lineæ*, has put me off that quest. I have therefore searched elsewhere.

I have nothing to add to these preliminary remarks but the following from a poem written after St. Anselm's death :—

> Relligio, morum probitas, et splendor avorum,
>   Littera, deliciæ, formaque cum facie,
> Vivere si facerent, non sic mea membra jacerent
>   Hâc constricta domo; sic erit omnis homo.

And these lines, written in his lifetime by his friend William of Chester :—

> Laudari proles procerum pede debet Homeri;
>   Da veniam, timui pondera tanta pati.
>   *   *   *   *
> Tu generosus homo, magnisque parentibus ortus,
>   Exsuperas morum nobilitate genus.

What was it, then, that made St. Anselm a *proles procerum* and a *generosus homo*? What was his *splendor avorum*? How came he to have *nobilitas generis* and *mediocritas natalium*? What did Eadmer know of his pedigree that he should say of his parents, 'nobiliter nati, nobiliter conversati sunt'?

§ 2. *On Gundulf's Ancestry.*

Towards the end of his life St. Anselm wrote a letter to Count Humbert II. of Maurienne, who enjoyed the additional titles of Count of Aosta and Marquis of Susa, in reply to a communication from that prince reminding him that they were *consanguinei*. They, therefore, had a common ancestor within seven steps from Count Humbert, who was considerably the younger man of the two. Now Humbert's paternal grandmother, Adelaide, was Marchioness of Susa in her own right, being the daughter of Manfred II., Marquis of Susa; and, as I cannot find that either the father's father or the father of Adelaide's husband married a Lombard, and as the former of those princes was a stranger from the far north when he settled in the Valley of Maurienne, I look for the common ancestor of Anselm and Humbert in the forefathers of the Marchioness, and not in those of her consort. It is possible, then, and I think probable, that the common ancestor of Anselm and Humbert is to be sought either in Adelaide's great-grandfather Arduin III., Marquis of Turin and Susa, or in his son and successor Manfred I.

Manfred I., then, Marquis of Susa, died 1101. Can he have been Gundulf's grandfather? Clearly he may have been, by the hypothesis. I believe that he was.

For if it be objected that some other person than the paternal grandfather of the Marchioness Adelaide may have been the common parent of St. Anselm and Humbert II., there is an answer at hand to the objection in the very letter to which I have referred. 'Your Highness does me a great honour, me, whose kinsmen rejoice in being your vassals, in saying that I am bound to you by the ties of blood ('consanguinitate copulari'). . . . My conscience tells me that I have always with heart unfeigned, before ever I saw you, held your prosperity and successes dear to me. For, mindful of the fact that *naturaliter à progenitoribus* I owe you the duty of a subject, I have never let the love of you be absent from my bosom.' In other words, Humbert's tie of consanguinity to Anselm was at the same time his tie of lordship, and as Humbert was Anselm's lord in virtue of territorial inheritance, it was to a territorial predecessor of Humbert's that one of Anselm's *progenitores* had been vassal. I conclude, therefore, that I am right in looking for the common ancestor in some earlier Marquis of Turin and Susa, or in some earlier Marquis of Ivrea.

Now Gundulf cannot have been the first of his race thus to pay homage to either such marquis, for a father is not a *progenitor*, but a grandfather is. A great-grandfather, again, would not, I think, have been called a *progenitor*, great-grandfathers being *antecessores*. If, then, Anselm's paternal grandfather was the first of his race to play the part of vassal to a contemporary prince, whether of Susa or Ivrea, and if his grandfather and that contemporary prince were sprung from the same stock, we may feel pretty safe in concluding (1) that the common ancestor of St. Anselm and the contemporary Count of Maurienne was either Manfred I. or Arduin, that prince's father, and (2) that the relation of lordship and vassalage between the two races was established in the persons of Manfred II. and the father of Gundulf.

Whether Gundulf's father did homage to Manfred II. in his own name or in his wife's is a question I cannot answer; but I incline to the former alternative, and believe him to have been that prince's brother, and to have been invested by him with part of the confiscated property of their ruined cousin Arduin, Marquis of Ivrea.

The following scheme, then, exhibits what I believe to have been Gundulf's relationship with the great houses of Ivrea, the house of Turin and Susa, and the house of Maurienne and Aosta, titles for the first time united in the person of Humbert II.:—

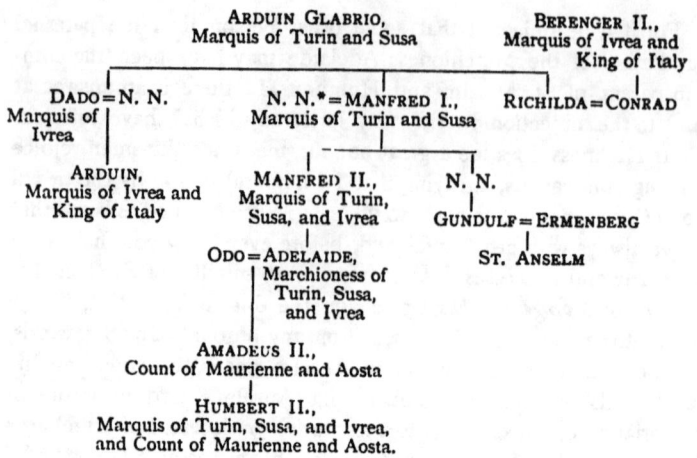

* Daughter of Atto, Count of Reggio, the paternal grandfather of Boniface, Duke and Marquis of Tuscany, the father of the illustrious Matilda.

§ 3. *On Ermenberg's Ancestry.*

I believe Ermenberg, the mother of St. Anselm, to have been a niece of Rudolf III., and thus a granddaughter of Conrad the Pacific, who preceded that prince on the throne of Transjuran Burgundy.

I also believe her to have been a niece of Anselm II., Bishop, and probably Count, of Aosta early in the eleventh century and until the year 1020, when he died. I proceed to justify these opinions.

I. In the year 1025 Conrad the Salic conferred the see of Toul upon his second cousin, Bruno of Ensheim, who happened to be with him in Lombardy while he was engaged in chastising the rebellious Milanese. Bruno lost no time in setting forth for his diocese, notwithstanding the remonstrances of the Emperor, who feared he might be molested on his journey through Lombardy, but took the precaution of detaching himself from the main body of his retinue and travelling some hours in advance of them with only a few attendants. His route lay along the *via regia*, which ran through Ivrea up the valley of Aosta as far as that city, and across the great St. Bernard. Passing unsuspected through Ivrea in broad daylight, he continued his journey for some nine or ten miles, when he alighted at Carema,[1] a little town on the border of the Valdostan territory, for he was in need of rest and was forty miles from Aosta.

[1] The Bollandists (April 19) read 'locus qui dicitur ad Cameram,' and add a note to say that the place meant is La Chambre, in Savoy. This explanation

The sun was already low in the west when his retinue entered Ivrea, intending to sleep there, but were at once surrounded by a crowd of eager and excited Lombards, who peered into the face of each, hoping to recognise Bruno. Perplexed by their failure, the Ivreans took counsel during the night, when some one bethought himself of the little group of travellers who had ridden through the town the day before. The fleetest horsemen that could be had were at once despatched in pursuit of them, and, galloping into Carema just as its gates were opened, learnt that there were travellers there sleeping heavily after a toilsome journey. They awoke them, secured them, and carried them back to Ivrea, rejoicing to think that Bruno was caught. No such thing. Heaven had interposed with what the biographer calls a *jocosum miraculum*; for Bruno, rising betimes but unwilling to disturb his jaded attendants, had set forth up the valley, intending to ride on at his leisure and let them overtake him, and was only a double arrow's flight out of the place by one gate when his pursuers entered it by the other. The story does not say what became of Bruno's retinue, but hastens to inform us that his wants were soon supplied by his sister-in-law, whose name is not given, but of whom it is enough to know that she was a niece of

takes no note of the preposition *ad*, and, what is worse, it involves an impossibility. Ivrea and La Chambre are about a hundred miles distant from each other, and are separated by a range of mountains. The place which they print 'ad Cameram' must have been somewhere in the valley of Aosta; of this there can be no doubt, and it must have been on or close to the line of demarcation between Italy and the county of Aosta. Now the Valdostan territory extended for forty Roman miles down the valley, measuring from Aosta, on the establishment of the colony under Augustus; and the boundary of the duchy embraced Carema, until in the year 1564 it was shifted so as to exclude it. Until 1564, that is to say, the boundary of the duchy would seem to have been identical with the boundary mentioned by Bruno's biographer as the limit of geographical Italy. The Valdostans are not Italians. But, however, Bruno crossed the boundary and entered Carema, or, as it seems then to have been called, 'ad Caremam.' This form 'ad Caremam' I suppose to have been the nearest Latin that could be found for the vernacular, whatever that may have been. But it is curious that the vernacular seems to have retained the preposition *ad*, and also the final *m* of a Latin accusative. I have never seen any conjectures about the name, and cannot say if the vernacular word represented by 'ad caremam'—possibly, however, it was 'ad carema'—was masculine or feminine. Philologists must know. But it is interesting to find that by the eleventh century there existed in the valley of Aosta a cognate word to the Italian *carema* and the French *carême*, with which we are all familiar. *Ad caremam*, or whatever the vernacular may have been, must have represented the classical *ad quadragesimum* (i.e. *ad quadragesimum lapidem*). The place lies, as I have said, forty Roman miles from Aosta. Similarly Quart and Nus are four and nine miles distant from that city.

King Rudolf III., and that her husband's name was Gerard, Count of Ensheim.

Now I believe Ermenberg to have been a younger sister of this lady, Countess of Ensheim and niece of King Rudolf.

II. King Conrad the Pacific, father of Rudolf III. and grandfather of the Countess of Ensheim, had been twice married, his second queen being Matilda of France, a daughter of Louis d'Outremer. Her dowry comprised the city and county, or city and exarchate, of Lyons, which, like Aosta, Lausanne, Vienne, Sion, and numberless other places in that age, was a *civitas episcopalis*. No sooner, then, did King Conrad receive this accession to his kingdom than he bestowed it upon a son, Burchard, issue of his first marriage, who retained his double dignity of ecclesiastical pastor and territorial prince for upwards of half a century, dying in the year 1031.

On the death, however, of Archbishop Burchard, a nephew of his who bore the same name as himself, and who, as being his nephew, was a grandson of Conrad the Pacific, hurried to Lyons and made himself master of the city, which he governed, as his uncle had done, in the double capacity of ecclesiastical and territorial ruler; for he was already a bishop with a diocese of his own in another part of the kingdom. But scarcely had he established himself in Lyons when his uncle King Rudolf died, bequeathing his kingdom to the Emperor Conrad the Salic, who at once made it his business to oust the new Archbishop of Lyons, whom he considered dangerous. Now, this new Archbishop of Lyons, grandson of Conrad the Pacific and nephew of the previous Archbishop, had been Bishop of Aosta since the year 1020. So that in the year 1025, when Bruno was succoured in his troubles, there were two grandchildren of King Conrad's at Aosta, who must either have been cousins or else brother and sister—namely, the reigning bishop and the Countess of Ensheim.

When the Emperor had ousted Bishop Burchard of Aosta from the archiepiscopate of Lyons, the claim was taken up by a certain nobleman, who put forward a mere child of his own, a *puerulus quidam*, as legitimate successor; and as it is hard to conceive what claim a mere child can have had but an hereditary one, the most obvious inference is that the *puerulus quidam* was Bishop Burchard's nephew, and that his father, a 'certain Count Gerard,' was Count Gerard of Ensheim. It is, therefore, reasonable to believe that Bishop Burchard of Aosta and the Countess of Ensheim were brother and sister; and, as their precise relationship does not affect my argument—as, I mean, it is indifferent to me whether they were brother and sister or cousins—I will adopt that belief as the more probable of two alternatives.

III. I said at the beginning of this note that Eadmer's description of the birth and state of Ermenberg invites us to believe that she was at least *generosior* by origin, and may have been royal. I incline to the latter alternative, for a reason which I must now give.

We have two letters of St. Anselm's to his maternal uncles Lambert and Folcerad, in each of which he calls them *reverendi domini*; a style which he never assigned—and his contemporaries seem to have followed the same rule—to any but princes, abbots, and bishops. We have letters of his to canons, to archdeacons, to all sorts of people; but, with the exception of abbots, bishops, and of course popes, none but princes are styled *reverendi domini*, none but princesses *reverendæ dominæ*. *Reverentia* was an old traditional term used to indicate royalty, like our 'highness;' and I suspect that to style a canon—Lambert and Folcerad were canons—*reverendus dominus* in respect of his canonry would have been much the same as it would be with us to say 'your grace' to an archdeacon.

This is, in my poor judgment, a fact of very considerable importance indeed, and encourages me to pursue the enquiry.

So much, then, for the present in recommendation of the opinion that one of Ermenberg's grandfathers was Conrad the Pacific, King of Burgundy. It is time to turn our attention to Anselm II., Bishop of Aosta, whom I believe to have been her uncle on one side, as I believe Rudolf III. to have been her uncle on the other.

IV. The ecclesiastical history of Aosta gives us three bishops of the name of Anselm in charge of that see in the course of about a century—namely, Anselm I., whom we meet in the year 923, and who was succeeded by Bishop Boso; after Bishop Boso Anselm II., whom we meet as late as 1002; and after Anselm II. the third of the name, who seems to have acted as coadjutor to the Bishop Burchard already mentioned.

Now Anselm I. was not only Bishop, he was also Count, of Aosta; a fact of considerable moment in our enquiry. For towards the close of the tenth century the privilege of hereditary succession was already so firmly established in Transjuran Burgundy that an attempt made to violate it in the year 1001 was the signal for a rebellion from end to end of the kingdom. I am not presumptuous, therefore, in supposing the second successor of Anselm I. in the earldom to have been a great-nephew. But not only were the great Burgundian fiefs hereditary; the great Burgundian counts had long been in the habit of disposing after their own pleasure of the bishoprics within their domains ; and if the second military successor of Anselm I. was a great-nephew, nothing is more likely than that his second ecclesiastical successor should also have been a great-nephew, and thus either the Count himself, or the Count's brother, or the Count's cousin. But this is immaterial; and the fact to which I now wish to direct attention is that the name of the father ot Anselm II. was Count Anselm, ånd that we have three Anselms in as many generations—Bishop Anselm I.; Count Anselm, his nephew, as I believe ; and Count Anselm's son, Bishop Anselm II. In short, Anselm seems to have been a family name.

V. Now Bishop Anselm II. was a relation of King Rudolf III. That prince in the year 1014 caused a deed to be executed in which he specified first his queen, Ermengard, then Counts Berthold, Rodolf and Robert, then Hugh of Sion, Henry of Lausanne, and Hugh of Geneva, and after these again ' Burchard of Lyons, Anselm of Aosta, and Pandulf, with the rest of (my) brothers.'

But Rudolf III. and Anselm II. were not sons of the same father ; neither were they sons of the same mother ; they must therefore have been brothers by canon law, the brother of one of them having married the sister of the other. And this is just the union I want (1) for the parentage of Bishop Burchard, who was certainly nephew to Rudolf III., and in all probability nephew to Anselm II., his predecessor in the see of Aosta, and (2) for the parentage of the Countess of Ensheim. Thus :—

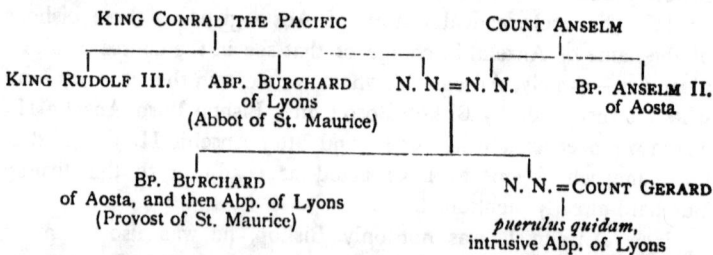

Now, what I want to do is to make Ermenberg the sister (1) of Bishop Burchard of Aosta and (2) of the Countess of Ensheim. And I think I may do so without presumption ; for I cannot see what can have entitled her brothers to the designation of *reverendi domini* but such relationship to the Kings of Burgundy as would thus be assigned to them.

I have only one more remark to make before proceeding to another branch of the subject. I do not know who Anselm III. was—the Anselm, I mean, who was *coepiscopus* of Aosta in Bishop Burchard's time—nor is the subject an important one. Still if we make him that prelate's brother, and bear in mind the fact that our saint had a nephew with the same name as himself, we have six Anselms in as many generations. Thus :—

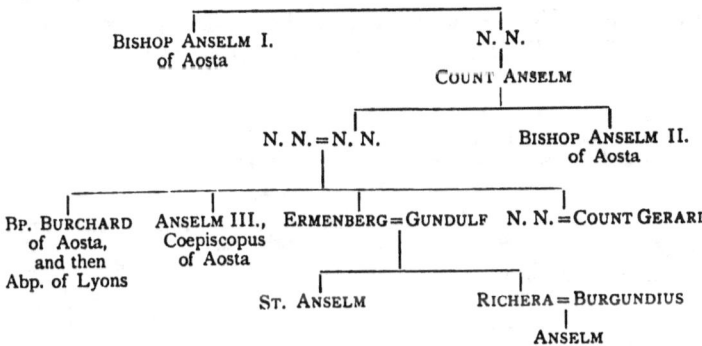

VI. I proceed with my argument. The house of Maurienne came into existence in 1000. Bishop Anselm II. died in 1020. In 1025 we for the first time find the title Count of Aosta borne by a Count of Maurienne.

Assuming, then, that Anselm II., like Anselm I., was Count of Aosta as well as Bishop, it follows that the secular title passed upon his death to the house of Maurienne. The ostensible reason of this transference may have been that there was no one of his own kin capable of performing military service for the Emperor, who was the designated heir to the crown of Burgundy; the real reason must have been that the new bishop and his family, who who were near relations to Rudolf III., might prove troublesome to Rudolf's alien successor. But that the transference was effected in open violation of all right, or that having been thus effected no record of the fact should survive, are improbable suppositions; nor is it likely that the Emperor would have invoked the certain disaster that would follow so outrageous an injustice by way of assuring his succession to the crown. I suspect, then, that the transference was effected by means of a matrimonial alliance, and that, just as in 1032 Turin, Susa, and Ivrea were handed over to the house of Maurienne by the marriage of the Marchioness Adelaide to Count Odo, so at an earlier date had the succession to the lordship of the valley of Aosta been secured to Odo's father, Count Humbert, by that prince's marriage with a sister of Bishop Anselm II. ; in which case the wife of Count Humbert I. no doubt bore a name proper to her race, Anci being no doubt a feminine cognate form with Anselm ; and the 'progenitores mei' of the saint's letter to his kinsman receives its strict literal interpretation of 'both my grandfathers.'

My ignorance of the name of Ermenberg's father cannot affect her relationship. He was not improbably the Pandulf who figures as a brother of Rudolf III. ; in which case her descent is to be tabulated thus :—

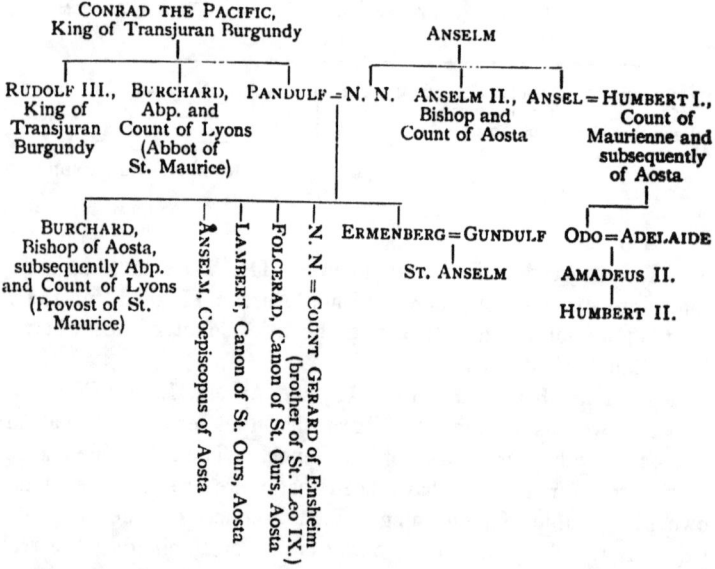

It would be an endless task to show all the relationships that might be established in virtue of St. Anselm's pedigree. It may, however, interest the reader to see at a glance what was the prelate's connexion with other descendants of his great-grandfather, Conrad the Pacific.

Conrad the Pacific = Matilda, daughter of Louis d'Outremer, King of France.
Matilda = Baldwin IV., Count of Flanders.
Baldwin V., Count of Flanders.
Matilda = William the Conqueror.

Conrad the Pacific = Matilda.
Gerberg = Herman II., Duke of Swabia.
Matilda = Frederick II., Duke of Lorraine.
Beatrice = Boniface, Duke and Marquis of Tuscany.
Matilda.

Conrad the Pacific = Matilda.
Gisela = Henry of Bavaria.
Henry II., Emperor.

Conrad the Pacific = Matilda.
Gerberg = Herman II., Duke of Swabia.
Gisela = Conrad the Salic, Emperor.
Henry III., Emperor.
Henry IV., Emperor.

Our saint was thus second cousin to the Conqueror's queen, second cousin to the mother of the Marchioness Matilda, second cousin to the Emperor Henry III., father of Henry IV. His mother was first cousin to the Emperor Henry II.

NOTE B (p. 94).

ON THE CANONICAL IMPEDIMENT TO DUKE WILLIAM'S MARRIAGE.

I know of no author who has explained the grounds of objection to William's marriage with Matilda. Whilst some have declared that there was no impediment at all, and others have thought fit to suggest that Leo IX. prohibited the marriage because there were political interests of his own which might have been thwarted by it, Mr. Freeman has adopted, with slight but immaterial modification, the argument advanced some thirty years ago by Mr. Stapleton in the 'Archæological Journal,' that Matilda was already another man's wife. He says, 'The panegyrists of William keep out of sight the fact revealed to us by a comparison of several documents and incidental statements that Matilda was the mother of a son and a daughter of whom William was not the father.' Why Mr. Freeman should accuse none but William's panegyrists of such reticence as this I will not stop to enquire. I note the rhetorical device, and pass on. 'She had already been married to Gerbod, a man of distinction in Flanders. To him she bore two children. . . . It is certain, though no one would have guessed it from any of the writers who record the marriage, that the bride of William was already the mother of two children by another man.'[1] 'Mr. Stapleton,' continues our learned and ingenious

[1] *Norman Conquest*, iii. 85.

historian, 'has, I think, convincingly made out' the proposition 'that Matilda was before her marriage with William the mother of Gerbod and Gundrade.'

Now, I do not doubt the truth of the proposition thus accepted by such an authority. I do not doubt it, for I deny it; and I deny it without reservation. There was not a drop of Matilda's blood in the veins of Gundrade. Further, I willingly concede that Gerbod and Gundrade were brother and sister, and I assert with confidence that there was not a drop of Matilda's blood in Gerbod.

Gundrade, I need scarcely say, was the wife of William of Warenne, the first of his race who bore the title of Earl of Surrey.

Earl William employs, or is reputed to have employed, the following words in one of the Lewes charters: 'Pro salute dominæ meæ Matildis reginæ matris uxoris meæ.' And William the Conqueror says, or is reputed to have said, in another document, 'Pro animâ . . . . Gundradæ filiæ meæ.' Mr. Stapleton and Mr. Freeman accept the first statement; but the brief they hold invites them to reject the second. I accept both one and the other; but whilst accepting them I still maintain that there was not a drop of Matilda's blood in the veins of Gundrade, and I also declare that neither was there a drop of William's blood in them.

But even if Mr. Freeman were right in his conjecture that Gundrade was a stepdaughter of the Conqueror's, he is as far as ever from the solution of the real difficulty. Even if he could prove that Matilda at the time of her espousals was not a maid but a wife, he would not therefore have explained away the concurrent testimony of contemporary historians that William and Matilda were *consanguinei*. The only impediment alleged by contemporary authors is that of consanguinity, and human testimony is at an end if we are not to give the most intelligible of words the only meaning it ever had or ever could have had.

No remarks of mine can be needed to give force to this objection. It is fatal, absolute, not to be gainsaid. The idea that, I will not say men like Orderic and William of Malmesbury, but that any man who ever wrote should have dreamt of explaining that Matilda was the undivorced wife of Gerbod by saying that she was the kinswoman of some other man, lies wide even of the limits of incredibility, and they are wide enough. It is as impossible as the square root of a minus quantity, and I shall waste no more words on it.

It must have been a sense of this objection that has led Mr. Freeman to enquire whether, after all, by the impediment of consanguinity that of affinity may not have been meant. 'Matilda's mother had been married, or rather betrothed, to William's uncle. . . . I am not canonist enough to say whether this would have been an impediment to a marriage between Richard's nephew and Adela's daughter.'[1] And again, 'It is by no means easy to see any reasonable ground for the prohibition on any of the usual ecclesiastical theories of affinity.'[2] On these sentences I need do no more than remark as follows :—

1. It surely requires no profound knowledge of canon law to consult such works, and even to understand them, as treat of cases like that of the betrothal of Matilda's mother to William's uncle, a betrothal not followed by cohabitation.

2. Our quest would be not for reasonable grounds, but for legal grounds, had such prohibition as Mr. Freeman suggests ever been issued.

3. The usual ecclesiastical theories of affinity are not the only theories that have ever been held. But, after all,

4. The marriage was not forbidden because the contracting parties were *affines*, but because they were *consanguinei*.

I do not know if Mr. Stapleton ever tried to discover William's relationship by blood to Matilda. All that Mr. Freeman says on this subject is that 'it is by no means easy to trace up the pedigree of William and Matilda to a common ancestor,' and 'there is no small difficulty in making out what the nearness of kin between William and Matilda was.'[3]

Be that as it may, the contemporaries of William and Matilda would not have left it on record that they had an ancestor in common if that had not been the fact.

I am not a canonist, but I cannot and dare not disdain, since the marriage was forbidden 'on the usual ground of nearness of kin,' to enquire what was in those days meant by nearness of kin, or consanguinity; and, curiously enough, all the information we require is to be found in the pages of history, not of canon law.

1. There is a passage in Orderic[4] which informs us that Henry I. forbade the union of his nephew William Clito with Sibylle, the daughter of Foulques, Count of Anjou, on the ground of consanguinity; and it proves them to have been *consanguinei* by a statement of which this is a tabular transcript :—

---

[1] iii. 650. [2] iii. 90. [3] iii. 650. [4] *Hist. Eccl.* iii. 11, § 19.

APPENDIX.

DUKE RICHARD I.

```
Duke Richard II.        Robert.
Duke Robert I.          Richard.
Duke William II.        Agnes.
Duke Robert II.         Bertrade.
William Clito.          Foulques.
                        Sibylle.
```

That is to say, although one of the parties was removed by five degrees, and the other by six, from a common ancestor, it would have been a violation of the Christian law under which they lived to be united as man and wife, 'diffinitum est eos secundum Christianam legem conjungi non debere.'

2. And if I might without presumption wander so far afield as to quote Yves of Chartres, I would remark that that prelate (Ep. 45) forbade the marriage of Robert, Count of Meulan, with Elizabeth the daughter of Hugh le Grand, because he was said to be descended by five generations from a common ancestor with that lady; and refused to allow so scandalous a union to be blessed in his diocese till satisfactory proof had been adduced in his presence that the common ancestor was as far removed from one or other of them as the eighth degree, 'nisi primùm in præsentiâ nostri consanguinitas hæc septimum gradum excessisse legitimè fuerit comprobata.' But there is as little need to consult Yves of Chartres as the 'Acta Conciliorum,' for the information I need may be obtained from domestic sources.

3. According to Orderic the Council of Rouen, held in 1072, decreed, 'Si infra septimam generationem aliqua consanguinitas inventa fuerit . . . . non conjungantur.'

4. William of Malmesbury informs us that, in the council held in London in the year 1075, marriage was forbidden between persons descended from a common ancestor at or within the distance of seven degrees—seven degrees, that is to say, on either side, '*ex alterutrâ parte*.'[1]

I am not a canonist, but it is notorious that, whereas nowadays marriages are forbidden between *consanguinei* as far as the fourth degree, in the eleventh century that older *jus* was still in force which extended the range of canonical consanguinity over a much wider field. Thus Nicholas II., the Pontiff to whom

[1] Guil. Malm. *De Gestis Pontificum Anglorum*, lib. i.

Lanfranc applied for the dispensation, decreed, 'Si quis infra septimum consanguinitatis gradum uxorem habet . . . . ab episcopo suo eam dimittere canonicè compellatur. Si verò obedire noluerit excommunicetur.'

It was for the violation of this immemorial law of Christendom that William and Matilda were punished. They broke that law deliberately, and in doing so defied the authority which had issued a special declaration of it to themselves by name. They knew what to expect; they provoked their chastisement. They knew perfectly well that they had at any rate one ancestor in common within seven generations; and Christendom knew it; we know it.

William the Bastard was in the fifth degree of descent from Duke Rollo, and Matilda was also descended from Duke Rollo through Adela, the wife of her great-grandfather Hugh Capet.

By the law under which they lived William and Matilda were *consanguinei*. I have stated that law, and have no more to say about it.

And now for Mr. Stapleton's discovery that Gundrade was Matilda's daughter by an earlier marriage. The discovery is a mare's nest. Had they been thus related no one would have thought of making a match between a son of Gundrade and a daughter of Henry I.; or had so scandalous a proposition been made—for scandalous it would have been accounted—it would have been met by a prohibition on the ground that the parties were cousins. Now, curiously enough, a proposal was once made that William of Warenne, second Earl of Surrey, should marry the daughter of Henry I.; and Archbishop Anselm forbade the alliance, not on the ground that the parties were cousins, as he would have done had the Earl's mother been the daughter of William the Conqueror or the daughter of his queen, but on the ground that the Earl was in the fourth generation, and the lady of his ambition in the sixth, from a common ancestor. I append St. Anselm's letter, and deem it unnecessary to say more in proof of my assertion that there was not a drop of Matilda's blood in the veins of Gundrade:—

'*Henrico charissimo suo domino Dei gratiâ regi Anglorum Anselmus archiepiscopus fidele servitium cum orationibus.*

'Gratias ago Deo pro bonâ voluntate quam vobis dedit, et vobis qui eam servare studetis. Quærit consilium celsitudo vestra quid sibi faciendum sit de hôc quia pacta est filiam suam dare Guillelmo de Vvarenne, cùm ipse et filia vestra ex unâ parte sint cognati in quartâ generatione, et ex alterâ in sextâ. Scitote absque dubio quia nullum pactum servari debet contra legem Christianitatis. Illi autem, si ita propinqui sunt, nullo modo legitimè copulari possunt, neque sine damnatione animarum suarum, neque sine magno peccato eorum qui hoc ut fiat procurabunt. Precor igitur et consulo vobis ex parte Dei sicut charissimo domino, ut nullatenus vos huic peccato misceatis neque filiam vestram eidem Guillelmo contra legem et voluntatem Dei tradatis. Omnipotens Deus dirigat vos et omnes actus vestros in beneplacito suo.'[1]

The common ancestor of the Earl and the King's daughter was the father or mother—perhaps both father and mother—of Gunnor, the mistress of Richard Sans Peur.

Still it may be urged that, after all, the first Earl William calls the Conqueror's queen 'mater uxoris meæ,' and that the Conqueror is at any rate averred to have written of Gundrade as 'filia mea.'

Precisely so. Matilda was Gundrade's *mater*, not her *genetrix*; and Gundrade was the Conqueror's *filia*, not her *nata*. Gundrade was Matilda's godchild. *Pater, mater, filius, filia* were the ordinary appellations of god-parents and god-children. Nothing was more common. Thus in the 'Life of Halinard,' who governed the diocese of Lyons in the course of the eleventh century, we are informed that he was loved with paternal affection by a certain Bishop Walter, *cujus filius erat in baptismate.* Here, it is true, we have the explanatory and qualifying words 'in baptismate'; but not so in every case. Thus St. Anselm writes to a canon of Beauvais (Ep. iii. 106), 'If you are elected with the advice of Bishops Yves of Chartres and Gualo of Paris, who were your *patres* and were charged with your education, you should not refuse the preferment.' And in the works of Yves of Chartres there is a letter (Ep. 178) to the clergy of Dol, in which the Bishop calls a certain Wulgrin his *filius*, whilst in another (Ep. 176), written on the same occasion, he says of Wulgrin 'eum de fonte suscepimus.' It is the knowledge of the fact that *filius* may mean, and very often does mean, godson which has enabled me to assure my readers that St. Anselm's maternal uncles Lambert and Folcerad were his godfathers, for he calls himself their *filius*.

I could adduce other instances, but these are sufficient; and I think I may without presumption affirm that I have proved two not unimportant propositions—first, that when contemporary writers condemned William's union with Matilda on the ground of consan-

---

[1] S. Anselmi Epp. iv. 84.

guinity, they knew and meant what they said; and secondly, that Gundrade was not a daughter of Matilda. Mr. Stapleton's theory is exploded.

P.S. Should the reader really care to enquire, Who, then, was Gundrade? I would refer him to the following passage in the 'Registrum de Bermundesei' (Harley, 231): 'A.D. M.XC.viij. Hôc anno Ricardus Guet frater Comitissæ Warene dedit manerium de Cowyk monachis de Bermondeseie.' There is a similar entry in the Bermondsey Chronicle.

This Cowyk is Cowickbury, now called, I believe, Quickbury, in the parish of Sheering, in Essex.

When the Domesday survey for Essex was made this place was held of Willelmus by one Ricardus. The superscription shows that the Willelmus was the William of Warenne; the Ricardus was, I presume, Richard Guet (Wet or Wette?), his brother-in-law.

NOTE C (p. 140).

ON THE PRAYERS AND MEDITATIONS.

Before setting down the few remarks which follow I think it right to say that, since my present work is biographical, not editorial, I do not profess to decide which of all the works assigned to St. Anselm, under the designation whether of prayers or meditations, are really his. I do not undertake to review or criticise these works one by one, even were I competent to the task; I only propose to say of some of them what I trust may be of service to a few of my readers, and not uninteresting to a somewhat wider circle.

I. And first, taking Dom Gerberon's edition as text-book, I will venture to say that I think the learned Benedictine has erred in styling some of them meditations and the rest prayers, to the exclusion in either category of the alternative designation; for several reasons.

St. Anselm seems to have made no such distinction, since in a collection of seven such compositions sent as a wedding present to a princely lady of his acquaintance, he says, 'I have added seven prayers' ('orationes'), 'the first of which is not so much a prayer as a meditation' ('non tantùm oratio quantùm meditatio') (Ep. iv. 121).

The 'Chronicon Beccense,' a document of unquestionable authority in this particular, whilst dividing his treatises into twelve groups, makes the eleventh consist of '*orationes contemplativæ*, which many people call *meditationes*.'

The prologue which in Gerberon's edition begins, 'Meditationes seu orationes,' and is prefixed by him to the twenty-one pieces which he calls meditations, begins in the Rouen and in the Subiaco collections, 'Orationes sive meditationes'—a preferable reading, as I believe—and refers indiscriminately to compositions which the Benedictine has separated in distinct groups.

II. All the compositions which Gerberon has published as prayers or as meditations of St. Anselm must not be too readily accepted as genuine.

Of the twenty-one pieces published by Gerberon as meditations we need not concern ourselves much with the last, which is a compilation from the 'Proslogion;' it does not contain a word which is not to be found in the authentic treatise. Still there is room to question whether St. Anselm either made or sanctioned the compilation. I doubt it. I am greatly inclined, on the other hand, to believe that he did issue the argument for the existence of the Supreme Being as it now stands in the second, third, and fourth chapters of the 'Proslogion' in a separate form. These three chapters are the nucleus of the comet; the rest are the tail.

The second meditation in Gerberon's collection is, as I believe, the product of St. Anselm's pen throughout. It begins, 'Terret me vita mea;' and Abbot Durand writes to St. Anselm, as we have seen, of a composition, or fragment of a composition, with this beginning. In the course, however, of my desultory enquiries I have found a meditation of considerable fervour, in the course of which are the words, 'Merito ergo terret me vita mea,' continuing with few and apparently unimportant variations from Gerberon's, and then ended with other matter. Is this piece to which I allude St. Anselm's? Is it his, I mean, from beginning to end? Was what Abbot Durand read only a fragment? or, if it was not a fragment, did Anselm himself work it up and incorporate it into a longer work? Or is the piece to which I refer an amalgam, partly Anselm's, partly some other person's?

These are not idle questions. Here is a parallel case. The second prayer in Gerberon's collection is, with the exception of some very bad readings which that editor found in his MS., identical with a very interesting copy with which I have happened to make acquaintance; identical, that is to say, for about two-thirds of its length, down to the words 'impietatibus meis.' But there the copy to which I refer ends. Which of the two is right? What follows in Dom Gerberon may or may not be Anselm's, but if it is Anselm's was it meant by him to be attached to what goes before in Dom Gerberon? This is no idle question, for it bears upon another—this, namely, For whose use was the shorter form written, if indeed the shorter form be a right one? But on that I will say no more in this place.

The seventh and eighth meditations in Gerberon's collection are, with the possible, but barely possible, exception of two paragraphs at the beginning of the former, not St. Anselm's, but some other writer's. I have some claim to speak confidently on this subject, for I have translated all the twenty-one pieces into English leisurely and with care, and I shall never forget the dreary hours I spent over this most melancholy, most inflated, and most obfuscated composition. I have found it amongst MS. copies of Bishop William du Puy's works, and it was published as his at Venice in 1591; published, I say, but published only in part, for after some thirty lines the editor has set a merciful '&c.' and spared the reader pages of dreary woe. With the slight possible exception which I have indicated, the seventh and eighth are not Anselm's.

The third is his, undoubtedly. I mention it to suggest a caution. It was not written *in propriâ personâ*. It may have been written, in the first instance, for a specific case; it may have been published in the hope of doing good in cases which must occur, even if rarely. But the assumption that Anselm wrote it for himself is simply intolerable.

The fifteenth, sixteenth, and seventeenth in Gerberon's collection of 'Meditations' were assigned by Luke Holstein to Ælred of Rievaulx. One or two passages, particularly in the seventeenth, may possibly be interpolated fragments from Anselm's writings, but these do not affect the question of the authorship of the work as a whole. For, in truth, the three pieces are one work. With the exception, then, of one or two irrelevant passages, which may or may not be Anselm's, the work as a whole is not his. Whoever wrote it must have written it *in propriâ personâ*. There can scarcely, at least, be a reasonable doubt of this. And if so it was not written by Anselm, for it was not written for Anselm's use. I say nothing about the style and manner of the work, but confine myself to the unquestionable fact that St. Anselm's youth was unstained by the sins which the writer of this work deplores.

Neglecting, therefore, the last of Gerberon's twenty-one 'Meditations' as one out of several *spicilegia* culled from the 'Proslogion,' five of the remaining twenty must be rejected—namely, the seventh, eighth, fifteenth, sixteenth, and seventeenth. The second, third, and eleventh are genuine. I believe the first, fourth, fifth, and sixth to be free from doubt, but cannot say as much for the ninth, tenth, twelfth, thirteenth, fourteenth, eighteenth, nineteenth, and twentieth. Were it my object to study particularly the devotional style of St. Anselm, I should confine my attention, for some time at least, to the first six and the eleventh in Dom Gerberon's collection.[1]

III. Of the seventy-five prayers published as Anselm's we may, without hesitation, accept as genuine the twentieth, twenty-third, twenty-fourth, forty-first, fiftieth, fifty-first, fifty-second, sixty-second,[2] sixty-fourth, sixty-fifth, sixty-seventh, sixty-eighth, sixty-ninth, seventy-first, seventy-second, seventy-fourth, and seventy-fifth, and perhaps the third, fourth, sixth, ninth, and thirty-fourth. The third and fourth are styled 'Meditations' in the Rouen collection.

The fiftieth and two following prayers are those of which St. Anselm wrote to his friend Gundulf (Ep. i. 20).

The seventy-first presents a peculiarity. Some copies make it an address to St. Martin, and others to St. Nicholas, whilst others again assign it to one or the other at the reader's discretion. I am inclined to believe that it was originally addressed to St. Martin, and that, whether St. Anselm ever did or did not sanction this alternative employment of it, he did compose a prayer to St. Nicholas, which was sent after him in rough copy across the Channel in 1092, and never returned to Le Bec. The popular devotion to St. Nicholas spread like wild fire at the close of the eleventh century, and it is quite conceivable that, pending the composition or the composition and publication of a prayer to him by the famous abbot—for by this time Anselm was known from end to end of Christendom—people should have made use of a previous composition of his which *mutato nomine* served their purpose.

IV. I have already alluded to a collection of seven prayers or meditations which Anselm sent to a royal lady, apparently on occasion of her marriage. Of these one was addressed to St. Stephen, the other to St. Mary Magdalene. They may have been the sixty-ninth and the seventy-fifth of Gerberon's collection; two, that is to say, out of the group of devotional pieces, some twenty in number, which I believe to be the set of meditative prayers mentioned in the 'Chronicon Beccense.' Of this it is impossible to speak confidently. But I think I have laid my finger on one of the seven—the

---

[1] St. Anselm's style is by no means easy of translation into English. Where, therefore, we find sentence after sentence turn itself, as it were, into English, we may be sure that it is not his.

[2] To St. John the Baptist.

second, namely, in Gerberon's edition—or rather so much of it as is comprised between the beginning and the sentence ending with 'propitieris omnibus impietatibus meis.' Whilst collating Gerberon's reprint with the copy which I have mentioned, I could not but observe, and with satisfaction, that *tumoris*, not *timoris*, must be the right reading in the following sentence : 'Memor perpetuæ nobilitatis semper fastidiam ventos hujus transitorii tumoris.' It recalled to mind passages in which *tumor* is used for the pride of birth, and I felt sure that *nobilitas* must here be used in the sense of royalty ; so that my investigations on this last word, however uninteresting they may be deemed, had not been made in vain. I felt sure that the prayer had been composed for the use of a royal personage ; and the assurance was only confirmed by what I next noticed, the numerous allusive references to royalty which occur in the prayer. I then remembered Anselm's letter to the Queen of Denmark, and on reperusing the prayer was struck with another fact to which I must now invite the attention of my readers.

It may be unnecessary to say that women, and communities of women, are not permitted in their devotional use, for example, of the Psalter, to change words of the masculine gender, which are susceptible of such change, into corresponding forms in the feminine. Thus it would be out of all order for a woman to say, ' Ecce enim in iniquitatibus concepta (instead of 'conceptus') sum.' Such changes are not permitted, have never been permitted, as I believe ; and the same remark holds good of all liturgical forms of devotion, hymns and prayers as well as psalms.

Now it is a remarkable fact, never as yet noticed, as I believe, that this second prayer, though it does not violate this general rule, is yet so composed as not to be subject to its application. There is nothing in it to betray the sex of the *persona loquens*. It is so composed as, while not violating the general rule, not to violate that character of absolute appropriateness which a lady who had been supplied with a prayer from the pen of such a man as St. Anselm would expect to find in it.[1] I have no doubt, therefore, that it was composed for the use of a princess. It may be one of the seven prayers sent to the Queen of Denmark.

The tenth prayer offers precisely the same characteristic, a most remarkable characteristic, to which justice can only be done by a

---

[1] There is one apparent exception in Gerberon's ' mihi reo videns congaude Eva,' but there can be little doubt that the *reo* is an interpolation. It is not in any MS. that I have examined.

careful perusal of all these pieces; and I have not the slightest doubt that it was written for the use of a woman—perhaps the Queen of Denmark, perhaps the Countess Ida, perhaps the Marchioness Matilda, perhaps Queen Matilda.

The twelfth prayer is in the same category; the *persona loquens* is characterised by no adjectives in the masculine gender, or by anything else that would be out of harmony with its use by a woman. But there is nothing in it to indicate the social rank of the person for whom it was composed.

The same may be said of the fourteenth, which was probably written for a widow, and perhaps of the thirty-eighth.

None of these five, neither the second, tenth, twelfth, fourteenth, or thirty-eighth, are included in the collection which I believe him to have put forth for the use of his monks while he was at Le Bec. Their issue was private, their destination personal.

V. If I am right in my conjecture about the prayers which constituted the *orationes meditativæ* put out by St. Anselm whilst he was at Le Bec, that collection can scarcely have contained one to St. Nicholas.

1. The devotion to this saint was new in the West in the year 1088, and can scarcely have reached Le Bec much before 1090, if so early.

2. St. Anselm's collection of prayers would seem to have been composed while he was prior—anterior, that is to say, to the year 1078. It would be an extravagance of literary scrupulosity to set their publication as late as 1090, within the last two years out of the thirty which he spent first as prior and then as abbot.

3. The saints addressed in those prayers are the Blessed Virgin Mary, St. John the Baptist, St. John the Evangelist, and SS. Peter, Paul, Stephen, Martin, Benedict, and Mary Magdalene. Guided by the late history of the monastery, I am inclined to think that there were altars to these several saints either in the church at Le Bec, in chapelries on the domain, or in dependent cells.[1]

[1] We have no information as to the number of altars at Le Bec at the time that the collection of prayers was put out. Six altars were consecrated in 1077, it is true; but there must already have been others, for the church had been in use for four years. In 1342 thirteen altars were consecrated in the newly built church to as many saints. I suspect that there were nine in Herlwin's church, and that the book of prayers was meant for use within its walls; for the nine saints whom I have named in the text had altars in 1342, our Lady having two and SS. Peter and Paul sharing one—the ninth. The tenth was to St. Nicholas, and I believe an altar to his honour to have been set up and consecrated some fifteen

4. There seems to have been an altar to St. Nicholas in the church as early as the year 1109, and how much earlier I cannot say; and a chapel on the way to La Baronnerie, or at any rate somewhere in the wood 'quæ vulgo dicitur Roboretum'—whence the modern Bosrobert, an adjoining commune—about the same time.

5. St. Anselm seems to have just finished a prayer to St. Nicholas when he left Le Bec in 1092. It was sent after him to England.

On the whole, then, I think it likely that the devotion to St. Nicholas was established at Le Bec in or about 1092; that the monks asked Anselm to compose them a prayer in his honour; that until such prayer should be composed they used *mutato nomine* that intended for St. Martin, which they already had in their collection of *orationes meditativæ*; that in the dismay and confusion which befell Le Bec on Anselm's appointment to the see of Canterbury they either forgot the prayer to St. Nicholas on which he had been engaged, or refused to ask him for it, or failed to get it, or, getting it, preferred to go on using what they had already used; and that their copies of it were never abundant at Le Bec. And it is thus that I account for the fact that there is no prayer proper to St. Nicholas in the published works of Anselm. Yet a prayer proper to St. Nicholas he certainly did compose, and I think I may have succeeded in finding it.

On reverting, after the lapse of a year, to the foregoing note, I find nothing to alter, although I have a little to add.

I. There can be no doubt that Dom Gerberon erred in dividing these devotional works into two distinct categories; for four or five examples, written during the saint's life or soon afterwards, which still survive, make no such distinction.

II. As to Oratio II., as Gerberon calls it, I have found a piece containing part of it, and thus entitled : 'Pars orationis Anselmi in fine.' It begins, 'Omnipotens Pater et misericors Deus per omnipotentes Filii tui' (ib. clviii. 859B), and ends 'omnibus iniquitatibus meis. Amen' (ib. 862C).

III. The first published collection contained, if I mistake not, the following prayers, neither more nor less :—

    1. To Christ, Or. 20.
    2. To the Holy Cross, Or. 41.
    3, 4, 5. To the Blessed Virgin, Or. 50, 51, 52.
    6. To St. John the Baptist, Or. 62.

years after the dedication of the church. The three remaining saints had received their honours subsequently to Anselm's day.

7. To St. Peter, Or. 64.
8, 9. To St. John the Evangelist, Or. 67, 68.
10. To St. Stephen, Or. 69.
11. To St. Martin or St. Nicholas, Or. 71.
12. To St. Benedict, Or. 72.
13. To Mary Magdalene, Or. 74.
14. To any patron saint, Or. 75.
15. A prayer for friends, Or. 23.
16. For enemies, Or. 24.
17. The *terret me*, Mad. 2.
18. The *deploratio*, Mad. 3.

In which case, as I have said, the church consecrated in 1077 had nine altars—the high altar, the Lady altar, and seven others.

But I say no more, lest the reader accuse me of neglecting biography for editorship.

NOTE D (p. 273).

ON RENOUF FLAMBARD'S SURVEY.

Orderic's account is as follows: 'Hic juvenem .... inquietavit regem, incitans ut totius Angliæ reviseret descriptionem, Anglicæque telluris comprobans iteraret partitionem, subditisque recideret .... quidquid inveniretur ultra certam dimensionem.' This must, at least, mean that he made a review of the Domesday Survey in order to deal with estates that exceeded a certain area. It cannot mean—for that would be absurd—that he made a survey of every little holding in the country, in order to curtail the large ones; nor need it mean that his reference to Domesday was made with a view to any estates but such as exceeded the proposed maximum. This was one part of his scheme.

The other is thus described: 'Annuente rege, omnes carrucates, quas Angli hidas vocant, funiculo mensus est et descripsit, postpositisque mensuris quas liberales Angli jussu Edwardi regis largiter distribuerant imminuit.' He grows obscure, however, when he adds 'et, regales fiscos accumulans, colonis arva retruncavit.' No augmentation of a tax can diminish the area of a field; and I suppose he means that the result of the enhanced taxation was much the same to small tenants as if their holdings had been curtailed. Before, however, this *retruncatio* was effected the earlier *imminutio* of the hide had taken place; and the explanation I have to offer of a confessedly difficult passage is, I think, justified by what follows, where the double process of the reduction of the unit of measurement and the augmentation of the assessment is described in other terms —'Ruris itaque .... diminutione et insoliti vectigalis gravi exaggeratione, supplices .... plebes indecenter oppressit'—and where by *diminutio ruris* we are, I apprehend, to understand the inevitable consequence of the *imminutio hidarum*, just as by *vectigalis exaggeratio* the means taken for the *accumulatio fiscorum*; not, that is to say, that the *rus* was lessened in area, but that for fiscal purposes it was subdivided into an immense number of diminished hides. That is to say, *imminuere hidam* is to cut down a liberally measured hide to a scanty one; and *diminuere rus* is to cut up, or parcel out, the land into areas rigorously kept down to the standard of the niggardly hide.

This account of the double process of *diminutio ruris* by means of *imminutio hidarum*, and of *exaggeratio vectigalis* resulting in *accumulatio fiscorum*, lends countenance to a literal interpretation of William of Malmesbury's 'duplum adjiciebat.' For if where the Confessor had counted six hides William Rufus counted ten, and where the Conqueror had imposed a tax of six shillings William Rufus imposed ten, the man who had once paid thirty-six shillings would now have to pay a hundred; and the effect of this surcharge of sixty-four per cent. in the new tax would be to retrench (*retruncare*) the available produce of the land; and this, as I hinted above, is the best sense I can make of 'arva retruncavit.'

All estates then, whether large or small, were afflicted with the *retruncatio arvorum*, which resulted from the double infliction of *imminutio hidarum* and *accumulatio fiscorum*.

But the cutting down to a prescribed limit would, on the other hand, affect only large estates. How many and what estates were thus treated I do not pretend to guess. It is a curious fact, however, that as early as the reign of Henry III. the lowy of Tunbridge had been greatly reduced from its original dimensions. Can it be that this was one of the properties that suffered?

To return, however, to Orderic.

I think that the best way of interpreting the whole passage is to make him mean to tell us that—

I. Renouf set the King upon making a careful review of the Domesday Survey, and going over for a second time the apportionment of the soil to which that document bore witness, the specific object being to cut down (*recidere*) all large estates to a certain area. This process, be it observed, related only to large estates, and could be carried out without any reduction of the unit of measurement. Actual survey, be the unit of measurement what it might, was all that was needed by way of information as to their extent. He set the King upon this, then.

II. But this was not all. He obtained the King's consent to another scheme, and that scheme was to affect all holdings. By it he reduced (*imminuit*) all the hides employed in the Confessor's time, some of which may have contained fifty, some seventy, some a hundred acres, to one restricted measure of, perhaps, from thirty to forty acres, and by this means cut up (*diminuit*) a few large taxable acres into many small ones. This done, he enhanced (*exaggeravit*) the assessment per hide, and then applying it to the *rus diminutum*—to the land, that is to say, which he had parcelled out into little hides—brought immense receipts into the royal treasure.

The first scheme, the scheme to which he prompted the King, was a *recisio telluris*, or carving off from this and that large estate all that exceeded a fixed maximum. The second scheme, the scheme which he induced the King to sanction, issued in a *retruncatio arvorum*, because its practical effect was to oblige landowners, great and small, to part with a large percentage of the produce of the land for the payment of an artificially augmented tax.

The first scheme aimed at a carving off of land, *recisio telluris*; the second issued in a retrenchment of crops, *retruncatio arvorum*. And just as *decimatio arvorum* would be a legitimate phrase by which to express the modern process of tithe commutation, so would *retruncatio arvorum* be for that which required a landowner to sacrifice an undue portion of his crops for the payment of a tax.

On the whole, then, I think that the passage under consideration may be satisfactorily explained by a careful attention to the meaning of the four words *recisio, imminutio, diminutio,* and *retruncatio*. To cut a piece off from an estate is *recidere* that estate; to reduce an unit of superficial measurement is *imminuere* that unit; to chop up an area into small portions is *diminuere* that area; to deduct an excessive percentage from the monetary yield of your crops is *retruncare* those crops.

NOTE E (p. 356).

ON SOME REMARKS BY MR. FREEMAN UPON ST. ANSELM'S PROMOTION TO THE EPISCOPATE.

It is not without reluctance that I call attention to some remarks made by Mr. Freeman upon St. Anselm's elevation to the Primacy of Britain. That gentleman says ('Norman Conquest,' vol. v. pp. 137 et seqq.), (1) 'Anselm's unwillingness was simply an unwillingness to accept the office under any form. . . .' (2) 'He received the staff from the King's hand.' (3) 'He became the King's man. . . .' (4) 'Nor do we find Anselm expressing the slightest scruple as to receiving the archbishopric by the gift of the King only, (5) without any reference to the elective rights of the monks of Christ Church or of any other ecclesiastical body. . . .' (6) 'Of any conscientious dislike to the way in which the archbishopric was conferred, repugnant as that way was to all the doctrines for which Hildebrand and his successors had been striving, we hear in the present stage of Anselm's history not a word.'

I. As to the first statement, Mr. Freeman adduces nothing in support of it. It is quite true that Anselm was unwilling to accept the archbishopric 'under any form,' whatever may be the precise meaning of those words; but it is sorry logic thence to conclude that he was indifferent to the ceremony with which it might be offered. I have spent five years in the study of St. Anselm's history; I have read and re-read all that Eadmer says of him; read and re-read, as I conscientiously believe, all his letters; read and re-read all that I have been able to find of contemporaneous record; and I feel that I am not guilty of presumption in declaring that the suggestion that Anselm, but for his unwillingness to be made Archbishop, would not have been unwilling to receive the crosier from the King's hand, has not even the phantom of a shadow upon which to rest.

II. But the suggestion sinks into insignificance before the astounding statement that he did so receive it—'he received the staff from the King's hand.' It is hard to believe that Mr. Freeman can have read either Eadmer's account or that of Gervase. Anselm did not receive the crosier from the King's hand. Eadmer says, 'Cùmque raperetur ad regem ut per virgam pastoralem investituram archiepiscopatûs de manu ejus susciperet *toto conamine restitit*' (clix. 366); and again,

'Rege autem ei baculum porrigente manum contrà clausit *et eum suscipere* nequaquam consensit;' Gervase ('Actus Pontiff. Cant.'); 'Cùmque ad regem renitens traheretur ut secundùm morem baculum susciperet pastoralem, *abhorruit Anselmus et quantum potuit renisus est.* Adjuncto tamen utcunque manui ipsius de foris baculo, præcepit rex,' &c. If a refusal, and not only so but a persistent refusal, to receive be the same thing as to receive, language is no longer the vehicle of human thought.

III. If, by the third statement, which is only separated by a semicolon from the second, Mr. Freeman wishes to suggest that Anselm became the King's man *pro archiepiscopatu*, I can only say that I know of no authority for the insinuation. Anselm did homage, it is true ; not, however, *pro archiepiscopatu*, but, as Mr. Freeman has failed to inform his readers, *pro usu terræ*, which is quite another thing. ' Ille igitur,' says Eadmer, 'more et exemplo prædecessoris sui inductus, *pro usu terræ homo regis factus est*' (clix. 372).

IV. As to the fourth statement, I must trouble the reader with a few quotations, to which Mr. Freeman's attention can scarcely, I should imagine, have been directed.

§ 1. Eadmer's account is as follows :—' Meanwhile all the good people present urged the King to release the common mother of the whole realm from her long widowhood by the appointment of a pastor ('instituendo illi pastorem'). He willingly consented. . . . The question thereupon arose, Who could best perform the duties of the post ? But as all present waited for a hint from the King (' cunctis ad nutum regis pendentibus '), he took the lead, and declared that Abbot Anselm was the most worthy of such a dignity, and the acclamation of all present, not one excepted, seconded his words (' prænuntiavit ipse et concordi voce subsequitur acclamatio omnium abbatem Anselmum tali honore dignissimum ') (ib. 365, 366).

This account represents the King as taking the lead, not as claiming, much less as exercising, a sole and exclusive power of nomination.

Apart, however, from this consideration we must remember that Eadmer here describes what took place in the presence of Anselm and his companions Eustace and Baldwin, and that it by no means follows that the subject had not already been discussed by the *primates regni* before their arrival at the Castle. The passages which I am about to quote will throw some light upon this subject. My main object, as I need scarcely remind the reader, is to show that

Mr. Freeman is mistaken in supposing that Anselm owed his promotion to 'the gift of the King only.'

§ 2. Orderic informs us (iii. 309) that Anselm mounted the throne of Canterbury after it had been three years vacant, and owed his promotion to *ecclesiastical election* ('ecclesiasticâ electione promotus'); to ecclesiastical election, not to the gift of the King only.

§ 3. Again, Orderic says (ib. 314), 'When Holy Church heard the royal order about the election of a metropolitan she rejoiced exceedingly, and assembling the *conventus seniorum*,[1] began to discuss the business about which they were gathered together. At length, regard being had to the holiness and wisdom of the venerable Anselm, *they unanimously elected him* in the name of the Lord ('omnes eum elegerunt in nomine Domini').

This is a very different account from Mr. Freeman's. The *ecclesia*—that is to say, as I believe, the episcopate or the bishops and abbots—and the *conventus seniorum*—or, as I suppose, the barons—made their choice of a successor to Lanfranc; the appointment was not a mere act of the King's. At what point in the story this election was made is an interesting question, but scarcely relevant at this moment.

§ 4. John of Salisbury informs us ('Vita S. Anselmi Cant.' cap. vii.) that after the King was taken ill he listened to the advice of his wise men, who suggested that Anselm should be promoted to the archbishopric, saying that he was most worthy to occupy that post of highest dignity ('languore tactus et sapientium motus consilio acquiescit ut in archiepiscopum promoveatur Anselmus, dicens eum summo honore dignissimum'). This passage receives elucidation from the next which I have to adduce.

§ 5. Matthew Paris ('Hist. Major,' s.a. 1094), when recording the attempt made by the Red King to extort a thousand pounds from Anselm a week or two after the consecration, informs us that the prince alleged as his excuse that he had received nothing for consenting to Anselm's promotion. ('Ad hoc alligabat, ut sibi videbatur causam justissimam quòd gratis promotioni suæ annuisset.') The promotion to which he consented cannot have been his own act. The appointment cannot be attributed to 'the King only.'

[1] What Orderic's *conventus seniorum* may be is a question of secondary importance in view of Mr. Freeman's statement. Whoever the *seniores* may have been, they were not the King. I suspect, let the idea be taken at its worth, that he means to say that the earls were summoned by the bishops to consult with them.

§ 6. The anonymous author of the 'Life of Bishop Gundulf, a prelate whom the biographer would seem to have known intimately, and from whom there can be little doubt that he had taken care to gain an accurate account of the whole business, tells us (Migne, clix. 826) that when the bishops and barons saw how great danger threatened the King they humbly begged him, seeing in what a predicament they were, to appoint a primate—not to elect; nor, if electing, to elect regardless of their wishes; but to appoint ('ut eis . . . . primatem constitueret')—and goes on to say that the King having listened to their advice, *they unanimously elected Anselm* ('omnes pariter providente gratiâ Dei Anselmum eligunt'), and having elected sent for him ('electum advocant'); and that when he came, although he resisted with all his might, they made him Archbishop—they, not 'the King only' ('vocatum licèt totis viribus renitentem archiepiscopum statuunt').

That is to say, they asked for a *congé d'élire*, and, having received it, chose Anselm. Whatever the distinction designed by the writer between their *statuere* and the King's *constituere*, it is evident that Anselm did not owe his promotion to 'the King only.' Whether the King had confirmed their election prior to Anselm's arrival at the Castle, or was prevented doing so before the subject was resumed in Anselm's presence, is irrelevant at the present moment.

§ 7. Nor is evidence wanting from the saint himself. In the very affecting letter which he wrote to his monks at Le Bec some little time before he accepted the archbishopric—I need scarcely say that he persistently refused to accept it for some five or six months after the date at which Mr. Freeman supposes him to have received it—he says, appealing to God, 'Thou seest, and be Thou my Witness that . . . . I cannot without sin tear myself free from the determination made by *my electors*;' and again, 'Whatever may be my own wish with regard to the accomplishment of what men have set on foot in *their election* of me, "lead me in Thy way"' (Ep. iii. 7).

§ 8. Is more needed? If so, I will adduce the King himself as a witness. Eadmer tells us ('H. N.' i.) that when the sovereign sent for Anselm soon after their interview at Rochester, he did so because he had two requests to make, the first of which was that he would no longer hold out in refusing to become Archbishop '*in pursuance of his election by the whole realm*' ('quatenus . . . . . . secundùm totius regni de eo factam electionem pontifex fieri ultro non negaret') (clix. 371).

I might stop here, were it not that I have two passages to adduce which will serve to convince the reader that had Mr. Freeman consulted St. Anselm's correspondence—the first ten letters of the third book all relate to the appointment—he would scarcely have ventured to make the assertion with which I am at present dealing.

§ 9. During the interval that elapsed between Anselm's appointment and his acceptance of the dignity Dom Osbern of Christ Church wrote him two letters, imploring him not to withhold his consent any longer. In the former of them he says, 'Knowing as I do your singular skill in the discernment of truth' (an allusive reference, no doubt, to Anselm's famous 'De Veritate') 'it seems to me a strange thing that in this one and only instance your tact and versatility in discerning truth should have played you false, and that you can blind yourself to the plain will of God, declared by the common voice of holy Church concerning you. If you mean to maintain that what has been proclaimed to be the will of God by the *general election* of you, or by the election, if not of all the electors, yet certainly of the overwhelming majority of them, and those the wisest ('generalis electio vel omnium vel certè quàm multò maximè plurium et eorum sapientissimorum'), is displeasing to God....' (Ep. iii. 2).

§ 10. My last evidence is good Bishop Gundulf himself, a *voluntarius co-operator*, and, not improbably, the chief conspirator. If any evidence be trustworthy, it is his; nor have we far to seek for it. It was he who broke the news to the good people at Le Bec, and as follows :—

'*Gundulfus gratiâ Dei . . . . servis Dei Becci consistentibus . . . .*'

'You know, my dearest friends, for how long a time the English Church has been bereft and deprived of her own proper pastor, how long she has lain desolate without the consolation of a father. Thanks to the unspeakable almighty power of God, our lord the King of the English has, with the advice and at the request of his peers ('principum'), and *at the prayer and by the election of clergy and people* ('cleri quoque et populi petitione et electione') conferred the government of the Church of Canterbury upon Dom Anselm, your abbot. There cannot be a doubt that this has been done by the all-merciful hand and guiding of God. We therefore humbly bid and earnestly entreat you, as our most dear brethren, to lay aside all sadness and all thought of grievance, if any there be; and, rather than oppose the will and handiwork of God and *the election of good men,* to give thanks to God and submit with joy and goodwill to what has taken place.'

To resume the evidence afforded us by the ten passages which I have cited :—

The first, it is true, says nothing about an election, but for the simple reason that it relates to events which took place subsequently (§ 1).

The seventh makes mention of electors, but gives no particulars; it is especially valuable, however, as coming from Anselm himself (§ 7).

The others are to this effect :—

(1) That Anselm became Primate by *electio ecclesiastica* (§ 2).
(2) That he was the elected of the whole realm (§ 8).
(3) That his promotion was the issue of a *generalis electio,* if not by all the electoral bodies, at any rate by the majority, and these the wisest of them (§ 9).
(4) That he was unanimously elected by *ecclesia* and by *conventus seniorum* (§ 3).
(5) That he was unanimously elected by the bishops and the *principes regni* (§ 6).
(6) That, recommended by the King's *principes,* he was elected by *clerus* and *populus*—clergy and laity (§ 10).
(7) That, the election made, the King's counsellors (*sapientes*) suggested to him that Anselm was the most fitting person for the dignity (§ 4).
(8) That the King acquiesced in the suggestion (§ 4).
(9) That he consented to the promotion (§ 5).
(10) That he did so without, as was his wont, exacting a pecuniary recognition (§ 5).

§ 11. It is to slay the slain to add more, and yet I will dare to do so. The following is Milo Crispin's account in his Life of Abbot William, St. Anselm's successor at Le Bec :—'When the King's life was almost despaired of, his bishops and barons admonished him for the saving of his soul to choose some good man and appoint him ('constitueret') Archbishop of Canterbury. "Whom?" he asked. "Abbot Anselm," was their reply. This pleased the King, who at once gave orders for him to be sent for. So then by the election of King and barons, by the acclamation of clergy and people, and by the evident disposition of Divine providence, he is chosen Primate of all Britain,' &c. (cl. 715).

So much, then, for Mr. Freeman's fourth statement that St. Anselm received the archbishopric by the gift of the King only, and yet expressed no scruple. As he did not receive the archbishopric by the gift of the King only, he can have had no such scruple to express.

V. As to the Christ Church monks, Mr. Freeman must know as well as anyone that they, of all people in the world, were the very men who most wished to have Anselm for Archbishop; and that had Anselm in the King's bedchamber, on the sixth of March, complained that their co-operation was necessary to his election, he would by the very fact of making such complaint have sealed his own fate. And Mr. Freeman must know as well as anyone who of all historians would in that case have been the readiest to call the poor saint by some very hard names. As it happens, however, when the moment came for doing so with propriety and without sacrifice of his proverbial prudence, Anselm *did* complain that the vote of the Christ Church monks had not concurred in his election.

VI. Mr. Freeman's sixth remark is a somewhat hasty deduction from the fifth, which in its turn is not likely to command the assent of anyone who is in the habit of revising his mental processes.

I am sorry to say, however, that it is scarcely accurate as a statement of facts. The truth is that 'Hildebrand and his successors' had not legislated on 'these matters'—that is to say, on lay investiture and homage—but only on one of them—that is to say, on lay investiture —and how Mr. Freeman can have slipped into the mistake of imagining that in 1093 the two things were in the same category surpasses comprehension; for the first Papal legislation upon homage took place, as Mr. Freeman ought to know, subsequently to that year.

What, then, was Anselm's conduct with regard to lay investiture? He rejected it. He absolutely refused to receive the crosier at the King's hand. What more would Mr. Freeman have had him do? Make a speech and aggravate the physical struggle in which he was already engaged by a wordy controversy in which he would certainly have been shouted down, and the most probable issue of which would have been to rend England then and there from Christendom? I know of one writer who, had Anselm been so foolish as that, could have found some very cruel things to say about him.

Surely Mr. Freeman's better judgment has by this time informed him of the frightful troubles which Anselm would have invoked by the utterance of any such 'word' as he fails to find. Nor need those of my readers who estimate sin as Anselm did be told that he was not the man to send a dying King into eternity with the guilt of schism on his soul.

END OF THE FIRST VOLUME.

www.ingramcontent.com/pod-product-compliance
Lightning Source LLC
Chambersburg PA
CBHW052137300426
44115CB00011B/1417